FIDEL CASTRO SPEECHES

FIDEL CASTRO SPEECHES

Cuba's Internationalist Foreign Policy 1975-80

PATHFINDER
New York   London   Montreal   Sydney

Edited by Michael Taber

Copyright © 1981 by Pathfinder Press
All rights reserved

ISBN 978-0-87348-609-5
Library of Congress Catalog Card Number 81-80717
Manufactured in Canada

First edition, 1981
Eleventh printing, 2025

COVER PHOTOGRAPHS: Fidel Castro, July 26, 1980 (Fred Murphy/ *Militant*)

PATHFINDER
pathfinderpress.com
Email: pathfinder@pathfinderpress.com

Contents

Fidel Castro   7

Introduction   9

**Part 1: Internationalism and
the Cuban revolution**   25

Internationalism and socialism: A condition for humanity's survival
  1. March 30, 1977   29
  2. April 2, 1977   34
  3. April 7, 1977   44

Twenty-fifth anniversary of Moncada *(July 26, 1978)*   55

Part 2: Solidarity with Africa: Angola   87

Closing speech to First Party Congress
  (December 22, 1975)   93
Angola: African Girón *(April 19, 1976)*   123
A duty fulfilled *(July 26, 1976)*   139

Part 3: Solidarity with Africa: Ethiopia   161

Cuba's aid to Ethiopia *(March 15, 1978)*   165
History is on our side *(September 14, 1978)*   181

Part 4: Defending Vietnam   191

Vietnam is not alone *(February 21, 1979)*   197

Part 5: The Nonaligned movement   213

At Nonaligned Ministerial Meeting
  (March 19, 1975)   219
Keynote to Sixth Summit Conference
  (September 3, 1979)   233
At the United Nations *(October 12, 1979)*   259

Part 6: Dialogue with the Cuban community in the U.S. 301
Dialogue with the Cuban community in the U.S.
    1. September 6, 1978 307
    2. November 20–21, 1978 318
    3. December 9, 1978 323
    4. Closing remarks *(December 9, 1978)* 329

Part 7: Cuba and the United States 335
Eulogy for seventy-three terror victims
    (October 15, 1976) 339
We do not negotiate principles *(December 24, 1977)* 357
Interview with CBS *(September 30, 1979)* 375
Speech to the fighting people *(May 1, 1980)* 389

Part 8: Nicaragua: The Sandinista revolution 417
The triumph of Nicaraguan independence
    (July 26, 1979) 421
In Nicaragua *(July 19, 1980)* 445
There is only one road to liberation: That of Cuba,
    that of Grenada, that of Nicaragua
    (July 26, 1980) 453

Appendices
Appendix A: Cuba in Angola: Operation Carlota
    by Gabriel García Márquez 485
Appendix B: Resolution on international policy 511
Appendix C: Cuba's view of the revolution in
    Latin America and the Caribbean 537

Index 543

Fidel Castro

Fidel Castro, born into a small landowning family in eastern Cuba in 1926, began his political activity while attending the University of Havana in the mid-1940s.

After Fulgencio Batista's coup d'état of March 10, 1952, Castro organized a revolutionary movement to initiate armed struggle against the U.S.-backed dictatorship. On July 26, 1953, he led an attack on the Moncada army garrison in Santiago de Cuba. Many participants were captured and murdered in cold blood; Castro and other survivors were imprisoned. Originally sentenced to fifteen years, he was released in 1955 together with his comrades as a result of an amnesty campaign. Following his release, the July 26 Movement was formed.

In July 1955 Castro left Cuba for Mexico, where he organized a guerrilla expedition to return to Cuba. On December 2, 1956, along with eighty-one other fighters, he landed in southeastern Cuba aboard the yacht *Granma*. For the next two years, Castro directed the operations of the Rebel Army and its expanding network of mass popular support from a base in the Sierra Maestra mountains. On January 1, 1959, Batista was forced to flee Cuba and shortly thereafter Rebel Army units entered Havana.

Castro served as prime minister of the revolutionary government from February 1959 until December 1976. He was president of the Council of State and Council of Ministers from 1976 to 2008, commander in chief of Cuba's armed forces from 1959 to 2008, and first secretary of the Central Committee of the Communist Party of Cuba from its founding in 1965 to 2011.

Introduction

Despite its small size, Cuba plays a major role in world politics. For over twenty years, revolutionaries throughout Latin America and the world have looked to the Cuban revolution as an example. For its part, Cuba has solidarized with liberation movements internationally, giving moral, political, economic, and in some cases military support to revolutionary struggles.

Cuba has played a prominent role in the United Nations and the Movement of Nonaligned Countries. When Fidel Castro, as chairman of the Nonaligned movement, spoke at the United Nations in October 1979, it was seen as an event of world importance. In addition to representing his own country, Castro today speaks on behalf of the masses of poverty-stricken peoples in the colonial and semicolonial world.

Cuba's impact is felt in the industrialized capitalist countries as well. The specter of the Cuban revolution, the first socialist revolution in the Americas, has haunted defenders of capitalism within the United States. Since the revolution came to power in 1959 the U.S. government has used every means at its disposal to isolate, weaken, and if possible overturn it: economic blockade; the military invasion at the Bay of Pigs in 1961; threat of nuclear annihilation during the 1962 missile crisis; spy flights; assassination attempts against Cuba's leaders; introduction of diseases to destroy Cuban crops and livestock; training and covering up for right-wing terror and assassination squads; and, above all, an unrelenting propaganda campaign to turn the American people against Cuba.

On April 9, 1980, speaking to the Caribbean/Central American Action group, then-President Carter candidly stated why the U.S. government has been so afraid of Cuba: "the real threat of Cuba is that they offer a model to be emulated by people who are dissatisfied with their lot or who are struggling to change things for the better."

While known by many in Latin America, the accomplishments of this Cuban "model" are not generally publicized in the U.S. Before the revolution, Cuba was a backward country with a one-crop economy and most of its people lived in abject poverty. Since then, the country has made some striking changes:

- Illiteracy, which once afflicted a quarter to a third of the population, has been eliminated, and free and universal public education instituted. Out of a population of ten million, three and a half million—of all ages—are currently enrolled in classes, one of the highest rates in the world.
- The Cuban health care system, by far the best of any underdeveloped country, is also free. Since the revolution, life expectancy has risen from under fifty-five years to over seventy.
- The chronic unemployment common to the rest of Latin America, with rates of up to 50 percent, is a thing of the past in Cuba.
- In 1958, 8 percent of the property owners held 75 percent of the land. Following the revolution, one of the most far-reaching agrarian reforms in the world was carried out, bringing better living conditions and cultural and educational opportunities to the country's agricultural workers.
- Racial discrimination, which had weighed on the backs of Cuba's Blacks and mulattos, was wiped out.

Cubans today feel a growing pride in their country's African heritage.
- Women in Cuba have made enormous strides. Whereas in 1959 the main "careers" open to women were those of domestic servant or prostitute, those categories have since been virtually abolished and increasing numbers of women are joining the labor force in a wide range of fields. Cuba has the most advanced system in the world of maternity benefits for women workers, quality childcare is being provided on a wide scale, and free birth control and abortion are available on demand.
- Long subjected to despotic regimes before the revolution, the working people of Cuba are now participating in running their own country through the system of People's Power and the mass organizations such as the Committees for the Defense of the Revolution, the Federation of Cuban Women, the trade unions, and the student and children's organizations.
- While the economic situation of most of the world's people has worsened over the last few years, Cuba, despite underdevelopment, the U.S. blockade, and a lack of natural resources, has been able to make progress in raising the living standard of its people.

The political framework for Cuba's foreign policy is summed up in the word *internationalism*. To Cubans this means that their country is only one part of a world revolutionary process; that they see their problems and opportunities in the context of world politics—not the other way around. As Castro stated in 1975: "The starting point of Cuba's foreign policy . . . is the subordination of Cuban positions to the international needs of the struggle for socialism and for the national liberation of the peoples." Along these lines, Cuba has put a priority on supporting struggles for social justice throughout the world.

Over the years, Cuba has at times taken political positions which have hurt them in an immediate economic sense. The Cubans know, for example, that by compromising their policies and abandoning their principles, they could have improved relations with the United States, entailing a lifting of the blockade and material improvements for the population. This they have refused to do.

An important aspect of Cuba's internationalism is its willingness to share the material fruits of its revolution. Fifty thousand Cubans—doctors, nurses, dentists, teachers, technicians, construction workers, soldiers—are currently serving abroad in thirty-seven countries with the aim of helping the people of those countries meet the basic health and education needs of their people, build up their economies, and defend themselves. All this is given without political conditions and is in most cases free of charge. This aid is especially remarkable given that Cuba is a poor country with pressing needs of its own. Aid is even sent to countries whose governments have a hostile attitude toward Cuba. For example, doctors and medical supplies were sent to Nicaragua under the Somoza tyranny following the devastating earthquake of 1972.

Explaining how Cuba sees its assistance to other countries, Castro said on April 7, 1977, ". . . it hurt us whenever we saw a Cuban child who was hungry, ill, or abandoned; but we have to be just as hurt on seeing an Angolan child who is hungry, ill, or abandoned—or a Vietnamese child, or a Mozambican child, or a child from any other country. . . . When these feelings begin to reach man's heart and conscience, then we are more than mean, egotistical individuals; we will have gone beyond individual, family, and even national egoism to reach the point of really acquiring an internationalist feeling." The idea that there is a "human family," that Cuba is simply one province within the world, is basic to Cuba's policies. This attitude contrasts sharply with the "national egoism" and chauvinism typical of relations among capitalist countries. And needless to say, Cuba finds it especially reprehensible when such egoism is also found in countries that claim to be revolutionary, socialist, or communist.

This internationalist spirit deeply permeates Cuba's people. For each person selected for an international assignment, there are many volunteers. Those returning bring back an awareness of the world's problems which is then disseminated to others. Schools, buildings, hospitals, and streets are commonly named after liberation fighters from other countries, including the United States. The unions, women's federation, and the Committees for the Defense of the Revolution, which encompass the bulk of the population, hold regular discussions and classes on international events. Even as little children, Cubans develop an internationalist consciousness. The model for Cuban youth is Che Guevara, who died attempting to help liberate other peoples. The motto of the Cuban children's organization, the Pioneers, is "We will be like Che." Combined with this internationalist spirit is a strong feeling of patriotism and pride in Cuba—pride in its history and accomplishments.

Because of its own history of colonial domination, Cuba is especially sensitive to the plight of the semicolonial and colonial countries, which contain the majority of the world's population. Upon winning its independence from Spain, Cuba was occupied by U.S. troops in 1898, and from then on was a virtual United States colony. At the time of the revolution, U.S. companies and businessmen owned 90 percent of Cuba's mineral wealth, 80 percent of the public utilities, practically all the industry and cattle ranches, and about half of the sugar production. The capital city of Havana was a center for gambling and prostitution, catering to U.S. businessmen, military personnel, and tourists. To top it off, the U.S. government possessed a naval base at Guantánamo in eastern Cuba which to this day is in the hands of the U.S. military against the will of the Cuban people.

Cubans also experienced the measures taken against them by the U.S. government after the revolution. On top of the military and terrorist attacks, Washington leveled an economic blockade whose effects should not be underestimated. Seventy-five to eighty percent of Cuba's trade was with the U.S., which meant that new markets and new suppliers had to be found. Virtually all industry was built by the U.S. and spare parts thus became unavailable, leading to breakdowns and big economic losses. Medicines, some of which were produced only in the U.S., could not be obtained. Instead of ninety miles, basic supplies had to be shipped an average of nine thousand miles, presenting Cuba with huge shipping costs. Many consumer items became unavailable, leading to problems of scarcity, speculation, and a black market—all of which had to be fought by the revolutionary government. In attacking Cuba, Washington wanted to issue a threat to other nations: this is what happens when a country tries to free itself from imperialist domination.

Thus, when the Cubans use the word *imperialism* they think of their own history: economic domination through foreign investment, unequal trade, appropriation of natural resources, the total distortion and subordination of their economy to the needs of another country; political subjugation; and the attempts to destroy them when they tried to achieve genuine independence.

While Cuba was able to free itself from imperialist domination, the majority of countries in the world still suffer the effects of it: disease, poverty, ignorance, desperation. And for most of them, the situation has been getting worse. The gap between the industrialized capitalist countries and the colonial and semicolonial countries grows wider every year. Already the per capita income in the industrialized countries is fourteen times greater. There are half a billion people hungry, a billion illiterates, and hundreds of millions dying each year from curable diseases. In several speeches contained in this book, Castro explains that these problems, created by imperialism, are leading to an international catastrophe.

From its own experience, Cuba sees political and economic independence as the precondition for solving these problems. Toward that end, it has attempted to challenge the governments of the semicolonial world to unite in a broad action front that could struggle for these objectives against imperialist domination. Cuba also believes that capitalism holds no solutions for the world's masses and that a radical change in the worldwide economic order is essential. Pointing to the problems of hunger, disease, poverty, and the threat of nuclear destruction, Castro remarked on April 7, 1977: "The analysis of all these elements leads to the question of how the problems of underdevelopment can be solved under these conditions. If there isn't a clear political idea and if neocolonialism, capitalism, imperialism, unequal trade relations, and all these problems aren't eliminated, how can the problem of underdevelopment, which affects billions of people in the world, be solved? It is clear that only socialism can find the answer to these problems—only worldwide socialism."

The year 1975 has been chosen to begin this collection of speeches because it marks a turning point internationally as well as for Cuba. In Castro's words, there was a "change in the balance of forces" in the world at that time. Of greatest significance was the victory of the Vietnamese revolution, resulting in the biggest political defeat for the United States government in this century. After spending tens of billions of dollars, sending troops who at the height of the war numbered over half a million, and using the most sophisticated instruments of destruction, Washington was unable to defeat the Vietnamese. In addition, the massive movement that developed within the U.S. against the war, and the resulting political crisis symbolized by the Watergate scandal, created the "Vietnam syndrome" among the American people. Direct U.S. military intervention in other countries became increasingly difficult for the immediate period.

Also occurring in 1974–75 was the revolutionary upsurge in Portugal, fueled by the crumbling of its colonial empire in Africa. The final collapse of Portuguese colonial domination unleashed a massive upsurge throughout southern Africa.

Along with these events came the first international capitalist economic crisis since the Great Depression of the 1930s. All over the world, an offensive was initiated by the capitalist class against the rights and living standards of working people. Gains won through years of struggle were taken away and many more were put in jeopardy. One of the effects of this crisis was a deepening radicalization of workers in the advanced capitalist countries, increasingly affecting the working class in the United States. Another effect was the devastating impact it had on the colonial and semicolonial countries. The increase in the cost of oil and manufactured goods hit these countries the hardest, forcing them deeper and deeper into debt. The consequences for the people of these countries was a further reduction in their already meager standard of living.

The combined effect of these objective world factors led to a new rise in revolutionary struggles and significant advances for the revolutionary movement during the middle and late 1970s. As a result, Cuba was given new openings to advance its revolutionary perspective and to give assistance to revolutions and national liberation movements.

Giving aid to revolutionary struggles was nothing new for Cuba. During the 1960s, it gave material and military support to a number of African liberation movements: in Mozambique, Angola, Guinea-Bissau, Cameroon, Sierra Leone, Guinea, Algeria, and the Congo. Cuban military personnel served in several of these countries, and Che Guevara himself fought in the Congo in 1965.

However, Cuba was most well known during this period for its support to guerrilla movements throughout Latin America. In 1967, it convened a conference of the Organization of Latin American Solidarity (OLAS) in Havana that issued a call for the creation of "two, three, many Vietnams" in Latin America.

Probably the most famous initiative was that of Che Guevara in Bolivia. In late 1966, along with a group of Cubans and other Latin Americans, Guevara went to Bolivia, where he established a guerrilla nucleus. The attempt ended in failure and Guevara was killed in October 1967. This defeat, along with similar ones in other Latin American countries, led to some rethinking on the part of the Cubans. They pulled back from their orientation to rural guerrilla warfare as a universal strategy for Latin America and began to direct increasing attention to the newly rising struggles of the urban working class in Argentina, Bolivia, Uruguay, Brazil, and, especially, Chile.

In the early 1970s, while involved in a reorganization of its economy and continuing efforts to break out of its

U.S.-imposed diplomatic isolation, Cuba continued its policy of supporting liberation movements. During the 1973 Mideast war, for example, Cuba sent 700 troops to Syria to help in the fight against Zionist Israel's invasion of that country.

Cuba also attempted to help push forward the revolutionary process in Chile while Salvador Allende was president. The Cubans gave economic assistance to Chile and waged a campaign against the U.S./CIA attempts to destabilize and overthrow the Allende government. At the same time, it attempted to influence the political course of the Chilean struggle in a revolutionary direction. During a month-long visit to Chile in 1971, Castro observed the development of the class struggle there. While Allende's regime looked to its alliance with sections of the military and the capitalists to prevent a right-wing coup, Castro pointed to the dangers in that approach. He noted that the growing boldness of the right wing was "based on the weakness of the very revolutionary process, on weaknesses in the ideological battle, on weaknesses in the mass struggle, on weakness in the face of the enemy."

On the eve of the September 1973 coup, Castro sent a letter to Allende urging him to rely on the organized strength of the working class to block the impending coup. Unfortunately, this was not done. After the murderous U.S.-backed military coup of Augusto Pinochet, Cuba launched a campaign denouncing the fierce repression. At a mass rally held two weeks after the coup, Cuba declared its continuing solidarity with the Chilean people and Castro spoke about the defeat: "The Chilean example teaches us the lesson that it is impossible to make the revolution with the people alone: arms are also necessary! And that arms alone aren't enough to make a revolution: people are also necessary."

In the period after 1975, Cuba was able to achieve successes in its foreign policy in Africa that would have been unimaginable just a few years before. Some of the speeches in this book explain the form and circumstances of Cuba's aid to Angola and Ethiopia. During late 1975, the Cuban government was asked by Angola to send troops to help beat back a U.S.-supported South African invasion, and to safeguard Angola's newly won independence. In Ethiopia in late 1977 and early 1978, Cuban soldiers once again were sent to stop another invasion. This time the Somalian government, with the backing of Washington, was attempting to reverse the deepgoing revolutionary process in Ethiopia. In both cases, Cuban support was decisive in ensuring defeats for the invaders.

Other speeches in this collection relate to Cuba's participation in the Nonaligned movement. Cuba's growing influence in this organization is another testimony to the changes in world politics following 1975. On the one hand, Cuba's prestige rose as a result of its actions in Africa and elsewhere. On the other, the growing crisis facing the semicolonial countries propelled some of the members of the Nonaligned movement to take more militant anti-imperialist positions, which were championed by Cuba.

An additional indication of the impact of Cuba's changing role has been seen within the United States itself. The establishment of a dialogue between Cuba and the Cuban exile community within the U.S. was an example of Cuba's efforts to begin to cut across the hostility that existed for years.

On top of all these developments, two events occurred in 1979 that had a profound impact on Cuba. On March 13, Eric Gairy, the dictator of the English-speaking Caribbean island of Grenada, was overthrown by a popular insurrection led by the New Jewel Movement, a revolutionary socialist party. Maurice Bishop became the prime minister of the new revolutionary government. Then, on July 19, the Sandinista National Liberation Front succeeded in ousting the U.S.-backed regime of Anastasio Somoza and installed a government representing the workers and peasants of Nicaragua. For the first time since 1959, Latin American and Caribbean countries had freed themselves from imperialist domination. Castro termed these two countries and Cuba "three giants rising up to defend their right to independence, sovereignty, and justice on the very threshold of imperialism."

Cuba responded immediately and enthusiastically to both revolutions. Cuban technicians, doctors, and other personnel were sent to Grenada along with millions of dollars worth of equipment to help build up Grenada's backward and stunted economy. In Nicaragua, material and human aid was sent including 1,200 teachers and 250 doctors. Cuba issued a challenge to all countries of the world to see who could help Nicaragua the most.

Combined with these two victories, other revolutionary upsurges were breaking out in Central America. Foremost among these was El Salvador, where an all-out civil war was developing between the workers and peasants on one side and the U.S.-backed oligarchy on the other. Throughout Central America and the Caribbean, growing popular unrest began to threaten imperialist control.

In response to the deterioration of its hold over this area and elsewhere in the world, Washington began to make serious preparations for military intervention. A Caribbean military command was created, military spending was increased, steps were taken to reinstitute the draft, military aid to repressive governments was increased, and, above all, with the help of the news media, propaganda was intensified to try to reverse the climate among the American people opposing further Vietnams. One of the central targets of this campaign was Cuba, pictured as a chief cause of Washington's problems. Cuba was portrayed as a "puppet" of the Soviet Union, a ridiculous charge to anyone familiar with Soviet and Cuban policy. While Cuba is dependent on Soviet economic and military assistance, without which it could not have withstood the attacks by the U.S. government, it has always prided itself on making its own decisions. As Castro stated during an interview with CBS-TV in 1979 regarding Cuban-Soviet relations: "At times we coincide. We don't always coincide." Nevertheless, the U.S. government has used this charge as an excuse for renewed military threats against Cuba.

In this climate of confrontation, there occurred the exodus of 125,000 Cubans to the United States in the spring of 1980 and the massive demonstrations in response by the Cuban people. These events are taken up in several of the later speeches in this book. Castro described the Cubans who left as people who did not have the revolutionary consciousness to stand up to the pressure and threats from the United States, nor to withstand the temptation of the greater availability of consumer goods in the U.S. He reiterated the Cuban government's position that socialism is a voluntary system and that all who wanted to leave were free to go.

In response to the claims by its opponents that the revolution had weakened and lost the support of the population, the Cuban people carried out the biggest mobilizations ever in support of the revolution and its policies. On April 17, 1980, one million people marched past the Peruvian embassy, where many of those wanting to leave had massed. On May 1, 1.5 million attended a May Day rally, and on May 17, five million Cubans, half the country's population, marched in a series of demonstrations across the island—the "March of the Fighting People." As Castro pointed out at the time, these actions were not simply in defense of Cuba, but also in solidarity with Nicaragua, Grenada, and other revolutionary struggles around the world threatened by U.S. intervention. In addition to expressing their continued support for the revolution, the Cuban people showed their determination to continue their country's internationalist policies.

For a quarter of a century, Fidel Castro has been the central leader of the Cuban revolution. His speeches, which reflect the collective thinking of the revolutionary leadership, are listened to, read, and studied throughout Cuba. Many of them are given to rallies of a million people or more and express the deep feelings and emotions of those present. In the speeches by Castro and the other revolutionary leaders, virtually all the major policies and actions of the government are discussed and motivated.

Given the extent of anti-Cuba propaganda in the United States and the lack of knowledge about Cuba, it is not surprising that a great deal of ignorance and misconceptions exist about its policies. Reading Castro's speeches is one of the best ways to get a better understanding of both the Cuban revolution and the feelings of the Cuban people.

Unfortunately, very few of Castro's speeches are readily accessible in English. What does exist in print generally dates back to the 1960s or even earlier. This book represents a step toward filling that gap.

As much as possible, we have tried to include the speeches in full. In the case of two speeches, excerpts were all that was available. Three others have been excerpted for reasons of space. Interjections from the audiences (i.e., applause, chants) have been included because they constitute an integral part of Castro's speeches. To assist the reader, notes have been added before each section to provide necessary background information. In the majority of cases, the translations have been taken from the English-language *Granma* weekly review, official organ of the Central Committee of the Communist Party of Cuba. Minor stylistic changes have been made to correct translation errors and for consistency and readability.

Michael Taber
FEBRUARY 1981

PART 1
Internationalism and the Cuban revolution

During March and April of 1977, Castro made a widely publicized tour of Africa. He visited Algeria, Libya, South Yemen, Somalia, Ethiopia, Tanzania, Mozambique, and Angola, stopping off in East Germany and the Soviet Union on the way home. All over Africa, he received tumultuous welcomes. Only a year before, Cuban troops had helped defeat the South African invasion of Angola. Cuba was widely viewed in Africa as a country that would put itself on the line in the fight against racism and colonialism.

The African trip made a deep impression on Castro. In his speeches during the trip he described the poverty and overwhelming economic problems that exist in many African countries and called on the Cuban people and anti-imperialist forces throughout the world to join with the peoples of Africa to overcome these problems. Castro's speeches during this trip are some of the best presentations of what Cuban revolutionaries mean concretely when they speak of internationalism.

July 26 is an important holiday in Cuba: the anniversary of the 1953 attack on the Moncada barracks, marking the beginning of the anti-Batista armed struggle. It has become a tradition for Castro to give a speech at the annual rallies on this date, and his address on July 26, 1978, the twenty-fifth anniversary, was an occasion to review Cuba's long history of struggle for independence and to evaluate the revolution's progress and policies.

Internationalism and socialism: A condition for humanity's survival

1. MARCH 30, 1977

Excerpt from a speech to Cuban civilian and military personnel in Luanda, Angola. The text is from *Current Problems of Underdeveloped Countries,* Oficina de Publicaciones del Consejo de Estado, Havana, 1979.

These feelings which we Cubans have already acquired will have to be shared by all people someday. Today it hurts us if a Cuban is hungry, if a Cuban has no doctor, if a Cuban child suffers or is uneducated, or if a family has no housing. It hurts us even though it's not our brother, our son, or our father. Why shouldn't we feel hurt if we see an Angolan child go hungry, suffer, be killed or massacred? Today we are hurt by the crimes that are committed against our people, by crimes committed against any Cuban, but as we progress and future generations have a higher consciousness than ours, the day will come when these feelings will go beyond the narrow horizons of a country's boundaries.

We have gone beyond individual and family egoism, and we are beyond the borders of national egoism. The day will come when these things I'm talking to you about have to be the prevailing feeling in every human family. You can't be utopian. I know that time hasn't come yet; there is still a great deal of egoism in the world; there is still a great deal of injustice and meanness. Part of humanity has freed itself and has started along this path, and we can feel that we are a part of this humanity.

We Cubans are now beginning to feel the problems of other peoples just as we feel our own problems. [*Applause*] We have begun to feel them and to do something about them. It isn't much, but we are doing what we can. If Cuba were only a richer country! If we only had great natural resources and could use those resources to help more than we are helping. It could be said that, today, our people's generosity goes beyond our material resources, beyond our strength.

I am convinced that the world's problems cannot be solved by capitalism or imperialism. Moreover, I believe humanity has lost a great deal of time—a great deal—that problems are accumulating and that they are graver and more serious all the time. Traveling through an area as big as Africa, you discover the situation of the people, their health situation, the food situation, the problems they have. Traveling through all these areas of the underdeveloped world you clearly understand the tragedy of the world and you ask, theoretically, how in the world these problems will ever be solved and how illiteracy, disease, unemployment, and poverty will be wiped out. How can human beings create minimal conditions for living with honor, decency, and dignity? How can you do this without revolution? How can you do it without socialism? What would the world be or what will the world be if it has to depend on the capitalist system to solve these problems?

These are very serious problems; and, we might add, what would the world be like if the capitalist model and capitalist consumer habits were to be spread throughout the world? If every individual were to have a car and aspire to all the luxuries of capitalist society? These luxuries that a minority has under capitalism, those luxuries that the most industrialized countries have. At what cost? At the cost of the rest of humanity starving to death.

Now a new problem, the problem of the oil-producing countries, of OPEC [Organization of Petroleum Exporting Countries], has arisen. Countries such as Saudi Arabia and Iran, that collect billions, do so in part from the price the capitalists pay them, but also in part from the price the countries of the Third World pay them. How do they invest that money? They lend it to capitalist countries. They buy all kinds of weapons from the capitalist countries and aid reactionary movements in the Third World. And, while it's true that the capitalist countries pay a higher price for oil, when they sell the underdeveloped world a piece of equipment, they cover the cost of that oil and more.

Today when we were meeting with the comrades who are providing technical assistance, we went over the cost of the equipment Angola has to buy: a dump truck, $40,400. That dump truck cost $10,000 a few years ago. Equipment, raw materials, medical instruments, medicines—everything is unbearably high.

There are countries such as Tanzania, which lives from

the sale of cotton, cashew nuts, and sisal, and their entire production of cashew nuts, sisal, and cotton—all together—isn't enough to pay for the 800,000 tons of oil they use. That is the situation in many non-oil-producing Third World countries.

Angola has a little oil and exports it. We are glad, because at least that oil is helping to consolidate the Angolan revolution; but the countries of the Third World that have no oil, that have to continue producing tea, rubber, coconut oil, cashew nuts, cloves, sisal. You know what sisal's like. In Cuba now there's almost no one who wants to work in sisal, no one. Zanzibar's economy is based on collecting flowers known as cloves from a very tall tree. The people in other countries make their living by climbing palm trees and picking coconuts in order to make copra. Many countries have to live from this. A ton of cashew nuts used to pay for fifteen tons of oil; now it pays for only four or five, so they're without energy; they have no fuel to develop transportation and industry. The unequal trade relations between the underdeveloped world and the developed capitalist world have worsened and now a part of the world—the major part of the underdeveloped countries—has also found that its trade relations with the oil-producing countries have worsened.

The conflicts and problems in the world are serious, really serious. You can look at them and see clearly what their origins are: capitalism, colonialism, imperialism. You go to the African countries, and how many students are there in a university? No, there aren't any universities—or if there is a university after fifteen years of independence, it has one-, two-, or three thousand students. There's one doctor for every twenty thousand inhabitants; Cuba's ratio is at least one doctor for every thousand.

There are many African countries that have one doctor for twenty-, or forty-, or fifty thousand inhabitants. Either they have no universities or the universities have two- or three thousand students.

It's truly a sad, difficult situation, and—I say this with more conviction than ever—these problems of humanity have no solution without revolution and socialism. [*Applause*] Marx, Engels, and Lenin saw these problems very clearly some time ago.

Of course, socialism doesn't yet prevail in the world; socialism in a number of countries coexists with capitalism in a great many countries. If a socialist community prevailed in the world instead of this egoism that is the rule in capitalist society—this wanting more and more luxury—the industrialized nations would have to throw themselves into speeding up the development of all the underdeveloped world. What is still happening, in fact, is that the industrialized capitalist countries are getting richer all the time, and there is an ever-greater distance, an ever-widening gap between the underdeveloped countries and the developed capitalist countries. Anyone who travels and works in these areas of the world knows their educational, hygienic, and food problems through and through and knows that this world—these billions of people who still live in abysmal conditions—will need the efforts of technology and the financial resources of the developed world.

Ours is a small country; its power is very relative, but we haven't the slightest doubt about the fact that we are meeting this responsibility as best we can; that we are working for, marching toward, and cooperating with the only solutions humanity has; and that without these solutions, not we, but the children and grandchildren of these generations—the future generations of Cubans and all other Latin Americans—would have truly insoluble problems.

2. APRIL 2, 1977

Speech given April 2, 1977 in Berlin, German Democratic Republic (GDR—East Germany). The text is from *Granma* April 17, 1977.

Dear Comrade Erich Honecker;
Dear comrades of the leadership of the party and the government of the GDR:

Let's see if between us the interpreter and I can do a decent job. It's the first time we've worked together.

When we started on our trip to several African countries, we really hadn't planned to visit the GDR. We toured Africa, made a long trip round the whole region, talking with revolutionary leaders and observing the situation in each place and the struggle between imperialism and the underdeveloped world, the struggle between capitalism and socialism, the struggle between oppression and freedom, the struggle between discrimination and equality.

Marxism-Leninism and socialism are studied in books. I, myself, got my first ideas of Marxism-Leninism from books, but also from life; traveling round the world a bit you learn a lot about Marxism-Leninism and about imperialism, colonialism, and neocolonialism. I have really learned a lot about these topics on this trip through Africa. Of course, I didn't visit reactionary, neocolonial, or racist countries; I visited progressive countries that are struggling for social change, revolutionary Arab countries, and countries of Black Africa.

Marx did research and wrote many brilliant things, but

the very revolutionary potential of what Marx analyzed was perhaps even more brilliant than what Marx himself foresaw. He conceived of socialism as the natural end-product of the laws of evolution of human society, after the development of capitalist society.

Lenin, who studied Marx in depth and gave his considered interpretation of Marx's thought, added the brilliant idea that many underdeveloped countries did not necessarily have to pass through the capitalist stage in order to build socialism.

And today we are witnessing this phenomenon in the world: countries that are going directly from underdevelopment to the construction of socialism. What is more: countries that are going from tribalism to the construction of socialism, countries that are going from nomadism to the construction of socialism. And these are truly interesting phenomena that enrich our doctrine and practice.

But we also saw all that capitalism, colonialism, and imperialism signified for a large part of humankind. We have seen those peoples that lived under colonialism and their present situation: incredible poverty, extraordinary technological backwardness, illiteracy, unemployment, diseases—above all the diseases. Nobody knows what percentage of babies die during the first year of life; there are no statistics. It might well be five, seven, ten times greater than the number of those who die in a developed country. Malaria, malnutrition, tuberculosis, all kinds of contagious diseases, and diseases due to deficiencies prevail in Africa.

On many an occasion a rare phenomenon can be observed: you see no old people in Africa. People don't live long enough to get old there. And we asked about doctors. One for every forty- or fifty thousand inhabitants or more. There are no technicians, no engineers, no teachers, and often no skilled workers. Either they have no universities at all, or there are a thousand to fifteen hundred students in the universities.

We ourselves, we Cubans, who consider ourselves an underdeveloped country, already have 105,000 university students and practically one doctor for every thousand inhabitants.

That's the picture we have in Africa, especially in Black Africa, which, in the present-day world, is the region where human beings live under the worst conditions.

It is truly cause for indignation to see how, after independence, the capitalists, the imperialists, tried to establish neocolonialism there; to see the attempt at capitalist development, the attempt to control natural resources through the monopolies.

The peoples of the underdeveloped world will find no solution along that road. How can the problems of illiteracy, disease, poverty, underdevelopment, and technological backwardness be solved by means of capitalism in those countries?

And the peoples of these regions of the world are beginning to understand this very clearly. Some of the governments of the underdeveloped world understand these problems and are working progressively along the socialist road.

Not even independence has been achieved in some countries of the region. Racism, together with capitalism and imperialism, still oppresses tens of millions of people. In Zimbabwe, 250,000 racists exploit and oppress six million Africans; in South Africa, two and a half million racists exploit and oppress almost twenty million Africans. A similar situation is to be found in Namibia.

There are, then, in the area we toured, two great political problems. In the Arab world, imperialist intervention, the struggle against the progressive movements and aggression via the Israeli state, in which the imperialists have the complicity of reactionary governments, with Saudi Arabia and Iran at the head. And in southern Africa, colonialism and racism—phenomena which subsist with the backing the imperialists give to the racists and through the complicity of the neocolonized governments of Africa.

But the struggle is on throughout the continent. I compare it with Latin America. In many countries of Latin America, the imperialists created an oligarchy, a reactionary bourgeoisie; they trained and organized reactionary armies and now maintain iron control. Fortunately, in Africa, as a general rule, there is no bourgeoisie they can count on; they're trying to create one, but I think it will be absolutely impossible. It's possible that the African countries will go over to socialism even before the countries of Latin America.

We have had the opportunity to observe the situation in this region of the world and draw many conclusions. Of course, ours isn't a contemplative stand; ours is a militant stand. I had the satisfaction of seeing Cuban technicians and doctors in many African countries, comrades who are devoted workers, true revolutionaries. That is the product of socialism. In our country before the revolution, we had no doctors to send to rural areas; the greater part lived in the capital and many had a bourgeois outlook. They were the product of capitalist society. The same thing happens in Latin America.

I will never forget an experience I had on my trip to Chile under the Popular Unity government. We arrived at an important city of over 100,000 inhabitants, in a region where the main wealth of the country was produced. There, the authorities asked me to send a number of specialists over: children's specialists, throat and eye specialists, surgeons, etc. There were twenty-seven in all. We said we were ready to send the specialists, but we couldn't send them in the end. The bourgeois medical association of Chile opposed the idea because they saw it as some sort of professional rivalry; and we couldn't send the specialists they asked us for in Antofagasta.

The capitalist, neocolonized countries of Latin America have universities; they turn out technicians and some engineers and doctors. The best brains are contracted by the United States and taken from their countries; and so, many bourgeois professionals trained in the universities can't even be used in the rural areas of their own country. There are no professionals, no doctors, among the peasants.

When the Cuban revolution came to power, half the university professionals left for the United States. That's what bourgeois society does. That's why it is cause for great satisfaction to us to know that not only do we have many more doctors than under capitalism, but that today we have doctors, technicians, and teachers who not only go to the countryside in Cuba but are also ready to go to Yemen, Tanzania, Somalia, Mozambique, Angola, or any African country. That's the product of socialism and the internationalist awareness that socialism forges in a people.

I had the opportunity of talking with many of our compatriots in Africa. I recall that a few days ago I met with 2,500 Cuban soldiers and civilians in Luanda, Angola. The whole scene seemed unreal, strange. Twenty years ago it would have been impossible. Twenty years ago the Cuban was known for his individualism, everyone for himself, the mean egoism characteristic of capitalism. After the individual came the family, the bourgeois family or bourgeois concept of the family. After that came the nation. With the advent of socialism in our country, we have gradually been eradicating selfish individualism; we have gradually been able to go beyond the egoistic meaning of the family, the egoistic concept of the bourgeois family. By now, the whole nation constitutes a great family with a deep sense of the fraternal and the humane. And we are already going beyond national egoism. Before, it would hurt to see a Cuban child suffer, go hungry, be sick or illiterate. And now it also hurts to see an African or Asian child sick, hungry, or ignorant.

In short, we are becoming internationalists. That isn't easy, it really isn't. There is a great deal of bourgeois selfishness and poison which capitalism, colonialism, and imperialism have instilled in the human being. I see that our compatriots are becoming internationalists.

The more we think about these problems, the more we admire the profound wisdom and extraordinarily revolutionary nature of the ideas of Marx and Engels. Before Marx and Engels, those who thought about brotherhood and justice among men out of simple reasoning or feelings were utopians. Once Marx and Engels had analyzed the history of human society and its evolution scientifically, we utopians were able to become revolutionaries. If Comrade Honecker had been born five hundred years ago, he would have been a utopian.

You and we had the privilege of being born after Marx, Engels, and Lenin. The revolutionary is a blend of human sensitivity and a natural feeling of rejection of injustice and oppression, and the scientific philosophy of Marxism-Leninism. I, myself, was a utopian before becoming a Marxist. I felt that capitalist society was complete madness, it was absurd. When I read the *Communist Manifesto* as a student, I began to cease being a utopian socialist to become a Marxist socialist. I still don't know to what extent I'm still a utopian and to what extent I've become a Marxist-Leninist—perhaps I may even be a bit of a dreamer. But I clearly see, very clearly, that socialism, revolution, and Marxism-Leninism are the only solutions for the problems of today's world. [*Applause*] The more my political awareness matures, the more I admire Marx, because he saw the solution with his heart and mind, with science and his conscience. And he saw humankind in the future as a single family, and the natural resources of the world at the service of all humankind, and the science and technology of the most developed nations working for the benefit of the poorest and most backward ones to create the bases for progress, well-being, and justice for all.

We like to recall recent history, and actually, humankind has made great progress since the glorious October revolution, whose sixtieth anniversary is upon us.

In these sixty years, the world has made greater progress than in thousands of years put together. Human society went through slavery, feudalism, capitalism, colonialism, and imperialism. And so many crimes were committed against humanity until very recently!

The European colonialist nations conquered America and exterminated a large part of the population; then they brought in millions of slaves from Africa and maintained a large part of the world under colonial rule until just a few years ago. Such absurd and incredible things! For example, why should Portugal, a small European nation, want to maintain control—and did so until very recently—over millions of square kilometers in Africa and tens of millions of oppressed Africans?

When I passed through Algeria before coming to the GDR, I was able to attend the First National Assembly in that sister nation. President Boumedienne gave a wise and intelligent speech with socialist content and discussed Algeria's development programs and the bright prospects for his people. He spoke in Arabic and I had a copy of

the speech in French. I don't know French all that well—
I can read it and if it is something political I can understand it, but those people understood Arabic. I could see the differences in culture, language, and traditions and I recalled that after the victory of the Cuban revolution—which was relatively recent—we would listen to news reports about the war in Algeria.*

The French colonialists killed a million and a half Algerians because they said Algeria was a French province. I ask myself, what did France have to do with Algeria? They killed a million and a half Algerians in order to hold on to that colony in Africa! Such incredible and absurd things, which happened until very recently.

Great changes have taken place in the world since the October revolution, but the tasks we face still are really enormous. Man has done a great deal so far, but he must do even more in the future. We still have imperialism, neocolonialism, and capitalism in a large part of the world, and it is our duty to continue struggling to transform society along the correct path, the revolutionary path, while we safeguard peace to prevent imperialism from destroying humankind out of desperation rather than witnessing the triumph of justice on our planet.

We maintain a resolute stand for socialism and against imperialism. Our country is a small nation with limited resources and forces, but we consider it our duty to struggle; it is our duty to cooperate in this struggle.

There are Cubans working in Asia and Africa and making their modest contribution. We aren't doing it for national prestige or out of vanity to play a role on the international scene. We're doing it out of a sense of internationalism.

---

* Algeria's war of independence lasted from 1954 to 1962. At the height of the struggle, half a million French troops were being used.

We live in the American hemisphere, and we have known the domination, oppression, and corruption of imperialism. We see how Latin America is oppressed by imperialism, and we deeply feel the need to struggle against that system; we feel it close by.

You, our friends in the GDR, understand this very well because you also have imperialism and capitalism close by. And, besides, because we feel and have a revolutionary outlook, we are inspired by the principles of Marxism-Leninism.

That's why, although the GDR was not on the itinerary of our trip—which will logically wind up in the USSR—toward the end I said, Let's go pay a visit to the GDR! [*Applause*]

This is not accidental. In Europe, you are in the front line of the socialist camp. You were blockaded for many years—imperialism tried to isolate you as it did Cuba. And you have developed a militant anti-imperialist awareness, just as we did. Like us, you are very concerned about all these problems in Africa and Asia, in the so-called Third World. We know this, we feel it, so we said, we'd like to tell our comrades in the GDR and Comrade Honecker about our impressions, at the end of our tour of Africa. [*Applause*]

Actually, I don't like to put people out. I sent Comrade Honecker a message with the idea of making almost no more than a technical stopover, a working visit. I don't know if the interpreter in Algeria didn't translate well or if the codes were mistaken; I really don't know what happened. You made my working visit an official visit, and because of me you have bothered the residents of Berlin and mobilized the leaders on a Saturday and Sunday.

When I was sweating a lot in some parts of Africa, in Dar es Salaam and Luanda—and sweating is not a bad thing, it's a physiological mechanism for adjusting the body temperature to the outside temperature—they would ask, "Aren't you hot?" "Yes, I am, but don't forget I don't come from Scandinavia; I come from a tropical country."

When I was on my way here, I was told to put my jacket on. And I said the cold wouldn't bother me. The protocol people asked me if I wanted to ride in an open or closed car. I asked myself, Will it be so difficult or self-sacrificing to ride in an open car? I went in an open car. But now I see that Comrade Honecker did think I came from a Scandinavian nation. I almost froze on that ride through Berlin and the only thing that encouraged and stimulated me was the affection, friendship, and fraternity of the residents of Berlin! [*Applause*]

Dear comrades of the GDR:

On this trip, I was also able to see the great confidence the underdeveloped nations, the nations of Africa, the countries which lived under colonialism, have in the socialist camp and especially in the Soviet Union. They know that in their struggle against imperialism, capitalism, and neocolonialism, they have only one hope and one friend; they have only one group of states from which they can expect cooperation in all fields: the socialist community, headed by the Soviet Union.

I was telling you that perhaps I am still a bit of a utopian and a dreamer; but I am also optimistic, and life has taught me to be optimistic. I have confidence in the future of the world. Justice, socialism, and peace will triumph, and one day the great ideas of Marx, Engels, and Lenin will be a universal reality. These ideas have already emerged triumphant in a large part of the world, and they are the foundation and example for the other peoples.

If any of those who have been kind enough and patient enough to listen to me this evening still think I am somewhat of a utopian, don't forget that Marx and Engels were born in this country and that many of their dreams have already been fulfilled.

Thank you very much! [*Applause*]

3. APRIL 7, 1977

Excerpt from a speech given to Cuban residents in Moscow at the Lomonosov University. The text is from *Current Problems of Underdeveloped Countries.*

I said in the GDR that we Cubans were becoming internationalists. In Luanda I spoke a long time about this problem of nationalism and internationalism, of the contradictions between the two.

You can be socialist yet at the same time develop a national egoism. It's possible. Socialism is the first chance to work for the community, to plan the economy, to help the country, and thus to feel a national egoism; all for your own country, and forget the rest of the world.

Marxism was conceived as a universal society: the working class of the entire world struggling for liberation against capitalism and against the bourgeoisie and closing ranks in order to one day create a society made up of a single human family. Of course, historically, this couldn't take place overnight; revolutions have to begin first in one country and then in another. At a certain time it seemed as if they were going to take place simultaneously, and the great forefathers of the socialist revolution thought so at one time.

But, when the first socialist revolution took place in this country and the revolutionary movement was crushed in other parts of Europe, the general circumstances were difficult and the Bolsheviks were faced with one alternative. What was it? The alternative of surrendering or that of building socialism even under very difficult conditions. This historical challenge, this enormous task, was imposed on them. They didn't surrender; they didn't consider themselves defeated by the fact that the revolution had been defeated elsewhere; and, considering the natural resources and the size of the country they opted to build socialism.

After World War II, the socialist camp was extended over an important part of Europe; then socialism emerged in other countries of Asia, and our socialism emerged in Latin America, and it is emerging in Africa, [*Applause*] precisely because of the fact that the first socialist revolution was consolidated.

The problems of the world can be solved. I'm absolutely convinced of that. And the problems of the future world are very great—very great. These children who are talking and yelling and crying now, and their children, are going to have a truly complex and difficult world, because the human population is growing at a very great rate; there will be some 7 billion human beings in the year 2000. To produce food for those living now is difficult; double this amount will have to be produced; in thirty more years, there will be 15 billion inhabitants. The best valleys, the most accessible land, the most arable soil is exploited. Technology and science can help solve these food problems but they can't be applied unless there are social changes. Under capitalism, colonialism, and neocolonialism, what comes first is population, not technology or science. Generally, we know what has to be done to produce more cane per hectare, and more rice and more corn and more of everything; we know how much herbicide, pesticide, fertilizer, and water and how many seed varieties are needed. The difficult problem isn't getting the knowledge but rather creating the conditions for applying it. In the world, in a large part of the world, population growth is much more rapid than the hope of applying technology and science and developing the industrial base required for producing all that food. Instead, a complex situation is developing. The sea, which was once everyone's domain, is now viewed by many in terms of 200 miles this way and 200 miles that way, so that the sea has also begun to be divided up. There's no telling what conflicts this can produce, because a ship within three miles of shore isn't the same as a ship fishing 200 miles offshore. Areas of conflict are going to increase as human needs increase and natural resources are limited. The population grows; important natural resources are exhausted.

There's the case of oil: a product accumulated over hundreds of millions of years, that man is liquidating in what amounts to half a century—fifty to sixty years; because it's from 1950 to the present that oil consumption has shot up. With this product—well, there are some countries with small populations and large amounts of oil; now they have organized an oil monopoly. They set whatever price they feel like setting—that's the reality—because they have a monopoly over this vital product. The industrialized capitalist countries manage because, after paying more for oil, they ask more for the trucks, tractors, equipment, and everything else they produce; or they sell arms, as the United States does, to Saudi Arabia and Iran—millions of dollars worth of arms they don't need. Later they send thousands or tens of thousands of technicians, who are also paid fabulous amounts, as advisors to people who are never going to learn how to handle or use those arms. The underdeveloped non-oil-producing countries suffer terribly from the consequences of this; they have to buy oil at five times its old price, while their products find no market and even drop in price. This is what has happened to almost all products, with certain exceptions, such as coffee, due to the great freeze that finished off the coffee in Brazil, and to the Angolan war.

I'll give you an example: Tanzania has 15 million inhabitants; we have 9.5 million. Tanzania consumes 800,000 tons of oil; to raise its development slightly, if it begins to produce cement, any mechanical industry, fertilizers, or whatever, it will have to begin to use more oil, because there is no development without energy, without increasing the consumption of electricity, transportation, and fuel.

We consume 8.5 million tons, or ten times what Tanzania consumes. Of course, we don't have any hydraulic energy sources or wood or coal. Everything in our country has to be produced with oil: sugar production, transportation, construction. Everything is done on the basis of oil.

How does Tanzania, which uses only 800,000 tons, pay for its oil at today's prices? Tanzania's three main export items are cashew nuts, sisal, and cotton. Those are the three main items. It produces a little coffee and also exports some of the cattle that isn't consumed internally to the rich Arab countries, and Zanzibar produces some cloves. But those are the three main items. A ton of cashew nuts used to pay for fifteen or sixteen tons of oil but now it only pays for about five tons of oil. All the cashews, cotton, and sisal Tanzania produces and exports are barely enough to pay for the 800,000 tons of oil it consumes, and it has 15 million inhabitants. You can imagine what it takes to gather a ton of cashew nuts; you can imagine what it is to produce sisal. We have a little sisal in Cuba—more or less what you see along the highway between Havana and Mariel and in the other direction, toward Matanzas, and between Matanzas and Varadero. Since the triumph of the revolution, nothing has been more difficult than to find people to work in sisal. [*Laughter*] It's hard, dangerous work because of the thorns. Then, cotton picked by hand. Hundreds, thousands of people working to get the cashew nuts, the sisal, and the cotton needed to purchase the oil that a handful of workers extract from a few wells.

What perspectives can an underdeveloped country have under such conditions? The other products are coffee, grains, and cloves. We visited Zanzibar and asked to be taken to see a clove tree, because we wanted to see how cloves grow. Well, they are trees as tall as that column, on which flowers blossom, and the flower has to be picked while it is blossoming, before it drops its seed—you have to be shackled to those trees to pick them. [*Laughter*]

They also produce coconuts, on trees that look like the royal palm. You have to climb up and get the coconuts and then husk them to extract a little coconut meat. Many countries live off this kind of work.

Sri Lanka supports itself on coconut oil, tea, and rubber, and it has the same problem as Tanzania when it comes time to buy oil: unequal trade relations. The man picking flowers, shackled there. When they go to buy a truck that was worth $5,000 a short time ago, they find it's now worth $35,000 or $40,000. We were talking to the comrades who are helping in Angola's foreign trade, and they told us that those little trucks cost $40,000 apiece. They need ever increasing amounts of their little clove flowers and their cashew nuts to buy a truck, a machine, X-ray equipment, dental equipment, a surgical room; they have to pay more and more each time; they have to provide more of that product. Now it isn't only to buy machinery from the developed capitalist world; now it's to buy oil, as well, because now unequal trade relations apply not only to machinery but also to energy.

I remember from my student days—that's been some time ago now—[*Laughter*] the slogans of the revolutionaries, the protest against the monopolistic price of oil. The monopoly enterprises were already making huge profits from oil at that time, and now oil has quintupled in price. A group of countries get hold of huge amounts of money. The capitalists manage with trade, by charging more for everything; but the oil producers ride roughshod over the underdeveloped non-oil-producing countries of the so-called Third World. Some oil-producing countries take that money and invest it well; at least they are investing it in their development, in doing something, in helping the people, the masses, their own masses. But others—the big producers, Iran and Saudi Arabia—use it to buy U.S. arms; they use those funds to support reaction; they are allies of imperialism; they play the role of gendarmes; since money talks, some of those countries are even increasing their influence in international policy. They see that ruin, that semiruin, and they give back a little of what they've stolen. That is, they take $300 million out of a country and then lend $50 million, with interest, back to the underdeveloped countries.

The situation has worsened. Now when countries impose a monopoly price on a basic raw material, they do so in detriment to all the other raw-material producers that sell on the world market. That is a mathematical fact. Some of these countries that have to buy whatever oil they use anyhow are left without a cent to buy other things: to buy sugar, for example, or to buy other raw materials, other foodstuffs, because they are paralyzed without oil.

The world cannot solve its problems this way: as the population increases, natural resources such as oil are exhausted; the environment is polluted. They say new energy sources will emerge. This year we are even going to begin building the first atomic plant, but the investments are very great. The technology still isn't sufficiently perfected; only part of the energy contained in uranium is used. All this energy development—which I think will undoubtedly have to be nuclear—involves other problems, including big investments, technological development, the transformation and accumulation of this energy—which isn't yet solved—transportation and the disposal of residues. So, when the population reaches 15 billion inhabitants and there isn't any oil, the number of nuclear plants that are required will be colossal. Then, too, the same raw material used to produce nuclear energy also produces the elements necessary for nuclear arms.

The analysis of all these elements leads to the question of how the problems of underdevelopment can be solved under these conditions. If there isn't a clear political idea and if neocolonialism, capitalism, imperialism, unequal trade relations, and all these problems aren't eliminated, how can the problem of underdevelopment which affects billions of people in the world be solved? It is clear that only socialism can find the answer to these problems—only worldwide socialism, because humanity would have to begin to work as a single family. The more developed countries will have to help the less developed ones—Marx and Engels and Lenin foretold this—as a means of working toward solving current problems.

Population problems cannot be solved without family planning and population control—but with humane, revolutionary methods, beginning with the education of the population; not, as is the case in some countries, because they want to sterilize women, men, and everybody. [*Laughter*]

But for whose benefit? The bourgeoisie's? The big landowners'? People can be told that there has to be such a policy for the benefit of all—their children, the present generation, and future generations—but, in a neocolonialist country, in a capitalist country, in a country of big landowners, in a country of the bourgeoisie, who's going to be convinced to stop having children or to have one instead of seven or two instead of eleven? To do that requires culture, education, planning, and above all, a clear idea that what is being done is for the good of the citizen, the people, humanity.

Natural resources have been squandered by the capitalist societies in untold amounts and they are being exhausted. The environment has been polluted. When all is said and done, the human family lives on this planet and has to continue living on it, because there doesn't seem to be any near possibility of moving from here to another planet. [*Laughter*] A certain number of inhabitants can be adequately, humanely accommodated in this physical space. If there are ten times as many, they can't live, and everyone will be poisoned. We aren't like mosquitoes. Mosquitoes reproduce constantly and adapt to DDT and everything else. We don't reproduce at that speed. Human evolution has been a matter of hundreds of thousands and millions of years. We humans are not adapted to withstand all these poisons that the industrialized capitalist societies have irresponsibly dumped on the world, in the sea, in the air, everywhere. These are scientific truths.

How can the human family solve this problem? Under capitalism? Under imperialism? Under neocolonialism? Only with socialism and communism; only as a universal family, using resources and technology universally, can future humanity find a solution to its problems. The more we meditate and think about this, the more convinced we are that this is so.

You learn as much Marxism by seeing these problems on a trip through Africa as in five years of reading Marxist books. That is, reality teaches a great deal and confirms all the predictions made by the creators of Marxism-Leninism at their best. All we have seen everywhere in the world reaffirms our convictions on this score.

I said that we Cubans are learning to think in a universal way, too. We are acquiring an internationalist spirit. That is the basic conclusion we have reached after observing our people's attitude today. I say that we are learning to be internationalists.

I said that, of course, it hurt us whenever we saw a Cuban child who was hungry, ill, or abandoned; but we have to be just as hurt on seeing an Angolan child who is hungry, ill, or abandoned—or a Vietnamese child, or a Mozambican child, or a child from any other country. The fact that it hurts us doesn't mean that we can solve these problems, but simply that it must hurt us, that we have to be sensitive to these realities. When these feelings begin to reach man's heart and conscience, then we are more than mean, egotistical individuals; we will have gone beyond individual, family, and even national egoism to reach the point of really acquiring an internationalist feeling.

When you travel through Africa today, you hear about tribes. No one doubts that tribalism should be surmounted—no one in the world. The day will come when no one will doubt that nationalism has to be overcome, too—because, really, what is the nation? A somewhat larger tribe doing much the same thing: [*Laughter*] the Cuban tribe, the Mexican tribe, the Venezuelan tribe, the Jamaican and Dominican tribes. The nation is somewhat more developed than the tribe; but, just as the whole world now recognizes the need to overcome the concept of the tribe, as a phase in society's development that has to be left behind, the same thing will happen with the nation and the national concept someday.

Again, what is the difference between a tribe and a nation, when there is national egoism, everything for the nation, fraternity within the nation, and unity within the nation?

In my view internationalism is the most beautiful essence of Marxism-Leninism. It isn't just a question of being a necessity as the result of a law of the evolution of human society. Socialism, internationalism, and communism are becoming a necessity for humanity's survival. That is the reality: a condition for humanity's survival!

Twenty-fifth anniversary of Moncada

July 26, 1978

Speech given to mass rally in Santiago de Cuba. The text is from *Granma,* August 6, 1978.

Distinguished guests;
Comrades of the party and the government;
People of Santiago de Cuba;
Compatriots:

This is the twenty-fifth time we have commemorated the 26 of July, 1953: in prison, in exile, in the mountains, and in our homeland liberated with the weapons that began the battle anew—the just, inevitable, and necessary struggle to follow a different and honorable course. Our people's struggle for liberation did not begin that day; rather the heroic march that Céspedes began in 1868 and was continued later by José Martí, intellectual author of the attack on the Moncada—that exceptional man born precisely 100 years before—was reinitiated.* [*Applause*]

---

* Carlos Manuel de Céspedes was the leader of the first Cuban war of independence, which began in 1868 and was known as the Ten Years

For millennia in the history of humanity, a system in which some were masters while others were slaves, serfs, workers, peasants, and people oppressed in all kinds of ways was imposed on humanity by the egoism of some, the impotence and weakness of others, and the objective process of the evolution of society—composed of human beings who also evolved from the most elemental stages of life to the marvelous physical and moral structure we have today—from the most primitive forms to its current stages.

Natural and social laws led to a merciless course that humanity followed unconsciously most of the way. What makes today's people privileged in comparison to those of other periods is the fabulous possibility they have for controlling nature and charting their own course of social development for the first time. This is precisely what makes some of the economic, social, and political forms that still persist in many parts of the world such a great crime; it is what may give the will of the peoples and their actions and struggles to change their lives the highest moral and heroic meaning and what gives the concept of revolution its fullest significance.

We also had our masters. Our Indian forebears even had their exterminators; our African forefathers, their slave owners; the descendants of both and of the masters, as well, their colonizers; the Cuban people, already constituted as a nation, their neocolonizers; our workers and peasants, their exploiting capitalists and landowners;

War; he was killed in the fighting. José Martí, an essayist and poet, founded the Cuban Revolutionary Party and initiated the second war of independence in 1895; he was killed the same year. A national hero in Cuba, he was the intellectual inspirer of Fidel Castro and the July 26 Movement.

our Black population and our women, their discriminators; our children, illiteracy and hunger and disease; our adults, ignorance and unemployment; our old people, neglect and oblivion.

Such were the injustices; and such the struggles. Against those systems, we had the uprisings and deaths of the Indians, the epic battles of the slaves, the heroic struggles of the oppressed, October 10, February 24, July 26.*

A long road lay behind when our generation earned the privilege of victory and the harvest of its splendid fruits. Thus, we can commemorate the date of our rebellion with the freedom, independence, and justice of which so many generations of our predecessors dreamed. Moreover, the ideas of liberty, independence, and justice weren't the same in each epoch. For the slave in his time, it simply meant removing that ignominious social and legal status; for the bourgeois, removing the fetters of colonialism; for the serf, obtaining full rights to the land and its fruits. For the worker, however, the concepts of freedom, independence, and justice were very different: the total elimination of all forms of man's exploitation of man, full and real equality for all human beings, and fraternity and cooperation among all the peoples of the world. Our revolution is of this epoch, the epoch of internationalism and socialism, of the fullest and most complete concept of liberty and fraternity among men.

Were we, perhaps, better revolutionaries than those who preceded us? It was the period, the objective conditions in society and in the world, that made us Marxist-Leninists, internationalists, socialists, communists. [*Applause*] At all

---

* On October 10, 1868, Céspedes proclaimed the independence of Cuba with the "Cry of Yara." On February 24, 1895, Cuba's second war of independence was launched with the "Cry of Baire."

times, in every country, during every epoch, revolutionaries have struggled and dedicated their best energies to the noble aim of human progress, so there is no reason for today's revolutionaries to consider themselves better than yesterday's. What can make the revolutionaries of today qualitatively different is their greater knowledge of the laws that govern the development of human society, for this places in their hands a great weapon for struggle and social change. Modern revolutionaries are indebted to the theoreticians of scientific socialism—Marx, Engels, and Lenin—for the immense treasure of their ideas. We are absolutely sure that, without them, our people would not have been able to achieve such a tremendous leap in the history of their social and political development. But, even with them, we would not have been capable of achieving it without the fertile seed and the unlimited heroism sown among our people and in our spirits by such giants of our country's history as Martí, Maceo, Gómez, Agramonte, and Céspedes.* [*Applause*]

That is how the real revolution was made in Cuba, based on its unique characteristics, its own traditions of struggle, and the consistent application of universal principles. These principles exist; they cannot be ignored.

There have been presumptuous people in the world who have wanted to nationalize and chauvinize Marxism; there have even been those who pretended to consider themselves superior to Marx, Engels, and Lenin, without taking into account the rigorousness of their

---

* Antonio Maceo, an important figure in Cuban history, was an outstanding general in both the first and second wars of independence from Spain. Máximo Gómez and Ignacio Agramonte were leaders of the 1868–78 war; Gómez played a leading role in the second independence war, as well.

research, the incomparable modesty that characterized those creators of our revolutionary doctrine, and the fact that men cannot erect their own monument for posterity; rather the people and objective facts assign each their role in history. [*Applause*] It was not without reason that the wisest of our patriots refused human vanity by teaching us that all the glory of the world fits in a kernel of corn. [*Applause*]

It is unnecessary, today, to relate well-known facts or stress the merits of an action which many of us who are here today witnessed or participated in.

First of all, let us say to our people and to the world youth who are fortunately with us on this anniversary that the triumph of an idea in any country is always the fruit of the efforts of many generations and of the contributions of all humanity. Here, within the walls of this fortress, following the armed action, dozens of young people like those who are meeting in our country this year were brutally tortured and finally assassinated by those who defended the interests of the exploiting class and the empire's monopolies, in a vain attempt to block the course of history. With the fury and hatred of those who neither tolerate nor pardon disrespect by the people, the oppressors—as in the days of Spartacus, the Paris Commune, Vietnam, and Chile—committed every iniquity against the brave revolutionary combatants. The reactionaries have always believed that their power was invincible and eternal. How far they were from thinking that one day in the first socialist country in the Western Hemisphere, in Santiago de Cuba itself and inside the walls of that military bastion, the representatives of the finest and most progressive world youth and of the people whose sons and daughters engaged in that unequal combat would meet to celebrate the victorious twenty-fifth anniversary of the attack on the Moncada and the Eleventh World Festival!* [*Applause*] This indicates that no just hope of the people is impossible to achieve, no setback is irreversible, no sacrifice is sterile, no reactionary regime is eternal.

Why explain to the youth of the world what oppression, underdevelopment, capitalism, colonialism, neocolonialism, racism, fascism, and imperialism mean, when many of them have felt and still feel them in their own flesh? Our experience was no different; our battles for freedom and progress were not unlike those that are taking place today in many parts of the world. Our struggle was the eternal struggle of all oppressed peoples; our enemies were and are the same enemies; our victories are the victories of all progressive humanity today and tomorrow. [*Applause*]

Without euphemism or exaggeration, the fact that, twenty-five years after that action which we are commemorating today and after a sustained, heroic, and victorious struggle, Cuba is successfully building socialism close to the most aggressive and powerful empire on earth is a success for the world revolutionary movement and an encouraging lesson for all peoples, no matter how much the imperialists and the shameless traitors to the cause of internationalism, who have now become lackeys and allies of the world's oppressors, try to ignore it. [*Applause*]

All the hatred of the Yankee empire was visited on our people. An implacable blockade that has now lasted for almost two decades was imposed on our homeland, and a foreign military base has been maintained in our country with insolent scorn for our national will and sovereignty. Conspiracies, plots, and acts of sabotage and aggression

---

* The Eleventh World Festival of Youth and Students was held July 28–August 5, 1978, in Havana, attended by 18,500 delegates from 145 countries.

of all kinds occurred for many years. Sinister plots for assassinating the leaders of the revolution—plots which have now been publicly acknowledged by the perpetrators themselves—were elaborated and carried out by the highest authorities in the United States. There was no means, procedure, or recourse, however illegal or dirty, that wasn't used against our country. The imperialists introduced disease and plagues that could wipe out useful plants and animals in our country.

The revolutionary vanguard also waged an epic ideological struggle against those who had been used to ruling, ordering, determining, and imposing their ways of thinking on the peoples of Latin America.

Why did the imperialists do this? What were they defending? What did they want to maintain in our country? Foreign control over our natural resources, our wealth, and what our people had produced with their sweat; corrupt and bloody governments that served their interests; landless peasants, exploited workers, and an illiterate, starving, despairing people; children without teachers or doctors, adults without health or medical care, fathers without work, hundreds of thousands of mothers who sometimes had no alternative to prostitution; discrimination based on race and sex; neglected old people; gambling houses, vice, corruption, and bloody political repression.

Compare our country now with the rest of Latin America. There is no imperialist or capitalist control, and we are the only people in the hemisphere free of unemployment, illiteracy, begging, prostitution, games of chance, and racial discrimination. We have the highest indices of public health, education, culture, and sports anywhere in the continent. [*Applause*] We are the absolute masters of our economic wealth and natural resources. We plan our development and are totally responsible for our people's economic, social, and cultural progress. Our difficulties are the same objective difficulties shared by any other underdeveloped country in the world, but we have the prerogative of determining the future, with austerity and modesty, yet with freedom and dignity. [*Applause*]

How did we Cuban revolutionaries achieve this victory? With determination; loyalty to principles; close ties with the masses; absolute confidence in the justice of our cause and in our people's virtues, their heroism, and spirit of sacrifice; international solidarity; and the cooperation of the progressive movement, the socialist community and especially the glorious Union of Soviet Socialist Republics. [*Applause*]

We said:
"No!" to discouragement in the face of adversity,
"No!" to difficulties,
"No!" to pessimism,
"No!" to fear,
"No!" to giving up,
"No!" to opportunism,
"No!" to ideological concessions,
"No!" to narrow nationalism and chauvinism,
"No!" to the abuse of power,
"No!" to violations of principles,
"No!" to corruption,
"No!" to self-glorification,
"No!" to the deification of leaders,
"No!" to the ridiculous cult of the personality, and
"No!" to the infallibility of revolutionaries.
And we were able to say:
"Yes!" to solidarity among men,
"Yes!" to Marxism-Leninism, [*Applause*]
"Yes!" to consistent anti-imperialism, [*Applause*]
"Yes!" to proletarian internationalism, [*Applause*]

"Yes!" to the need for a vanguard party, [*Applause*]

"Yes!" to collective leadership and revolutionary democratic norms, [*Applause*]

"Yes!" to self-criticism and recognition and rectification of errors, [*Applause*]

"Yes!" to modesty,

"Yes!" to complete dedication to the people,

"Yes!" to admiration and respect for those whose past struggle made today's homeland a possibility, and

"Yes!" to eternal gratitude to those who expressed their solidarity with us and whose disinterested and noble support helped us to win out over imperialism's aggressions. [*Applause*]

The Cuba you see today is nothing like the one that existed twenty years ago. Casinos, beggars, unemployed men, and brothels made the first impression on visitors then. Today those things no longer exist. But don't think the postrevolutionary change was necessarily pleasing to every visitor. During the time of the Popular Unity, the flagship of the Chilean navy visited us. Many cadets, educated in a bourgeois, capitalist mentality, were displeased at not being able to find brothels in Havana, like they found in all the other capitals of Latin America, in the United States, and in Western Europe.

Before the Cuban revolution, the brothel and the gallows existed side by side—as in Chile now. [*Applause*]

That underdeveloped neocolonialist, and capitalist way of life imposed on the nation was maintained by pure force and was the hallmark and basic achievement of imperialist control over our country. The imperialists didn't train doctors or teachers, but they trained henchmen in the art of torturing, kidnapping, and murdering opponents and revolutionaries—as is done today in Nicaragua, Chile, Uruguay, Paraguay, and other unfortunate countries of America and the world, with the far more refined techniques of the Pentagon and the CIA. They taught how to persecute a communist, how to split a trade union and put in their own man, how and what to write for a newspaper, what movies to see, what radio programs to listen to, what books to read. They determined when to invest and what the profits would be; that was their role as absolute masters of our finances, our best land, and the rest of the country's natural resources. They outlined our policy and our future.

What is even worse, because its effects remain and are more difficult to uproot, they imposed the consumer habits and customs of the developed capitalist world on our poor and underdeveloped country. Their development was achieved on the basis of the most merciless exploitation of their own people and the rest of the colonized and neocolonized world and the most brutal and unequal trade relations with economically backward countries.

Bourgeois society creates its bourgeois tastes and its bourgeois landscape in urban and rural areas, and they cannot be those of the workers' societies. Along with the millionaires' palaces go the slums, and, along with the modern throughways where luxury cars drive at high speed, are muddy roads that the humble peasants travel on foot. Bourgeois countries offer statistics on per capita rates of consumption but say not a word about the tremendous difference between what a millionaire consumes and what a worker, one of the unemployed, or a beggar gets.

In our cities, you won't see huge, flashy billboards with advertising, because we don't try to use conditioned reflexes to inculcate our citizens with what soft drinks should be consumed or what cigarettes should be smoked, as is done in the societies that, ridiculously, pretend to be free. Instead, in many parts of our countryside you will see the electric lights in the classrooms of our thousands of rural schools, our polyclinics, and our peasants' houses. In our papers you won't see ads, wedding announcements, or stories about the parties and recreational activities of the rich—that never interest the worker, the only true creator of social wealth. Nor do our radio and television stations constantly interrupt their programs to offer commercials, because our mass media serves information, education, and culture, not social vanity or vulgar mercantile interests.

Sometimes we may even lack paint for our most important buildings, but teachers and books will never be lacking in any schools, and all the children and other citizens of our country will have doctors and medicines in our hospitals when they need them. [*Applause*]

You won't see our streets crowded with modern, noisy cars that consume fabulous amounts of energy, because we are promoting and developing collective transportation and view the private car simply as an instrument that can support the social services that technicians, doctors, teachers, and other workers in our society provide.

I have often wondered what would happen to the world and its energy and other natural resources if every family in Asia (China or India, for example), Africa, and Latin America had a car, in line with the fictitious, absurd ideal that the developed capitalist societies have created. Someone once said that man does not live by bread alone. Today we can say, "Man does not live by (and for) cars alone." [*Applause*]

That which irrationally engendered capitalism and exploitation can never be the model for the 7 billion inhabitants the world will have twenty-five years from now. We consider that oil and other essential resources should be used first to provide food, lodging, health care, education, culture, and other basic requirements for the well-being of people who have another concept of life, society, and the fruits of human work. We are dedicating our modest resources to that end in the midst of the cruel and relentless economic blockade that the powerful and rich United States has imposed on our heroic country.

In spite of it, however, nobody can be unaware of Cuba's advances, which show what can be done even when you're poor, provided the justice of socialism exists. [*Applause*]

You'll see everyone in our country with a book under their arm, because we all want to study, learn, and correctly interpret the world in which we live. We never tell anyone to believe; we tell everyone to think, study, and decide. [*Applause*]

The imperialists foolishly attempt to present our country as having a system upheld by force. Of course there is force, but this strength lies not in weapons or laws or state institutions; it resides in the people, [*Applause*] in the masses, in revolutionary convictions, and in the political education of every citizen. Our strength is not in lies or demagoguery but in sincerity, truth, and consciousness. In addition, the weapons are in the hands of the people and they use them to defend the revolution without torture, crime, death squads, missing persons, illegalities, or arbitrary acts such as occur every day in the countries in which imperialism keeps unjust, oppressive, reactionary regimes in power. Even our most bitter enemies have begun to acknowledge this now—the fruits of our having planted seeds of principle and revolutionary ethics at the time of the Moncada, seeds that flourished during the war of liberation and the subsequent development of the revolution. Rising above the mountains of imperialist slander, our historical reality stands firm and invincible.

Our country plans to continue its just march forward. We are now drawing up our second five-year plan. Serious studies are being made on our perspectives for economic, social, and cultural development up to the year 2000. Fairly soon, we will have a twenty-year prognostic plan. Each province, city, and municipality will know with the greatest possible precision what its future will be like and what national development tasks it will be assigned. Just to give you an idea of what the future holds in store, I will say that, this year alone, 18,000 Cubans have been graduated as teachers and professors. [*Applause*] For those who think Cuba is becoming a country of soldiers, it is good to point out that there were twenty times as many teachers and professors graduated as there were officers for our armed forces this year, [*Applause*] even though it is a very high honor for a Cuban to be a soldier or an officer, because the arms borne in our homeland and even outside it are used in the most noble cause of the revolution and internationalism. [*Applause*] When it comes right down to it, we are all soldiers of the revolution, but it is more difficult to know how to teach than how to die. More than once, our men fought and died for this right, for men must also know how to die so that humankind may live. [*Applause*]

We are advancing resolutely toward becoming a country with a high level of culture. In this field, our road has no limits. We will live on what our technology, natural resources, and sweat can create, and we won't be egoists, like a snail closed in its own shell; we will give the world everything within the reach of our revolutionary and internationalist generosity. [*Applause*]

What is our life without you; what is Cuba without the rest of the world? If our dreams of yesterday have become today's realities, our dreams of today will come true tomorrow, and this will be true for the whole world, if we can dream together of a better future. [*Applause*]

Since realities cannot be overlooked, it must be said that humanity faces serious problems today. First of all, there is the vital matter of overcoming the risks of nuclear warfare. In other eras, men settled their political conflicts by using stone axes, lances, bows and arrows, swords, cannon, and even planes, warships, and tanks. However, no other era in history has had such deadly weapons of mass destruction as those that exist today. What might have been called irresponsible ambition yesterday—something the privileged classes could be party to in defense of their interests and their aims to carve up the world and wipe out the advance of progressive ideas, as was true of World War II—becomes universal suicide and a crime against humanity today, with modern, sophisticated means of mass destruction. It remains to be seen whether humanity will be able to survive the diabolical weapons it has produced.

If we make a basic analysis of realities, we will see that humanity's political and social advancement as a whole falls short of its capacity for destruction and extermination. The progressive and revolutionary forces are not the ones that have created this dreadful and dangerous situation. Vladimir Ilyich Lenin launched the slogan of peace and coexistence among all nations at the time of the birth of the first socialist state. [*Applause*] Socialism, whose basic economic objective is the development of the productive forces and the equitable distribution of the fruits of labor, has absolutely no need for wars, for carving up the world, or for an arms buildup. The planned development of the economy and basic human requirements in no way necessitate the investment of infinite human and material resources in a sterile arms race. The first socialist state did not declare war on nations with different social systems; the imperialist powers were the ones that decided to use intervention and blockade to do away with the first workers' and peasants' state and, at the same time, crush the revolutionary movement throughout the world. This policy produced fascism and World War II. The crusade against the Soviet Union waged by Hitler's Germany, armed with the collaboration of the other imperialist powers, cost the first socialist state the lives of 20 million of its finest sons and daughters. The peoples of the imperialist countries also had to pay a high price for their governments' rash anticommunist, profascist adventurism.

Can anyone deny these historic truths? Can anyone hide the fact that the capitalist countries were basically responsible for the outbreak of that war? Who can forget that it was socialism that kept fascism from gaining control of the world? What country but the United States, virtually replacing Hitler's Germany, started a crusade of anticommunism and counterrevolution in the world? What other country is a real threat to world peace? Who practices a policy of force? Who has spread military bases all over the world? Who promotes the arms race? Who needs the military industry to handle internal economic problems and satisfy powerful monopoly interests?

Those who blame the socialist countries for their defense programs forget the lesson of fascism and the historic truth that it is imperialism, through its aggression, blockades, and threats, that has forced our countries to invest considerable resources in military expenses completely foreign to the needs and objectives of the socialist system. [*Applause*] As a principle, we Marxist-Leninists know that social change cannot be imposed from abroad; nor can it be prevented when the people decide to obtain it by any means necessary. The socialist peoples do not try to export revolution. No one exported socialism to the Soviet Union, and no one exported socialism to Cuba. Since the birth of socialism, only the imperialist countries have tried to export their system—capitalism, reaction, counterrevolution, and fascism.

What interest can humanity have in the arms race? Why waste on arms what people need in food, housing, health care, education, and recreation? Each year, hundreds of billions of dollars are spent on military hardware. Mountains of deadly weapons are stockpiled every year before the horrified eyes of a world with mountains of problems: underdevelopment, hunger, excessive population growth, unemployment, disease, illiteracy, the growing scarcity of food and natural resources, and environmental pollution.

It is clear that there is only one final solution for this tragedy: humanity must go beyond its capitalist and imperialist phase, and social justice and cooperation must be developed on a world scale. But this is a task for the people of each country.

Humanity must be preserved for a better future. A pessimistic position concerning the need for and possibility of peace, such as that held by those who predict the inevitability of war—and even encourage it, perhaps believing they will be the only survivors—is inadmissible and absolutely irresponsible.

The peoples have the duty to struggle for peace and, at the same time, for social change. Will we let threats intimidate us? No, because we are optimists and because we know, as Karl Marx taught us, that the oppressed have nothing to lose but their chains. [*Applause*]

The U.S. government is currently vaunting human rights. We Marxist-Leninists, who have made the material and spiritual well-being of the people and their economic, social, and political rights, the raison d'être of our lives and who are struggling to do away with all forms of man's exploitation of man, will always, naturally, be in favor of true human rights. We will even be glad if Carter's preachings have any influence on some of his intimate allies, such as Nicaragua, El Salvador, Guatemala, Haiti, Chile, Paraguay, Uruguay, Argentina, Brazil, Zaïre, South Africa, Saudi Arabia, Iran, South Korea, and others of their ilk in persuading them to cease their genocidal practices and their systematic torture, murder, and kidnapping of fighters for democracy and progress. [*Applause*] If they should have any such influence, the capitalist, neocolonialized, proimperialist regimes and that of the United States itself would be a little less inhuman. However, it is yet to be shown that a bellicose, imperialist, bourgeois regime can promise true human rights to anybody in the world, whether within or outside its own country, because such a system exists only to place all its resources and means—both domestic and foreign—at the service of the rights and interests of big capital.

On what moral grounds can the rulers of a nation in which millionaires and beggars exist; Indians are exterminated; Blacks are discriminated against; women are prostituted; and huge numbers of Chicanos, Puerto Ricans, and other Latin Americans are scorned, exploited, and humiliated, speak of human rights?

How can the rulers of an empire in which the Mafia, gambling, and the prostitution of minors run rampant and in which the CIA draws up plans for worldwide espionage and subversion and the Pentagon creates neutron bombs that can preserve property while wiping out human beings—an empire that supports reaction and counterrevolution everywhere and protects and stimulates the monopolies in their worldwide exploitation of natural and human resources, unequal trade relations, a protectionist policy, an incredible waste of natural resources, and the system of hunger for the world—raise this cry?

How can the representatives of a capitalist and imperialist society based on the exploitation of man by man, combined with egoism, individualism, and the total absence of human solidarity, do this?

How can those who train and provide military supplies to the bloodiest, most reactionary, and most corrupt governments in the world, such as those of Somoza, Pinochet, Stroessner, the gorillas in Uruguay, Mobutu, and the shah of Iran, to cite just a few examples, mouth this slogan?

How can those who maintain close relations with the racists of South Africa—who oppress, discriminate against, and exploit 20 million Africans—and those who supply large quantities of sophisticated arms to the Zionist aggressors who expelled the Palestinian people from their land [*Applause*] and refuse to return to the Arab countries the territories wrested from them by force, speak of such rights?

How can the leaders of a state whose intelligence agencies organized assassination attempts against the leaders of other countries and whose armies dropped explosives in Vietnam equivalent to hundreds of atom bombs such as those exploded over Hiroshima and Nagasaki and who murdered millions of Vietnamese without even deigning to apologize to the country or pay indemnity for the lives lost—the leaders of a state that has traditionally intervened in Latin America, subjects the peoples of this part of the world to its exploiting yoke, and is responsible for the deaths of hundreds of children every year due to illness and starvation—how can they speak of human rights?

In short, how can the imperialist government that forcibly maintains a military base in our territory and subjects our people to a criminal economic blockade speak of human rights?

It would be wonderful if President Carter were to be true to his preachings and decree the freeing of Lolita Lebrón, [*Applause*] and the other Puerto Rican patriots who have been unjustly imprisoned for more than twenty-five years, and the Wilmington Ten,* who have been jailed arbitrarily, and an amnesty for the thousands of U.S. Blacks who have been forced by discrimination, unemployment, and hunger to commit criminal acts. [*Applause*]

Every U.S. ruler has had his own rhetorical phrase for Latin America or the world: one spoke of a "Good Neighbor Policy"; another, of the "Alliance for Progress." Now the watchword is "human rights." Nothing has changed in U.S. policy toward the hemisphere and the world; everything is just the same; gunboat and dollar diplomacy, the law of the mighty, has always prevailed. The phraseology is just as fleeting as the administrations. The only constant in the Yankees' policy is their propensity to lie. [*Applause*]

We were saying that imperialism supported fascism in Latin America, apartheid in Africa, and neocolonialism all over, but imperialist policy is also something much more subtle: it promotes the split between socialist countries, abets nationalist currents, fans chauvinism, and seeks allies in the progressive movement. Imperialism—which used to fight nationalism tooth and nail as a manifestation of the peoples' spirit of independence against the colonial system and used to fight and still does fight it as an expression of anti-imperialist struggle and of the defense of the legitimate interests of each country—cherishes the hope that the exacerbation of this same sentiment—that

---

* Lolita Lebrón was one of five Puerto Rican nationalists imprisoned in the U.S. in the early 1950s for armed proindependence actions. She and the three other surviving prisoners were released in 1979; Cuba was widely credited with playing a major role in winning their release. The Wilmington Ten were convicted in 1972 of arson and conspiracy, in a case evoking worldwide charges of racism. Rev. Ben Chavis, the last of the Ten remaining in prison, was released in December 1979.

is, chauvinism—will clash with the principles of socialism and internationalism. It believes that this current will always be more powerful than the revolutionary, internationalist spirit in Asia, Africa, and Latin America.

For the rest, they trust to their technologies as industrialized countries, to the monopoly of their international loan agencies, and to the enormous monetary reserves still held by the capitalist West. To the gold accumulated during centuries of the exploitation of their own workers and of the colonized, neocolonized, and other underdeveloped countries is now added the multimillions amassed by such states as Saudi Arabia and Iran, that extract part of their fabulous gains from countries that are economically backward. With these resources, they seek to wipe out the progressive movement in the nations of the so-called Third World.

It is true that the effects of the world economic crisis are felt strongly in countries with progressive governments and few resources, tied down with debts and mercilessly subjected to the whiplash of financial problems. As a result of economic difficulties, right-wing forces win electoral victories in some countries, while the reaction resorts to fascism to face those same difficulties with the most brutal repression. The International Monetary Fund and other loan agencies that are traditional tools of U.S. policy impose onerous conditions, weaken the popular base of the governments that aren't to their liking and undermine their political stability. These circumstances are favorable for pressure being exerted and people giving in—and, thus, for transitory victories for reaction in some countries of the world.

We would be dishonest if we denied that the progressive and revolutionary movement itself was facing serious difficulties. The repugnant betrayal of the cause of internationalism perpetrated by the Chinese leadership, its insane political conduct, and its shameful alliance with the imperialist powers, have been a harsh blow to the progressive forces of the world.

Vietnam, Angola, and Cuba—small countries that won solid, recognized prestige in the world with their acts of heroism, past and present, in their resolute, firm, unwavering struggle against imperialism—are now victims of brutal attacks, [*Applause*] hostility, and slander from the traitorous Chinese leadership. After nearly twenty years of aggression and harassment of our country by the United States, which never succeeded in bringing us to our knees, we are now witnessing the present Chinese leadership's incredible and infamous attempts to justify the economic blockade of Cuba and the presence of a Yankee naval base on our territory.

There is no longer any difference at all between the imperialist wire services and those of China, in terms of their crude and scheming language and the perfidious, base arguments they employ in attacking Cuba. Soviet cooperation, so decisive for the consolidation and survival of the Cuban revolution in its most difficult years, when the imperialists deprived us of their market for our sugar and halted shipments of foods, medicines, fuel, spare parts, and raw materials which were essential for us, is vilely slandered. Along with the decisive economic support we have received, we will never forget the fact that the weapons we used to defend ourselves against the imperialist aggressors at Playa Girón [Bay of Pigs] were supplied by the Soviets. [*Applause*] The fact that the United States was unable to commit genocide against Cuba in a direct attack was due in large part to the solidarity and support of the USSR. History cannot be so grossly distorted. Human speech was created for more noble ends.

Cuba's internationalist policy; the unlimited generosity of our people whose sons fought in Angola against the South African racists so that the Angolan people's independence—won in fifteen years of heroic struggle—would not be snatched away; and our solidarity in the Ethiopian revolution's battle against foreign aggression, promoted by the United States, the other NATO powers, and the Arab reactionary forces, are described by the Chinese leaders in the same gross, base terms as those used by imperialism's spokesmen and in even worse—less subtle, more overtly false—language.

Internationalism and its ideals of solidarity and fraternity among peoples form the beautiful essence of Marxism-Leninism. Without internationalism, the Cuban revolution wouldn't even exist. Being internationalists is one way of paying our debt to humanity. [*Applause*]

Even though we don't like to be the ones to speak of the irreproachable way in which the Cuban revolution has fulfilled its internationalist duty, it should be recalled that our military cooperation with Angola and Ethiopia was not something new. Cuban soldiers went to the sister republic of Algeria in 1963 to support it against foreign aggression when, in the months following the victory of its heroic struggle for independence, attempts were made to grab a part of its territory. Cuban soldiers went to Syria in 1973 when that country requested our help right after the last war waged against the Zionist aggressors. Cuban fighters fought and died to help free Guinea-Bissau and Angola from Portuguese colonialism. It is no secret that worthy comrades from our guerrilla struggle in the Sierra Maestra died with Che in Bolivia. [*Applause*]

This internationalist tradition of the Cuban revolutionaries goes back to before the triumph of the revolution, when more than a thousand volunteer fighters, many of them communists, left for Spain to fight against fascism. [*Applause*] The communists' international solidarity and spirit of sacrifice and struggle have had particularly deep and beautiful roots in the world revolutionary movement since the glorious days of the Paris Commune.

The Yankee imperialists practice solidarity with reaction, the bourgeoisie, and fascism. Hundreds of thousands of U.S. soldiers and military specialists are in Western Europe, Turkey, Saudi Arabia, Iran, South Korea, Japan, the Federal Republic of Germany, and scores of other countries. Why is it that imperialists are allowed to cooperate among themselves but revolutionaries aren't? [*Applause*]

Our military specialists in Africa and other parts of the world have been requested by sovereign governments. The United States, however, has tens of thousands of soldiers in Panama against the will of that people. The United States has thousands of sailors stationed in a part of Cuba's national territory against the will of our homeland. What right does the United States have to demand the withdrawal of our military personnel from Africa, when they are there at the expressed wish of completely independent, progressive, and revolutionary governments?

Politically and morally, how can you describe those who support these demands by imperialism?

Ever since a foolish mortal was turned into a god in the People's Republic of China and the party and its best cadres were destroyed in the days of the crazy adventure of the Cultural Revolution and the ruling circles let themselves be swayed by the petty-bourgeois spirit and great-power chauvinism that led them to betray internationalism and to turn a socialist state into a nepotic satrapy, in which the wives and sons-in-law of the rulers become members of the political bureau, we have seen that anything can happen.

What is strange about the Chinese government today supporting Pinochet's bloody fascist regime and the other repressive and reactionary military governments of Latin America? What is surprising about its collaborating with Mobutu along with the NATO interventionist forces? What is surprising about its joining South Africa against Angola, Somalia in its attack on the Ethiopian revolution, Egypt in its sell-out and separate peace policy, the conservative and reactionary forces of England and the Federal Republic of Germany, NATO in Europe, and Yankee imperialism all over, or its dangerous and stupid assumption of the inevitability of a third world war?

However, the most reprehensible crime committed by the Chinese leadership is its hostility to Vietnam. Nobody is unaware that Maoism and the Chinese ruling clique are behind Cambodia's extremism; nobody is unaware that they are behind the acts of provocation against Vietnam; nobody is unaware that they are behind the artificially created "problem of the Hoa." An enormous chauvinistic propaganda campaign is now being waged in China against the Vietnamese, and all economic cooperation has been suspended. In this criminal and unscrupulous way, Vietnamese efforts to rebuild their country, so cruelly devastated by the imperialist war, are being sabotaged.

These actions by the Chinese government remind us of Yankee prepotency against Cuba. In the first years of the revolution, the imperialists also tried to bring in ships without our authorization to take out U.S. citizens; they promoted the emigration of tens of thousands of Cubans, mainly professionals, specialists, and skilled workers; they launched an enormous slander campaign against Cuba and adopted severe measures of economic blockade.

Vietnam—the homeland of the most modest and consistent Marxist-Leninist of our times, the unforgettable and beloved Ho Chi Minh—[*Applause*] Vietnam, the patriotic and revolutionary feats of whose thousand-times-heroic people have amazed the world, is now, as well, the victim of China's betrayal and aggression.

Some days ago, the wire services reported violations of the Vietnamese border by squadrons of Chinese military planes. If the criminals' hands are not stopped in time, we will be witness to more serious acts of aggression and military provocation by China against heroic Vietnam. This is why we should offer the people of Vietnam our most determined solidarity and support. [*Applause*] Our party proposes to reactivate the Committees of Solidarity with Vietnam in the face of the threats of imperialist aggression, this time orchestrated—absurd as it may seem—by imperialism's brand-new allies in the camp of counterrevolution.

Scorn for the peoples and for norms and principles must have a limit; it must be stopped at some point; it must come up against a solid resistance in the universal conscience.

Not even Albania, a small socialist country that supported it in the first days of the split in the revolutionary movement, follows China today. And economic assistance to Albania has also been withdrawn.

Sooner or later, the hard-working, militant, self-sacrificing, heroic, and revolutionary Chinese people will settle accounts with the traitors who have dropped their beautiful internationalist banners at the feet of imperialism. [*Applause*]

There are two paths in the world: that of reaction and that of progress. A choice must be made; neutrality is impossible.

Recently, as a result of the problems that have arisen in the revolutionary movement, opportunism, unprincipled policies, and a tendency to compromise with imperialism have gained some strength. Opportunism, economic difficulties, chauvinism, demagoguery, and political cowardice have led to vacillation on many key issues.

It is impossible to be neutral concerning the Arab people's struggle to recover their occupied territory and to have the rights of the Palestinian people recognized; [*Applause*] it is impossible to be neutral in the struggles between the peoples of Africa and their neocolonizers, between Angola and its invaders, between the Saharan people in the defense of their rights and the occupiers of their territory, [*Applause*] between the Ethiopian revolution and the Somalian aggressors, [*Applause*] between the Yemeni revolution and Arab reaction, [*Applause*] between the progressive Arab countries and the reactionary Arab countries, [*Applause*] between Vietnam and those who threaten and harass it, [*Applause*] between the South African racists and the African people of South Africa, [*Applause*] between the Patriotic Front of Zimbabwe and Ian Smith, [*Applause*] between Mozambique and the Rhodesian and South African fascists, [*Applause*] between Namibia and its colonizers, [*Applause*] between the people of Cyprus and the foreign occupiers, [*Applause*] between the progressive forces and the rightist forces of Lebanon, [*Applause*] and between Allende and Pinochet; [*Applause*] it is impossible to be neutral on such questions as Panama's sovereignty over the canal, [*Applause*] the right of the peoples of Belize and Puerto Rico to independence, [*Applause*] and the blockade of Cuba and the Yankee naval base at Guantánamo; it is impossible to be neutral concerning imperialism, colonialism, neocolonialism, racism, fascism, and any of the situations that come up in the political, economic, and social struggle between the reactionary forces and the progressive forces of the world.

Our revolution is known for its rejection of all kinds of political opportunism. This militant, clear, firm, and determined line of Cuba's, in solidarity with the just cause of the peoples, and its growing authority and prestige in the international arena worry certain people—especially Yankee imperialism, which vainly tried to isolate and destroy our revolution.

According to news reports coming from the United States the government of that country has approached fifteen Nonaligned countries with a view to contesting Cuba's role in that movement. However, the Movement of Nonaligned countries is not the OAS [Organization of American States], the ministry of colonies in which imperialism, as the ruler of this hemisphere, makes all the decisions. It would be good to know which fifteen foreign ministries the United States contacted and what their replies have been.

Since when does the United States have the right to advise and orient the Nonaligned countries? Which are the shameless governments that lend themselves to this?

We have always thought that the Nonaligned movement—which Cuba, along with Nasser, Nehru, Nkrumah,* and other leaders, many of whom are, unfortunately, dead, helped to found—should be characterized by quality rather than quantity. We have always opposed and will continue to oppose having countries that belong to military pacts participate in this movement. [*Applause*] We have always opposed and will continue to oppose having

---

* Gamal Abdal Nasser was president of Egypt 1956–70; he nationalized the Suez Canal and was known as an advocate of Arab unity. Jawaharlal Nehru was prime minister of India from its independence in 1947 until his death in 1964. Kwame Nkrumah helped lead the Gold Coast (renamed Ghana) to independence and was prime minister and later president (1957–66); a proponent of Pan-Africanism.

fascist, reactionary governments, pawns of imperialism, introduced as Trojan horses in the heart of that force. [*Applause*] We have always thought and will continue to think that the Nonaligned movement should not be an amorphous, opportunistic, weak-kneed current but should be an anti-imperialist, anticolonialist, and progressive force that can have a positive influence on world policy. It was created with this spirit, and it cannot be conceived of in any other way. [*Applause*]

Cuba is a Nonaligned country because it does not belong to any military pact, but it is decidedly against reaction, imperialism, colonialism, neocolonialism, fascism, racism, Zionism, unequal trade relations, and the exploitation of the underdeveloped countries. [*Applause*] Cuba resolutely supports the liberation movements, the just causes, and the progressive forces of the whole world, essential objectives for which the Nonaligned movement was created.

Why is the United States so interested now in the Sixth Summit Conference, to be held in Havana? Why is it trying to sabotage it? Who is going along with this maneuver? What objectives do they seek in our movement? It is clear that the United States, the traitors, the opportunists, the neocolonized, the fence-sitters, and those whose principles are negotiable are worried by the militant, firm, staunch, and honest role of Cuba. [*Applause*]

There are governments that sell out, but the government of Cuba can never be bribed. [*Applause*] The United States knows this.

We will make no concessions; we will not betray our internationalist principles; we will never bend to the exigencies and blackmail of imperialism. [*Applause*] We do not pursue chauvinistic interests. Our international policy is not up for negotiation. We are ready to resist the imperialist blockade selflessly and with dignity for as many years as it may be necessary. Others may give way, accept bribes, and engage in betrayal, but Cuba will continue to set an example as a revolution that does not surrender, does not sell out, and does not go on its knees. [*Applause*]

The prospect of struggle does not put us off; never, since we first took the paths of revolution, have we been discouraged. No real communist has ever been afraid of difficulties. Our homeland was forged with indomitable revolutionary steel. The purest ideas of Marx, Engels, and Lenin teem in our minds and beat in our hearts. [*Applause*] The blood of the heroes of '68, '95, and '53; [*Applause*] of Céspedes, Martí, Maceo, Abel Santamaría, Frank País, Camilo, and Che;* [*Applause*] of the heroes of Yara, of Baire, of the Moncada, of the *Granma*, of the Sierra, of Girón, of the October Crisis, and of the internationalist heroes of antifascist Spain, Angola, and Ethiopia [*Applause*] runs in our veins. [*Applause*]

When our people are asked to volunteer for internationalist missions, not tens of thousands, but rather hundreds of thousands of combatants seek the honor of being chosen. [*Applause*] The same response is given by Cuban doctors, teachers, engineers, technicians, and other workers whenever the cooperation of civilians with Africa and other parts of the world is requested. This reflects the spirit of our people; it shows our political level, the complete triumph of revolutionary ideas, the com-

---

* Abel Santamaría was a leader of the Moncada attack in 1953 and was tortured to death after being captured. Frank País was a leader of the July 26 Movement's urban underground; he was assassinated in 1957. Camilo Cienfuegos was a guerrilla commander and one of the central leaders of the revolutionary war; he was killed in a plane crash in October 1959.

munist spirit of solidarity of the men and women of our homeland. [*Applause*]

The world revolutionary movement has taken great strides in the present century. Its forces are growing, its ranks are strengthened, and its experience has been enriched. The treason, insanity, weakness, and blindness of those whose vanity, pride, petty-bourgeois stupidity, chauvinism, and opportunism kept them from taking the splendorous path of the revolution will never halt the victorious advance of humanity. [*Applause*]

In the epoch in which we live, humanity as a whole has no middle way between war and peace. Peace along with civilized, peaceful coexistence between different social regimes are the wisest and only real ways out. Meanwhile, every people must determine its economic and social destiny for itself, without any interference, and this must necessarily be that of progress, that of a just world of solidarity in which—as Marx and Engels said—man is no longer a wolf to man.

The forces of socialism and of peace are strong enough now to keep imperialism from imposing its policy of hegemony, war, and regression in the world. These forces, including our beloved sister, the glorious homeland of Lenin, constitute a very strong, invincible curb to the appetites, adventures, and excesses of reaction in the present stage. These forces keep Asia, Africa, and Latin America and their natural resources from being once more carved up and colonized by the imperialists.

Humanity will not go back to the past; peace will be preserved; the peoples will advance along the paths of progress, and nothing and nobody can prevent this.

The Moncada is an example, and the Cuban revolution stimulating proof of this truth. The Eleventh World Festival of Youth and Students for peace, anti-imperialist solidarity, and friendship, [*Applause*] which we are holding for the first time in the Western Hemisphere—with optimism, with great hopes in the world of tomorrow and with the absolute conviction that the future belongs completely to progress, to freedom, to justice, and to brotherhood between men and peoples—is irrefutable proof of this.

Patria o muerte! [*Our homeland or death!*]

Venceremos! [We will win!] [*Ovation*]

PART 2
Solidarity with Africa: Angola

For over 400 years, Angola had been a part of the Portuguese empire, which imposed a particularly brutal form of colonial rule. Beginning in the 1960s, an armed struggle for independence was waged by three groups: the MPLA (Movimento Popular de Libertação de Angola—People's Movement for the Liberation of Angola) led by Agostinho Neto; the FNLA (Frente Nacional de Libertação de Angola—Angolan National Liberation Front), led by Holden Roberto; and UNITA (União Nacional para Independência Total de Angola), led by Jonas Savimbi. The United States gave arms and support to the Portuguese imperialists, who were carrying out fierce repression and killing thousands of Angolans. At the same time, the Portuguese government was trying to put down revolts in its other African colonies, most importantly Mozambique and Guinea-Bissau.

In 1974, a revolutionary upsurge broke out in Portugal, largely provoked by the costly and increasingly unpopular colonial wars. As a result, the Lisbon regime was forced to withdraw its forces and concede independence to its African colonies. In January 1975, the three Angolan groups signed an agreement to establish a coalition government. This broke down in April, was reinitiated in June, but within a month, full-scale civil war broke out with the MPLA on one side and the FNLA and UNITA on the other.

As insurance against a Portuguese defeat, the CIA had given aid to the FNLA since the 1960s. After Portugal announced its decision to withdraw, Washington began to step up this aid, and also began to aid UNITA—all with the intention of defeating the MPLA and ensuring the existence of a proimperialist regime. South Africa was also encouraged to enter the conflict. In August 1975, South African military units first crossed into Angola from Namibia. And, in October, in alliance with the FNLA, UNITA, and the government of Zaïre, South Africa launched an invasion and began advancing rapidly on the capital city of Luanda, which was in the hands of the MPLA. At this point, the MPLA-backed government requested that Cuba send troops.

Cuba had had relations with the MPLA since 1965 at the time when Che Guevara was fighting with guerrillas in the Congo (now Zaïre). In October 1975, Cuba began to send military equipment and instructors. Then, in response to the MPLA's request, the Central Committee of the Communist Party of Cuba and the Cuban government decided on November 5 to send troops to defend Angola's right to self-determination against the South African invasion.

Hundreds of thousands of Cubans volunteered to go and an estimated 10–20,000 were sent. Many of the troops were Black, reflecting the large percentage of Blacks in Cuba's population. Within several weeks of their arrival the tide began to turn, and the South Africans were eventually routed. On March 27, the last South African troops crossed back over the border into Namibia.

The U.S. government, its goals blocked by Cuba's actions, launched a propaganda campaign referring to the Cubans as "mercenaries" and branding Cuba an "international outlaw." But within Africa itself, there was little support for Washington's demand that Cuban troops be withdrawn. This was all the more true given the role of the CIA in the war. In addition to funneling aid to the FNLA and UNITA, U.S. pilots were involved in airlifting weapons and the CIA recruited foreign mercenaries, including Americans.

The victory over Portuguese colonialism and the defeat

of South Africa and the United States were an inspiration to Africans. One of the immediate results was the upsurge in the Zimbabwean and Namibian liberation struggles and the explosion of the struggle in South Africa in 1976, beginning in the township of Soweto.

In spite of their defeat, the U.S. and South Africa have continued to try to undermine the Angolan government. Aid was given to the remnants of UNITA and the FNLA to carry out terrorist operations, and South African troops have repeatedly attacked Angolan villages under the pretext of "pursuit" of Namibian guerrillas. In May 1978, South African troops killed at least 600 Namibian refugees near Cassinga in Angola. In June 1980, several thousand South Africans crossed into Angola, killing several hundred civilians. There have also been numerous bombing raids.

For its part, Cuba vowed to keep its troops there until the Angolan government felt it would be able to adequately defend itself, and it has urged international solidarity with Angola in the face of the continued attacks. For further information on Cuba's role in Angola, see Appendix A ("Cuba's Role in Angola: Operation Carlota" by Gabriel García Márquez), p. 485.

Closing speech to First Party Congress

December 22, 1975

Speech given to the closing session of the First Congress of the Communist Party of Cuba held in Havana December 17–22, 1975. The text is from *Granma,* January 11, 1976.

Distinguished guests;
Dear comrades:
 The time has come to close our historic congress. Not much can be added to all that has been done, agreed upon, and said here. Of course, at a time like this we must control our emotions.
 The day we gave the report to the congress, we said that there might have been some omissions. And indeed there were some omissions. For instance when we referred to those who had visited our country, the name of a very important visitor was missing: that of the leader of the Palestine Liberation Organization, Comrade Arafat, [*Applause*] whom we deeply love and admire in our country, and to whom we have always shown our solidarity, and

whose visit to our homeland was a great honor for our people. I take this opportunity to rectify that involuntary omission. [*Applause*]

At the same time, although this was not an omission— in fact, when we were working on the report, we were pressured by its great length and we tried to set down the general aspects of our policy without going into details— I take this opportunity to express our party's stand and support for the worldwide demand for the release of Luis Corvalán in Chile, [*Applause*] since Luis Corvalán is, for all of us, a symbol of the revolutionaries imprisoned in Latin America. He represents all the communist, socialist, and progressive combatants of the whole continent, for whose liberation we must fight untiringly. [*Applause*]

We would like to say a few things about the Central Committee of our party.

In a country where there are so many men and women with the merits, with the ability, with a communist spirit, it is not easy to draw up a list of those who should belong on the Central Committee. In the first place, it was necessary to replace certain comrades. And that, of course, was not easy, because among the comrades replaced, one or the other had made mistakes, but that was neither the main factor nor the general factor which determined that a group of comrades be replaced. It was rather the need to act according to the method, to the principles of renewing and of replacing part of the Central Committee.

And when that moment comes, one finds comrades with an exceptional record and extraordinary personal merits, who, nevertheless, have to be replaced in order to follow a sound principle.

At that moment, when ballots are proposed, a thoroughgoing analysis has to be made as to which comrades— according to the work they have done, according to the functions they have—should remain on the Central Committee, and which comrades are those whose replacement less affects the Central Committee.

And that is why we want to express our acknowledgment, our respect, our affection, and our consideration for those comrades we have replaced on the Central Committee. [*Applause*]

At the same time, all of us who form part of the Central Committee should now be aware that when the next congress is held, we will again have to go through the painful duty of replacing some of the members of the Central Committee. From the point of view of the functioning of the party it is convenient and healthy, because new qualities and new cadres arise, whom the revolution should promote. The renewal of our leading cadres is a vital law. It is useful to the party, it is good for the party. And even if all were to do their utmost and were to do a perfect job, inevitably at the next congress we would have to renew part of the Central Committee. [*Applause*]

On the other hand, to decide which new comrades should be included on the Central Committee was not an easy task. Undoubtedly, as no human labor is perfect, as no selection is perfect, we believe that what is important in this case is the effort that is made to ensure the best possible selection among so many comrades that could have been picked for that nomination.

We have seen to it that, for instance, women are represented on the Central Committee and, if not on the Central Committee, at least among the alternate members of the Central Committee. We have seen to it that all activities, all basic work fronts are represented so that our Central Committee is a representation of our party in its countless activities: the provinces, the country's defense, production, and the mass organizations. And we believe that the decision taken and the ballot approved and the comrades elected introduce principles that are very noble in our society and our process. Because you do not run for a post on the Central Committee; that is principle number one. It must be up to the party to decide. In our pure, really pure society no one should ever propose himself. [*Applause*] In our society and in our party one principle must prevail: that of merit, ability, modesty. And public office must never involve any kind of privilege! [*Applause*] And the esteem of our society for our militant revolutionaries can involve no preferences.

The comrade members of the Central Committee have this function by virtue of their abilities and merits, but our party and our society elevate thousands, tens of thousands, hundreds of thousands, millions of ordinary people, even though they are not members of the Central Committee. Thus there are innumerable Heroes of the Sugar Harvest, dozens of Heroes of Labor, thousands and thousands of anonymous heroes. Let us say that our revolution esteems the anonymous hero more than anyone else—[*Applause*] the common man, the modest fighter who performs his duty out of sheer consciousness, without ever expecting recognition for his merits! [*Applause*] That is the model of a communist. [*Applause*] And what matters is that the party and the people feel they are represented in their Central Committee.

Election to the Central Committee is attained in our country in a truly fine way. To think of comrades such as Comrade Pedro Rodríguez Peralta, [*Applause*] who won that honor by fighting in the liberation movement side by side with the Guinea-Bissau patriots and who, seriously wounded and taken prisoner by the enemy, endured years of confinement in the Portuguese fascist prisons [*Applause*] and remained unflinching and firm like a true communist in the face of maltreatment and all kinds of pressure when he was one man alone in a cell thousands of kilometers from his homeland. [*Applause*] How far he must have been at that moment from thinking that one day his people would have the opportunity of expressing their admiration for such solid communist virtues! [*Applause*]

Reinaldo Castro shows us that by cutting sugarcane in the canefields, the right to be a leader of our party can be attained. [*Applause*] Pilar Fernández teaches us that by working humbly in a factory, managing that factory efficiently, with a lifetime dedication to the well-functioning of a production center, the honor of being chosen a member of the Central Committee can be attained. [*Applause*] Or by devoting oneself to science and saving lives, like Zoilo Marinello; [*Applause*] or by writing popular and revolutionary poetry for dozens of years, like Nicolás Guillén. [*Applause*] Other examples can be added, such as Facundo [Martínez Vaillant], [*Applause*] who wore his first pair of shoes at the age of fourteen and who devoted his life to the working-class and peasant struggle.

Militant revolutionaries—wherever they may be, whether in the country or abroad—by simply working and fulfilling their duties, symbols of the tens and hundreds of thousands or even millions of Cubans also doing just that, may be entitled to the extraordinary honor of becoming a member of the Central Committee, an honor which was not thought of by the comrades to whom it was granted, and for which they did not strive. Because each of us has a central committee which far excels the Central Committee of our party; and it is the central committee of the consciousness of each and every one of us! [*Applause*]

I repeat that we have been most careful in our proposals to the congress, so that the party is worthily represented.

And the party's opinion is expressed in the election, in

the practically unanimous way in which the leaders of the Central Committee have been elected. And when we refer to unanimity, we are by no means criticizing those comrades who stated their opinions freely; for that honesty, that freedom, and that spirit with which each expresses his opinion is what we had been aiming at, what we aim at, what should exist within our party. [*Applause*]

And that is why the principle of creating the proper conditions and facilities has been established. But for the next congress we should have even more facilities. We think that those poll booths or boxes—or whatever they are called—should be improved and provided with additional facilities, a small table and everything necessary, so that everyone can express their opinions freely, [*Applause*] for this is precisely what we are striving for.

But we want more than that: we want every party leader never to think of this election when fulfilling his duty; we want him to act justly and firmly and, at the same time, humanely—for, above all, our party should be humane—and to act firmly and unflinchingly when fulfilling his duty, [*Applause*] without ever thinking of elections, even if the price of fulfilling one's duty is not obtaining a single vote. [*Applause*]

These are the criteria that should prevail in a party as pure as ours. And it has been proven. The purity of our party has been proven in the ideas and conduct of its members. And we want to combine these things: purity, honesty, a spirit of criticism, and freedom of opinion! [*Applause*]

We believe, comrades, that a good Central Committee has been elected. And after this congress, this Central Committee will have very important functions in directing the party. [*Applause*]

Just as the Central Committee has been enlarged, so

has the Political Bureau. We followed the congress closely, and we see the great confidence you show for the members of the Political Bureau. [*Applause*]

That bureau is enlarged. And it is enlarged with comrades such as Blas Roca, [*Applause*] whose life is a monument to simplicity, to modesty, to work, to identification with the cause of the workers [*Applause*] and, moreover, a monument to ability and efficiency. A comrade who has displayed exceptional activity in all tasks assigned to him by the party throughout these years.

It is enlarged with Comrade Machadito [José Machado Ventura]—as most of us call him—[*Applause*] whose merits, whose character, whose prestige, and whose authority are known to all.

It is enlarged with Comrade Carlos Rafael Rodríguez, [*Applause*] whose ability is proverbial because even during capitalism, Carlos Rafael was spoken of very respectfully, [*Applause*] who has worked tirelessly in all tasks assigned to him by the revolution, and who has brilliantly headed our party's Foreign Relations Department. [*Applause*]

It is enlarged with Comrade Pedro Miret, [*Applause*] one of the first university students who joined the struggle that started this process, appointed by the FEU [Federation of University Students] to give the combatants military training; who opened wide the doors of that Aula Magna for training the cells that later attacked the Moncada; who heroically fought at the Moncada; who, while in Mexico, was not able to join us because he was arrested by the police; who in prison had to bear the agony of seeing his comrades depart, and who, besides the merits he attained in the war once he was able to join us again in the Sierra Maestra, has modestly worked in the tasks assigned to him during these seventeen years of revolution. [*Applause*]

And Comrade [Arnaldo] Milián, [*Applause*] whose brilliant work at the head of Las Villas Province is well known. [*Applause*]

The Political Bureau is enriched by this enlargement by the entry of these comrades, because they bring with them to the Political Bureau their experience in very different fields. Comrades such as Milián and Machadito, who have spent years in the provinces, heading the party in the provinces, and who know all the problems concerning party direction in the provinces—aside from Comrade [Armando] Hart and Comrade [Juan] Almeida— [*Applause*] bring that experience and that practice to the Political Bureau.

Moreover, in all this process of institutionalizing and restructuring the country, we can count on comrades who have authority as members of the Political Bureau to work in the various regions of the country—Oriente, Las Villas, and Havana—in all this transition period, in which cadres are required who are able to facilitate change.

We can fully understand that saying that Las Villas is divided into three provinces is not enough; for a period of time a great number of tasks have to be coordinated among those three provinces. And we need comrades who, on behalf of the party, help and cooperate in the changes and the fulfillment of the tasks relevant to each of those provinces. We need them in Las Villas, we need them in Havana, and we need them in Oriente; and it is really wonderful that the party can count on such comrades.

Moreover, in the party's international relations, in its representation at international events, at congresses of other parties, in the attention given to guests, a lot of energy, time, and effort is required. And this enlargement of the Political Bureau will be of great help to us. Eight members were actually too few for all these tasks.

We already explained at the meeting of the new Central Committee how the working Secretariat is maintained. We still have to elect the Control Commission, according to the statutes, a task to be undertaken at a future date by the Central Committee.

Lastly, comrades, concerning leadership, our party elected as its second secretary the comrade who, doubtlessly, possesses all the qualities, the ability, and the merits to hold this post. [*Applause*]

It is known that in our party and in our revolution family favoritism cannot exist and will never exist, that is known! [*Applause*] Sometimes two cadres concur: the case of Raúl [Castro] and Vilma [Espín] [*Applause*] who now have family ties. And there are cases of other comrades. But in our party, where merit must prevail, neither friendship nor kinship are, or ever will be, factors to be taken into account. [*Applause*]

We have the case of José R. Fernández and Comrade Asela [de los Santos]: [*Applause*] both have been elected to the Central Committee. But we are not to blame for this! It is only merits, exclusively the merits of each that counts.

In the case of Comrade Raúl, it is indeed a privilege for me that, besides being an outstanding revolutionary cadre, he is also a brother. [*Applause and shouts of "Fidel!" "Raúl!"*]

He gained those merits in the struggle, and from the very beginning. Family relationship served to enroll him in the revolutionary process, to invite him to take part in the Moncada. Ah, but when a military patrol arrived at the Santiago de Cuba Court and took them prisoner, if Raúl had not done what he did then—which was to snatch the gun from the officer's hand and take the patrol that had taken them prisoner—[*Prolonged applause*] there would have been no Raúl a long time since. If he had not done that, they would all have been murdered within hours of the attack on the Moncada. And that was the beginning. And prison, and exile, and the *Granma* expedition, and the difficult moments, and the Second Front, and the work carried out during these years.

I say and stress this because it is necessary to express to what extent the criterion that prevails and always will prevail in our revolution is merit, and never any consideration of friendship or family ties. We Cubans understand this well, but it is also necessary that this be understood abroad.

We believe that the congress has worked well as regards the election. I'm not going to say that work has been excellent because we must not forget that the one who is speaking has also been elected. [*Applause*]

Actually—well, since I have mentioned it I should say a few things on the subject. First, when Comrade Fabio Grobart spoke and mentioned the reasons why it had been decided to propose me for secretary of the Central Committee, I sincerely believe that what he expressed is more than I deserve. [*Shouts of "No!" prolonged applause, and exclamations of "Fidel, Fidel!"*] Now it seems as if the conduct of some of us is deserving of special merits, but we cannot forget, even for one moment, that more than men with great merits, we are men to whom chance and history have granted excessive privileges. How many individuals fought over such a long period of time, from Carlos Manuel de Céspedes, Agramonte, Maceo, Martí, Mella!* So many who fought to see the country free one day, to see their dreams fulfilled, and historical factors, terrible adverse forces made it impossible for them to live to see their efforts crowned, to see the day in which their

---

* Julio Antonio Mella was a founding leader of the Communist Party of Cuba in 1925; he was assassinated in 1929.

dreams were to come true. Many of them were not able to see the homeland free, they were not able to see the entire country united, independent, sovereign, revolutionary, democratic, just, victorious. They were not able to see it despite their exceptional personal merits!

And we are a handful of men with a few merits and with exceptional privileges as heirs of those who did the greater part of this task. We are, more than men with merits, privileged heirs of what others did. [*Applause*]

The forces of history helped us, the world balance of forces helped us. And that is why we have been able to see, we have been able to gather here the efforts of so many who fought so hard and who were not able to see their dreams come true. And that is how it is, as we see it and as we ought to see it.

I know, comrades, that some of you were hurt as we analyzed our mistakes. I know that some comrades, in particular, were especially hurt when we spoke of how those of us who embarked on the path of revolution through purely intellectual ways often suffered from petty-bourgeois hangovers and chauvinism. But if we were not proletarians, many of us; if we were not exploited peasants; if our class origin did not objectively make revolutionaries of us, how else could we embark on the path of revolution if not through thinking, vocation, and human sensitivity? Perhaps because we may even have had some revolutionary genes. It is possible that I inherited it from my great-grandparents, exploited peasants in Galicia. It is possible. [*Laughter and applause*] This is what we wanted to say, and it is true. We could not say that the world is full of revolutionaries, but in turn, we could say that the world is full of petty bourgeois. And we can truly say that the world is plagued by many people who through purely intellectual ways come to adopt revolutionary stands, but who carry with them traces of their class origins, certain hangovers. There are many such people in Latin America, in Europe, everywhere, and that is a fact. And we come across this spirit constantly. We cannot but acknowledge that fact. And what better way to show that we are getting rid of, overcoming, or wiping out those hangovers, than realizing that we have them?

It is not self-criticism for the sake of it. We have made a just analysis of our mistakes, but we have not exaggerated. If we were to be more exhaustive, we would find many more mistakes. We have simply covered the main ones. And besides, comrades, as a revolutionary principle, self-criticism is always a thousand times preferable to complacency. [*Applause*] And being humble is always preferable to praising oneself! [*Applause*]

We really believe that we revolutionary leaders must constantly subject ourselves to scrutiny and self-criticism, if not publicly, in private. [*Applause*] We must always be settling accounts with our conscience. [*Applause*] And we should never be self-satisfied, because he who feels self-satisfied is not a revolutionary. [*Applause*]

And what is it that we need? Praise? No. Those who have the confidence of the collectivity and of their people—those who even have great power because of the position in which their compatriots have placed them—need no praise.

What does history prove? That men have had power and have abused power. Even in revolutionary processes certain individuals acquire extraordinary power, especially in this phase, especially in the first few years. When the revolutionary process becomes institutionalized, when there is already a party, when the rules are already established, when these rules are embraced by the community, then there is no danger.

But in this phase of the revolutionary process through which we have all lived, there were great dangers: the danger of vanity, the danger of conceit, the danger of deification, the habit of having authority, the habit of holding and exercising power. How many risks are involved! And how many mistakes have been made throughout the history of humanity because of this. [*Applause*]

Therefore, it was very important throughout this period—and it will always be—that men invested with authority, men with great responsibilities granted them by their compatriots, were duty-bound to be firm and demanding of themselves. And we believe that this is a principle that should always be observed by our party, even though in our party and in our future, as individuals, men and leaders become less and less important. [*Applause*]

In the past, a town doctor obtained all he wanted. He was the party delegate there. If a councilman was to be elected, it was he who was elected. If a mayor, it was he. If a representative, it was he. If a senator, it was he. The only one in the town who knew anything was the doctor. But what would have happened in that town if everyone were a doctor? And that is what happens in the revolution.

At a given moment, certain individuals play a role, they play a very outstanding role. Everyone believes in them. The masses are ignorant, illiteracy prevails everywhere; then, a few, just because they had the privilege of attending a university, know a little more than the rest.

That is why in almost all revolutionary processes which have taken place up to now, those who worked out the ideas did not frequently come from the most humble strata; but since they had access to the university, which the worker, the peasant, the common man from among the people could not attend, they played a great role. Marx and Engels themselves were not proletarian. They could study at the university. The workers who toiled for sixteen or seventeen hours in a factory could not work out the Marxist-Leninist theory.

But with the revolution the doors to the university are opened to all, culture is available to all, and there comes a time when knowledge is no longer the patrimony of a few but of the masses.

And our revolution, like all socialist revolutions, follows the road along which knowledge gradually becomes the patrimony of the masses. Then those enormous differences between the knowledge gained by a few and the knowledge of the masses will not exist. And the time will come when those differences between the knowledge of those leading and that of those being led will be minimal.

Humanity has no geniuses as such. There are brilliant individuals. You may have read that some persons are awarded such and such a prize; genius is not within individuals; genius is within the masses. [*Applause*] When someone was outstanding in mathematics it was because hundreds of thousands did not have the opportunity to study mathematics. And someone was outstanding in economy or in history or in any branch of human knowledge because the rest did not have the opportunity to study. But when the masses have access to culture, when they have the opportunity to study, when they have access to knowledge, then differences disappear, because instead of one genius, there are a thousand, there are ten thousand geniuses. And where there are ten thousand geniuses there is no one genius at all, there is a collective genius. [*Applause*]

We are already entering a phase of institutionalization of the revolutionary process, a phase of security, a phase of great guarantees, because guarantees are no longer given by men but by institutions. And we men are frail: we disappear and fade away over little things, indigestion or a car accident, not to speak of the tenebrous and truculent assassination plans of the CIA.

There was a most difficult period—and we explained what happened during that period today in the Central Committee—in which the leaders had to be greatly protected because they were playing a decisive role. Those were critical times. Then I said: Well, if they kill me, there is still Raúl, and they are not going to annihilate the revolution. All this has been changing. Today I may be gone, Raúl may be gone, but the revolution will go on; the Political Bureau may be gone, but the revolution will go on. Isn't that really extraordinary? [*Applause*] The Central Committee may be gone but the revolution will go on. [*Applause*] If that wall were to collapse and the entire Central Committee were to disappear, we are sure that you would assemble and would elect another good Central Committee. [*Applause*] But I will go further. If this congress is gone, that is to say, this assembly of delegates, the revolution will go on. [*Applause*]

It is true that the country's leading cadres are here, the main cadres of the party, of the armed forces, of the Ministry of the Interior. All of them. But if that hypothetical case were to materialize, those who remained there, at the grassroots level, in the party nuclei, in the regions, municipalities, and provinces, the lieutenants and the captains of military units and of the Ministry of the Interior would carry forward the revolution. [*Applause*] Because the 200,000 communists who are not present here and the whole people are behind them. [*Applause*] They are also backed by a just cause and by revolutionary ideas! [*Applause*]

That is what the party means, and what institutionalization of the revolution means.

Despite this security we have, we did not fail to take measures to protect this theater. Let that be clear! The MINFAR [Ministry of the Revolutionary Armed Forces] and the Ministry of the Interior and the organizers of the congress took all the necessary measures in case they sent an airplane full of bombs here. And although everything would have gone on, as I said before, the initial disorganization would have been considerable, wouldn't it? [*Applause*] I withdraw that statement of initial disorganization. I withdraw it because it is not correct. It would be better to say that the tragedy would have been great, that it would have been a great loss for the country because of the experience gained by all the men and women in this theater. And all the necessary measures were taken!

Anyone who reads the history of the CIA operations knows that these measures are not exaggerated, and that the beaten and desperate enemy is capable of resorting to anything, and often does. And here they had the chance of getting all the cadres of the party, the state, the mass organizations, and the defense apparatus of the country, and moreover, many very distinguished guests. [*Applause*]

Just think of Giap,* whom they could neither capture nor encircle during thirty years of war, [*Applause*] what if imperialism were to get him here at the Karl Marx Theater?

We couldn't give them any chance and that is why all the necessary measures were taken. That is why congress sessions finished relatively early, because at night the defense of this hall became a bit more complex. But during all these days our air force, our navy, and our security forces have been preventing the enemy from having

---

* Vo Nguyen Giap, Vietnam's minister of defense and deputy premier, was a leader of the Vietnamese forces during the French and U.S. military interventions.

the slightest chance of coming here to wipe out the party leadership and the congress. [*Applause*] Because we know what they are capable of scheming up in a moment of desperation and defeat. We have taken all the necessary measures because it was right to protect this congress by all means possible.

But our basic idea is that as the party develops, ideas are embraced by the entire people. As the revolution becomes more institutionalized, individuals come to play a less important role; cadres individually come to play a less important role. And that makes all of us very happy, because the revolutionary work is ensured. We can all be confident. All of us! Every citizen, even the most humble citizen of this country and those who have just been born today, as this congress comes to a close. The revolution is already ensured against all possible contingencies.

One of our principles should be the spirit of criticism and self-criticism. And what should be of concern to all of us when we hold our next congress is the balance sheet of our achievements and mistakes.

But we were saying that the conditions have been created so that all mistakes can be prevented if foreseen in time, and in the event of actually being made, quickly corrected. [*Applause*]

Those are the conditions that have been created and the conditions that have been consolidated at this congress.

Aside from that, comrades, we, all of us—I speak on behalf of all the comrades on the Political Bureau and the Central Committee, with whom you have been so effusive, affectionate, and warm—feel deeply moved and we will never feel conceited because of it. We always keep in mind one of the great truths expressed by Martí: "All the world's glory fits into a kernel of corn." [*Applause*]

The trust you have placed in us, the honors you confer

on all of us, will only serve to make us feel further committed and even more obliged to our party and our people. It will encourage us to increase our efforts to maintain the honesty, the purity, the human and fraternal spirit of our party and our revolution. Because someone once said that the revolution was like Saturn, who devoured his own children. But this revolution does not devour its own children; we, the men who started this revolution, are here. [*Applause*]

And those who continued it later on are here; gathered here are those with the most years at the service of the revolution, those who started before us, such as Fabio Grobart and [Ladislao González] Carvajal, Blas and Carlos Rafael, those of us who were at the Moncada, who came together in exile, who came together in the Sierra, who were together at the triumph, old and mature men and women, and young men and women, from Fabio to [Orlando] Domínguez; we are all here. [*Applause*] And this revolution has not devoured and will never devour its own children. [*Applause*] But without this implying overindulgence, a lack of strictness necessary in a revolution.

But the humane character of our revolution—fraternal and generous but at the same time firm—pleases us and makes us all proud. And that course, that future, is guaranteed by our party and by this congress, and herein lies its true significance. A new stage of the revolution begins after the First Congress. [*Applause*]

We know who are the ones assembled here and what they represent as regards merits and ability. We know how many Heroes of Labor, how many men and women who have received awards by the revolution, how many comrades awarded with twentieth anniversary medals attend this congress. We also know what the selection process has been like and the extraordinary qualities of those present here today. And we are sure that some day, just as we speak today of what happened fifty years ago when a handful of men organized the first Communist Party of Cuba, we are sure that within fifty, within a hundred years, your grandchildren, your great-grandchildren, and your great-great-grandchildren will also speak of the First Congress.

We have passed wonderful resolutions. Exceptional documents have been drawn up to set out guidelines and chart the course of what is to be done in the years to come. This is the result of seventeen years of experiences. Some of you wonder why this congress was not held before. We are fortunate to be holding it now! Fortunate indeed! [*Applause*] This way the quality of the congress is endorsed by seventeen years of experience. Just think, seventeen years of experience! When we have corrected a great number of mistakes, when the revolutionary process has attained real maturity. And we have been able to hold a serene, truly mature congress. We have been able to hold a great congress now! And, of course, we will from now on, periodically hold subsequent congresses of the party every five years.

I am not going to expand on the subject. We have seen the papers presented. Our unanimity did not come from blind discipline; the documents have been thoroughly discussed by the mass of the people. Each one of the basic documents was discussed with the people and with the party. All the people were able to contribute their ideas and give their opinions, and all were able to make amendments. Finally, the documents were discussed in the commissions. And this explains why practically all the decisions were adopted unanimously, except for a word that was misused, and a comrade correctly pointed out that it was misused. This was the democratic procedure used for discussing all the resolutions.

I will not take much longer. We are having a mass rally afterward. We have held the party congress and we will now hold the people's congress. [*Applause*] But before the congress ends, I wish to take up a matter of foreign policy. And to analyze it calmly, objectively.

While this congress was being held, the president of the United States declared that, as a result of our aid to the sister people of Angola, any prospects or hopes or possibilities of improving relations between the United States and Cuba were—more or less—cancelled.

It is odd that the president of the United States, Mr. Ford, should threaten us with that. Before, when we did have relations, they cut them off; when there was a sugar quota, they cut it off; when there was trade between the United States and Cuba, they cut it off; but now they have nothing else to cut off, and now they cut off hope. [*Laughter and applause*] This could be called "the hope embargo" on the part of the president of the United States. [*Laughter*] He has actually embargoed that which no longer exists. [*Laughter*]

They were already indignant at the holding of the Conference of Solidarity with Puerto Rico, claiming that it seriously affected any possibility of improving relations. But if we must renounce this country's dignity, renounce this country's principles in order to have relations with the United States and improve relations with the United States, how can we possibly have relations with the United States?

Apparently, according to the mentality of the U.S. leaders, the price for improving relations, or for having trade or economic relations, is to give up the principles of the revolution. And we shall never renounce our solidarity with Puerto Rico. [*Applause*]

What kind of people do they think we are? What country do they think they are dealing with? The old Cuba?

No! This is the new Cuba, and this is a different country! [*Applause*] And until they get this fact into their heads, I cannot see any possibility of improving relations, because we shall never desert our Puerto Rican brothers and sisters even if there are no relations with the United States for a hundred years. [*Applause*]

Now it is not only Puerto Rico; now it is also Angola. In all our revolutionary process we have always followed a policy of solidarity with the African revolutionary movement. One of the first things the revolution did was to send arms to the Algerian combatants who were fighting for their independence. This impaired our relations with the government of France, which was indignant at the fact that we were sending arms to the Algerian combatants and supporting them in the United Nations and in every international forum. But we were firm in that policy and we helped them.

After the victory of the revolution, when the new Algerian state had to face certain risks and certain dangers, we did not hesitate in sending them our help, and we did send it.

As regards those who fought in Guinea-Bissau—we have the case of Pedro Rodríguez Peralta, member of the Central Committee, who was fighting side by side with the patriots of Guinea-Bissau.

We have given our support to the progressive governments and revolutionary movements in Africa since the very moment of the victory of the revolution. And we will continue supporting them! [*Applause*]

This assistance has taken different forms: sometimes we have sent weapons, or on other occasions we have sent men; we have sent military instructors, or doctors or construction workers, and sometimes we have sent all three: construction workers, doctors, and military instructors. [*Laughter*] Loyal to its internationalist policy, what the revolution has been doing since the beginning is to help wherever it can help, wherever it may be useful and, moreover, wherever this help is requested.

Similarly, we are helping the MPLA and the people of Angola, [*Applause*] with whom we have had relations and have been cooperating since the very beginning of their struggle for independence against Portuguese colonialism. Many of the Angolan cadres studied in Cuba.

But, what happens? Undoubtedly, Ford's statements are occasioned by the fact that the imperialists are irritated with us. And why are they irritated? Because they had it all planned to take hold of Angola before November 11.

Angola is a territory rich in natural resources. Cabinda, one of the Angolan provinces, has large oil deposits. This country has great mineral wealth—diamonds, copper, iron. This is one of the reasons why the imperialists want to take hold of Angola.

And the story is perfectly well known: many years ago, when the imperialists realized that these colonies would some day fight for their liberation, they began to organize their movements. Thus, they organized the FNLA, with CIA people. We are not the ones who say so; it has just been exposed by the *New York Times* in detail that the FNLA was organized by the CIA.

When the Angolan people were about to attain independence—just as Guinea-Bissau, Mozambique, Cape Verde, and other countries attained their independence—imperialism worked out a way to crush the revolutionary movement in Angola. They planned to take hold of Cabinda, with its oil, before November 11; to seize Luanda before November 11. And to carry out this scheme, the U.S. government launched South African troops against Angola.

You know that South Africa is one of the most hated

and most discredited states in the world, for three million whites oppress fourteen million Black Africans. And there they have established one of the most ignominious, shameful, and inhuman regimes that could ever be thought of, condemned by the whole of the world progressive movement, condemned by all Nonaligned countries, and condemned by the United Nations.

South Africa not only maintains this fascist and racist regime in the south, but also occupies the territory of Namibia, where it has established a kind of protectorate.

And the U.S. government, absolutely devoid of all scruples, launched the South African regular troops against Angola. Thus Angola was being threatened on the north by the FNLA and was attacked on the south by regular troops organized into armored columns. Everything was ready to take over Angola before November 11. And the plan was very solid; it was a solid plan; the only thing was that the plan failed. They had not counted on international solidarity, on the support given to the heroic people of Angola by the socialist countries, in the first place, and by the revolutionary movements and progressive governments of Africa, or the support we Cubans, among the world's progressive governments, also gave Angola. [*Applause*]

The imperialists did not count on that. What was the result? On November 8 they launched an offensive against Cabinda and were crushingly repelled. What they went through in Cabinda was a sort of Girón: in three days, in seventy-two hours, the invaders were annihilated. In Luanda, they were twenty-five kilometers from the capital on November 10; they attacked with armored columns; now they are more than a hundred kilometers from Luanda. The South African armored columns which had been attacking since October 23 and had advanced some

700 kilometers in less than twenty days, in a sort of military parade, were halted at more than 200 kilometers from Luanda and have not been able to advance any further.

That is, the heroic struggle of the Angolan people, supported by the international revolutionary movement, has made the imperialist plan fail.

And that is why the imperialists are irritated with us, among others. Some of them wonder why we help the Angolans, what interests we have there. They are accustomed to thinking that whenever a country does something, it is in pursuit of oil, or copper, or diamonds, or some other natural resource. No! We are not after material interests, and, logically, the imperialists do not understand this, because they are exclusively guided by chauvinist, nationalist, and selfish criteria. We are fulfilling an elementary internationalist duty when we help the Angolan people! [*Applause*] We are not looking for oil, or copper, or iron; we are not looking for anything at all. We are simply practicing a policy of principles. We do not remain passive when we see an African people, a sister people that the imperialists all of a sudden want to swallow up, and that is brutally attacked by South Africa. We do not remain passive, nor will we remain passive!

Thus, when the imperialists ask us what are our interests, we will have to say: "Look, read a manual on proletarian internationalism so that you may understand why we are helping Angola."

That is the cause of their irritation and threats.

Can you imagine what this country's future would be like if the price of renewing relations with the United States were a return to the past? [*Shouts of "No!"*]

That this country refrain from expressing its solidarity with its revolutionary brothers in the rest of the world? [*Shouts of "No!"*]

That we refrain from expressing our solidarity with the Vietnamese, the Laotian people, the Cambodians, the Africans, the Yemenis and the Arabs, and with Syria, Algeria, Guinea, and all those countries? [*Applause*]

Our policy of solidarity is no secret. And one of the factors, one of the finest elements of this congress was international participation. On the one hand, the presence of the representatives of the countries which have helped us, and among them the delegation of the Soviet Union, [*Applause*] which has given us great proofs and great lessons of internationalism. Because, in spite of the distance between us, the Soviet Union did not allow imperialism to stifle us, to swallow us up, and to destroy us, because it sent us oil when they left us without oil, because it sent us weapons when we were threatened with aggression, because it also sent us men when they were needed. [*Applause*]

And numerous representatives of prestigious countries have been present. They have spoken and have addressed our people with great affection and with great respect, and have made us feel that we belong to a great revolutionary family, and that that family is a powerful one. [*Applause*]

The representative of Algeria spoke here. The representative of the Republic of Guinea spoke here. The representative of Guinea-Bissau spoke here. The representative of Somalia spoke here. The representative of Yemen spoke here. The representative of the Congo spoke here. The representative of Syria, a country at the vanguard of the struggle against imperialism in the Middle East, spoke here. [*Applause*]

And it is no secret to anyone that at a given moment of danger and threat for the Republic of Syria, our men were in Syria. [*Applause*] It is also no secret that at a moment of danger for the Republic of Algeria, our men were in Algeria. [*Applause*] And the cooperation of our people and our armed forces with numerous countries in Africa and Asia has been very broad. And to the Vietnamese we said: "For Vietnam we are willing to give our own blood!" [*Applause*]

Thus this revolutionary family has been forged. What is imperialism aiming for? That we break with this family? [*Shouts of "Never!"*] That we stop being a people in solidarity with those sister peoples fighting against imperialism? [*Shouts of "Never!"*] Then, which hopes or possibilities or prospects are embargoed by the president of the United States? Because at that cost, then, there will never be relations with the United States! [*Applause*] Despite the fact that the policy of our revolution is a policy of peace and of relations and coexistence with regimes of different ideologies and of different social systems. But they are not satisfied. It is as though we were to tell them they had to carry out an agrarian reform or to nationalize the electric power company in order to establish relations with us. What sort of conditions does imperialism intend to impose on our country?

We practice our solidarity with Angola, we are helping Angola. And we will continue to help the people of Angola! [*Applause*] And what we ask of the congress of our party is simply to support the policy adopted by the leadership of the party of helping the heroic people of Angola in all possible ways and with all possible means! [*All delegates, standing, raise their credentials. Prolonged applause and shouts of "Angola, Angola, Angola!"*]

Let the imperialists know what the stand and the line of our country is. On the other hand, a more stupid policy than that which the imperialists are following in that country cannot be conceived. It is stupid, for they have just come out of the adventure of Vietnam and they are getting involved in one as serious as that of Vietnam. Why? Why? We want to give you some facts.

South Africa, that is to say, the racists, fascists of South Africa, are hated tremendously by all the peoples of Africa. To say South Africa in Africa is to say Israel among the Arab countries. The policy of the United States supporting the aggression and encouraging the aggression of South Africa against Angola divorces them from and makes them the irreconcilable enemies of all the peoples of Africa.

But there is something else. The province of Cabinda is firmly in the hands of the MPLA. As I told you before, the attack on November 8 was vigorously repelled. From that moment on, the popular forces have grown in strength, and it will not be easy for the imperialists to take hold of Cabinda. There is, however, large-scale oil production in Cabinda, on the shelf, and there are installations along the coast. There are many U.S. citizens working in oil extraction. And, in spite of the war, production has not stopped one single day. And these are U.S. enterprises, and it is the combatants of the MPLA who watch over those facilities and have offered security and guarantees to the U.S. citizens working in those facilities at Cabinda. While the United States arms mercenary armies, while the United States launches South African troops against Angola, the MPLA combatants guarantee and give security to U.S. facilities and citizens in Cabinda.

In our opinion, this policy is correct. It evidences calmness, it evidences wisdom, it evidences maturity on the part of the African revolutionary movement. Those facilities are difficult to operate. The technology of oil exploitation on the coast is very complex. And what has been the policy followed by the Angolans? To give security, to give guarantees, to facilitate the development of this work.

This also proves the common sense of the Angolans,

the intelligent way in which they conduct their policy. And it proves that the African revolutionary movement is willing to negotiate the exploitation of any natural resources when it is to their convenience to do so.

Something the African revolutionary movement will never negotiate with is racism, apartheid; it will never negotiate with the occupation of Angola by South Africa. Because the occupation of Angola by South Africa represents a grave danger for the whole of Africa; the occupation of Angola by the racists of South Africa represents a grave danger for Zambia, it represents a grave danger for Mozambique, for Zaïre, and for the People's Republic of the Congo, it represents a grave danger for the whole of Africa. And Africa is determined to support the movement of the MPLA, the struggle of the MPLA. And there are ever more governments and more countries in Africa willing to send weapons and to send men to fight against the South African racists. Africa is not going to let itself be devoured by South Africa. And the Cuban people will be side by side with the African people in that struggle! [*Applause*]

If South Africa insists on its policy, on its attempt of getting hold of Angola, it will have to face the struggle with all Black Africa.

I do not think the European countries would do such a stupid thing as to associate with South Africa in that fascist and racist crusade; and it is undoubtedly an act of great stupidity on the part of the U.S. government to associate itself with that campaign, when the Angolans themselves are giving proof of their sober and correct policy to the extreme—I repeat—that it is the MPLA combatants who are now guaranteeing the oil installations and U.S. citizens in Cabinda.

We do not understand how the Ford administration will be able to justify that before the U.S. public opinion, or what pretext he may have in carrying out that policy of aggression against Angola, in connivance with the South African racists.

This is the foreign policy issue we wanted to discuss; we want to tell the imperialists that we are not after anything there, that we practice our traditional internationalist policy; that we are helping the people of Angola, and that we are firmly determined to help them! [*Applause*] And that we, of course, greatly regret that Mr. Ford finds himself in the need of having to "cancel" and "embargo" the hopes. As far as we know, those hopes, in the context of such a policy, had no grounds.

Comrade delegates, in a few minutes we shall assemble with our people, who, in an enthusiastic and exemplary way, have supported this congress through their work and with the encouragement they have given us. They have followed the congress closely. We have not the least doubt that our people will make the resolutions of the congress their own, with revolutionary fervor and passion.

We wish to express our deepest gratitude to the eighty-seven guest delegations, who have contributed with their presence to the significance and prestige of this congress. [*Applause*] We are really much encouraged by this.

To know that they take with them a good impression of the quality of our congress also encourages us.

Comrades, we have all lived through unforgettable days. We have all experienced exceptional emotions. We have all felt happy. And we have all been proud of the work of the revolution and of the work of our party. We have all experienced the confidence in the future this congress has given us. All of us, over three thousand delegates, have felt that during these days we have been working for the future of our country, that we have been making our contribution to history.

We shall never forget the impressions of this congress. We shall never forget such fraternal spirit, such human warmth, such purity and unity as we have seen in this congress.

We have a party closely united in ideology and in common purpose. We have a closely united leadership. That is why we can say that never was the revolution stronger, never were the party and the people more united, never was our revolutionary consciousness greater.

That is why, I repeat, we have felt proud of our party and of our congress.

We are grateful to you all, comrades, for the effort made during these days; your conduct, the perfect organization, the exemplary discipline, and, above all, the political consciousness you have shown before our guests during these days.

On behalf of the Central Committee and the Political Bureau, we embrace you all.

Patria o muerte!

Venceremos! [*Ovation*]

Angola: African Girón

April 19, 1976

Speech given in Havana's Karl Marx Theater to commemorate the fifteenth anniversary of the Cuban victory at the Bay of Pigs (Playa Girón). The text is from *Granma*, May 2, 1976.

Dear Comrades:

Precisely fifteen years ago, at this very hour, you could still hear the echoes of the last shots of the battle that smashed one of Yankee imperialism's most sinister and traitorous actions against a Latin American people. Girón went down in history as the first defeat of Yankee imperialism on this continent.

It would be useless to try to find the slightest ethical principle in a system whose every act is characterized by exploitation, plunder, deceit, and crime. How many pages has the United States of America written in its relations with the Latin peoples of this hemisphere, from the time it stole more than half of Mexico's territory until it fostered the criminal fascist coup in Chile that culminated in the assassination of its illustrious revolutionary and noble President Salvador Allende? [*Applause*] On those pages are written the occupation of the Isthmus of Panama, the sordid and piratical armed intervention in numerous countries of Central America and the Caribbean, the murder of Sandino, and the landing of the Yankee marines in Santo Domingo to wipe out Francisco Caamaño's revolution,* all in the same style of prepotency, deceit, treason, and violence.

By these treacherous means, it seized the wealth of all America, imposed a relentless system of exploitation on our peoples, and initiated neocolonialist methods of domination in this continent, for the first time ever in the world.

Everything concerning the Girón episode was treacherous, a flagrant violation of international law, a perfidy, and a crime. The sinister CIA invested tens of millions of dollars to recruit, train, and equip mercenaries: landowners, bourgeois elements, traitors, war criminals, drug addicts, common criminals, and lumpen. Its strategy was accompanied by hair-raising plans to assassinate leaders of the Cuban revolution, in which they did not hesitate to use known Mafia leaders, poison, bacteria, explosives, and the most refined criminal methods. Beforehand, at every hour of the day and night, in planes or boats, scores of agents and thousands of arms were systematically brought in. They established their training bases in one Central American state and the embarkation points and air bases in another.

---

* U.S. forces were first sent to Panama in 1908. Augusto César Sandino, leader of a Nicaraguan national liberation army, was assassinated by the U.S.-organized National Guard in 1934. In April 1965, tens of thousands of U.S. troops invaded the Dominican Republic to crush a popular uprising whose main leader was Lt. Col. Francisco Caamaño Deñó.

One quiet, clear dawn, on April 15, 1961, Yankee bombers bearing Cuban insignia attacked our air bases where a few rickety old planes, with barely half a dozen pilots, constituted our air forces. With unparalleled cynicism, the United States representative declared in the United Nations that those planes were part of our own air force that had rebelled.

Everything was done with the tacit complicity and in many cases with the collaboration of the majority of the Latin American governments and the approval and support of the loathsome and repugnant OAS. Never before in the history of our continent were such corruption, shamelessness, cowardice, immorality, and crime brought together to carry out a military and political action. That is what the mercenary attack on the Bay of Pigs symbolizes. What took place is now known in all its details, as revealed by its planners and direct participants. Thus, the history of imperialism is written, without, however, the opportune and forced confession of its crimes implying the slightest principle of rectification on its own part, or on the part of its miserable accomplices. Girón, Watergate, the alleged incidents of the Tonkin Gulf,* the plans to assassinate foreign leaders, the destabilization of governments by the CIA, fascist coups d'état, the universal practice of bribing rulers and officials carried out by the Yankee monopolies, and other similar deeds, today known to world public opinion, do not mean that such practices will cease while imperialism exists.

The United States has established throughout the world a system of military pacts, bases of aggression, centers of

---

* The Tonkin Gulf incident of August 1965 was a staged attempt by the U.S. government to provoke a North Vietnamese attack on U.S. destroyers, that was used as a pretext for U.S. military escalation in Vietnam.

corruption, bribery, subversive propaganda and espionage, overt or covert actions, terror, and threats, which imperialism, because of its rapacious and exploitative nature, cannot do without.

In those institutions of war, aggression, espionage, and bribery, the United States today invests more than $120 billion, a figure twice that of the national budgets of all Latin American countries put together.

Experience, nevertheless, shows that, in spite of these fabulous resources placed at the service of reaction, subversion, and crime, imperialism cannot hold back the victorious march of the peoples. Girón, Vietnam, Laos, Cambodia, Guinea-Bissau, Mozambique, Angola, and other comparable examples are irrefutable proof of this truth.

At times, imperialism holds back the course of liberation in certain countries such as Chile; at times it promotes coups d'état or draws certain governments into committing treason, either to smash the revolutionaries in a specific nation or to divide progressive forces, as is happening within the Arab nationalist movement. Shamelessly furthering this strategy are those who from the ranks of the revolutionary movement itself betray the principles of proletarian internationalism through vanity, ideological inconsistency, personal ambitions, or simple decadence and senility, as in the case of the arrogant, demented clique that governs the destiny of China. But there is absolutely no doubt that those imperialist victories are passing. No imperialist policy, no cowardice, no betrayal will be able to hold back the inexorable march of history and the triumph of revolutionary ideas.

No work of humankind is perfect, and that goes, of course, for revolutions, which are made by men, with all their limitations and imperfections. Humanity's march toward the future must necessarily include sorrowful experiences, but that future belongs to principles, to revolutionary solidarity among peoples, to socialism, to Marxism-Leninism, and to internationalism.

The option between the past and the future, reaction or progress, treason or loyalty to principles, capitalism or socialism, imperialist domination or liberation, was what was decided at Girón, on April 19, 1961. Three days earlier, at the grave of the first martyrs of that brutal aggression, the people proclaimed the socialist nature of our revolution, and the men and women of our homeland expressed their readiness to die for it. No one knew how many mercenaries there were; no one knew how many Yankee marines and soldiers would come in after them, how many planes, how many further bombings it would be necessary to bear. Never, as at that moment, was the slogan of "Patria o muerte" more dramatic, real, and historic. The decision to win or die, embodied in a whole people, was stronger than all the risk, suffering, and danger. This made that day doubly historic, because our Marxist-Leninist party was really born at Girón; [*Applause*] membership in our party is recognized from that day on; from that day on, socialism was cemented forever with the blood of our workers, peasants, and students; from that day on, a new and completely different destiny opened up before the people of this continent because of the liberty and dignity that one of them had conquered in the face of aggression from the powerful empire that subjected all. Because, say what you will, after Girón, all the peoples of America were a little bit freer.

The spectacle of a valiant, heroic, victorious people shook the foundations and changed political psychology, the old formulas and thinking habits of this continent. Even the government of the United States found itself forced to declare new policies and methods to block the revolutionary advance. The Alliance for Progress emerged, and many governments on this continent that hadn't received the slightest consideration up to then, were honored with a White House reception, long-term loans, and bank credits. Many bourgeois Latin American governments capitalized on the blood of those who died at Girón, as they had capitalized earlier on the aggression against our sugar quota. Terms such as agrarian reform, fiscal reform, redistribution of income, housing, educational and public health plans for the peoples of Latin America—words which up to that moment had never appeared in Washington's vocabulary—became fashionable. A whole philosophy was drawn up in the midst of the panic of the imperialists, landowners, and bourgeoisie in order to block the social revolution in Latin America. In Chile "revolution in liberty" was invented, to demonstrate that social justice was possible without socialism, which is like demonstrating that there can be justice under imperialist domination, under the capitalist system, the dictatorship of the bourgeoisie, and the exploitation of man by man.

Today, after those deceitful, ridiculous, utopian exercises, the only thing left to imperialism is fascism. The people understand this clear and naked truth. Today there aren't even any classic models of "representative democracy," as there were for a long time, to gladden liberals and the ignorant, in Uruguay and Chile. There is only fascist dictatorship, torture, and crime. What does this represent if not the prelude to the truly radical and deep-rooted changes our peoples need? And what's left to imperialism after fascism?

In commemorating this, the fifteenth anniversary of the heroic, glorious victory at Girón, our people have an additional reason to be proud, which constitutes their finest expression of internationalism and transcends the boundaries of this continent: the historic victory of the people of Angola, [*Prolonged applause*] to whom we offered the generous and unlimited solidarity of our revolution.

At Girón, African blood was shed, that of the selfless descendants of a people who were slaves before they became workers, and who were exploited workers before they became masters of their homeland. And in Africa, together with the blood of the heroic fighters of Angola, Cuban blood, that of the sons of Martí, Maceo, and Agramonte, that of the heirs to the internationalist tradition set by Máximo Gómez and Che Guevara, [*Prolonged applause*] also flowed. Those who once enslaved man and sent him to America perhaps never imagined that one of those peoples who received the slaves would one day send their fighters to struggle for freedom in Africa.

The victory in Angola was the twin sister of the victory at Girón. [*Applause*] For the Yankee imperialists, Angola represents an African Girón. At one time we said that imperialism had suffered its great defeats in the month of April: Girón, Vietnam, Cambodia, etc. This time the defeat came in March. On the twenty-seventh of that month, when the last South African soldiers crossed the Namibian border, after a retreat of more than 700 kilometers, one of the most brilliant pages in the liberation of Black Africa was written.

Ford and Kissinger are irritated by the defeat. And like two little thundering Jupiters, they have made terrible threats against Cuba.

Ford, in an electoral campaign rally in Miami, competing for the votes of the Cuban counterrevolutionary colony with his rival Reagan, who, to be sure, is much more reactionary, called the prime minister of Cuba an international outlaw because of the aid our people gave to Angola. Even some United States press columnists were surprised to hear such epithets emerge from the illustrious mouth of Mr. Ford. Moreover, perhaps as one indication of Ford's low level of development, which is becoming proverbial, he declared on one occasion that Cuba's action in Angola was similar to what happened in Ethiopia in Mussolini's time. And later on, not satisfied with that most original historical simile, he compared the events in Angola to Hitler's dismemberment of Czechoslovakia after Munich.

The war in Angola was really Kissinger's war. Against the advice of some of his closest collaborators, he insisted on carrying out covert operations to liquidate the MPLA through the counterrevolutionary FNLA and UNITA groups, with the support of white mercenaries, Zaïre, and South Africa. It is said that the CIA actually warned him that such clandestine operations could not be kept secret. Aside from the fact that from the time it was founded, the FNLA was supported by the CIA, a fact now publicly acknowledged, the United States invested tens of millions of dollars from the spring of 1975 on to supply arms and instructors to the counterrevolutionary, secessionist Angolan groups. Instigated by the United States, regular troops from Zaïre entered Angolan territory in the summer of that same year, while South African military forces occupied the Cunene area in the month of August and sent arms and instructors to UNITA bands.

At that time there wasn't a single Cuban instructor in Angola. The first material aid and the first Cuban instructors reached Angola at the beginning of October, at the request of the MPLA, when Angola was being openly invaded by foreign forces. However, no Cuban military unit had been sent to Angola to participate directly in the fight, nor was that projected.

On October 23, also instigated by the United States, South African regular army troops, supported by tanks and artillery, invaded Angolan territory across the Namibian border and penetrated deeply into the country, advancing between 60 and 70 kilometers a day. On November 3, they had penetrated more than 500 kilometers into Angola, meeting their first resistance on the outskirts of Benguela, from the personnel of a recently organized school for Angolan recruits and from their Cuban instructors, who had virtually no means for halting the attack by South African tanks, infantry, and artillery.

On November 5, 1975, at the request of the MPLA, the leadership of our party decided to send with great urgency a battalion of regular troops with antitank weapons [*Applause*] to help the Angolan patriots resist the invasion of the South African racists. This was the first Cuban troop unit sent to Angola. When it arrived in the country, the foreign interventionists in the north were 25 kilometers from Luanda, their 140-millimeter artillery was bombing the suburbs of the capital, and the South African fascists had already penetrated more than 700 kilometers into the south from the Namibian border, while Cabinda was heroically defended by MPLA fighters and a handful of Cuban instructors.

I do not mean to relate the events of the Angolan war, the later development of which is generally known to everyone, but rather to point out the occasion, the form, and the circumstances in which our aid began. These facts now form part of history.

The enemy has talked about the number of Cubans in Angola. It is sufficient to say that once the struggle began, Cuba sent the men and the weapons necessary to win that struggle. [*Applause*] To give due honor to our people, we must say that hundreds of thousands of fighters from our regular troops and reserves were ready to fight alongside their Angolan brothers. [*Applause*]

Our losses were minimal. In spite of the fact that the

war was fought on four fronts and that our fighters fought alongside the heroic MPLA soldiers in the liberation of almost a million square kilometers [*Applause*] that had been occupied by the interventionists and their accomplices, fewer Cuban soldiers were killed in action in over four months of fighting in Angola than in the three days of fighting at Girón. [*Applause*]

Cuba alone bears the responsibility for taking that decision. The USSR had always helped the peoples of the Portuguese colonies in their struggle for independence, provided besieged Angola with basic aid in military equipment, and collaborated with us when imperialism had cut off practically all our air routes to Africa, but it never requested that a single Cuban be sent to that country. The USSR is extraordinarily respectful and careful in its relations with Cuba. A decision of that nature could only be made by our own party. [*Applause*]

Ford and Kissinger lie to the people of the United States and to world public opinion when they try to place the responsibility for Cuba's action in solidarity with Angola on the Soviet Union.

Ford and Kissinger lie when they seek to blame the Congress of the United States for the defeat of the interventionists in Angola because Congress failed to authorize new funds for the FNLA and UNITA counterrevolutionary groups. Congress made those decisions on December 16, 18, and 19. By that time, the CIA had already supplied large amounts in arms, Zaïrean troops had been repulsed in Luanda, Cabinda had been saved, the South Africans were contained and demoralized on the banks of the Queve River, and no shipment of arms from the CIA would have changed the already inexorable course of events. Today the arms would be in the hands of the revolutionary forces, like many of those the CIA supplied earlier.

Ford and Kissinger lie to the people of the United States, and especially to the Black population of that country, when they hide the fact that the fascist and racist troops of South Africa criminally invaded Angolan territory long before Cuba sent any regular unit of soldiers there.

There are some other lies on the part of Ford and Kissinger in relation to Angola which need not be analyzed now. Ford and Kissinger know perfectly well that everything I say is true.

In this solemn commemoration ceremony, I am not going to say what I think of the insolent epithets Ford has used in his political campaign through the South of the United States and of other cynical aspects of his imperial policy; I will confine myself, for now, to replying that he is a common liar. [*Applause*]

True, events in Angola resemble those of Ethiopia, but in reverse. In Angola, the imperialists, the racists, the aggressors symbolized by the CIA, the South African troops, and the white mercenaries did not win victory nor did they occupy the country; victory was won by those who were attacked, by the revolutionaries, by the heroic Black people of Angola. [*Applause*]

True, events in Angola resemble those of Czechoslovakia after Munich, but also in reverse: the people who were attacked received the solidarity of the revolutionary movement, and the imperialists and racists could not dismember the country or divide up its wealth or assassinate its finest sons and daughters. Angola is united, its territory is unified, and today it is a bulwark of liberty and dignity in Africa. The swastika of the South African racists does not fly over the palace of Luanda. [*Applause*]

We advise Mr. Ford to study a bit of true history and draw the correct conclusions from its lessons.

With the imperialist defeat in Angola, Mr. Kissinger

scarcely has time enough to run from place to place whipping up fear of the Cuban revolution. Some days ago he traveled through half a dozen Latin American countries and now he has announced a new trip to several countries of Africa, a continent he never deigned to look at before his African Girón.

No Latin American country, whatever its social system, will have anything to fear from the armed forces of Cuba. It is our deepest conviction that each people must be free to build their own destiny; that each people and only the people of each country must and will make their own revolution. The government of Cuba has never thought of taking revolution to any nation of this hemisphere with the arms of its military units. Such an idea would be absurd and ridiculous. Nor is it Cuba who stole the major part of its territory from Mexico, landed 40,000 marines to crush the revolution in Santo Domingo, occupies part of Panamanian territory, oppresses a Latin people in Puerto Rico, plans assassinations of foreign leaders, or exploits the wealth and natural resources of any people in this hemisphere.

No country of Black Africa has anything to fear from Cuban military personnel. We are a Latin-African people—enemies of colonialism, neocolonialism, racism, and apartheid, which Yankee imperialism aids and protects.

They say that Kissinger wants to meet in Africa with the representatives of the liberation movements of that continent. Anything is possible in Black Africa after the Girón of Angola. [*Applause*] But what kind of hypocritical, cynical, and pharisaical words can Kissinger speak to the African liberation movements, to the representatives of the oppressed peoples of Rhodesia, Namibia, and South Africa—he who represents the empire that unscrupulously supported Portuguese colonialism and today aids, protects, and supports with economic and political means the South African and Rhodesian racists, in brazen violation of United Nations agreements and resolutions?

Ford and Kissinger have the inveterate habit of using blackmail and threat as a tool of foreign policy. Not long ago they threatened the oil-producing countries with military measures. Now they are using the same cynical and shameless language against Cuba. They are not the first Yankee rulers who have used, to no avail, these intimidating tactics against our homeland. Eisenhower, Kennedy, Johnson, and Nixon all tried to intimidate Cuba. All, without exception, underestimated the Cuban revolution; all were mistaken. [*Applause*] Cuba cannot be intimidated by bellicose threats. It is possible to know when and how a war on Cuba can be started; four madmen could decide that at anytime; but what is impossible to know is when and how it would end. [*Prolonged applause*]

Only peoples who have no dignity can be intimidated. We have already lived through the October Crisis of 1962, and scores of atomic weapons pointed at Cuba did not make our people—not even the children—hesitate. [*Applause*] The people of Cuba can answer Kissinger's threats with the verses of a classical Spanish poem:

> And if I fall,
> What is life?
> I already
> Gave it up for lost
> When,
> Fearlessly,
> I tore off the yoke
> Of the slave. [*Applause*]

The Yankee imperialists have hundreds of thousands of soldiers abroad; they have military bases on all continents and in all seas. In Korea, Japan, the Philippines, Turkey, Western Europe, Panama, and many other places, their military installations can be counted by the dozens and the hundreds. In Cuba itself they occupy by force a piece of our territory.

What moral and legal right do they have to protest that Cuba provides instructors and assistance for the technical preparation of the armies of African countries and of other parts of the underdeveloped world that request them?

What right do they have to criticize the aid and solidarity we give to a sister people of Africa such as Angola, who have been criminally attacked?

The imperialists are pained that Cuba, the attacked and blockaded country they tried to destroy fifteen years ago by a mercenary invasion, is today a solid and indestructible bulwark of the world revolutionary movement, whose example of bravery, dignity, and determination gives encouragement to peoples in their struggle for liberation. [*Applause*]

On the other hand, our revolutionary action is in keeping with the world balance of forces and the interest of world peace. We are not enemies of détente or of peaceful coexistence between states with different social systems based on strict respect for the norms of international law. We would even be willing to maintain normal relations with the United States on the basis of mutual respect and sovereign equality, without renouncing any of our principles and without giving up the struggle on an international level to ensure that the norms of peaceful coexistence and respect for the rights of each nation are applied to all the peoples of the world, without exception.

The United States occupies a piece of our territory in Guantánamo; the United States has maintained a criminal blockade against our country for more than fifteen years.

Cuba will never bow before this imperialist policy of hostility and force and will struggle against it tirelessly. We have said that there can be no negotiations while there is a blockade. No one can negotiate with a dagger at his chest. It doesn't matter if we spend a further twenty years without relations with the United States. [*Applause*] We have learned to live without them, and by basing ourselves on our solid and indestructible friendship with the USSR we have advanced more in these years [*Applause*] than any other country in Latin America. While trade with the United States might perhaps mean certain advantages and a faster rate of development, we prefer to move less rapidly but with our heads held high and the flag of dignity fully unfurled. [*Prolonged applause*] We will not exchange the revolutionary birthright we hold as the first socialist revolution in the Western Hemisphere for a plate of lentils. [*Applause*] We can also say, like the Christians, that man does not live by bread alone.

Some days ago, coinciding with the Yankee threats made by Ford and Kissinger, pirate ships, whose crews the entire world knows come from the United States, attacked two Cuban fishing boats. Once again, a humble worker of the sea was savagely assassinated. This is a flagrant violation of the Memorandum of the Agreement on Air Piracy between Cuba and the United States. If such occurrences do not cease and if their authors are not duly punished, that agreement will be terminated. [*Applause*] Let it not be said later that the government of the United States was not warned in time of the consequences of its irresponsible acts.

A long time has passed since Girón. Our Revolutionary Armed Forces today have an incomparably greater potential. Our soldiers and officers have acquired a vastly superior training. More than half a million men make up the reserve of our military units. [*Applause*] The most modern equipment, supplied by the USSR, constantly updates and improves our combat ability. The country is much stronger in every sense. Our party, virtually born, as I said, at the time of Girón is today a formidable and deeply rooted vanguard organization. The people and the state are organized on increasingly broad and solid bases. "Whoever tries to conquer Cuba," as Maceo said, "will gain nothing but the dust of her blood-soaked earth if he doesn't perish in the struggle first!" [*Prolonged applause*]

Let us bow our heads with respect and eternal gratitude to the heroes who, with the victory of fifteen years ago, made possible the worthy, brave, indestructible homeland of today.

Patria o muerte!

Venceremos! [*Ovation*]

A duty fulfilled

July 26, 1976

Speech given to mass rally in Pinar del Río to commemorate the anniversary of the Moncada attack. Also present was Angola's President Agostinho Neto. The text is from Granma, August 8, 1976.

Dear Comrade Agostinho Neto and other members of the delegation from the MPLA and the People's Republic of Angola; [*Applause*]
Comrades of the party and government;
Guests;
People of Pinar del Río:
Cubans: [*Applause*]

The province of Pinar del Río was honored with the privilege of being the site of the main celebration of the twenty-third anniversary. Under capitalism, no region in Cuba was more neglected, no people in Cuba were made the object of greater indifference—of scorn, we might even say—in spite of the fact that this province played a principal role in the last war of independence and these lands were the scene of many of the most brilliant armed actions carried out by the Army of Liberation under its glorious General Antonio Maceo, [*Applause*] and in spite of the fact that countless sons and daughters of this province died either in the struggle or in concentration camps or were victims of the crimes committed by colonialism.

As many of you recall, the situation in Cuba by July 26, 1953, was becoming unbearable. This province was the headquarters of the lowest, most reactionary, most avaricious latifundists. The great majority of the peasants, who worked the land as sharecroppers, were forced to turn over as much as 50 percent of the crops—and sometimes even more. We are familiar with the struggles waged by the peasants of Pinar del Río against the abuses, the injustices, the crimes, and the evictions to which they were subjected. There were no schools in the countryside. Only 33 percent of the youngsters between six and twenty-four attended school. The illiteracy rate was over 30 percent. Unemployment, poverty, the shantytowns in the cities—a product of the peasants' emigration from the countryside—abounded in every part of this province. We have no idea of what the rate of infant mortality was, since nobody ever bothered to keep a record. It could have been sixty, seventy, eighty, and even one hundred out of every thousand babies born alive. The province had only one senior high school. And a university branch was simply out of the question!

Today, things are completely different. Today there are no longer reactionary large landowners exploiting the peasants. Nor is there eviction, unemployment, or illiteracy. And the infant mortality rate—not only for the entire country but also for this province, which was one of Cuba's poorest and most backward—is lower than that of any country in Latin America. [*Applause*]

If, according to historical data, the province of Pinar del Río had, prior to the revolution, 140 doctors, 35 dentists, and 50 nurses, today there are in this province, working in the cities and in the countryside, three times as many doctors and dentists and twenty times as many nurses and public health aides. [Applause]

One hundred percent of the children of elementary school age are attending school. There isn't a single place in the province, regardless of how remote it may be, that doesn't have a classroom and a teacher. [Applause] Whereas before the revolution only 4,000 residents of Pinar del Río Province had graduated from high school, by the end of the coming school year there will be 41,000 students attending high school in this province. [Applause] Close to 250,000 of the 600,000 residents of Pinar del Río Province, including those in adult education, are studying. [Applause] Pinar del Río already has a university branch [Applause] which will have a student body of more than 4,000 during the next school year. [Applause]

Agriculture is no longer limited to tobacco. Of course, tobacco—and plenty of it, too—which, by the way, is the world's best, continues to be grown. [Applause] But important rice projects have also been developed. And, whereas prior to the revolution the province turned out between 14,000 and 18,500 metric tons of rice, it is now producing more than 90,000 metric tons. [Applause] In the past, there were only a handful of citrus fruit groves; now the province has some 17,500 hectares of land planted to citrus fruit trees, and the area will be extended to more than 26,000 hectares by 1980. [Applause] There was hardly a single poultry farm with the means for modern production; today the province is one of the country's highest producers of poultry. An important hog-raising project has also been developed on the basis of the most modern techniques. Milk production keeps increasing year after year. And, as far as forestry is concerned, a total of 250 million trees have been planted since the triumph of the revolution, [*Applause*] which is equivalent to a third of all the trees planted in the country throughout this period. A vast network of roads has been built, and there's practically no place in the province without this means of communication. A thruway is now under construction between Pinar del Río and Havana. [*Applause*] The province's central railroad will be rebuilt in the future, [*Applause*] and the construction of a modern airport near Pinar del Río will get under way in the coming months. [*Applause*]

As you can see, the face of the province is changing. There didn't used to be a single reservoir in this province, but dozens of dams have been built in the last few years, steadily increasing the province's reserves of water. And we are sure you won't stop until our watchword of "Not a single drop of water to the sea!" is met. [*Applause*]

The face of the province is changing. Dozens of junior and senior high schools in the countryside and polytechnic institutes are being built. This province already has a very modern Technological Institute of Forestry, with facilities for over 1,000 students. [*Applause*] Changes can be seen right in the city of Pinar del Río, where tall buildings are going up: [*Applause*] dozens of apartment buildings; a school for teachers, with a capacity for 2,000 students, already operating fully; [*Applause*] and a vocational school, which will be ready this year with a capacity for 2,500 students. [*Applause*] You already have a magnificent stadium and, next to it, a fine school for teachers of physical education, [*Applause*] who, in this year's nationwide emulation, took first place in their category. You also have a new Technological Institute of Health. [*Applause*]

The young people of Pinar del Río Province are responding to this effort made for them by the revolution by applying themselves to their studies. In four different nationwide emulations, schools in Pinar del Río placed first this year: [*Applause*] the Antonio Guiteras Senior High School in the Countryside, [*Applause*] which came in first in the nation for the third consecutive year; [*Applause*] the Camilo Cienfuegos Military School; [*Applause*] a rural junior high school; [*Applause*] and a vocational school. [*Applause*]

With us here today—and they are worthy of our recognition—are the students of the junior high school in the countryside in Las Villas Province that won first place on the national level. [*Applause*]

This year, Pinar del Río Province has brought in the largest tobacco harvest of all time, [*Applause*] amounting to some 34,500 metric tons, [*Applause*] or double the 1971 harvest.

This is the result of a growing productive effort that has been made for several years. In the last five-year period, overall social production in Pinar del Río increased by 64 percent. The agricultural sector increased its production by 61 percent; industry by 66 percent; and construction by 200 percent. [*Applause*]

As a result of this, per capita income in the province rose during that five-year period from 404 pesos to 530 pesos per year. [*Applause*] Women's participation in productive activities and social services now constitutes 30 percent. [*Applause*] There are now 217,000 workers in the province. [*Applause*]

And this year, not only did the tobacco harvest set an all-time record; the sugarcane harvest was also the largest ever in the history of Pinar del Río. [*Applause*]

There are now over half a million head of cattle in the province, and rice production also set an all-time record. Just about all the plans for the first half of this year were fulfilled. [*Applause*] And the value of what was produced in the first half of 1976 was 18 percent higher than that of what was produced in the corresponding period of 1975. [*Applause*]

These achievements are the result of the excellent job of leadership done by our party; [*Applause*] by its magnificent provincial leadership team; and especially by its first secretary, Comrade Camacho Aguilera. [*Applause*]

We are very pleased by the demonstration of affection and trust that you have given Comrade Camacho, [*Applause*] because we remember his revolutionary history. We remember that, at the time of the *Granma* landing, he led a handful of combatants in the attack and capture of one of the tyranny's garrisons in the Guantánamo region. [*Applause*] We remember the tremendous job he did—his political work with the military men who sympathized with our cause—which resulted in the heroic uprising of Cienfuegos on September 5, 1957. [*Applause*] We remember the arduous tasks and the tremendous risks which Comrade Camacho assumed in the underground struggle—a struggle whose story has not yet been written but which contains many interesting anecdotes, such as the fact that the movement's penetration in the ranks of the enemy was so great that, on more than one occasion during the war, Comrade Camacho, who was in hiding and being pursued, walked right into Camp Columbia, the main bulwark of the tyranny, to make contact with military men. [*Applause*]

Those times have passed. Others came which called for even more arduous, more dedicated, and we might even say more difficult work: that of rebuilding the country, the job of developing our homeland economically and socially, the job of building socialism. And Comrade Camacho is devoting himself to this task with the same enthusiasm with which he had thrown himself into the struggle against the tyranny—with that same enthusiasm, or we might say with even greater enthusiasm—[*Applause*] because one of his characteristics, in addition to his sense of responsibility, his modesty, and his seriousness, is his inextinguishable enthusiasm. [*Applause*] How much he has worked and struggled to help this province advance! [*Applause*] And in our opinion, this is one of the factors that explain this success of yours.

But the fundamental factor is you, the people of Pinar del Río; [*Applause*] you, the masses of Pinar del Río; [*Applause*] you, the self-sacrificing members of the party in Pinar del Río; [*Applause*] you, the nearly 30,000 members of the Young Communist League in Pinar del Río; [*Applause*] you the hundreds of thousands of members of the Committees for the Defense of the Revolution, [*Applause*] workers, peasants, [*Applause*] members of the Federation of Cuban Women, [*Applause*] students and Pioneers; [*Applause*] you who belong to and work in our mass organizations. Without your work spirit; without your enthusiasm; without your trust; without your self-sacrifice; without your discipline; without the revolutionary awareness of you, the people of Pinar del Río Province, these successes could never have been achieved. [*Applause*] And we are glad to be able to proclaim it, here at a July 26 celebration in this province, a province that gave one of the best contingents for the beginning of the revolutionary armed struggle: [*Applause*] young people from Artemisa, from Guanajay, and from the city of Pinar del Río [*Applause*], which used to constitute united parts of Pinar del Río Province. This is why we are always aware of the support given by this region of Cuba to the revolutionary struggle both before and after July 26; [*Applause*] before and after January 1; [*Applause*] yesterday, today, and tomorrow! [*Applause*]

We think that this is the best tribute that can be paid to the seventeen combatants from Pinar del Río who were killed in the events surrounding the attack on the Moncada [*Applause*] and those killed in later struggles. Some of those who participated in the attack on the Moncada also took part in the *Granma* landing and in the struggle in the Sierra and are always with us: Julito Díaz and Ciro Redondo symbolize them. [*Applause*] They struggled for the freedom and progress of the present; for their whole homeland and in its heart, their province: Pinar del Río. [*Applause*]

Since the congress of the party, our revolution has been working on new tasks. The vast majority of the people approved our socialist constitution on February 24. [*Applause*] The election of delegates to People's Power* will be held in October. [*Applause*] A big effort is being made to prepare the conditions for the implementation of the System of Economic Management. [*Applause*] And we are sure that you, the people of Pinar del Río, will be in the vanguard in the many tasks that lie ahead. [*Applause*]

We all have a lot of work to do. A lot has already been done in this province, but a lot—a great deal—still needs to be developed. The battle we must wage with nature is a great one, as is the effort needed to rebuild the forests decimated by capitalism, to harness water and store it in reservoirs, to drain the swampy areas, to irrigate the largest possible areas, and to keep on developing our tobacco industry—raising the quality as well as increasing quantity. There are possibilities for building new sugar mills in this province, and this will have to be done sometime in the future. Mining possibilities are being studied and look

---

* People's Power is the Cuban system of elected representative assemblies on the local, regional, and national levels.

promising. There are many natural resources, including the natural beauty of this province, which will lead to a greater development of tourism in the future. [*Applause*]

In the terms of social progress, there are many schools still to be built, hospitals to finish, children's day-care centers to build. But, above all, there is the tremendous need for housing that is felt all over the country, including here in Pinar del Río Province. [*Applause*]

With the new political-administrative division of the country, the provinces will be more or less equal. There won't be big provinces and little provinces; all the provinces will have more or less the same population and be of more or less the same size. In the future, the fourteen provinces in the country will have optimal conditions for emulating with one another. [*Applause*] And we don't think the people of Pinar del Río will want to fall behind [*Applause and shouts of "No!"*] or have less enthusiasm than any other province. [*Applause and shouts of "No!"*] And we believe that this spirit, this tremendous spirit, this enthusiasm that you have shown with regard to July 26 and in this rally will be kept up always. [*Applause and shouts of "Yes!"*] But, in addition to Pinar del Río's having the honor of being the site for the main ceremony held on this July 26, our country and the people of Pinar del Río have been given the immense honor of having with us today the revolutionary leader and president of the People's Republic of Angola, Agostinho Neto. [*Applause and shouts of "Cuba, Angola, united will win!"*]

This isn't a matter of courtesies, of paying compliments; rather, it is a question of analyzing the facts, of understanding their meaning, and of expressing our most sincere feelings.

Agostinho Neto is a man whose name will go down in history as one of the revolutionary leaders who have demonstrated great worth in the eyes of their people and the world revolutionary movement.

At times, history evolves before our very eyes, yet we fail to understand it in all its meaning. We Cubans can understand it best by comparing it with our own experiences. What was Cuba in the last century, but a Spanish colony? What has Angola been until very recently, but a Portuguese colony? Two nations belonging to the same peninsula, and two equally exploiting and cruel colonial systems. And how did the independence of Cuba come about? What obstacles did our compatriots in that epoch not have to surmount in order to achieve independence? With how many hundreds of thousands of soldiers did they have to fight? The Cuban nation still didn't exist as such; the feeling of nationhood evolved in the course of the struggle.

We have infinite admiration for Martí because of the gigantic tasks he assumed of forming a revolutionary awareness in our people. We admire Martí because he was a brilliant intellectual, a man of tremendous culture, a poet of exquisite sensitivity, who dedicated his talent to the revolutionary struggle, who dedicated his life and his pen to this struggle; he was a man of both word and action. We are grateful to him, and always will be, for what he meant and what he symbolized.

But this same history of our homeland at the end of the last century is also the present history of Angola, [*Applause*] a country colonized for more than 400 years; a country in which the colonialists exploited, developed, and exacerbated all manner of divisions; a country in which, as Neto has explained, the colonialists used racism, tribalism, and regionalism, and resorted to all kinds of weapons to keep an Angolan nation from being forged, so as to maintain their colonial rule indefinitely.

And here we have a man who also has dedicated his life to the effort to free his homeland, who had to confront enormous difficulties; and, to make the situations even more similar, Neto is also a man of tremendous culture, of great intellectual capacity, and an extraordinary poet who has dedicated his life and his pen to his people—to his discriminated against and enslaved brothers and sisters—to forge political awareness in the Angolans. [*Applause*]

Just as Martí wrote many of his best works, including much of his best poetry, amidst suffering—the inextinguishable suffering of one who is aware of the meaning of freedom and will not stand for man being treated as a slave—so did Neto write most of his best poetry amidst his suffering in prison and exile and as a result of the slavery of his brothers and sisters. [*Applause*] Martí and Neto have been the makers of countries.

But not only did Neto awaken an awareness. Like Martí, he also outlined the means for struggle and set a course—the only course for Angola, as it was for Cuba yesterday—that would lead to independence: the heroic struggle of the people, the people's armed struggle. [*Applause*] And, for many years, he has directed that struggle. Neto is also one of the most unassuming, noble, and honest men I have ever known.

Neto suffered the rigors of prison on many occasions. The first time was in 1951, and the second in 1955—from February 1955 to June 1957. So, when we, the assailants of the Moncada were in prison on the Isle of Pines, in February 1955, Neto and his comrades were also imprisoned in the colonialist jails of Angola. [*Applause*] By the time Neto was released from prison in 1957, as a result of the tremendous pressure exerted by world public opinion and the world progressive movement, among whom Neto already enjoyed great prestige as an intellectual and as a revolutionary, those who had participated in the attack on the Moncada—and who had also been released as a result of the tremendous pressure exerted by our people—were fighting in the Sierra Maestra. [*Applause*]

At that time we had no relations with either Comrade Neto or his movement. In those days of February 1955, we spent time in our cells thinking about the future and preparing ourselves for the future struggle. A lot of time has gone by since then: more than twenty-one years! And who would have said then—only those who had faith in the future could have done so—that one day the fighters of the July 26 Movement and those of the MPLA, [*Applause*] representing socialist Cuba and a sovereign and free Angola, all the way from Cabinda to Cunene, an Angola on the way to the construction of socialism, would meet here, in Pinar del Río on a July 26. [*Applause*]

However, the road to this meeting was a long one, indeed. We had already triumphed by 1959, but Neto was still the victim of persecution and repression. He was imprisoned for the third time in 1960 and again in 1961, in the days of Playa Girón. And several weeks after Playa Girón Agostinho Neto was imprisoned for the fourth and last time.

We had just emerged from that difficult test following the victory of Playa Girón, which represented the first defeat of Yankee imperialism in America. [*Applause*] And if we hadn't defeated Yankee imperialism in April 1961, we wouldn't have been able to give our help to invaded Angola in late 1975. [*Applause*]

This is why when a people fights for its rights and for a just cause, it also fights for the just cause of others. In their struggle against imperialism, the Vietnamese were also fighting for us. In their struggle against imperialism, the Angolans were also fighting for us. [*Applause*] And we

Cubans, in our struggle against imperialism at Girón, were also creating the conditions so that, one day, Angolans and Cubans, fighting shoulder to shoulder, could inflict upon the imperialists an African Girón. [*Prolonged applause*]

This is why we appreciate the profound significance and the extraordinary symbolism of Neto's presence in this rally. To us, it is a living page of history that brings to mind the history of our country.

After all, who were our people, our nation? Who but Africans, to a great extent, constituted our nation? And who but the old African slaves—or their descendants—fought in great numbers in our wars of independence in 1868 and 1895? [*Applause*] And who knows how many descendants of Angolans were among them!

When Comrade Neto and I were discussing sports—I wanted to know what his ideas were in this regard and the conversation came about on account of all the expectations surrounding the Montreal Olympics—he said to me, "It'll be a long time before we're able to participate in the Olympics." And I said to him, "Just think, Comrade Neto, that the Angolans are also represented at the Montreal Olympics [*Applause*] by many of our athletes. Who knows how many of them are descendants of Angolans?"

Many things bind us to Angola: the cause, common interests, policy, ideology. But we are also united by blood ties. [*Applause*] And I mean this in two ways: by the blood of our ancestors and the blood we have shed together on the battlefield! [*Prolonged applause*]

Comrade Neto spoke wise words of profound significance when he said that it is not geography that separates or unites peoples and that the common revolutionary struggle should unite our peoples more and more, independently of geography.

We have fulfilled our elementary internationalist duty

with Angola. By fulfilling a duty we are not doing a favor but simply fulfilling a duty. We've always thought that if a man cannot sacrifice himself for others, he is incapable of sacrificing himself for anything; [*Applause*] a people that cannot sacrifice itself for other peoples is incapable of sacrificing itself for its own sake; [*Applause*] a people that is not willing to fight for the freedom of others will never be ready to fight for its own freedom. [*Applause*]

We have fulfilled our internationalist duty with the sister people of Angola and we feel proud of having done so. [*Applause*] We are proud of our revolutionary people, who were willing and ready to enlist hundreds of thousands of their fighters if necessary. [*Applause*] We are proud of our revolutionary reservists and soldiers who fought shoulder to shoulder with the Angolans with the same heroism and the same courage that would characterize their action in our own country. [*Applause*] We are proud of those soldiers, who, 10,000 kilometers away from our country and under the battlecry of "The struggle continues, victory is certain!" proclaimed their own battlecry of "Patria o muerte, venceremos!" [*Applause and shouts of "Venceremos!"*] and were fully justified in doing so, because their fighting side by side with their Angolan brothers was tantamount to fighting for their own country! [*Applause*]

There has been a great deal of talk in international circles about our aid to the Republic of Angola and about Cuban military personnel in Angola. The whole matter is very clear and very simple.

As we all know, our country has been gradually withdrawing whatever military personnel is no longer necessary in Angola, given the present conditions. However, by virtue of an agreement between the government of the People's Republic of Angola and the government of Cuba, the Cuban military units and weapons necessary to support the People's Republic of Angola in case of aggression from outside still remain in Angola. [*Applause*] And they will remain for as long as it is necessary.

And what, in the opinion of the governments of Angola and Cuba, the MPLA and the Communist Party of Cuba, does "as long as it is necessary" mean? Well, we'll say it again; whatever time it takes for the armed forces of the People's Republic of Angola to be organized, equipped, and trained, [*Applause*] and until the day they no longer need us to repel any invasion like the one that took place recently. And the day will come when they will no longer need such military aid! Just as in our case, since we have been able to organize powerful means of defense.

One of the most shameful crimes perpetrated by the imperialists in recent times was precisely the invasion of Angola, in which they used the regular troops of the South African fascists in a silent, dirty war. But in Angola, the South African fascists met their match! [*Applause*] Therefore, let no one be deceived or confused. Angola has sufficient military aid! [*Applause*] And, if another invasion should occur, Cuban soldiers will again fight shoulder to shoulder with the Angolan people! [*Prolonged applause*]

There's speculation among some circles as to the content of the talks between Comrade Neto and us—whether the talks have to do with military matters. Actually, the least we have talked about is military matters. These matters were discussed a long time ago. [*Applause*] Everything in its time, we say. Angola is now going through a phase that is not essentially military. It's still faced—just as we were, following the triumph of the revolution—with the struggle against counterrevolutionary bands. Needless to say, the imperialists are trying—the same way they did in Cuba for years—to harass, sabotage, and disturb the peaceful work in Angola. But, to tell the truth, the counterrevolutionary organizations, the FNLA and UNITA, are completely demoralized and will never again get back on their feet. Now they devote themselves to two different types of warfare: A war of "statements" in some capitals, with a lot of talk about going on the offensive, battles, victories, etc., that exist only on paper. The fact remains that what these groups of bandits—with which we are more than familiar, because, as you all remember, here in Cuba they devoted themselves to murdering teachers, doctors, workers, and peasants—are really doing is the following: they come into a hamlet and try to sow terror among the people, they murder women by cutting their bellies open and murder children by leaving them to burn to death inside the houses they set on fire. That's the kind of heinous crime they are committing, earning for themselves more and more hatred from the population. These groups of bandits haven't got a chance in Angola, nor will they ever be able to put up a fight against FAPLA [Popular Armed Forces for the Liberation of Angola].

Angola is faced now mainly with tasks of a civilian character. The time has come for the Angolans to rebuild and develop their country and to carry the revolution forward. They are faced with an immense number of tasks amidst very difficult conditions.

What did colonialism leave in its wake in Angola? The colonialists never bothered to teach Angolans how to drive a truck or a tractor. They didn't teach them anything at all. They didn't even train them as skilled workers.

In Angola, colonialism left an illiteracy rate of 90 percent in its wake. Moreover, the colonialist property owners abandoned the farms, the factories, everything, taking the technicians with them. The kind of aid that Angola needs most today is of a civilian character, of a technical character. And the talks between the Angolan and Cuban delegations have dealt with this type of collaboration.

We will collaborate with the Angolans in every field; in the political field, in the military field, helping to organize and train their armed forces, helping to train cadres for the struggle against sabotage and counterrevolution! And we will collaborate with the Angolans in many other fields in which we are able to do so.

Of course, aid to Angola can be managed only through the collaboration of all the socialist countries. And the socialist countries have expressed their willingness to collaborate with Angola, some in one field, others in another.

We have been studying Cuba's collaboration with Angola in the field of public health. A contingent of doctors and public health aides is already working in Angola and it is our intention to further this kind of collaboration. This is a field in which we have experience and in Angola the struggle against illness is very great, because the colonialists did nothing at all in the field of public health. This is why we will make an important contribution to public health.

We will also give Angola the benefit of our experience and our aid in the field of construction. As you all know, we have made extensive progress in this field, too, and we are able to collaborate with the Angolans. We will also cooperate with them in the fields of education, fishing, sugarcane, the sugar industry—they have four sugar mills and, by the way, they have already started their sugar harvest—and coffee. Of course we will cooperate in any other field if it is necessary. We will have to work in this direction.

The heroic stage, the stage of war, has passed. This is the stage of peace and it calls for heroes of peace! [*Applause*]

There are several hundred Cubans working in various fields, but we believe that the time will come when two or three thousand and even more will be needed. [*Applause*]

As I said before, among the problems facing the Angolans today is one stemming from the fact that the colonialists never bothered to teach them even to drive motorized vehicles. For example, now the Angolans are faced with harvests, the transportation of crops, etc.; they can acquire the trucks they need—but they have no drivers for these trucks. At times they need a driver to drive the truck and, at the same time, teach an Angolan how to drive it. Or they need a bricklayer who will teach an Angolan his trade while he is on the job. Or they need a construction foreman who will not only do his job but will also teach it to an Angolan. And of course, they are in need of doctors, engineers, architects, teachers, and so on.

In sum, they are badly in need of technicians of every kind.

It is in this field that our country can give Angola help. Actually, it won't be the kind of aid that costs a great deal from an economic viewpoint, because it's not a matter of tons of sugar or tons of commodities, since Angola is a country that has vast natural resources and a great economic potential. The aid they need now is human aid, from trained men and women. [*Applause*]

This is why we expect from our people, our workers, and, particularly, our young people, that, just as hundreds of thousands were ready to fight in Angola, so tens of thousands will be ready now to give Angola civilian help. [*Applause*]

This doesn't mean that we are going to send every person who wants to go to Angola. We will send only a small number of those who are ready to go. To us, what counts is the spirit of solidarity, the spirit of collaboration.

Let no one think that a people loses something when it helps another. When a people helps another it is not a loss but rather a gain. [*Applause*] Our country loses nothing by sending a doctor to some country—like those we have had practicing their profession in Algeria, Yemen, Tanzania, Somalia, or Angola itself. In fact, the country gains by doing this, because it gains a professional who becomes more conscientious, more revolutionary. [*Applause*]

Our country didn't lose anything by sending 900 construction workers to Vietnam. Instead, we gained by doing that, because today those workers constitute enthusiastic and magnificent nuclei in our construction industry. When they returned from Vietnam they were sent to work on our country's most important, top-priority projects. Our country loses nothing when one of its technicians leaves to carry out an internationalist mission. Instead, our country gains a great deal. [*Applause*] Our revolutionary awareness and our political development gain from it. And this attitude on the part of our people to be ready to fight and to be ready to help in one field or another is a source of pride for any revolutionary party, for any country, and it constitutes a good indicator of our people's maturity and revolutionary awareness. [*Applause*]

This is why the imperialists are always wrong about Cuba, because they don't have the standards with which to measure such moral issues. [*Applause*] They simply cannot gauge the spirit and the conscience of a people. [*Applause*] They were wrong at Playa Girón. And they made another mistake when they planned the invasion of Angola. [*Applause*] They couldn't even imagine that Cuba, a country separated from Angola by a distance of 10,000 kilometers, could lend Angola the kind of collaboration it did. Ten thousand kilometers! [*Applause*] This was because they thought that the people subject to a blockade, the people they have tried so hard to ruin could not provide that kind of aid. And they were wrong!

First of all, there were our fighters; the crewmen and the ships of our merchant marine; our passenger planes [*Applause*] and our aviation workers. And all of them responded quickly and effectively to the appeal of the MPLA and the People's Republic of Angola. [*Applause*]

The imperialists never reckoned on that. This is why the most important thing about a country is not its wealth—the imperialists have plenty of it, but they have neither conscience nor spirit—the most important thing about a country is its conscience and its spirit! [*Applause and shouts of "Fidel!"*]

It has been twenty-three years since the attack on the Moncada barracks. And the one thing that made possible the progress of our struggle was precisely the conscience and spirit of the assailants.

Truthfully speaking, when we began that struggle we had no money, no weapons, no military training, nothing. But, in spite of all the difficulties, nobody ever thought that such an act would be impossible. And it was possible! When I witness the spirit of our people today, I recall that this was exactly the spirit of our comrades in those days. [*Applause*] Except that today it is no longer a matter of the spirit of a handful of men but of that of an entire people! [*Applause*] And if the spirit of a handful of men could not be crushed, much less can the spirit of an entire people ever be defeated! [*Applause*]

Let us proclaim on this July 26 that our party, whose ranks are composed of the revolutionary vanguards of men and women of various ages—ranging from those who have been fighting for the revolution for dozens of years to the young people who join our ranks every day—is proud of the attitude, the mettle, and the awareness of our people. [*Applause*]

Comrade Neto, this is why in the name of our people

we say to you that, just as Angola received our aid in the difficult and heroic days, in this arduous stage of construction, of the development of the country and of the march toward socialism, Angola can also depend on our utmost collaboration. [*Prolonged applause*]

We take this opportunity to extend to our fighters and our workers and civilian technicians in Angola the recognition, the greetings, and the admiration of all our people. [*Applause*]

Cubans are also engaged in a vigorous struggle in another field, the field of sports, at the Olympics. They sent us a beautiful message today. And to them we say that we too are proud of their efforts, we congratulate them and wish them new victories. [*Applause*]

And you, the people of Pinar del Río, allow us to express to you the extraordinary impression we have had today [*Applause*] and to thank you for something that we will remember forever: the enthusiasm, the seriousness, the discipline, and the warmth with which you celebrated July 26. [*Applause*]

People of Pinar del Río: let us make the Angolan watchword "The struggle continues; victory is certain" our watchword for the years of work that lie ahead!

Patria o muerte!

Venceremos! [*Ovation*]

PART 3

Solidarity with Africa: Ethiopia

In 1974, a popular revolution swept away the semifeudal regime of Ethiopian Emperor Haile Selassie, who had been in power for close to half a century. The revolution brought with it the deepest agrarian reform ever carried out in Africa, large-scale nationalizations of industry and land, and a campaign to begin to eliminate illiteracy, which affected 90-95 percent of the population. As the revolution unfolded, a section of the junior officer corps came to power, led by the Armed Forces Coordinating Committee, also known as the Dergue. After a series of purges, Lt. Col. Mengistu Haile Mariam emerged as the dominant figure in the government.

As the revolution took more and more radical measures, the U.S. and other imperialist powers began to see it as a threat. In 1977, the U.S. government cut off aid to Ethiopia and began arming neighboring Somalia, which under President Siad Barre had previously been receiving Soviet arms and had even claimed adherence to socialism. With the support of Washington, Somalia launched a full-scale invasion of Ethiopia in the Ogaden region of eastern Ethiopia in July 1977. Because many inhabitants of the Ogaden were themselves Somalis, the Somalian government claimed it was only aiding these Somalis to win national liberation. This claim rapidly lost credibility as Somalian troops advanced into Ethiopia far beyond where the Ogaden Somalis lived.

During his African tour in March 1977, Castro visited both Somalia and Ethiopia, and convened a meeting between the leaders of those countries in an attempt to prevent the approaching war. In a speech given in Somalia, Castro warned Siad Barre: "What does imperialism count on to fight against the revolutionary movement? It always tries to divide the peoples. It wants to divide the Arab and African peoples, it wants to have the peoples fight each other, and it even wants to have progressive peoples go to war against each other."

After it became apparent that the Somalian invasion could deal a major blow to the Ethiopian revolution, Cuba once again responded to an Ethiopian request by sending thousands of troops beginning in December 1977 and January 1978, quickly reversing the course of the war. By March 14, the last Somalian troops had been driven out. Once again, Cuba had given aid to a popular revolution fighting against an invading force supported by imperialism. A renewed U.S. slander campaign against Cuba was initiated.

One of the important issues in the Ethiopian revolution has been the Eritrean struggle for national independence. Forcibly annexed to Ethiopia in 1962, the Eritrean people had waged a long struggle against Haile Selassie and had received Cuban support. With the triumph of the Ethiopian revolution, the Eritreans thought that at last they would be granted their freedom. Instead, the new regime began large-scale military actions to suppress the Eritrean struggle. For its part, while pulling back from its support to the Eritrean liberation struggle, Cuba repeatedly stated its support for a political, not military, solution to the question. It emphatically denied that Cuban troops were involved in Ethiopia's Eritrean campaign, a fact confirmed by the Eritrean liberation forces themselves. For more information on Cuba's position on Eritrea, see pages 223-224.

Cuba's aid to Ethiopia

March 15, 1978

Excerpt from a speech given to a Santiago de Cuba rally commemorating the one hundredth anniversary of the Baraguá Protest, when Antonio Maceo refused to accept a cease-fire with the Spanish colonialists to end Cuba's first war of independence. The text is from *Granma*, March 26, 1978.

I was saying that a detailed report was published yesterday. We might point out that it has been a tradition in our revolutionary process to report on the facts and tell the truth. Every citizen who read those reports yesterday knew there wasn't a single lie there. This has always been our practice from the time of our struggle in the Sierra Maestra and all during these twenty years: the truth, confidence in the people, and information for the people. The revolution works with the masses, merges with the masses and the truth. That's why nobody had any doubts that what *Granma* said yesterday was the truth and nothing but the truth. [*Applause*]

Some imperialist news agencies have said that the Cuban people officially found out about our internationalist aid to Ethiopia yesterday. Well, if they want to say "officially," yes, we admit it; but unofficially—in the way we know about things and the way we do things and know how to do them among ourselves—everybody knew about it a long time ago. [*Prolonged applause*]

It was the same with our internationalist aid to Angola. The people know about it because we don't do things any other way than with the people. Of course, there are situations in which certain things can't be published officially, because if you must undertake a complicated and dangerous operation you must do so in a discreet manner; there is no need to go around telling everybody about it. [*Laughter*] But who if not the workers and peasants of our reserve forces and the soldiers and officers of our regular forces fulfilled this mission? [*Applause*] All the combat units knew about it and so did all the reserve units. And, as was the case with Angola, there weren't a thousand or ten thousand but hundreds of thousands of our compatriots who were willing to fulfill this internationalist mission. [*Applause*]

We never do anything behind the backs of the people. Very often the masses are told about many things that are not published on the front pages of the newspapers through the party and the mass organizations.

What would the party and the leadership of the party be able to do without the masses? We are glad that our masses are very discreet, [*Applause*] because there are times here when a secret is known to millions of people and nobody else besides those millions of Cubans finds out the secret. [*Applause*]

That is the revolution; that is the spirit of our people, the heritage from Maceo and the Baraguá Protest. That is the spirit of 1868 and 1895, which is present in our people.

We don't speak of the heroes of the past as if they were tourists in history or mere passive onlookers of the feats of others. Our people can speak of those heroes because they have many present-day heroes. [*Applause*] They can speak of their brave *mambí** independence fighters because they are a people of *mambí* fighters. [*Applause*] They can speak of their heroes of the past because they are a people of present-day heroes who fulfill their duties without ostentation! [*Applause*]

Our revolution isn't seeking glory or prestige; it simply fulfills its internationalist postulates and principles! [*Applause*]

Of course, we couldn't discuss our internationalist aid to Ethiopia publicly until the Ethiopians did. As long as they felt that keeping quiet was the right thing, we did likewise. When the Ethiopians discussed the matter publicly, we, our party, were then in a position to do the same. It wasn't going to be a secret known to millions of people forever. Now it's a national and international secret. [*Laughter*]

Fine. We mustn't boast about this. We have no intention of boasting about anything. First of all, we would like to say that we deeply regret the conflict between Somalia and Ethiopia; we did all we could to avoid it. Roughly a year ago, around this time—perhaps it was later than March 20, I don't remember exactly—we organized a meeting in Aden between the leaders of Ethiopia, Yemen, and Somalia and ourselves in an effort to solve the problems between Somalia and Ethiopia, precisely to avoid a war; to avoid a development which would constitute a betrayal

---

* Cuban independence fighters during the first war of independence against Spain.

of the international revolutionary movement; to prevent the leadership of Somalia, with its territorial ambitions and aggressive attitude, from going over to imperialism. We weren't able to prevent it.

In Somalia, there were two forces: forces of the right and forces of the left. For many years they talked to the masses about socialism and progress, but there was a powerful reactionary group in the government, right-wingers who advocated an alliance with imperialism, Arab reaction, Saudi Arabia, Iran, etc. They gradually caused the left-wingers to lose ground in the country, upholding, as reactionaries always do everywhere, the banner of chauvinism. Since they lack a social, political, and revolutionary doctrine, reactionaries resort to playing upon people's basest instincts, and they especially resort to chauvinism.

History is filled with examples of this. What did fascism do in Italy and Germany? It extolled racial prejudice. Instead of combating racial prejudice, which is what the revolution does, fascism exalts prejudice and turns it into hatred. That's what the fascists did in Nazi Germany. In the name of nationalism, territorial ambition, and racial prejudice, they unleashed the occupation of Europe and the invasion of the USSR. What were German soldiers doing in Stalingrad, 1,500 kilometers inside the border of the USSR? How can men be dragged into such madness? On behalf of narrow nationalism, chauvinism, hatred between nations, and territorial ambition.

All reactionaries throughout history have resorted to those methods. Those were the banners upheld by the reactionary faction in the government of Somalia: national hatred, chauvinism, territorial claims, the idea of a Greater Somalia—which would include Djibouti, a third of Ethiopia, and part of Kenya—when all African states, with a great sense of the practical, have wisely agreed on the inviolability of the borders left by colonialism. Those who are familiar with the situation in Africa know that in every African nation there are tribes who live on either side of a border. There are many African states that haven't left the tribal stage completely behind yet. Setting the precedent that a country could use force to seize territory which it was claiming, would have been disastrous for Africa as a whole. That's why the African states have said that there must be no border changes, much less border changes through the use of force.

Chauvinism, however, isn't the only thing which explains the timing of the attack. Ethiopia was ruled by a feudal regime for many years, and that regime was done away with by the Ethiopian revolution. Ethiopia is a country in which peasants make up 85 or 90 percent of the population. Before the revolution and practically up to 1973, even slavery existed in Ethiopia. Those who weren't serfs or peasants tied to the land and oppressed by the landowners might well have been slaves.

Thus, the Ethiopian revolution meant an extraordinary change for the people of Ethiopia; many millions of exploited peasants were liberated, and the bondage of the exploited masses ended. They didn't have a very large working class, but it was also liberated by the revolution. Women, who were especially oppressed and subjected to terrible injustices, were liberated by the Ethiopian revolution.

The Ethiopian revolution not only did away with feudalism; it also decided to advance toward socialism. [*Applause*] One of the most important events to take place in Africa during the last few years was precisely the Ethiopian revolution.

Ethiopia is a country that has suffered a great deal. It was one of the few African countries that was able to maintain its independence for centuries, fighting resolutely until the Italian fascists, who at all costs wanted colonies of their own, invaded Ethiopia in complicity with the colonial powers of Europe. But Ethiopia is a nation of fighters. By the end of the last century they had already defeated the Italians, who were unable to take over the country. However, in 1935, thanks to their technical superiority, the availability of many resources, and the complicity of imperialism, the Italian fascists seized Ethiopia. The Ethiopians fought very hard during the years of occupation, for the Ethiopian people are characterized by their courage and fighting spirit.

Given those circumstances and at the exact moment when the revolution took place—rather, not exactly then, but when the most radical and revolutionary people took power—was when Somalia launched the attack.

Previously, Ethiopia with its emperor was an ally of the United States, of imperialism. During all those years the right-wing faction in Somalia never dreamed of invading Ethiopia. Why? Because they didn't want to mess with imperialism. When the revolution took place but its exact nature hadn't been defined yet, they still didn't dare attack Ethiopia.

In February 1977 the most important, radical, and revolutionary elements, headed by Comrade Mengistu Haile Mariam [*Applause*] took over the leadership of the Ethiopian revolution and announced their intention to build socialism, and it was then that the ties between Ethiopia and imperialism were broken. It was at that precise moment that the right-wing faction of the government of Somalia felt the time to invade Ethiopia had come, because they knew that invading Ethiopia meant cooperating with imperialism in the destruction of a great revolution and that imperialism would be delighted. Furthermore, they knew that the NATO powers would also be delighted if Somalia helped eliminate the Ethiopian revolution.

Today we realize that when we met with Somalia's leaders in March of last year in Aden they had already worked out the plan—which they later put into practice—to invade Ethiopia, because they felt that the historical opportunity had arrived, since Yankee imperialism and the NATO nations would welcome news of the invasion of Ethiopia with open arms.

You know that there are many revolutionary Arab countries but that there is also a group of reactionary Arab countries. These reactionary Arab countries were also delighted with the attack on Ethiopia to destroy the revolution. One of those countries, Saudi Arabia, which is ruled by an archaic monarchy, was one of the most interested in the destruction of the Ethiopian revolution because when you see your neighbor's house on fire you take precautions. Since an emperor had been overthrown, the emperor, or king, or whatever they call him, of Saudi Arabia, was very worried about the downfall of the Ethiopian emperor.

The same thing happened in Iran, a reactionary ally of Yankee imperialism with a criminal and repressive government, a country also ruled by a shah—shah means emperor, king, or, well, I'm not exactly sure what it means. [*Laughter*] It is another feudal monarchy, an absolute monarchy that was also bent on destroying the Ethiopian revolution and encouraging Somalia to attack.

In view of these favorable circumstances for them, the reactionary faction, who hoped to get a flood of petrodollars from Saudi Arabia and Iran, and economic aid from NATO and the United States, took advantage of the fact that there was a revolution in Ethiopia and foisted on this country their policy of war and aggression. This is the Somalian leadership's great crime: invading Ethiopia to destroy a revolution on behalf of the reactionary nations of the area, NATO, and imperialism.

But at the Aden meeting the leaders of Somalia solemnly pledged, solemnly committed themselves not to invade Ethiopia ever, not to attack Ethiopia militarily. In fact, they already had everything planned, and the attack began in July.

Ethiopia is a big country, it has a large population, it has soldiers, and very good soldiers at that. That's why, in answer to their request, we initially decided to send them a few dozen instructors and advisers—the figure might have come to a few hundred—to train units and teach them how to handle modern weapons of a type they weren't familiar with. Since the emperor was an ally of the United States, the Ethiopians had U.S. weapons; then they started to receive supplies from the socialist countries which they didn't know how to handle.

We felt that helping them to train their army would be a provisional measure, because when the Ethiopian army has been trained and well armed you can be sure that nobody—nobody—will bother them. You can be sure of that! [*Applause*]

Why did it become necessary for us to send fighters? Because of the scope and magnitude of Somalia's aggression. Somalia had been preparing itself for a number of years. It had even been upholding the banners of socialism; it claimed to be a progressive country, an ally of the progressive world—I'm talking about the Somalian government—and all along it had been building up an army. Somalia had hundreds of tanks, hundreds of artillery pieces, planes, many motorized infantry brigades, and nearly all those weapons and units were used during the invasion of Ethiopia.

At that time, Ethiopia had to struggle all over the country against groups of counterrevolutionary bandits aided from abroad and directed by feudal elements, and against the secessionist movements in the north, that are still getting help today from reactionary countries in the region. Ethiopia was faced with a very difficult situation, with no time to spare. If the Ethiopians had had a little more time, they would have learned how to handle all those tanks, artillery pieces, and other modern weapons. We, along with other socialist countries, would have contributed to training personnel. But the critical situation created by the invasion in late November led the Ethiopian government to make an urgent request that we send tank, artillery, and aviation specialists to help the army, to help the country, and we did so.

As *Granma* explained, our specialists started arriving in Ethiopia in mid-December and early January. We sent tank, artillery, and aviation specialists, since the Ethiopians didn't have the time to learn how to handle that weaponry in view of the situation. They really didn't need infantry; there were plenty of infantrymen. If some Cuban medium-sized units such as battalions were sent to the east, it was to ensure cooperation with the tank and artillery contingents operated by Cuban personnel, since you must bear in mind the language problem and the fact that there are times when a tank unit must have cooperation with the infantry assured.

But actually our main support for Ethiopia involved sending specialists. The Ethiopians already have artillery and tank units, and I'm sure that soon they'll have excellent cadres to handle that equipment. They have more than enough soldiers, and training an infantryman is easier than training a tank or artillery specialist. We might add that the Ethiopian infantry is made up of very brave and courageous soldiers who have tremendous fighting potential.

Our cooperation became indispensable, the specialists were sent, and, as was reported in *Granma*, Cuban motorized infantry units participated in the final stage of operations alongside the Ethiopian infantry. [*Applause*]

We might point out—as was published yesterday—that in seven weeks practically all the occupied territory in Ogaden was liberated, an area of more than 320,000 square kilometers. [*Applause*] The invaders had overrun 320,000 square kilometers, an area three times the size of Cuba! From January 22 to March 14, practically the entire area was liberated; only a few towns were left and their capture was just a matter of time, since the Ethiopian forces didn't have enough vehicles and in many of those places they had to go on foot. So, for all practical purposes, the war on the eastern front has ended.

Cooperation between Ethiopians and Cubans was magnificent. There were artillery units made up of Cuban specialists and Ethiopian personnel. In a few days they started to understand one another by using signs and numbers, and the artillery group was operating smoothly. In spite of the language differences, they got along very well, and there was a great deal of comradeship, confidence, and brotherhood, and problems were solved smoothly.

I repeat that we don't want to seem as if we are boasting, as if we were indulging in exaggerated praise for our fighters, but we do think that it's only fair to say that the Cuban internationalist fighters stood out for their extraordinary effectiveness and magnificent combat ability. [*Applause*] It is really admirable to see how many sons of our people were capable of going to that distant land and of fighting there as if fighting in their own country. That is proletarian internationalism! [*Applause*] Brave and efficient revolutionary soldiers soon struck up a wonderful friendship and close ties with the admirable Ethiopian revolutionary fighters; they were welcomed in an extraordinarily affectionate manner by the Ethiopian people, and I know their leaders are very grateful to our people for this help.

The war against the invaders is practically over. Ethiopia has publicly stated it will not cross Somalia's border. This seems to us completely just and correct, because the war was fought not to invade another country, much less to seize land which belongs to others. It was an absolutely just, defensive war to protect territory invaded by foreign aggressors until such a time as those aggressors could be thrown out. Of course, this means that the attacks on Ethiopia from Somalia will cease, because we can't imagine that any country would be willing to tolerate attacks launched from the borders of another country indefinitely without responding appropriately. But we know the Ethiopian government was absolutely sincere in its assurance that its troops would not cross the Somalian border. Actually, from the military point of view there is no need to do so, since the attacking forces have been completely defeated, and we fully support the position of the Ethiopian government.

What will happen in Somalia? There's no telling. But it is clear that the right-wing faction, which imposed its aggressive and adventurist line on the government of Somalia, has suffered a great defeat. Naturally, even amidst defeat the imperialists are trying to encourage this group and are maneuvering. However, there are also progressive and left-wing forces in Somalia, and we shall see what happens in the coming weeks. Of course, this is a matter that concerns only the people of Somalia, not any of us or any other country.

The imperialists have assumed a very hypocritical position during the conflict, because they knew that Somalia was invading Ethiopia right from the start, in July. The United States and the NATO countries knew about it and remained silent; they didn't say a word and they were delighted. They provided weapons for the aggressors—weapons from the United States and from NATO member states—by way of Saudi Arabia, Iran, and other countries, and as the Somalis advanced they didn't say a word. When Somalia had occupied nearly all of Ogaden, the imperialists were optimistic; but when the Ethiopians began receiving internationalist aid, when they started to get weapons from the socialist camp, and internationalist Cuban fighters began to arrive, the imperialists raised a real hue and cry. Then they insisted that there had to be a meeting of the OAU [Organization of African Unity], the UN, etc., etc., and they talked about the need for a cease-fire. When, though, did they start talking about a cease-fire? When the aggressors started to lose the war.

As long as Somalia's forces advanced, the imperialists didn't say a word. When things started to change after the Ethiopians' first successful battles, when they realized that the situation could change quickly, then they raised the hue and cry and unleashed a propaganda drive all over the world, talking about the Cuban internationalist fighters—the Cuban troops as they call them—in Ethiopia. When the tables began to turn, they started to talk about a cease-fire, something which they hadn't done for all those months when the reactionary aggressors advanced. Of course, the Ethiopian government quite correctly said that there could be no cease-fire as long as part of its territory was occupied. That's also our revolutionary philosophy: there can be no cease-fire as long as there is occupied territory. [*Applause*]

The first counterattacks and the offensive followed,

and the enemy troops were roundly defeated. They had to pull out in great haste, leaving behind tanks, cannon, artillery, all kinds of weapons, to escape being surrounded and captured, because they had been defeated, completely defeated. We must point out that there was nothing voluntary about the withdrawal of Somalia's troops. If they had stayed four more days, just four more days, virtually all their troops in Ogaden would have been surrounded. Due to the way the revolutionary forces advanced and captured the main communication centers, if the enemy hadn't undertaken a speedy withdrawal, the remains of Somalia's army would have been surrounded in Ogaden. Thus, the aggressors have been forced to leave. They can't fool anybody at all by saying that the Somalian government made the gesture of withdrawing its troops, because had the Somalis not done so they would have lost what little they had left. That's the situation: they left as a result of the military operations in which they were defeated.

That's the truth; there's no need to lie. We feel that the war between Somalia and Ethiopia has ended for the time being since the territory has been liberated. I don't think the Somalis will be stupid enough to fall into the temptation of attacking Ethiopia again on their own; but just as reactionary countries, NATO states, and imperialism encouraged them once, they might do so again.

We sincerely advocate peace between the two countries. The aim of the war was to liberate occupied territory. We sincerely hope that the people of Somalia will now be able to live in peace and march down the real path of progress and socialism. The people of Somalia have great merits and virtues. As *Granma* explained, Somalia's soldiers aren't cowardly. It is fair and right to say this. They were tough and showed real fighting spirit. They were undoubtedly fooled and poisoned by that chauvinism and the idea of a Greater Somalia. Nobody should think that Somalian soldiers are weak or incompetent—but they were defeated. The enemy did not appraise the situation well and made errors of leadership. There's no doubt that the Somalian leaders made serious political errors and some military ones, which explain the defeat—not to mention the fact that they were trying to commit a great crime against history. The effectiveness of the revolutionary forces greatly reduced their casualties in combat. It must be said that due to their effectiveness and magnificent combat training, our internationalist fighters suffered very few casualties.

We are also giving Ethiopia civilian aid. In all, counting doctors, technicians, and other health personnel, we've sent—most of them are there—more than 300 medical workers. The country has a population of 30 million, it is very heavily populated, and health conditions are still very poor. We have talked about this on other occasions.

I don't need to say more on this subject. We felt that its importance and implications justified our dealing with it today.

Dear comrades, let's dedicate the last minutes of this ceremony to the Baraguá Protest and Antonio Maceo. From the bottom of our hearts, let's dedicate the work of the revolution to them. To Maceo, Gómez, Céspedes, Agramonte, Martí, Yara, Baraguá, and Baire we offer the tribute of our revolutionary efforts, of our generation's revolutionary efforts. To them we dedicate the Moncada, the *Granma*, the Sierra, the thirteenth of March,* Girón, and the heroic internationalist missions in Angola and Ethiopia. [*Applause*] To them we dedicate our efforts and struggles.

---

* On March 13, 1957, the student-based Revolutionary Directorate led an unsuccessful attack on Batista's Presidential Palace.

On such a day, let's pledge to continue marching forward as we've marched so far, enriching the pages of Cuban history.

Many tasks and efforts await us. Our fighters must intensify their combat training, and our workers must step up their efforts to fulfill all the goals we have ahead of us.

Taking our inspiration from our ancestors, from deeds like this and from Antonio Maceo, let's faithfully fulfill our present-day duties!

Patria o muerte!

Venceremos! [*Ovation*]

History is on our side

September 14, 1978

Speech given at the opening ceremony of the International Conference of Solidarity with the Struggle of the African and Arab Peoples Against Imperialism and Reaction held in Addis Ababa, Ethiopia, attended by representatives from 110 countries. Castro visited Ethiopia September 12–19, 1978. The text is from *Granma*, September 24, 1978.

Dear Comrade Mengistu Haile Mariam;
Distinguished delegates and guests:

The privilege of attending the celebrations of the fourth anniversary of the Ethiopian revolution has given me the chance to be with the leader of the Ethiopian revolution, Comrade Mengistu Haile Mariam, at the opening ceremony of this conference.

The problems of Africa and the Middle East stand at the center of today's international situation and your decisions will not only influence the question of international détente, on which concern throughout the world is focused.

But in addition they will determine the destiny of the African peoples and of the Arab people of Palestine, and hence the course of the struggle of the countries which are fighting in Asia, Africa, and Latin America to achieve, consolidate, and develop their national independence; and thus, with full equality and rights, to join the tide of progress carrying humanity towards higher economic and social goals.

This conference is being held at a time when Africa is the chief concern of the most aggressive imperialist forces, who would wish to hold back the uncontainable advance of the African peoples.

In the days following the defeat of Nazi fascism in World War II, the crisis of the colonial system led to the legal independence of dozens of African countries. The Arab countries of the north, and a significant group of countries of Black Africa including Guinea, Senegal, and Ghana, achieved this legal independence without the need to resort to a final armed confrontation with their former colonial oppressors.

But the imperialists used their former ties of economic dominance and their political influence in order to transform that formal beginning of independence into a sad reality of neocolonial systems. Sometimes by assassinating great figures like Patrice Lumumba,* sometimes by means of reactionary coups, at other times by means of political penetration and economic corruption—the imperialists gradually substituted colonial vassalage with the more

---

* Patrice Lumumba, president of the Congolese National Movement, became premier and minister of defense of the Republic of the Congo (later Zaïre) after independence from Belgium in 1960. With the help of the CIA, he was overthrown by Mobutu Sese Seko that same year, arrested, and later killed.

subtle, but no less sinister system of socioeconomic neocolonialism. Just a few isolated regimes were left fighting heroically to maintain their independence.

However, in the seventies we have seen the resurgence of the struggle for national independence. To an appreciable degree this has been influenced by the fact that neocolonial imperialism does not have anything better to offer the peoples it tries to dominate. But the heroic and resolute struggle of the African peoples also has a decisive influence. Foremost are those whose struggles brought about the crisis and defeat of Portuguese colonialism, such as Angola, Mozambique, Guinea-Bissau, and Cape Verde, as well as the valiant and resolute determination of the peoples of Zimbabwe, Namibia, and South Africa to rid themselves of the shameful and brutal domination of colonialism, the bloodthirsty and oppressive white minorities, and apartheid.

In Angola the imperialists tried to use the abominable South African racist regime and their puppet governments in countries bordering Angola to crush the MPLA government led by Agostinho Neto and bring about a new reverse like that of the fifties, which would restrict the independence of Angola, Mozambique, and Guinea-Bissau and would once again isolate Tanzania, Zambia, the Republic of Guinea, and other democratic and progressive governments.

The victory in Angola prevented this historic reverse from taking place, and the heroic and victorious action of the Ethiopian people in introducing a profound and authentic revolution to the northeast of Africa, to a strategically situated country with an ancient culture and more than 30 million inhabitants, made a decisive contribution to the struggle of the Black and Arab countries of Africa. These victories have converted the African continent, as we said, into an area that is decisive for the confrontation with imperialism by the peoples both here and in Latin America and Asia, who are waging the final battle for real independence and for the profound, just, and humane social changes that history demands.

The African people's solidarity with one another, solidarity between the African peoples and the Arab countries of Africa and the Middle East, the solidarity of all the underdeveloped and developing peoples with their brothers in this part of the world, as well as the solidarity of the progressive forces of the whole world, the socialist countries, and the working class and progressive forces in the developed capitalist countries with the cause of Africa and the Arab countries, are an indispensable part of this historic battle. Solidarity has had a special significance for the African and Arab struggles in our times.

The imperialists and their reactionary agents attack the presence of Cuba in Africa, when it is no more than an expression of this necessary and courageous solidarity which you yourselves defend and practice. [*Applause*] We could answer them by repeating the words of various African heads of state, who have said that there is not a single Cuban in Africa who has not been asked to come by an independent state exercising its sovereignty and in order to defend a just cause. [*Applause*]

We have come here to say to you, the representatives of the progressive and revolutionary organizations of the peoples of Africa, the Middle East, and other parts of the world, that we are with you in your decision in favor of solidarity which has inspired this enthusiastic gathering. [*Applause*]

To those who accuse us of promoting armed confrontation by the African peoples against their oppressors, we say that Cuba is not opposed to any peaceful solution to the struggle for independence of the African peoples, essentially in Zimbabwe and Namibia, so long as the solution is a fair one and is accepted by the peoples' legitimate representatives—the Patriotic Front and SWAPO [South West Africa People's Organisation]—and by the African states that have supported them. [*Applause*] But at the same time we say that the main responsibility for the failure to achieve a peaceful solution lies in the fact that while the Anglo-American leaders talk about peace, they seek to achieve it maintaining intact the repressive and reactionary structures created by Smith and Vorster to impose their hateful white minority and apartheid regimes.

While this situation continues, and those fighting in Zimbabwe and Namibia go on risking their lives in this arduous struggle, the Patriotic Front and SWAPO can count on the same resolute cooperation they have received from revolutionary Cuba until now. [*Applause*]

The imperialists persist in supporting the Zionist reactionaries and their illegal occupation of Arab territories—in particular, of Palestinian territories.

The Camp David talks are a desperate attempt to maintain the diplomacy of conceding the Arab and Palestinian peoples their rights in partial installments, and to prevent the presence of the Arab countries and their allies at the Geneva negotiations, which they hope to cancel.*

The difficulties are many, but in Africa and in all parts of the world the struggle of the peoples advances. In Latin America there is no future for the regimes that have taken

---

* The Geneva negotiations were first held in December 1973 with Egypt, Israel, Jordan, the Soviet Union, the U.S., and representatives of the United Nations participating; a dispute soon developed over the issue of Palestinian representation in the talks. On September 17, 1978, the Camp David agreements between Israel, Egypt, and the U.S. were announced.

the road of fascism—a road that has been renovated by the CIA and the transnational corporations. Panama has won recognition of its right to the canal. A glorious chapter of Nicaraguan history is being written by the Sandinista Front, and the country's entire people have joined the uprising against the tyrant Somoza. In its Special Committee on Decolonization, the UN has acknowledged that Puerto Rico is a Yankee colony.

We could add (leaving the text for a moment) that this great victory won by our people, won by Latin America in particular, which opposes the annexation of Puerto Rico and opposes the devouring of the Latin American community by U.S. imperialism—that this victory was achieved with the aid of countries which firmly supported the just position and as a result of two great events: the victory of the Ethiopian revolution and the victory of the revolution in Afghanistan. [*Applause*]

We must say here at this solidarity conference that one of the most inspiring examples of internationalist spirit and political honor given us by Comrade Mengistu and the Ethiopian revolution was his decision to vote for the just position on the Puerto Rican question at the Special Committee on Decolonization.

In the same way we must salute the courageous stand taken by the government of Afghanistan, which also supported the resolution.

And so the revolutionary family grows year by year, [*Applause*] and the correlation of forces changes in favor of the independence of the peoples, in favor of our struggles.

As we speak here today, we recall speaking in Algeria in 1973. At that time Guinea-Bissau, Angola, and Mozambique were still fighting. Just a few years have passed, and today these countries are in the vanguard of the world's progressive movement, and they are not with us here as liberation movements but as independent, sovereign, and revolutionary states. [*Applause*]

And who would have dreamt just four years ago that feudal Ethiopia, an ally of imperialism, would today be one of the most resolute bastions of the progressive movement and liberation movement in the world?

In the same way, I am sure that before long Namibia and Zimbabwe will also be represented at this conference as independent and sovereign states. [*Applause*] And that, by perhaps a somewhat more distant date, the brutal, repugnant, and hateful colonialism, fascism, and racism will have disappeared from South Africa.

Near here Afghanistan has overthrown feudalism and advances like a second Ethiopia, while the people of Iran fight valiantly for their freedom.

Now not even the imperialists—the imperialists who talk so much about human rights and support the shah of Iran, one of the most repressive regimes in the world—now not even the imperialists are sure that this regime will survive.

The most important thing in this struggle is to maintain the unity of the forces that are fighting and of the countries that are supporting them. Historically the most important weapon the imperialists have used against the peoples of Africa and every part of the world has been division. Division between countries, division between races, division between revolutionary forces. If there is anything we would wish to emphasize in this brief speech, it is that unity must be the constant watchword of all those who oppose the system of domination that imperialism is trying to preserve.

Precisely here lies the vile significance of the role of the Chinese leadership. If those who fight for democracy and national independence of the peoples have righteously condemned the Chinese leaders for supporting the murderers of the Chilean people, for their aggression against heroic Vietnam, for encouraging fratricidal war in Indochina, and for their attacks on Angola and Ethiopia, then the Chinese leaders merit such denunciation even more for their devious and obscene divisionist policy.

We visited Ethiopia for the first time eighteen months ago. We came to meet the leaders of this revolution, in which we had seen from afar an example of the most profound social changes in the African continent. Because it must not be forgotten that there was slavery in Ethiopia until the revolution. In the Addis Ababa exposition we have seen the iron and steel fetters used to chain tens of thousands of this country's citizens. But we also came with the purpose of trying to find just political solutions that would prevent divisions and war between the peoples of the Horn of Africa, and the shedding of blood in internal struggles. We did not succeed because of a great charlatan—who I will not mention by name, nor is there need to—who posed under the banner of socialism but believed that Ethiopia was militarily so weak that he would be able to carve it up, realize his expansionist dreams in opposition to the decision of the African countries, and at the same time be of service to the imperialists he had already sold out to.

Eighteen months later we have come back to Ethiopia, now victorious thanks to the heroism of its warrior sons and to the support of international solidarity, as Comrade Mengistu put it two days ago. What's more, it is a now powerful Ethiopia. The massive parade on Tuesday has given proof of the enormous tide of people who keep pace with the revolutionary change. And yesterday's military parade has shown us the degree of organization and discipline achieved by the combative and courageous sister people of Ethiopia. [*Applause*]

Let us remind those who are ignorant of some things in this world, that one of the most combative, courageous, and heroic soldiers in the world is the Ethiopian soldier. [*Applause*]

We reaffirm today our close and indestructible alliance with the Ethiopian revolution, and our certainty that the Ethiopian leaders will be able to find revolutionary, just, and Marxist-Leninist solutions to their problems, and that they will be able to preserve not only the territorial integrity of Ethiopia, but also the union of all in a great revolutionary Ethiopia. [*Applause*]

Comrades, permit me to salute you, the representatives of the best forces from all continents, and on behalf of my people to thank you for the solidarity you have always shown us. Also let me convey to you the Cuban revolution's message of struggle and encouragement, and urge that your duty be fulfilled.

Revolutionary internationalism is one of the laws of our struggle. We cannot triumph in isolation. Large-scale assistance or the simplest support of popular rebellions strengthens us all, since they are the expression of a new humanity, which fights for a more just society.

We join with you in condemning the racist and aggressive regimes of South Africa, Zimbabwe, and Israel, and the bloody regime of the shah of Iran. With you, we support the Polisario Front [of Western Sahara], the Patriotic Front of Zimbabwe, SWAPO, and the South African organizations. And like you, we also condemn the imperialist powers who use NATO as their advance guard to intervene militarily in Africa and give political support to the antipopular and reactionary regimes of Africa and the Middle East.

We are infinitely more powerful than the imperialists

and their agents, because we are the standard-bearers of social progress and justice. History is on our side; our scientific and just ideas are invincible.

Long live solidarity between the peoples! [*Ovation*]

PART 4
Defending Vietnam

During the U. S. government's war in Indochina, Cuba was among Vietnam's staunchest defenders. In 1963, Vietnam solidarity committees were set up in Cuba, the first such committees in the world, which educated people about the war, organized blood donations, and carried out other solidarity activities. Cuba publicly called on all forces to aid Vietnam, appealing especially to Moscow and Peking to close ranks against Washington's aggression. Cuba repeatedly offered to send its own troops to fight if the Vietnamese so desired, and Cuba's support to Latin American guerrillas under the slogan of "create two, three, many Vietnams" was aimed partly at taking some of the pressure off Vietnam.

In April 1972, during the height of the U.S. bombing, Cuba sent a medical contingent to North Vietnam, and in 1973 it sent 1,000 workers and technicians. Castro himself visited Vietnam in 1973, touring liberated parts of South Vietnam.

Throughout this period, Cuba recognized the significance of the antiwar movement in the United States and internationally. At the First Congress of the Communist Party of Cuba in 1975, Castro spoke about the impact of this movement within the U.S.; "The war against the Vietnamese people, which began with mass support inside the United States, soon generated an anti-imperialist and antiwar consciousness in U.S. universities, in the country's most prominent circles, and even in ever-growing sections of the working class deceived by the advantages of the ruthless exploitation of other countries . . ."

In April 1975, the Khmer Rouge of Kampuchea (Cambodia) captured the capital city of Phnom Penh and the Vietnamese liberation forces took Saigon. Immediately, however, the political paths of the two countries began to diverge. The Vietnamese instituted a program to reconstruct their devastated country and over a period of time, the workers' state in the North was extended into the South, culminating in nationalizations of most of the remaining capitalist enterprises in 1978.

The Kampuchean regime, on the other hand, took an opposite course. Within hours of their victory, the dominant wing of the Khmer Rouge, led by Pol Pot, ordered a forced evacuation of the population from all the cities. They established forced labor camps in the countryside, instituted the seven-day workweek and child labor, and virtually eliminated all education and medical care. In addition, a mass extermination campaign was directed against oppositionists and suspected oppositionists, with a particularly devastating effect on the working class and intellectuals. It has been estimated that 2–3 million people died under the Khmer Rouge regime. Rather than moving toward socialism, the Pol Pot government sought to crush and disperse the forces capable of carrying out a socialist transformation. Frightened by the extension of the Vietnamese socialist revolution, the regime launched military attacks on southern Vietnam and, by late 1978, began to increase its ties to the imperialist powers and their allies.

Pol Pot's most open supporter was the Chinese government. In the early 1970s, Mao Tse-tung's regime achieved its long-standing desire for a rapprochement with the U.S. government, and its foreign policy began more and more to openly echo Washington's line. Among the U.S.-backed dictators who received Chinese support were the shah of Iran, Somoza in Nicaragua, Pinochet in Chile, Mobutu in Zaïre, and others.

As the Vietnamese revolution deepened in the late seventies, Peking became more hostile toward it. When the remaining Vietnamese capitalists, many of them of Chinese ancestry, were expropriated in 1978, Peking began a campaign in their defense. Massive numbers of Chinese troops gathered at Vietnam's northern border. At the same time, Pol Pot's forces were carrying out border incursions into Vietnam.

Seeing signs that Pol Pot was forging ties with Washington and fearing an attack on two fronts, Vietnam decided to act. On December 19, 1978, 100,000 Vietnamese troops along with 20,000 Kampuchean insurgents crossed over into Kampuchea and drove the Pol Pot forces out of Phnom Penh on January 7. A new government headed by Heng Samrin was installed. Throughout the country, the Kampuchean rebels and their Vietnamese allies were greeted as liberators.

Immediately, Washington and its allies launched a storm of protest and rushed to take sanctions. Pol Pot received arms, supplies, and sanctuary in Thailand, a close ally of the U.S. government. Washington backed the Pol Pot regime in the United Nations and the deposed Khmer Rouge regime began to openly appeal for imperialist support.

As part of the anti-Vietnam campaign, China's leader Deng Xiaoping arrived in the U.S. January 28, 1979, and discussed with President Carter China's plans for "punishing Vietnam." Almost immediately after his return, Peking sent 170,000 Chinese troops into Vietnam with the objective of forcing the Vietnamese to withdraw from Kampuchea. The United States government, claiming neutrality, echoed Peking's call for Vietnamese withdrawal. To further demonstrate its support for the Chinese invasion, Washington went ahead with the formal opening of diplomatic relations with China in the middle of the war.

Nevertheless, the invasion was a failure. Under stiff resistance from the Vietnamese, China was forced to withdraw, without achieving its objective of forcing Vietnam out of Kampuchea.

While many of Vietnam's allies questioned U.S. neutrality claims, Cuba was the most explicit in pointing an accusing finger at Washington's role in the affair.

Vietnam is not alone

February 21, 1979

Speech given in Havana to the national rally in solidarity with Vietnam. The text is from *Granma*, March 4, 1979.

Compatriots:

I wasn't supposed to speak at this rally. I came just as you did, to express my own solidarity with the people of Vietnam. [*Applause*] The main speech was given by Comrade Jaime Crombet, and he spoke very well; [*Applause*] but since they've put me up here on the platform (I think it was the decision of the master of ceremonies), I'm going to say a few words.

In reality, this is not just any moment we are living through. We've gotten together many times. There have been problems in the world of late; but without a doubt this is one of the most serious, if not the most serious of these times, and it means everybody must think long and deep.

This aggression against Vietnam is certainly one of the

most repugnant, cowardly, miserable actions that we have ever come across—it would be difficult to find one to top it. If there was serious crime or crimes before this, this crime overshadows them all. Because we're not dealing in this crime with a question of colonialists or Japanese imperialists or French colonialists or Yankee imperialists; it's a question of a country that up until a few years ago was seen as a bulwark of the world revolutionary movement, was seen as a socialist country, an anti-imperialist country, as a friend of the revolutionary movement, a country, as we've said before, whose revolution all the peoples of the world and all the progressive forces of the world have watched with hope.

We've known all along about imperialism, we've known about colonialism; but until a few years ago never would one have thought such a thing as this could happen. It is the most abhorrent case of treason against the revolutionary movement in all the history of humanity.

We are certainly not going to say that it is the Chinese people who have perpetrated this treason. It is not the Chinese people; it cannot be the Chinese people; it is a band of villains, of fascists, who have taken over the command of the Chinese people. [*Applause*] We really do not believe the Chinese people capable of such a thing. We don't believe it! Certainly not a people with the qualities and revolutionary spirit of the Chinese people.

That people does not even know what is happening at this moment. That people does not know at this moment that Vietnam is being attacked, that Vietnam is being invaded. That people is being contemptuously tricked through all the mass media—radio, television, newspapers—in the hands of that gang. But it's not so easy to trick a people.

So I ask myself at this hour why the Chinese leadership hasn't talked to the people about that war of aggression, that barefaced invasion that it is waging against the Vietnamese people. They are talking about a Vietnamese aggression against China: a Vietnamese aggression against China! They're talking about a Chinese counterattack.

Well, there hasn't been any exaggeration in what's been said here concerning the methods that government is using. It goes without saying that what is going on inside China isn't even known; it's not known: the problems, the splits, which faction is calling the shots at this moment, which ones are responsible, which of the factions is responsible for this war, for this incredible adventure; though to all appearances, to all appearances, the man who's at the head of this skulduggery, this crime, the number one man responsible seems to be this numbskull, [*Laughter*] this puppet, this brazen Deng Xiaoping; they purged him once, he came back, they purged him again, he's back again, and one fine day they'll purge him once again. It could happen. One just doesn't know. The factions have gone back and forth purging each other for years. They're purged, they're rehabilitated, they're purged again, and they're rehabilitated again, until one fine day the Chinese people will purge them all once and for all. [*Applause*] Ah, but they're dangerous, infinitely dangerous!

This evening, Comrade Jaime pointed out what *Granma* had said concerning the methods, how the methods follow to the letter fascist methods, Hitler's methods, how these events follow to the letter those others, that began with the same kind of adventure and ended in a world war: the invasion of Poland by Hitler's troops in September 1939. Exactly the same case.

Afterwards the documents became known, as did those who participated, those who planned that operation; there have even been films made explaining how the incident was brought about, how the Nazis pulled some common prisoners out of jail, dressed them up in Polish uniforms and had them attack a German radio station, and how they immediately unloosed the invasion.

China's harassment of Vietnam had been going on for days.

Everybody knows the Vietnamese! The intelligence, the prudence, the wisdom of the Vietnamese. [*Applause*] Who can imagine Vietnam being interested in a conflict with China? Nevertheless, there were hundreds of acts of harassment on the part of the Chinese all along the border.

But this was not a plan of the moment. This plan had been in the works for some time. Those Ping-Pong games between China and the U.S., those visits of Kissinger to Peking, those visits of Nixon while imperialist aggression against Vietnam intensified, have all been made clear now. It was all part of a plan; it was all a maneuver. The Chinese weren't interested in an independent Vietnam, in a united and revolutionary Vietnam. They wanted no part of that.

We recall how they invaded some islands belonging to Vietnam when the puppet government was still in the South. While the Yankees were still there, they didn't invade a single tiny island off the South of Vietnam; but when the Yankees left, they invaded the islands, because they knew the islands to be rich in natural resources, that there might be oil, etc. When the South still hadn't been liberated but the Yankees had gone, they attacked and occupied islands that belong to Vietnam. Later they turned their efforts to Kampuchea, on the pretext of helping the Kampuchean revolution. They wormed their way into Kampuchea and got control of the movement, with people sworn to them, some of Chinese origin and others connected to Chinese, related to Chinese, married to Chinese. And in this way they went about taking over the leadership of the revolutionary movement in Kampuchea.

What did they do there? What they did was that in the name of the revolution, in the name of socialism, they set up one of the most monstrous regimes of modern times; they emptied the cities at bayonet point. This doesn't mean that a city can't ever be evacuated at a given moment, in a given situation, out of a given need. The revolutionary method is to persuade the people, the masses, when there is a real necessity—of a military type or of any type—that makes it essential. They evacuated the cities at bayonet point. They separated members of families from each other; they set up gigantic concentration camps. They even went so far as to establish marriage by—I don't know if it was by decree. No, no, strange, strange things. They told each person whom they had to marry. Forced marriages. On the other hand they separated the men from the women, children from their families, and they got rid of practically all the professionals in the country. They committed unbelievable massacres. The whole world knows this. This isn't anything new. In fact it's said that they murdered three million people in two and a half or three years. This was Maoism put into practice. This was Maoism, a Maoism the Chinese did not even practice in China; they practiced it in Kampuchea. It was true genocide. No government could sustain itself on such a basis. It was absolutely impossible. It was a policy of extermination on the one hand and of tightening the noose around Vietnam on the other. They goaded the Kampuchean fascists into aggression against Vietnam. The aggression began from the south across the Kampuchean frontier. That's where there are documentaries showing the massacres of tens of thousands of Vietnamese: men, women, children. One of the most brutal, criminal, genocidal governments ever known.

It had to blow up one day, and it did. It couldn't have

kept going, not in Kampuchea or in any other part of the world. And I think that one of the best things that could have happened was the overthrow of that fascist and genocidal group in Kampuchea, [*Applause*] that well known Pol Pot-Ieng Sary clique, swept aside by the people; that gang collapsed like a house of cards, in a way that meant not just the liberation of Kampuchea, of a people who couldn't go on living under such conditions, but meant as well a tremendous political defeat for the government of China.

The Yankee imperialists, who were the masters of sham and hypocrisy—and I say "were" because they've now been done one better—began to raise the rooftops, since obviously because of the relations with China, the rapprochement between China and the United States, both regimes were interested in encircling Vietnam.

The government of the United States talked on about human rights, and at one point it was proposed in the U.S. Senate that there be international intervention to stop the genocide taking place in Kampuchea. What was going on came out repeatedly in the world press and in the U.S. press itself.

Nevertheless, no sooner was that genocidal regime overthrown than they began a violent worldwide campaign against Vietnam, because of the solidarity of Vietnam with the Kampuchean revolutionary movement, with the aim of presenting Vietnam to world opinion as the aggressor country, as a country that violated the independence of another people. To negate the real fact that the Kampuchean regime was untenable; it couldn't stay in power. All this, I repeat, meant a tremendous blow to the leading gang in China. And from that instant the aggression and harassment against Vietnam along the border was stepped up and troops were amassed. The whole world knows that the Chinese government was concentrating troops on the Vietnam border.

The visit of Deng Xiaoping to the United States took place in the midst of this situation. In what was the height of hypocrisy he declared there that Vietnam and Cuba had to be taught a lesson. That's what he said, that Vietnam and Cuba had to be taught a lesson. He was saying to the Yankees: you teach Cuba a lesson. Look what things have come to; look what they have come to.

The government of a country that trained kids, Pioneers, to stab with bayonets at a straw effigy that was Nixon, the United States, imperialism. That's right, Nixon himself; they stabbed him in his straw belly, that's right, yes, Pioneers—before their final about-face.

That country that sent so many telegrams to revolutionaries all over the world. "A billion Chinese"—no, in those days it was 800. "Eight hundred million Chinese support you; you have the solidarity of 800 million Chinese." And they bragged about the 800, and later about the 900, and so on.

Of course, there were some pretty strange things about the Chinese leadership from early on. For example, at the time of the October Crisis, when the world was at the brink of war. In such an extremely serious situation, the Chinese kept their mouths shut and turned around to make a little war on India, to take from India a piece of territory. But they kept their mouths shut during that whole period of the October Crisis. They never said a word.

At a later period they began to make statements, to make accusations, and try to stir up intrigues about the whole problem of the October Crisis.

But who would have thought then that China, that the government of China would end up by telling the Yankees that Cuba had to be taught a lesson, that Vietnam had to be taught a lesson? This is what Deng Xiaoping said in the United States. And he said it again about Vietnam in Japan, that Vietnam had to be taught a lesson.

And as soon as—it's known today because an internal report reached the hands of a foreign journalist and they published it. The day after Deng Xiaoping got back, he met with the Military Commission of the Chinese Communist Party, which he heads. He met with them over three or four days, and that's where it was decided to quickly send large troop reinforcements to the frontier with Vietnam and attack Vietnam. Immediately after his return from the United States.

What did Deng Xiaoping discuss with Brzezinski? What did Deng Xiaoping discuss with Carter? Did the government of the United States know about the Chinese plan of aggression and invasion of Vietnam or not? Were they privy or not? That is a very important question. What explains his meeting with the Military Commission and ordering the invasion of Vietnam as soon as he got back?

It's a fact that the U.S. government has associated itself politically with the invasion of Vietnam, it associated itself politically. What's more, a U.S. senator recently stated that Brzezinski had told him that the Vietnamese must now withdraw from Kampuchea. It was a statement. And so the U.S. government, which unquestionably knew what was going to happen, and which without any doubt has associated itself with this adventure of Peking's, says that the Vietnamese must withdraw from Kampuchea, for the Chinese to withdraw from Vietnam. With this invasion the Yankee imperialists have made common cause with the Chinese rulers. They have made common cause over this crazy, preposterous adventure. It's a sign that both the United States and China are hoping to restore the genocidal Pol Pot-Ieng Sary regime in Kampuchea. This is the political objective: attack Vietnam precisely so that all the cooperation and all the solidarity that Vietnam has shown to the revolutionary government of Kampuchea should come to an end, in order to restore the genocidal regime and encircle Vietnam on both sides again, to the south and to the north. This is the policy of the United States, which meanwhile pretends to wash its hands of the problem.

What cheek! The way the whole question has been presented to the world, the way the Chinese have presented it: that the Chinese were invaded by Vietnam and that they counterattacked.

They haven't even followed Hitler's example very well. It can be said that in this affair Deng Xiaoping has virtually become, not a Hitler, but a sort of caricature of Hitler. Because from this internal information bulletin that came to be published, we know—in this bulletin it says—at what hour they attacked, how they attacked by surprise, how artillery and aerial preparation was carried out at three in the morning, how the invasion was launched. And in this same bulletin they don't hide the casualties they have suffered, they can't hide them. They say two interesting things, two interesting things in the bulletin. That they have suffered some 3,000 casualties. Which were the same figures as the Vietnamese were giving up till that moment. Of course, they didn't say that they had lost dozens of tanks. They didn't say they had suffered some serious setbacks either. The only other thing they said in the bulletin was that the different sections and the aviation and the infantry had not coordinated well and that as a result there had been difficulties in the advance. In other words, on the one hand they say that they were attacked and that this is a counterattack, while on the other hand they put out a bulletin for limited internal circulation explaining what happened.

What cheek, what cynicism, so similar, so incredibly similar to Hitler's methods! Both in the outrageous criminal invasion of a small country, and in the way the issue is presented to the world.

A very dangerous situation has now been created, an extremely dangerous situation. They have taken a leap into the dark. With what aims? How far are they prepared to go? How will this crisis be resolved? What extremes could this crisis reach? Since they have launched themselves into this crazy adventure, this really crazy and dangerous adventure.

This solidarity with Vietnam, this mobilization of all the revolutionary peoples and all the progressive and peace-loving peoples of the world is not in vain! Quite the contrary. We have taken part in many meetings of solidarity but I am sure that none has ever been of such worldwide significance, none has ever been more important, more necessary, than this solidarity. [*Applause*]

The progressive forces, the peoples of the world must mobilize to stop this adventure, to stop this danger, to stop this madness, since the whole world could find itself embroiled in this situation. The consequences of this kind of adventure may be terrible for the world. This is no exaggeration! Because Vietnam cannot be sacrificed just like that. It's not possible. There can be no other alternative for these proud and arrogant mandarins but retreat, no other alternative but defeat. But world opinion must rise up to contribute to bringing to a halt an adventure that could lead the world into a catastrophic war.

This is a moment of truth for all those throughout the world who call themselves revolutionaries, for all those throughout the world who call themselves progressives,

[*Applause*] for all those throughout the world who call themselves peace-loving. This is not the time for vacillation, for ambiguities; this is not the time for half measures; this is not the time for viewing Vietnam and China in the same light; this is the time for defining who's who, for defining who's who. [*Applause*] Because no peace-loving person in the world, no progressive person, no revolutionary or those who consider themselves revolutionaries in this world can fail to condemn the criminal adventure by the Chinese government in the most energetic and categorical way. [*Applause*]

However, we must be calm. Precisely at those moments of greatest danger for the world, we must act with the utmost calm, with the utmost presence of mind. All the socialist states and progressive peoples in the world have a duty to act with the utmost calm and presence of mind. This is not the moment for losing one's head, for losing control, because if certain processes are set in motion, they could be irreversible.

It's absolutely necessary to defeat this adventure, to defeat this madness. It must be defeated; it must be defeated! [*Applause and shouts of "Fidel, Fidel, Fidel!"*] These crazy neo-fascists, this mad faction, yes, this mad, neofascist faction that rules China at this moment must be prevented from getting its own way in its wish to embroil the world in a nuclear war. They must be defeated and stopped from getting their own way.

We must pay great attention to the course of developments in Vietnam, we must keep up with all the reports, all the news coming from Vietnam.

We are not going to overestimate China's strength. There's no reason to. Nor are we going to underestimate Vietnam's strength. [*Applause*] Technically, from the military point of view, with all the insanity and "cultural revolutions," people purged and purged again, people rehabilitated and rehabilitated again, the Chinese army has continued to be backward as regards weapons. A Chinese tank cannot be compared with one of the tanks Vietnam has, [*Applause and shouts*] a Chinese antiaircraft missile cannot be compared with a Vietnamese antiaircraft missile, Chinese antiaircraft weaponry cannot be compared with Vietnamese antiaircraft weaponry, [*Applause and shouts*] Chinese artillery cannot be compared with Vietnamese artillery.

They can brag about hundreds of millions and even a billion but it's not so easy to lead a people to slaughter. It's not so easy. What's more, a soldier needs to be motivated. Beyond any doubt, when the Chinese soldier fought the reactionary forces in the liberation war, he was an excellent, courageous soldier. Beyond any doubt, when the Chinese soldier fought Yankee troops in Korea, he was an excellent, courageous soldier. He was motivated: he was confronting imperialism and he had a deep-rooted revolutionary reason for fighting. [*Applause*] I wonder how these fascists are going to motivate the Chinese soldier to defy death. And if the Chinese soldier can be persuaded to go to battle, as if he were a tin soldier, how are they going to persuade him to kill Vietnamese women and children, to wipe out entire Vietnamese families, to commit acts of genocide? What instructors are going to be able to encourage this army to commit these crimes? I question the fighting morale of those Chinese soldiers invading Vietnam, however much they try to deceive them. All the more so because Vietnam will not be sitting back idly, because Vietnam has an extraordinary degree of combative experience, because Vietnam has magnificent weapons, and because Vietnam is not alone. [*Applause and shouts of "No!"*]

What a monstrous crime against this people! How many feats of heroism they have been called upon to perform in recent decades! First there were the Japanese invaders, then there were the invaders of the French neocolonialist expeditionary force, then there were the Yankee invaders. And now, finally, Chinese invaders. In these struggles the Vietnamese have acquired a great deal of experience. There is no people in the world who understand the tactics and strategy of the liberation struggle better than the Vietnamese people, [*Applause*] because they have always had to confront very powerful enemies. And the Vietnamese know more about tactics and strategy than the Chinese do. [*Applause*] A revolutionary war isn't the same as a genocidal war. A revolutionary war like the one the Chinese waged against the Japanese occupiers and reactionary forces, is not the same as a genocidal, criminal war against a courageous people who are defending their cause, their homeland, their revolution, their independence, and their existence, as the Vietnamese people are doing today. [*Applause*]

What's more, the Vietnamese are very wise, they know very well what they are doing, how far they can let an enemy penetrate, how to fight him, when, and in what way. They know what they are doing. And let me tell you that I have infinite confidence in these qualities of the Vietnamese people. [*Applause*] Although this neofascist faction that rules China brags about the billion people, it would not be at all surprising if they suffered a resounding defeat in Vietnam; it would not be at all surprising. [*Applause*]

And it is for this reason that I say that these criminals have launched themselves into a crazy adventure that will lead to a dead end. And that's why this situation is a risky one. It really is a dangerous, complicated situation that requires the utmost calm, the utmost presence of mind, and at the same time the utmost solidarity and support for Vietnam, and the utmost determination. [*Applause*]

What are we convinced of? The Vietnamese defeated the Japanese, the Vietnamese defeated the French, the Vietnamese defeated the Yankees, who were much more powerful, incomparably more powerful than the Chinese fascists. [*Applause*] Although the Yankees surrounded the country with aircraft carriers and thousands of planes and strategic bombers, they still ended up defeated. We are convinced that the Vietnamese will defeat the fascist Chinese invasion. [*Applause*] We are convinced of this! It's irrespective of whether they have penetrated ten kilometers or fifteen kilometers, a little more or a little less. Many penetrated, and you all know how they ended up.

As I said, our people must follow the events closely; we must pay attention to all the news. Our press, our television, and our radio services must make every effort to offer our people as much information as possible so that they can judge for themselves and so that they should be ready for everything. For everything! [*Applause*]

Crises are nothing new for us. A few years ago we went through the October Crisis, when many nuclear missiles were pointed our way, and yet nobody lost any sleep over it. I don't know anybody who didn't sleep soundly. In fact I think that during those days the people slept better than ever before. [*Applause*] And it's the same now. We have to be ready for everything. We don't know how long this crisis will go on. At this moment nobody can predict how it is going to develop. We must be ready for anything. [*Applause*]

We must strengthen our solidarity and increase our information and awareness, and at the same time we must remain calm and not lose any sleep. Let us cry with more feeling and determination than ever: Long live proletarian internationalism! [*Shouts of "Long live!"*]

Long live the thousand-times heroic people of Vietnam! [*Shouts of "Long live!"*]

Patria o muerte!

Venceremos! [*Ovation*]

PART 5
The Nonaligned movement

The Movement of Nonaligned Countries held its first conference in Belgrade, Yugoslavia, in 1961 with twenty-five member nations. By the time of the Sixth Summit Conference in 1979, membership had grown to ninety-five governments and liberation movements. While these governments defend different social systems and hold different political outlooks, most of the countries do share a common trait: economic domination and superexploitation by the imperialist powers. Corresponding to its heterogeneous composition, the movement has been confronted with varying positions on what attitude to take towards imperialism, ranging from capitulation to resolute struggle.

As a founder of the movement, Cuba was its first Latin American member. From the beginning, the Nonaligned movement opposed the U.S. economic blockade and the military occupation of Guantánamo and affirmed Cuba's right to determine its own future. That stand was a blow to Washington's efforts to isolate Cuba.

Cuba has participated in the movement to advance its own line of consistent anti-imperialism. As a central issue within the Nonaligned, it has raised the demand for a new international economic order: for an end to imperialist exploitation of the colonial and semicolonial countries, for the right of each country to control its own wealth, for a $300 billion development fund contributed by the industrialized countries, and for cancellation of the massive foreign debt that keeps the semicolonial countries in an inescapable situation of economic subjugation.

At the Second Congress of the Communist Party of Cuba in December 1980, Castro commented on the significance of these proposals: "The battle for a new international economic order is really a continuation of the struggle for emancipation from colonial rule and imperialist plunder." Pointing to the proposals' impact on world politics, Castro noted that "the struggle for a new international order . . . has had the positive result of uniting the underdeveloped countries in a single front—a phenomenon that, in view of their tremendous economic, political, and social heterogeneity, can be explained only on the basis of a generalized contradiction between them and imperialism, a contradiction that includes the governments of countries that are allies of imperialism on the periphery of the underdeveloped, dependent world, but [who] are no longer ready to accept unchanged the system of inequality and exploitation to which the monopolies of the capitalist powers subject them."

Mexico is an example of a country with a capitalist government whose newly acquired oil wealth has led to conflicts with Washington. In attempting to avoid total domination of its economic resources by the U.S. monopolies, and in response to the deep going anti-imperialist sentiment of its people, the Mexican government has traditionally taken independent positions on certain questions. For example, Mexico never broke relations with Cuba, and has maintained good economic ties with it. Mexico has also opposed U.S. military intervention in Latin American countries, such as the Dominican Republic, Nicaragua, and El Salvador. Cuba sees the value these positions have for the struggle for Latin American self-determination and recognizes the potential importance that Mexico's oil has for the economic future of Latin America.

At the 1973 summit conference of the Nonaligned in Algiers, Castro called for the movement to focus all its fire on imperialism and he opposed the efforts of some to make the axis one of opposing equally the U.S. and Soviet "superpowers." Referring to an attempt to condemn the Soviet Union as imperialist, Castro pointed out that the Soviet Union had no foreign investments, owned no foreign wealth, and exploited no resources in other countries, and stated that "the invention of a false enemy can only have one purpose: to flee from the real one."

During the 1970s, the Nonaligned movement adopted anti-imperialist positions on a growing number of questions and, correspondingly, Cuba's role and influence within it began to grow. The high point was the September 1979 Nonaligned Summit Conference in Havana, which included delegations from 138 countries with 55 heads of state or government—a defeat for Washington's twenty-year campaign to isolate Cuba. At the conference, Cuba led the fight for a clear anti-imperialist platform. Among the resolutions adopted were those calling for the independence of Puerto Rico; demanding the withdrawal of U.S. troops from Cuba, Puerto Rico, and Korea; denouncing Zionism and the Camp David agreements between Israel, Egypt, and the U.S.; opposing U.S. and British aid to the white-settler regimes in southern Africa and supporting the liberation struggles in those countries; and hailing the revolutions in Nicaragua and Iran. The conference also voted to withdraw recognition from the reactionary Pol Pot regime in Kampuchea.

From the beginning, Washington supported attempts by the Somalian and Yugoslav governments to move the conference site away from Havana. When that failed, it launched a campaign against Cuba as a "Soviet puppet" and announced the discovery of a Soviet "combat brigade" in Cuba. It urged countries not to attend.

On the floor of the conference itself, Grenada's Prime Minister Maurice Bishop revealed the nature of the U.S. maneuvers: "Last week, shortly before coming to this conference, we received a cable from the secretary of state of the United States which said that if we participated in the conference we would be in the front ranks of the efforts by Cuba to try to destroy and divide the movement. They said these were efforts aimed at destroying the OAS and undermining the pacifying role of that organization, and it was hoped that we in Grenada would join with other forces to prevent that from happening."

However, these efforts ended in failure.

Following the conference, Castro, as chairman of the movement, went to New York to report to the United Nations on the decisions adopted. Castro had addressed the UN General Assembly previously in 1960, when he delivered a devastating point by point denunciation of U.S. actions against Cuba and other underdeveloped countries, creating an international sensation. This time, Castro's speech was greeted with enthusiasm and repeatedly interrupted by applause. It received worldwide publicity and was widely seen as a victory for the Cuban revolution.

At Nonaligned Ministerial Meeting

March 19, 1975

Speech given at the closing session of the Third Ministerial Meeting of the Coordinating Bureau of the Nonaligned Countries, meeting in Havana. The text is from *Granma,* March 30, 1975.

Distinguished members of the Coordinating Bureau of the Nonaligned Countries;
Distinguished observers:

It is a signal honor for our people that this meeting of the Coordinating Bureau has taken place in Cuba. We appreciate in all its worth the presence of the representatives of the valiant, fighting peoples that have distinguished themselves internationally for their contribution to the struggle for the independence and progress of their homelands, world peace, and the success of the noble objectives of the movement that brings us together here.

The Coordinating Bureau is meeting a year and a half after the Algiers summit conference; and each day that has passed since then confirms the importance and the role of the Nonaligned movement and the diagnosis of the international situation made in the resolutions of that conference.

Important international events have occurred since then, some adverse, many favorable. The most immediate to that event, which took place just following it, was the criminal fascist coup that imperialism perpetrated in Chile. We recall that President Allende was unable to come to Algiers because at that time he was confronting the subversive actions and sabotage of the reaction. Foreign Minister Clodomiro Almeyda and other spokesmen of the progressive movement denounced these actions and pointed out the active intervention of the imperialist government of the United States in Chile's internal policy. President Allende's cause found deep sympathy and broad solidarity in that conference. It would have been practically impossible to imagine that barely seventy-two hours after the closing of the Algiers summit, President Allende would die heroically while resisting the fascist blow that put an end to that admirable effort to make the revolution through institutional and peaceful means, an effort which the world followed with particular interest. Today, CIA participation in those events is no longer simply a charge or a hypothesis, because it has been openly admitted and, what is even worse, justified by the government of the United States itself.

In the enormous wave of world solidarity with the Chilean people that followed the fascist coup, along with the socialist countries, which almost unanimously broke with the usurper regime, and the world revolutionary and progressive movement, the Nonaligned countries have been militantly present. The fascist junta, today internationally ostracized, crushingly discredited, abhorred by the masses, and drowned in the blood of its own people, has no alternative other than defeat.

Following close on the heels of those events came the heroic battle of the Arab peoples to liberate the occupied territories in October 1973, ending the myth of the invincibility of the aggressor Israeli state, giving rise to a new balance of power in the Middle East, and also to a new phase in the struggle of the Arab peoples to recover their legitimate territories and restore the national rights of the heroic Palestinians, criminally oppressed and expelled from their native land.

Today, imperialism is making desperate efforts to counteract this situation and is perfidiously maneuvering to divide the Arab countries, isolate the courageous Syrian people, cheat the Palestinians of their rights, and extend its presence and influence in the Middle East in order to impose the onerous peace conditions that most suit its interests and those of its allies in the aggression against the Arab peoples. For that reason, any type of playing around with imperialism by any Arab country is dangerous, because political opportunism cannot replace frank, open, and revolutionary diplomacy—and sometimes, it leads to flagrant betrayal. The present situation in the Middle East cannot be alien to the interest and deepest concern of the Nonaligned countries.

A series of equally important events also took place during 1974.

After ten years of dedicated struggle, the peoples of Guinea-Bissau, Mozambique, and Angola brought the fascist, colonial regime of Portugal to the crisis point. As a result, revolution erupted in the metropolis itself and the road was opened for the liquidation of Portuguese colonialism in Africa and the liberation of all the peoples it oppressed on that continent. This year will bring with it the official declaration of independence of the peoples still under Portugal's formal domination.

At the same time, it is noteworthy and encouraging for the world progressive movement that the revolutionary process is being deepened and consolidated in Portugal. Until a short time ago the seat of a fascist state which was the instrument of the most obsolete colonialism, combated and rejected by world opinion, that country stands today as a revolutionary hope in Western Europe. The Movement of Nonaligned Countries should greet this historic event with jubilation and firmly support the people and present government of Portugal as new allies in the common cause of liberation and world progress.

In Greece, the fascist military regime, allied with NATO and in obvious collusion with the Pentagon, played the principal role in the Cyprus adventure, overthrowing the legitimate government and threatening the independence and integrity of that country, which holds a distinguished and honorable position in the Nonaligned movement. This brought about the immediate reaction of Turkey, another member of NATO, which proceeded to occupy a part of the island militarily.*

The irrational adventure and its failure were more than the tottering Greek dictatorship could stand and, unable to resist the situation thus created, it crashed with a resounding thud. Although this did not produce a revolutionary situation, as in Portugal, an institutional and legal regime has been established in that country and we greet it with satisfaction.

---

* In July 1974, the Greek military dictatorship helped carry out a coup d'état in Cyprus. In response, the Turkish government sent troops to the island, precipitating the fall of the Greek regime and its replacement by a civilian capitalist government.

Still, as a result of the adventures, battles, and conflicts among the NATO governments, Cyprus—a Nonaligned country—has remained divided de facto by the military intervention of foreign powers, and its integrity is threatened. The Nonaligned movement cannot be indifferent to this situation without diminishing its prestige. It is necessary that we support the independence and integrity of Cyprus without any hesitation, demanding a solution that takes into account the rights, the collaboration, and the understanding of the national minorities involved in the problem.

From a progressive and revolutionary point of view, the events in Ethiopia, which also took place last year, are both of great interest and historic importance. That country, which, by the way, is also a member of the Nonaligned family, was suffering from a terrible situation of misery and social backwardness. As a result of that situation, aggravated by natural calamities, hundreds of thousands of persons have died of hunger in recent years, while an unscrupulous, exploiting class of landowners appropriated up to 80 percent of the production of the peasants. A continuation of that state of affairs could not be in keeping with the times or with the aspirations of today's world. That is why it was inevitable that a revolutionary situation would sooner or later develop in that country. As a revolutionary, I cannot but rejoice, because I think that not only should the exploitation of some nations by other nations disappear from the world, but all forms of exploitation of man by man as well.

Unfortunately, a fratricidal struggle between the new government that destroyed the old structures and a national liberation movement is now being waged within that very state. The situation in which two causes of a progressive character are confronting each other is indeed complex. Therefore, what is the duty of the Nonaligned? Is it perhaps to stand idly by or to support one side to the detriment of the other? To urge the war on? Decidedly not. The least that should be done is to make a serious effort and seek a peaceful and just solution that is acceptable to the parties in the conflict which is separating and pitting against each other the Ethiopian revolutionary process and the liberation movement of Eritrea. Only recently, OPEC worked to seek peace between Iraq and Iran. Why don't the Nonaligned countries do the same thing in Ethiopia?

In Cambodia, despite United States aid, the usurper regime of Lon Nol is in its death throes. The resolute and heroic struggle of the Cambodian revolutionaries is relentlessly advancing to a victorious outcome and nothing can stop it, because such is the inexorable course of events in the world of today.

During this period, we have seen in South Vietnam the outrageous sabotage of the Paris agreement on the part of the puppet [Nguyen] Van Thieu and his Yankee masters. This has prevented that tormented country from enjoying peace and from establishing a democratic and legal regime, which would permit the South Vietnamese to decide freely on their form of government and on integration with their brothers and sisters of the North. But the maneuvers of imperialism have been shattered by the resolute, heroic purpose of the Vietnamese patriots, whose cause is growing stronger day by day while the Saigon regime is deteriorating and drawing closer to the sad end which history reserves for traitors.

The Provisional Revolutionary Government of South Vietnam and the [Khmer Rouge-led] Royal Government of National Union of Cambodia are two states which, by their presence, do honor and bring prestige to the Nonaligned movement, which should offer them its most energetic and resolute support.

In the international field, the Sixth Special Session of the United Nations General Assembly demonstrated the immense strength which the Nonaligned movement has today; indeed, every one of the international forums has now turned into a scene of their struggles. Such was the World Food Conference in Rome, and such is the Conference of the United Nations for Industrial Development, which is now ending in Lima. Dakar received the representatives of the [Group of] 77* to establish the program for the defense of fair prices and the markets required for basic products.

The most serious problem the Nonaligned countries movement is faced with is the current international economic crisis. This crisis began in the developed capitalist world with galloping inflation, to which has been added a serious economic recession. For the students of Marx, Engels, and Lenin, this fact comes as no surprise or mystery. Economic crisis is inherent in the capitalist system, and is aggravated in this case by the policy of cold war; the arms race, and the repression of the national liberation movement which U.S. imperialism fostered after World War II; by unequal trade and the ruthless plunder of the natural resources of the underdeveloped countries by the developed capitalist societies.

The ideologists of imperialism, disregarding the historically and scientifically proven laws inherent in the system, claimed that capitalism could march forward with-

---

* The group of 77 is a governmental bloc of underdeveloped countries that prepares proposals and resolutions on economic and development questions for various United Nations organizations. Founded in the 1960s with 77 members, it numbered 122 in 1981.

out limit, without economic crisis; spending, moreover, fabulous sums on armament; waging unpopular wars such as the one in Vietnam without bothering to levy taxes for its bellicose purposes; approving deficit budgets; printing paper money; squandering resources in order to put on a display of wealth. All of which was even more insulting because it happened in the midst of a great part of the underdeveloped, hungry world lacking the most indispensable things, yesterday colonized and subjected by imperialism and today exploited by unequal trade and the ruthless pillage of its raw materials.

Sooner or later, such a policy had to lead to a serious world economic crisis which, needless to say, hurts neither the bourgeoisie and the financial oligarchs of the developed capitalist world nor the feudal lords and the wealthy classes wherever they exist in the underdeveloped world, but rather the industrial workers and the humble laborers of city and countryside in both groups of countries— even though poverty and misery really make themselves felt more acutely in the underdeveloped world.

Of course, the only real solution to the economic crisis is the disappearance of capitalism from the world. This, of course, will happen some day and partially as a result of the crisis. But what concerns us are the present-day serious problems in an underdeveloped world subject to the voracity and the machinations of imperialism, which, although in crisis, still has enough powerful economic, technical, political, and military resources to try to impose its solutions and shove the burden of the crisis on the shoulders of its own workers and those of the economically backward countries.

This is the challenge facing the Nonaligned countries movement and the rest of the underdeveloped world today.

Of course, we, the group of the underdeveloped countries, do not constitute a homogeneous whole. Some oppose imperialism and struggle against it; others, in turn, are very close to imperialism and in many cases even act as its allies. There is a great range of different situations. That is why it is difficult to draw up a common policy to safeguard the fundamental interests of our peoples within this essential contradiction between the underdeveloped countries and imperialism. Nonetheless, the Nonaligned countries movement has succeeded in uniting a considerable number of countries of different political shades which have demonstrated the possibility of joint action in a series of important questions. It could be affirmed that the future of this movement depends largely on the clarity and the decision with which it acts today in solving the economic problems now affecting the underdeveloped world.

Even the unity of the Nonaligned countries is now being put to trial by imperialism. The issue revolves around the economic crisis and the energy problem. Imperialism seeks to divide the underdeveloped countries into oil-exporting countries and oil-importing countries and, likewise, to split the Nonaligned countries into those that export oil and those that import it. And imperialism may succeed if a close unity of interests is not obtained between the oil-producing and non-oil-producing underdeveloped countries.

The facts must be examined objectively.

In the case of OPEC, for the first time in the history of international relations a group of underdeveloped countries has managed to set their own trade terms for their basic raw materials vis-à-vis the developed capitalist world. Undoubtedly, we see this as a great victory.

In the same way, for the first time in history a relatively small group of underdeveloped countries are accumulating extraordinary amounts of surplus funds formerly under the exclusive control of the developed capitalist countries. This is also a victory, for it opens up new possibilities of resources to the underdeveloped world.

But oil, among all raw materials, has a privileged status. Unlike iron, aluminum, zinc, lead, nickel, copper, tin, and others which are practically not used by the underdeveloped world and which are neither so scarce nor play the role of energy in the developed capitalist world, oil is a product of obligatory world consumption. Absolutely no country can do without it. No other raw material of the underdeveloped world could wield the might of oil to demand so big an amendment in the terms of trade.

The developed capitalist countries are transferring a substantial part of the new costs of oil to the underdeveloped world by raising to unprecedented heights the price of technology, equipment, manufactured and semimanufactured products, fertilizers, synthetic materials, and many others that developing countries must import.

The non-oil-producing underdeveloped world is paying much more for energy and, in 1974, it spent $10 billion more for that purpose alone.

Furthermore, the non-oil-producing underdeveloped world is paying much more for the technology, equipment, and products they import from the developed capitalist world.

Unequal trade for the non-oil-producing underdeveloped countries has become more onerous for both the industrial products they import from the developed capitalist world and the energy they must import for their subsistence. In short, new unequal trade has emerged for the underdeveloped world.

With few exceptions, the prices for the raw materials and products which are essential to a great majority of non-oil-producing countries have been falling considerably in recent months. As a result, while a great number of underdeveloped countries are seeing the prices of their export products reduced, they, in turn, must pay much more to obtain industrial products and energy. The effect of the world economic crisis is bearing down terribly on them.

On the other hand, surplus funds of approximately $60 billion in the possession of the oil-exporting countries accumulated in 1974, which—according to estimates published by capitalist financial sources themselves—were invested as follows: in the European financial market, $21 billion; in the United States, $11 billion; in Great Britain, $8 billion; in public loans issued by developed capitalist countries, and direct investments of the oil-producing nations in those countries, more than $10 billion; in international financial institutions, $3.5 billion. And only $2 billion were effectively transferred to underdeveloped countries during this period. That is, while the bulk of these surpluses in one way or another went to the developed capitalist world, the underdeveloped world did not even receive 5 percent of them. It is evident that, except for isolated and individual actions, the oil-producing countries do not have a strategy of economic cooperation with the underdeveloped world, something of basic importance in approaching and confronting, correctly and solidly united, the political and economic risk that the situation implies for all.

Surplus funds gave birth to imperialism. To the extent that the oil-producing countries invest their surplus funds in the developed capitalist world, their interests will inevitably be identified with the interests of imperialism and not with the cause of the exploited peoples of the world. Furthermore, as we said on another occasion, that capital would serve as a hostage in imperialist hands.

Naturally, financial surpluses must circulate throughout the world's economy. Yet, the economies of all the countries, including developed countries, can be aided and a crisis of catastrophic dimensions averted only to the extent that a substantial portion of these funds passes through the underdeveloped world and is converted into technology and development.

I am talking about financial surpluses, not resources that the oil-producing countries ought to invest on a priority basis in their own economies. Neither am I talking about donations or gifts, nor direct investments—for that would repeat the history of imperialism—but about credits given under conditions adequate for the development of the countries that need them, and provided, of course, that such funds are really and truly used by those countries for development, for the benefit of their peoples, and not in the interest of tiny minorities or foreign monopolies.

This is the policy which we encourage among the Nonaligned movement and all the other underdeveloped countries.

On September 28 of last year, I said: "If all underdeveloped countries are to make the battle for oil their battle, it is essential that the oil-producing countries make the battle of the underdeveloped world theirs."

I know that several oil-producing countries, among them Venezuela, Algeria, and Iraq, have shown in various ways their interest in encouraging and defending a correct policy of this type. Others have opened up credit operations for development. At the OPEC summit conference in Algiers it was also stated that the oil-exporting countries wanted to work together with the rest of the underdeveloped countries in the struggle against unequal trade terms and in the defense of all the raw-material producers. We hail these initiatives and statements because they are proof of the growing awareness of the seriousness and scope of these problems.

Some oil-producing countries, the weakest demographically and militarily, are seriously threatened by imperialist aggression. We do not believe that the statements made by the president of the United States were intended merely to intimidate by threat; we believe they were also intended to pave the way if he should decide to act. We spoke about this danger at the Algiers summit conference, at the time when the present energy situation had not yet been created. Even before the last Middle East crisis, U.S. troops were being trained by the United States for desert military action. The present world balance of power is far from favorable to imperialism's warmongering ventures, but we must not underestimate the extremes to which desperation can lead.

History has proven that the firm union of the peoples and world opinion, plus the will to vigorously resist aggression, are factors that can put an end to imperialist threats. Cuba has proven it in facing up to these risks and threats ninety miles away from the United States. Our people have victoriously and resolutely withstood the blockade and aggression with international solidarity and the firm and determined aid of the Soviet Union.

The revolutionary government of Cuba follows a policy of principles in its international conduct and therefore, at the same time that it is concerned over and expresses itself frankly and honestly about the errors that may be committed by the underdeveloped countries themselves, it reaffirms its determination to close ranks with the Nonaligned countries, OPEC countries, and the rest of the economically backward world in order to carry out a correct joint policy in the face of economic crisis, unequal trade terms, plunder of our natural resources, and imperialist threats and blackmail, and exhorts all the Nonaligned countries to work in this direction.

Please forgive me for having spoken extensively. I do not want to conclude without recalling that in many parts of the world other peoples are struggling for their claims and rights in a battle against imperialism and reaction. Some I mentioned at the beginning of this address. Others we cannot fail to recall: the people of North Vietnam are devoting themselves to the task of reconstructing their country devastated by the barbarous Yankee air raids. Why not create a fund to help that heroic country, which has sacrificed itself so much for the cause of all the peoples of the world? In Korea, a self-sacrificing people bear the country's division imposed by imperialist intervention and presence in the South. In Africa, the odious policy of discrimination, which has been the constant concern of the Nonaligned countries, continues against numerous peoples and nations. In Latin America, Puerto Rico is awaiting the solidarity of all in its struggle for freedom; Panama claims its sovereign rights over the usurped Canal territory; Peru carries forward its revolution in the face of imperialist stratagems and conspiracies; Venezuela is nationalizing iron and oil, exploited over decades by foreign monopolies. To all of them let us offer our firmest solidarity.

The overall account of the advances of the liberation movement and the peoples' victories is encouraging. New conditions and possibilities have been created for the further advancement of humanity along the roads of justice, freedom, progress, and peace.

We are certain that the Nonaligned countries, closely united with all world progressive forces, will know how to fulfill the duty that the present and the future of the peoples we represent here demands.

Many thanks.

Keynote to Sixth Summit Conference

September 3, 1979

Speech given at the opening of the Sixth Summit Conference of Nonaligned Countries meeting in Havana. The translation is by Prensa Latina.

Your excellencies;
Guests;
Comrades:

I would like to ask that the first moments of this solemn event be dedicated to the memory of a beloved friend whom we all admired, a hero of his country's liberation and revolution who guided the Algiers summit conference brilliantly in 1973 and who did much for the strength and prestige of the Nonaligned movement—the late president of Algeria, Houari Boumedienne. How it grieves us that he cannot be with us in Cuba to share this occasion in our movement's history. I ask this worthy conference to observe a minute of silence in his memory.

Mr. Chairman, Junius Jayawardene, I would like to express my sincere recognition of your constant concern for the future of our movement and democratic respect for the dissimilar components of this powerful association of countries and the wise prudence you have shown in every difficult situation our Nonaligned countries have had to face in the past three years—which have not been easy times. In spite of distance and economic problems, your small country has made a noble and worthy effort to live up to the honorable responsibilities entrusted to it.

I thank all of you for the tremendous honor you do us with your presence here. I greet all of you warmly and welcome you on behalf of our people.

I would also like to fraternally greet the new countries that are joining our powerful movement at this conference: Iran and Pakistan have become members following the toppling of the shah's throne and the breaking up of the aggressive, reactionary CENTO [Central Treaty Organization] military alliance; Surinam, Bolivia, tiny Grenada, and the indomitable people of Nicaragua, whose heroic, self-sacrificing fighters have left recent signs of their historic march that brought freedom to Sandino's homeland and dignity to our America.

Ethiopia and Afghanistan now accompany us with a new revolutionary character, and the Patriotic Front of Zimbabwe has full member status.

Our family is growing and increasing in quality, which is the way it should be.

The Philippines, St. Lucia, Dominica, and Costa Rica are new observers and we have a number of guests, including Spain, whose gesture of sending a delegation to this conference for the first time we view as a hope for friendly and useful relations with all the peoples of the world, without allowing itself to be drawn into the aggressive NATO military bloc, which would only serve to compromise and alienate the brilliant future of that self-sacrificing people whose historical, cultural, and blood bonds with the nations of our America are so solid. We also need friends in industrialized Western Europe that are not tied to the imperialist wagon.

Ninety-four states and liberation movements are represented here as full members of this Sixth Summit Conference. This summit conference is, therefore, the one with the largest attendance and with the greatest number of Nonaligned and national liberation movement leaders ever held. This is not something for which our modest country should take credit; rather it is an unmistakable sign of the vigor, strength, and prestige of the Movement of Nonaligned Countries.

All efforts to sabotage the Havana summit conference have proved futile. All pressures, hectic diplomatic efforts, and intrigues to prevent the conference from being held in our country were in vain.

The Yankee imperialists and their old and new allies—in this case I refer to the Chinese government—didn't want this conference to be held in Cuba.

They also engaged in dirty scheming, saying that Cuba would turn the Movement of Nonaligned Countries into a tool of Soviet policy. We know only too well that the U.S. government even got hold of a copy of the draft final declaration, drawn up by Cuba, and made feverish diplomatic contacts in an effort to modify it. We have irrefutable proof of this.

We believe that the draft—which was submitted to all the member countries earlier than at any other conference and was even modified to include many of their suggestions—is a good draft, subject to improvement. Improvement means strengthening, not weakening it. Since when does the United States have the right to involve itself in the Nonaligned movement and decide how our documents should be drawn up?

What is the reason for the reactionary opposition to Cuba?

Cuba isn't exactly a country that is inconsistent toward the imperialists. Cuba has never ceased to practice a policy of close solidarity with the national liberation movements and all other just causes of our times. [*Applause*] Cuba has never hesitated to defend its political principles with determination, energy, dignity, honesty, and courage, nor, in over twenty years, has it ever stopped fighting against the aggression and the blockade imposed by the most powerful imperialist country in the world simply because Cuba carried out a genuine political and social revolution just ninety miles from that country's coast.

It is all too well known—and has been admitted and officially published in the United States—that the authorities of that country spent years organizing and methodically plotting to assassinate the leaders of the Cuban revolution, using the most sophisticated means of conspiracy and crime.

Nevertheless, despite the fact that these deeds were investigated and publicized by the U.S. Senate, the U.S. government has not yet deigned to give any kind of apology for those vituperative and uncivilized actions.

The true measure of a revolutionary people, the unblemished honor of a country that cannot be bribed, bought, or intimidated, is given by the imperialists' hatred. [*Applause*]

In our international relations, we express solidarity with deeds, not fine words. Cuban technicians are now working in twenty-three countries that belong to our movement. In the vast majority of these countries, because of their economic limitations, this cooperation is provided without charge, in spite of our own difficulties. Right now,

Cuba has twice as many doctors serving abroad as does the UN World Health Organization.

Noble, self-sacrificing Cubans have died thousands of miles from home while supporting liberation movements, defending other people's just causes, and fighting against the expansion of the North American racists as well as other forms of imperialist attack on human dignity and the integrity and independence of other nations. They express the purity, selflessness, solidarity, and internationalist consciousness that the revolution has forged among our people.

What charges can be brought against Cuba? That it is a socialist country? Yes, it is a socialist country, [*Applause*] but we don't impose our ideology or our system on anyone, either inside or outside the movement, and being socialist is nothing to be ashamed of. That we have a radical revolution in Cuba? Yes, we are radical revolutionaries, but we don't try to impose our radicalism on anyone, much less on the Nonaligned movement.

That we maintain fraternal relations with the Soviet Union and the rest of the socialist community? Yes, we are friends of the Soviet Union. [*Applause*] We are very thankful to the Soviet people, because their generous cooperation helped us to survive and overcome the very difficult and decisive periods in our people's life, when we were even in danger of being wiped out. No people has the right to be ungrateful. We are grateful to the glorious October revolution because it ushered in a new era in human history, made it possible to defeat fascism, and created a world situation in which the peoples' self-sacrificing struggle led to the downfall of the hateful colonial system. To ignore that is to ignore history itself.

Not only Cuba but also Vietnam; the Arab countries under attack; the peoples in the former Portuguese colonies; the revolutionary processes in many other countries throughout the world; and the liberation movements that fight against oppression, racism, Zionism, and fascism in South Africa, Namibia, Zimbabwe, Palestine, and elsewhere owe a great debt of gratitude to socialist solidarity. I wonder whether the United States or any other NATO country has ever helped a single liberation movement anywhere in the world. [*Applause*]

In fact, I am convinced—and I have said so on other occasions—that without the power and influence which the socialist community exerts today, imperialism, harassed by the economic crisis and by the shortage of basic raw materials, would not hesitate to divide the world up again. It has already done so more than once. It is even threatening to do so again and, in point of fact, is creating special intervention forces aimed menacingly at the oil-exporting countries. To cite just one example of this, the United States has unilaterally decided to respect no more than a three-mile limit of maritime sovereignty.

If membership in the Nonaligned movement depended on betraying our highest ideas and convictions, it would not be honorable for me or for any of you to belong to it. No revolutionary has the right to be a coward. [*Applause*]

There are some who have made an art of opportunism. We Cuban revolutionaries are not and never will be opportunists. We are prepared to sacrifice our own national economic interests whenever necessary to defend a just principle or an honorable political position. We Cubans will never renege on what we said yesterday, nor will we say one thing today and do something else tomorrow.

We are firmly anti-imperialist, [*Applause*] anticolonial, antineocolonial, [*Applause*] antiracist, [*Applause*] anti-Zionist, [*Applause*] and antifascist [*Applause*] because these principles are part of our thinking, they constitute the essence and origin of the Movement of Nonaligned Countries and have formed its life and history ever since its founding. These principles are also very fresh in the life of the peoples we represent here.

Was any country that now belongs to our movement really independent more than thirty-five years ago? Is there any member that hasn't known colonialism, neocolonialism, fascism, racial discrimination, or imperialist aggression; economic dependence; poverty; squalor; illiteracy; and the most brutal exploitation of its natural and human resources? What country doesn't bear the burden of the technological gap, a lower standard of living than the former metropolises, unequal terms of trade, the economic crisis, inflation, and underdevelopment imposed on our peoples by centuries of colonial exploitation and imperialist domination?

Cuba will be in the front line defending these principles, independence, and the unique, prestigious, fraternal, and ever more constructive and influential role of the Nonaligned movement in international life, so that the energetic and rightful voice of our peoples may be heard. [*Applause*]

Moreover, I believe that if you thought Cuba was not completely independent or lacked the loyalty and honesty it owes to the movement in line with its concepts and goals, you would not have given your generous cooperation, confidence, interest, and enthusiasm to this Sixth Summit Conference. [*Applause*]

Throughout our revolutionary life, no one has ever tried to tell us what to do. No one has ever tried to tell us what role we should play in the Movement of Nonaligned Countries. No one told us when or how to make the revolution in our country, nor could anyone have done so. By the same token, no one except the movement itself can determine what it should do and when and how to do it.

We have worked tirelessly to create the material and political conditions to make this event a success. We have respected and we will continue to totally respect the rights of all members of the movement. We have fully and scrupulously fulfilled our duties as host country and will continue to do so. Our views will not always coincide with those of each and every one of you. We have many close friends at this conference, but we don't always agree with the best of them. We hope that everyone will speak out with the greatest freedom and honesty, and feel that he is being heard with interest, respect, and concentration. The combined experiences of all of us gathered here can produce tremendous results. If certain topics displease anyone, please understand that we do not mean to hurt or wound. We will work with all member countries—without exception—to achieve our aims and to implement the agreements that are adopted. We will be patient, prudent, flexible, calm. Cuba will observe these norms throughout the years in which it presides over the movement. I declare this categorically. [*Applause*]

We have grown and advanced. Fortunately, Mozambique, Angola, São Tomé and Príncipe, Guinea-Bissau, and the Cape Verde Islands are now fully independent countries, after a heroic and unequal struggle. Today, as sovereign states, they are prestigious and influential members of our movement. Just six years ago, at the Algiers summit conference, they were only liberation movements.

Vietnam is united and free after thirty years of extraordinary and admirable struggle.

The shah is no longer the shah, [*Applause*] CENTO no longer exists, Somoza is no longer in power, [*Applause*] and the fascist Gairy no longer rules tiny, heroic Grenada. [*Applause*] These are unquestionable victories for independence, progress, and freedom. Our causes triumph because they are just.

Growing numbers of peoples are joining our ranks as they break the bonds of colonialism, neocolonialism, fascism, and other forms of oppression and dependency. In one way or another, all these struggles have been supported by the Movement of Nonaligned Countries, and these are victories for us as well. [*Applause*]

Nevertheless, imperialism has not ceased its tenacious effort to maintain its subjugation, oppression, and occupation of other peoples and countries, whose causes demand our resolute support. First of all I refer to the long-suffering, courageous Palestinian people. No more brutal pillage of a people's rights to peace and justice has occurred in this century. Please understand that we are not fanatics. The revolutionary movement has always learned to hate racial discrimination and pogroms of any kind. From the bottom of our heart, we repudiate the merciless persecution and genocide that the Nazis once visited on the Jews, but there is nothing in recent history that parallels it more than the dispossession, persecution, and genocide that imperialism and the Zionists are currently practicing against the Palestinian people. Pushed off their lands, expelled from their country, scattered throughout the world, persecuted and murdered, the heroic Palestinians are a vivid example of sacrifice and patriotism, living symbols of the most terrible crime of our era.

Piece by piece, Palestinian lands and the territories of neighboring Arab countries—Syria, Jordan, and Egypt—have been seized by the aggressors, armed to the teeth with the most sophisticated weapons from the U.S. arsenal.

The just Palestinian and Arab cause has been supported by world progressive opinion and our movement for nearly twenty years. [*Applause*] Nasser was one of the prestigious founders of this movement. Nevertheless, all UN resolutions have been scornfully ignored and rejected by the aggressors and their imperialist allies.

Imperialism has sought to impose its own peace, using betrayal and division. An armed, dirty, unjust, bloody peace will never be a true peace.

The Camp David agreement is a flagrant betrayal of the Arab cause and of the Palestinian, Lebanese, Syrian, Jordanian—all the Arab peoples, including the Egyptians. [*Applause*] It is a betrayal of all the progressive peoples of the world who, at the United Nations and all other international forums, have always supported a just solution to the problems of the Middle East, one that would be acceptable and honorable for all and guaranteed by all.

True peace in the Middle East will never be built on such injustice, such a Machiavellian policy, such betrayal, and such flimsy bases.

Instead of one gendarme for the Middle East, the Arab world, and Africa, imperialism now wants two: Israel and Egypt. If peace really exists between Egypt and Israel, why does Egypt need all the weapons it is getting—even though they aren't as sophisticated and modern as the ones that are going to the Israelis? How will these arms be used, except against the peoples in the area, including the Egyptians themselves?

International policy should be ethical. The Movement of Nonaligned Countries should roundly denounce the Camp David agreement. Moral censure, at least, is essential. [*Applause*]

We have witnessed ten years of imperialist maneuvers, deceit, and crimes in Zimbabwe. Six million Africans there are oppressed by a tiny, arrogant, and genocidal racist, fascist minority. We should firmly denounce and reject the so-called internal settlement and Muzorewa's puppet regime,* which is a mockery of Africa's conscience, and give the Patriotic Front of Zimbabwe—the legitimate representative of its people—the Nonaligned movement's all-out support and solidarity. [Applause]

The people of Namibia are also suffering from South Africa's scorn, mockery, and disrespect for United Nations orders and resolutions—and South Africa is fully supported by the NATO powers, including the United States. Racist South African troops that have no right to be there are depriving the Namibian people of their independence and imposing a Bantustan system on that long-suffering country, in defiance of the international community and world public opinion.

South Africa itself constitutes the most shameful blot for the peoples of Africa and the world. Human dignity cannot help being offended by that repulsive stronghold of the Nazi-fascist spirit that remains in the southern cone of Africa, where 20 million Africans are oppressed, exploited, discriminated against, and repressed by a handful of racists. [Applause] Who spawned that system? Who supports it? They say the South African racists even know how to make atom bombs. I ask: Against whom are they likely to be used? Against the Black ghettos of Pretoria? Will they perchance be used to block the just and inevitable liberation of the people?

Why are the Rhodesian and South African racists al-

---

* The internal settlement was a plan by the white minority government in Rhodesia (Zimbabwe) to institute nominal Black rule while maintaining the economic and political structure of white domination. Under this set-up, Abel Muzorewa, a Black minister, was installed as prime minister in June 1979. Lacking support from the Black majority, the internal settlement collapsed, and after British-supervised elections in March 1980, Robert Mugabe of the Patriotic Front became prime minister.

lowed to bomb Mozambique, Zambia, Angola, and Botswana almost daily, murdering with impunity thousands upon thousands of refugees and citizens of those countries as well? Why are the Zionist aggressors allowed to bomb the Palestinian refugee camps and Lebanese towns daily? Who has given them that right? Who has given them that power? Why are they allowed to use the most sophisticated weapons of destruction and death? Who supplies them? Isn't this undeniable proof of imperialism's aggressive role and the type of peace and order it wants for our peoples? Isn't it a crime to kill a child, an old man, a woman, a Black adult, a Palestinian, a Lebanese? Can these methods and these concepts be differentiated from the methods and concepts that fascist Germany once used? Reports of genocidal acts of this nature are broadcast daily, even by the imperialist press agencies, as if to accustom us to accepting such needs with resignation and weakness.

Another problem that concerns African and world opinion is that of Western Sahara. Cuba has no particular dispute with Morocco, whose government maintained diplomatic and trade relations with us even in the most critical period of the blockade of our country. But looking at the matter from a principled point of view, Cuba expresses its total support for the independence of the Saharan people, [*Applause*] considering the occupation of their territory to be utterly unfounded and their desire for free self-determination to be unquestionably just. Cuba was a member of the UN commission that investigated the desires of the Saharan people prior to the conflict and can attest to the fact that 99 percent of the inhabitants want independence. We congratulate Mauritania on its courageous decision to renounce all territorial claims [*Applause*] and hope that Morocco will reconsider its policy on Western Sahara, a policy that not only isolates and weakens its international position but also exhausts and impoverishes it economically. The right to independence of the valiant Saharan people and the Polisario Front, their legitimate representative, should be recognized by all.

We support the people of Cyprus in their struggle against the foreign occupation of a part of their territory and for the development of peace and fraternal coexistence by all components of that sister country's population.

Cuba's position on the problems in Southeast Asia is crystal clear. For our people, Vietnam is sacred. [*Applause*] We once swore that we were willing to die for Vietnam.

No other people of recent times has paid such a high price in sacrifice, suffering, and death in order to be free. No people has made a greater contribution to the national liberation struggle. No other people has done so much in this period to create a universal anti-imperialist consciousness. Four times as many bombs were dropped on Vietnam as were used in World War II. The most powerful imperialist country had its claws cut off in Vietnam. [*Applause*] Vietnam taught all oppressed nations that no force can defeat a people that is determined to fight for its freedom. The struggle in Vietnam reinforced the respect and unity of all our peoples. [*Applause*]

Now, when Vietnam has been made the victim of intrigue, slander, and encirclement by the Yankee imperialists and of betrayal, conspiracy, and aggression by the government of China, Cuba offers it its firmest support.

With all their talk about the problem of the Vietnamese refugees—who are the direct result of colonialism, underdevelopment, and the thirty-year war of aggression—why don't the U.S. government and its allies even mention the millions of Palestinians scattered all over the world and the hundreds of thousands of Zimbabwean, Namibian, and South African refugees who are dispersed, persecuted, and murdered in Africa? [*Applause*]

What right does China have to teach Vietnam a lesson, invade its territory, destroy its modest wealth, and murder thousands of its people? The Chinese ruling clique, which supported Pinochet against Allende, which supported South Africa's aggression against Angola, which supported the shah, which supported Somoza, which supports and supplies weapons to Sadat, which justifies the Yankee blockade against Cuba and the continued existence of the naval base at Guantánamo, which defends NATO and sides with the United States and the most reactionary forces of Europe and the rest of the world, has neither the prestige nor the moral standing to teach anybody a lesson. [*Applause*]

We also support the Laotian People's Republic against the Chinese government's threats of aggression and expansionism.

Cuba's position on the problem of Kampuchea is known. We recognize the only real, legitimate government of Kampuchea, which is the People's Revolutionary Council of the People's Republic of Kampuchea, and we endorse Vietnam's solidarity with that fraternal country. [*Applause*] People keep saying that Vietnam sent fighters to support the Kampuchean revolutionaries. Why don't they say that the bloody clique that had seized control of the country, in complicity with China and imperialism, provoked and attacked Vietnam first and that there is indisputable documentary proof of mass murders perpetrated against Vietnamese women, old people, and children?

With all our energy, we condemn the genocidal government of Pol Pot and Ieng Sary. [*Applause*] Three million dead accuse them. Even Sihanouk has admitted that some of his relatives were murdered. It is a shameful thing for the progressive forces of the world that such crimes could ever have been committed in the name of the revolution and socialism.

Nevertheless, Cuba, mindful of its obligations as host country, offered the facilities for both parties to be present in Havana until the movement comes to a decision in this regard. It is inexplicable that, while some oppose the expulsion of Egypt, which allied itself with the United States and Israel, openly betraying the noble Arab cause and the Palestinian people, efforts are being made to condemn Vietnam for its acts of legitimate defense against aggression and the fiction is maintained that Pol Pot's bloody government, an affront to all humanity, still exists.

The movement should preserve its unity and always seek a peaceful solution to any difference that may arise among its members. But it is equally bound to maintain impartiality, realism, and political logic in its decisions. [*Applause*] Tanzania was also obliged to defend itself against Uganda's aggression and to support the patriots of that country against the repressive regime.* Now, the legitimate, revolutionary government of Uganda is represented in the conference. [*Applause*] Why should we deny this right to People's Kampuchea? [*Applause*]

We firmly support the Korean people's struggle for the unification of their country. We denounce the unjust division and virtual occupation of a part of their territory by U.S. troops. [*Applause*] We denounce the inconsistency and hollowness of the U.S. government's promises, for, far from reducing those troops it is reinforcing them and increasing their aggressive potential.

---

* Under the government of Idi Amin, Ugandan forces invaded Tanzania in October 1978, later withdrawing. In February 1979, Tanzanian troops invaded Uganda; Amin fled in April.

In our America, we reiterate our firm and staunch solidarity with the fraternal people of Puerto Rico, [*Applause*] whose right to self-determination and independence is stubbornly denied by the colonizing power. Puerto Rico—just like Zimbabwe, Namibia, South Africa, Palestine, and other countries—needs our help. And we must give it unhesitatingly and unswervingly, in spite of the strong pressures that the United States constantly brings to bear on all countries in this regard.

We support Panama's right to full autonomy over the canal [*Applause*] and we condemn the reactionary maneuvers to obstruct the laws for the implementation of the new treaty.

We support Belize's right to independence, [*Applause*] which is today thwarted principally by the opposition and threats by the cruel and pro-Yankee satrapy that oppresses Guatemala. The people of Belize, from the ethnic, cultural, and historical points of view, are completely different from the people of Guatemala and both are in need of freedom.

The new Nicaragua requires the utmost cooperation from the international community for the reconstruction of the country, destroyed by almost half a century of the Somoza dynasty, fathered by the U.S. Marines. It is just that we offer them our solidarity. [*Applause*]

The aspiration of Bolivia, whose territory was mutilated a century ago in a war stirred up by imperialist interests, for an outlet to the sea is absolutely justified and vital. Therefore, we consider it our duty to support it. [*Applause*]

We are opposed to the continuance of any type of colonial enclave in this hemisphere, wherever it still exists.

Cuba also needs solidarity. Our country is the victim of a criminal and cruel economic blockade imposed by the United States, which includes even medicines; and a piece of our national territory remains occupied by force.

Does the United States have the right to try at all costs to block our development? Does it have the right to possess military bases in another country against the wishes of that people?

In all these issues and struggles, which are cause for our concern and call for our solidarity, there is a constant and invariable element: the action of imperialism. Can our movement ignore this? Is it just extremism on our part to clearly bring the deeds to light?

Although the underdeveloped countries, with great poverty, a very low living standard and life expectancy, are the ones who have the least to lose in a war, we cannot be insensitive to the need for peace in our planet. This would be tantamount to renouncing the hopes for a better future for the peoples. We do not agree with the thesis that a nuclear war is inevitable. Such a fatalist and irresponsible attitude is the best way to assure that humanity will be annihilated by a universal holocaust. Never before in the history of humanity has such a real technological possibility existed. It is not possible for us to be so insensitive as to ignore this. For the first time in history, it has fallen to our generation to confront such risks.

In our world of today, mountains of more and more deadly arms accumulate alongside mountains of problems of underdevelopment, poverty, food shortages, squalor, environmental pollution, school and housing shortages, unemployment, and an explosive population growth. Such natural resources as land, water, energy, and raw materials are beginning to be in short supply in various parts of the world.

The developed capitalist societies not only created wasteful and untenable models for standards of living and consumption but also led countries in our area to conceive of development only as the aspiration to get to be and live like New York, London, or Paris.

One way or another, the world economic crisis, the energy crisis, inflation, the depression, and unemployment oppress the peoples and governments of a large part of the earth. Very few, if any, of the members of our movement are free of these difficulties, because we bear the brunt of these calamities.

The struggle for peace and for a just economic order and a workable solution to the pressing problems that weigh on our people is, in our opinion, increasingly becoming the main question posed to the Movement of Nonaligned Countries.

Peace, with the immense risks that threaten it, is not something that should be left exclusively in the hands of the big military powers. Peace is possible, but world peace can be assured only to the extent that all countries are consciously determined to fight for it—peace not just for a part of the world, but for all peoples. Peace, also, for Vietnam, the Palestinians, the patriots of Zimbabwe and Namibia, the oppressed majorities in South Africa, Angola, Zambia, Mozambique, Botswana, Ethiopia, Syria, Lebanon, and the Saharan people. [*Applause*] Peace with justice. Peace with independence. Peace with freedom. Peace for the powerful countries and the small countries. Peace for all continents and all peoples. We understand perfectly well that we will not achieve it without a tenacious, resolute struggle. But we should believe in the possibility of achieving it in spite of imperialism, neocolonialism, racism, Zionism, expansionism, and the other regressive elements that still exist in the world. The strength of our united countries is very great. Never before have the forces of progress and the advanced political awareness of the peoples attained such high levels. Even within the imperialist, reactionary countries themselves, important progressive sectors are determined to struggle for the same ends. The important role that the people of the United States and world opinion played in ending the criminal imperialist war against Vietnam should not be forgotten.

We must demand peace, détente, peaceful coexistence, and disarmament. We must demand and win them, because they will not come about by spontaneous generation, and there is no other alternative in today's world if we are to preserve the very existence of humanity.

Likewise, we must encourage all progress in this field. Thus, we must greet with satisfaction the SALT II agreements between the Soviet Union and the United States, as well as other steps in this field. We must also denounce the reactionary forces which advocate a cold-war policy and are involved in the dirty arms trade business, destruction, and death. They also oppose ratification of the treaty by the U.S. Senate.

However, we recognize that these steps, positive and important though they be, are still a long way from the ideal of gradual denuclearization leading to the total disappearance of nuclear weapons, which in the end would be the only equitable and just solution for all nations, and to a halt to the arms race.

The day must come when humanity resolutely condemns the manufacturing and trade of arms.

Statistical publications indicate that the world spends more than $300 billion a year on arms and military expenditures, and this is probably a conservative estimate.

The forces of the United States alone use up, for example, 30 million tons of oil, which is more than the total expenditure of energy by all the nations of Central America and the Caribbean put together.

Three hundred billion dollars is enough to build 600,000

schools a year with a capacity of 400 million children; or 60 million comfortable homes with a capacity of 300 million people; or 50,000 hospitals with 18 million beds; or 20,000 factories to provide employment for more than 20 million workers; or make possible the irrigation of 150 million hectares of land, which with an adequate technical level could provide food for a billion people. That's what humanity wastes on military expenditures every year. We must also bear in mind the huge drain on manpower, in the blood of youth, scientific and technical resources, raw materials, and other goods. This is the price for there not being a true climate of confidence and peace in the world.

As far as we Marxists are concerned, war and weapons are inseparably linked in the course of history to the system of the exploitation of man by man and the tremendous greed of that system to take over the natural resources of other peoples. As we said one day at the UN, "Halt the philosophy of plunder and the philosophy of war will be halted."

Socialism as a system does not require arms production for its economy. It doesn't need armies to seize the resources of other people. Had unity and fraternity among peoples and men been a reality there would have been no need for arms to attack or oppress anybody, nor for arms to win and defend freedom.

Regardless of how long and utopian the path may seem, regardless of the setbacks and even the betrayals in the progressive movement, we must never be discouraged nor cease our effort to achieve these objectives. At all international organizations and platforms we must demand a shift from rhetoric to action.

The questions lead us directly to the topic of economics. More and more statesmen and leaders in our movement are stating the need to place this matter at the center of our concerns. [*Applause*] You are statesmen who wrestle every day with the knotty economic questions of your countries. You know full well what the great difficulties are: the constantly rising foreign debt, a shortage of foreign currency, the soaring prices of fuel and other import products, unequal terms of trade, low prices on the foreign market that constantly and increasingly rob us of the products that are the fruit of our people's labor, inflation, the rise of domestic prices, and all the social conflicts that arise from this state of affairs.

Progressive governments that are making a noble effort to develop and increase the well-being of their countries are overwhelmed and may even be wiped out by economic difficulties and unfair, unpopular conditions imposed by the international credit agencies. What political price haven't many of you had to pay because of the rules laid down by the International Monetary Fund? We Cubans, who are excluded from that institution because of an imperialist dictate, aren't quite sure whether that exclusion was a punishment or a privilege. [*Applause*]

Some governments placed in power by the people's revolutionary struggles suddenly find themselves faced with horrifying conditions of poverty, indebtedness, and underdevelopment that prevent them from responding to even the most modest hopes of their peoples.

I'm not going to tell you half-truths, nor am I going to hide the fact that social difficulties are much greater when, in any of our countries, a small minority controls the basic wealth and the majority of the people are completely dispossessed. In short, if the system is socially just, the possibilities of survival and economic and social development are incomparably greater. Some countries present the phenomenon of growing economies with equally growing poverty, illiteracy, the number of children with no schools to go to, malnutrition, disease, begging, and unemployment—all of which show in no uncertain terms that something is wrong.

The underdeveloped countries—some optimistically prefer to call them developing countries, when, in fact, the gap separating their per capita incomes and standard of living from those of the developed countries is constantly widening—contain 65 percent of the world population but account for only 15 percent of total world production and only 3 percent of industrial production. The conglomerate of countries in this category which have no natural energy sources, now have a foreign debt of over $300 billion. It is estimated that around $40 billion a year goes to servicing this foreign debt—more than 20 percent of their exports. Average per capita income in the developed countries is now 14 times greater than in the underdeveloped countries. In addition, the underdeveloped countries contain more than 900 million illiterate adults. This situation is untenable.

One of the most acute problems facing the non-oil-producing underdeveloped countries—the vast majority of the members of our movement—is the energy crisis. The oil-exporting countries—all of which are in the underdeveloped world and almost all of which belong to the Movement of Nonaligned Countries—have always been supported by the rest of our countries in their just demands for the revaluation of their product and an end to unequal terms of trade and the wasting of energy. These countries now have a much greater economic potential and negotiating capacity with the developed capitalist world.

This is not the case of the non-oil-producing underdeveloped countries. Sugar, bauxite, copper, and other solid minerals, peanuts, copra, sisal, tea, cashews, and agricultural products in general are terribly underpriced on the world market. The developed capitalist countries selfishly raise their tariffs against those few products that our countries manufacture and even subsidize goods that compete with ours, whenever possible. The European Economic Community and the United States do this, for example, with sugar.

The prices of the equipment, machinery, industrial articles, and semifinished products that we import are raised constantly. The privileged exporters of these goods charge ever higher prices for them. It is easier for them than for the underdeveloped countries to pay for fuel. They even export tens of billions of dollars' worth of arms annually and often buy oil with this money. The shah of Iran was one of their favorite multimillionaire clients, until he was rightly overthrown not long ago. Most of the surplus money from oil sales is deposited and invested in the richest, most developed capitalist countries. The funds are also used to supply them with fuel. But what recourse do the non-oil-producing underdeveloped countries have?

It is absolutely necessary to be aware of this reality, because the situation of many countries, a large number of which are members of this movement, is truly desperate. We should consider and discuss this matter. A solution must be found. Imperialism is already maneuvering to divide us. It is trying to isolate the oil-producing countries from the rest of the underdeveloped world, blaming them for the economic crisis—whose cause really lies in the unjust order established in the world by the imperialist system. And, what is even more dangerous, it is looking for pretexts and covering up its aggressive plans against the oil-exporting countries.

Cuba isn't bringing this topic up in order to defend interests that affect it directly. Of course, we suffer from the indirect effects of the international economic crisis and the low prices established for our products in Western markets, but we have an assured supply of oil which we purchase with sugar, whose price is directly proportional to the price of oil and other articles which we import from the socialist area.

Nevertheless, we should point out that, if all the sugar produced in Cuba—nearly eight million tons in the 1979 harvest, the largest production of cane sugar in the world—had been sold to the Western world at the price now being paid on the so-called world market—around eight cents a pound—it wouldn't have paid for the fuel that Cuba uses, at its present price.

We must look for solutions to the energy crisis, but not only for the developed countries, which already use most of the energy produced in the world. Basically, we must also find solutions for the underdeveloped countries.

We appeal to the sense of responsibility of the large oil-exporting countries in our movement, asking them to strike out courageously, firmly, and boldly in implementing a wise and farsighted policy of economic cooperation, supplies, and investments in our underdeveloped world, because their future depends on ours. [Applause]

I am not asking you to sacrifice your legitimate interests. I am not asking you to stop all-out efforts to develop and raise the well-being of your own peoples. I am not asking you to stop trying to safeguard your future. I am inviting you to join us and close ranks with us and struggle together for a real new international economic order whose benefit will extend to all. [Applause]

No money can purchase the future, because the future lies in justice, in our consciences, and in the honest and fraternal solidarity of our people. [Applause]

The solution to the economic problems faced by our

countries requires a tremendous, responsible, conscious, and serious effort of a world nature.

Those of us meeting here represent the vast majority of the peoples of the world. Let us close ranks and unite the growing force of our vigorous movement in the United Nations and in all other international forums to demand economic justice for our peoples and an end to foreign control over our resources and the theft of our labor. [*Applause*] Let us close ranks in demanding respect for our right to development, to life, and to the future. Enough of building a world economy based on the opulence of those who exploited and impoverished us in the past and who exploit and impoverish us today, and of the poverty, the economic and social underdevelopment of the vast majority of humanity. May a firm determination to struggle and concrete plans of action come out of this Sixth Summit Conference: deeds, not just words. [*Applause*]

Perhaps this speech inaugurating this conference has been somewhat undiplomatic, not quite in line with protocol, but no one should doubt the complete loyalty with which I have spoken.

Thank you. [*Ovation*]

At the United Nations

October 12, 1979

Speech given to the Thirty-fourth Session of the United Nations General Assembly. The translation is based on the UN's simultaneous translation corrected against the Spanish original and is copyright © 1979 by *Intercontinental Press/Inprecor*. It is reprinted from *Fidel Castro at the UN*, Pathfinder Press, 1979.

Most esteemed president;
Distinguished representatives of the world community:

I have not come to speak about Cuba. I am not here to denounce before this assembly the aggressions to which our small but honorable country has been subjected for twenty years. Nor have I come to injure with unnecessary adjectives the powerful neighbor in his own house.

We have been charged by the Sixth Conference of Heads of State or Government of the Movement of Nonaligned Countries to present to the United Nations the results of its deliberations and the positions to be derived from them.

We are ninety-five countries from all the continents,

representing the immense majority of humanity. We are united by the determination to defend the cooperation between our countries, free national and social development, sovereignty, security, equality, and self-determination.

We are associated in our determination to change the present system of international relations, based as it is on injustice, inequality, and oppression. In international politics we act as an independent world factor.

Meeting in Havana, the movement has just reaffirmed its principles and confirmed its objectives.

The Nonaligned countries stress that it is imperative to do away with the enormous inequality that separates the developed countries from the developing countries. We are struggling to eradicate poverty, hunger, disease, and illiteracy, from which hundreds of millions of human beings still suffer.

We aspire to a new world order, one based on justice, on equity, and on peace. One that will replace the unjust and unequal system that prevails today, in which, as proclaimed in the final declaration of Havana, "wealth is still concentrated in the hands of a few powers, whose wasteful economies are maintained by the exploitation of the workers as well as the transfer and plunder of the natural and other resources of the peoples of Africa, Latin America, Asia, and other regions of the world."

Among the problems to be debated in the present session of the General Assembly, peace is a concern of the first order. The search for peace also constitutes an aspiration of the Movement of Nonaligned Countries and has been the subject of its attention at the Sixth Conference. But for our countries, peace is indivisible. We want a peace that will equally benefit the large and small, the strong and weak, peace that will embrace all regions of the world and reach all its citizens.

Since its very inception the Movement of Nonaligned Countries has considered that the principles of peaceful coexistence should be the cornerstone of international relations, constituting the basis for the strengthening of peace and international security, for the relaxation of tensions and the expansion of that process to all regions of the world and to all aspects of international relations, and must be universally applied in relations among states.

But, at the same time, the Sixth Summit considered that these principles of peaceful coexistence also include the right of peoples under alien and colonial domination to self-determination, to independence, sovereignty, the territorial integrity of states, the right of every country to put an end to foreign occupation, to the acquisition of territory by force, and the right to choose its own social, economic, and political system.

Only in this way can peaceful coexistence be the foundation for all international relations.

And this cannot be denied. When we analyze the structure of the world today, we see that these rights of our peoples are as yet not guaranteed. The Nonaligned countries know full well who our historic enemies are, where the threats come from, and how to combat them.

That is why in Havana we resolved to reaffirm that "the quintessence of the policy of nonalignment, in accordance with its original principles and essential character, involves the struggle against imperialism, colonialism and neocolonialism, apartheid, racism—including Zionism—and all forms of foreign aggression, occupation, domination, interference, or hegemony as well as the struggle against great power and bloc policies."

Thus it will be understood that the final declaration of Havana also linked the struggle for peace with "political, moral, and material support for the national liberation movements and joint efforts to eliminate colonial domination and racial discrimination."

The Nonaligned countries have always attached great importance to the possibility and necessity of détente among the great powers. Thus the Sixth Conference pointed with great concern to the fact that in the period that elapsed after the Colombo summit conference there was a certain stagnation in the process of détente, which has continued to be limited "both in scope and geographically."

On the basis of that concern the Nonaligned countries—who have made disarmament and denuclearization one of the permanent and most prominent objectives of their struggle, and who took the initiative in the convocation of the tenth special session of the General Assembly on disarmament—examined the results of negotiations on strategic arms and the agreements known as SALT II. They feel that these negotiations constitute an important step in the negotiations between the two main nuclear powers and could open up prospects for more comprehensive negotiations leading to general disarmament and relaxation of international tensions.

But as far as the Nonaligned countries are concerned, those treaties are only part of the progress toward peace. Although negotiations between the great powers constitute a decisive element in the process, the Nonaligned countries once again reiterated that the endeavor to consolidate détente, to extend it to all parts of the world, and to avert the nuclear threat, the arms buildup, and war is a task in which all the peoples of the world should participate and exercise their responsibility.

Mr. President, basing ourselves on the concept of the universality of peace, and on the need to link the search for peace, extended to all countries, with the struggle for national independence, full sovereignty, and full equality among states, we, the heads of state or government who met at the Sixth Summit Conference in Havana, gave our attention to the most pressing problems in Africa, Asia, Latin America, and other regions.

It is important to stress that we started from an independent position that was not linked to policies that might stem from the contradiction between the great powers. If in spite of that approach, which was objective and uncommitted, our review of international events became a denunciation of the supporters of imperialism and colonialism, this merely reflects the essential reality of today's world.

Thus, having started the analysis of the situation in Africa, and having recognized the progress made in the African peoples' struggle for their emancipation, the heads of state or government stressed that a fundamental problem of the region is the need to eliminate from the continent, and especially from southern Africa, colonialism, racism, racial discrimination, and apartheid.

It was indispensable that we stress the fact that the colonialist and imperialist powers were continuing their aggressive policies with the aim of perpetuating, regaining, or extending their domination and exploitation of the African nations.

And that is precisely the dramatic situation in Africa. The Nonaligned countries could not fail to condemn the attacks on Mozambique, on Zambia, on Angola, on Botswana, the threats against Lesotho, the destabilization efforts that are constantly being made in that area, the role played by the racist regimes of Rhodesia and South Africa. The pressing need for Zimbabwe and Namibia to be completely liberated quickly is not just a cause of the Nonaligned countries or of the most progressive forces of our era, but is already contained in resolutions and agreements of the international community through the United Nations, and it implies duties that must be taken up and whose infractions must be denounced internationally.

Therefore, when in the final declaration the heads of state or government approved the condemnation by name of a number of Western countries, headed by the United States, for their direct or indirect collaboration in the maintenance of racist oppression and South Africa's criminal policy, and when on the other hand they recognized the role played by the Nonaligned countries, the United Nations, the Organization of African Unity, the socialist countries, the Scandinavian countries, and other democratic and progressive forces in supporting the struggle of the peoples of Africa, this did not involve even the slightest manifestation of ideological leaning. It was simply the faithful expression of objective reality. To condemn South Africa without mentioning those who make its criminal policies possible would have been incomprehensible.

More forcibly and urgently than ever, the Sixth Summit Conference expressed the need not only to end the situation in which the Zimbabwean and Namibian peoples' right to independence is denied and the Black men and women of South Africa's pressing need to attain a status in which they are considered as equal, respected human beings is denied, but also to guarantee conditions of respect and peace for all the countries of the region.

The continued support for the movements of national liberation, the Patriotic Front [of Zimbabwe] and SWAPO, was a decision that was as unanimous as it was expected. And let us state very clearly now that this is not a case of expressing a unilateral preference for solutions through armed struggle. It is true that the conference praised the people of Namibia, and of SWAPO, which is their sole and authentic representative, for having stepped up the armed struggle and for advancing in it, and called for total and effective support for that form of combat. But that was due to the fact that the South African racists have slammed the door on any real negotiations, and the fact that the efforts to achieve negotiated solutions go no further than mere maneuvers.

The attitude toward the Commonwealth's decisions at its Lusaka meetings last August to have the British government, as an authority in Southern Rhodesia, call a conference to discuss the problems of Zimbabwe, confirmed the fact that the Nonaligned countries are not opposed to solutions that may be achieved without armed struggle, so long as they lead to the creation of an authentic majority government and so long as independence is achieved in a manner satisfactory to the fighting peoples, and that this be done in accordance with the resolutions of such bodies as the Organization of African Unity, the United Nations, and our own Nonaligned countries.

Mr. President, the Sixth Summit once again had to express its regret over the fact that Resolution 1514 of the General Assembly of the United Nations, concerning the granting of independence to colonial countries and peoples, has not been applied to Western Sahara. We should recall that the decisions of the Nonaligned countries and the resolutions of the United Nations, and more specifically General Assembly Resolution 3331, have all reaffirmed the inalienable rights of the people of Western Sahara to self-determination and independence.

In this problem Cuba feels a very special responsibility since it has been a member of the United Nations commission that investigated the situation in Western Sahara, and this enabled our representatives to verify the Sahraoui people's total desire for self-determination and independence.

We repeat here that the position of the Nonaligned countries is not one of antagonism against any country. The welcome that we gave to the agreement between the Republic of Mauritania and the Polisario Front and to the Republic of Mauritania's decision to withdraw its forces from the territory of Western Sahara is in keeping with the application of our principles and the agreements of the United Nations, as is our deploring the extension of Morocco's armed occupation of the southern part of Western Sahara, previously administered by Mauritania.

Therefore the conference expressed its hope that the ad hoc committee established at the Sixteenth OAU Summit Conference would make it possible to ensure that the people of the Sahara would be allowed to exercise their right to self-determination and independence as soon as possible.

That same principle and that same position determined the resolution on Mayotte and the Malagasy Islands and the need for them to be reintegrated into the Comoros and Madagascar respectively.

Mr. President, there can be no doubt that the problem of the Middle East has become one of the situations that give rise to the greatest concern in today's world. The Sixth Summit Conference examined it in its twofold dimension.

On the one hand the conference reaffirmed that Israel's determination to continue to follow its policy of aggression, expansionism, and colonial settlement in the occupied territories, with the support of the United States, constitutes a serious threat to world peace and security.

The conference also examined the problem from the standpoint of the rights of the Arab countries and of the Palestinian question.

For the Nonaligned countries the Palestinian question is the very crux of the problem of the Middle East. They both form an integral whole and neither can be settled in isolation from the other.

No just peace can be established in the region unless it is based on total and unconditional withdrawal by Israel from all the occupied Arab territories as well as the return to the Palestinian people of all their occupied territories and the restoration of their inalienable national rights, including their right to return to their homeland, to self-determination, and to the establishment of an independent state in Palestine in accordance with Resolution 3236 of the General Assembly.

This means that all measures taken by Israel in the occupied Palestinian and other Arab territories, including the establishment of colonies or settlements on Palestinian land or other Arab territories—whose immediate dismantlement is a prerequisite for a solution of the problem—are illegal, null, and void.

As I stated in my address to the Sixth Summit Conference, ". . . we are not fanatics. The revolutionary movement has always learned to hate racial discrimination and pogroms of any kind. From the bottom of our heart, we repudiate the merciless persecution and genocide that the Nazis once visited on the Jews, but there is nothing in recent history that parallels it more than the dispossession, persecution, and genocide that imperialism and the Zionists are currently practicing against the Palestinian people.

"Pushed off their lands, expelled from their own country, scattered throughout the world, persecuted and murdered, the heroic Palestinians are a vivid example of sacrifice and patriotism, living symbols of the most terrible crime of our era." [*Applause*]

Can anyone be surprised that the conference, for reasons that stemmed not from any political prejudice, but rather from an objective analysis of the facts, was obliged to point out that the United States policy, in aligning itself with Israel and in supporting it and working to attain partial solutions that are favorable to Zionist aims and to guarantee the fruits of Israel's aggression at the expense of the Palestinian Arab people and the entire Arab nation, played a major role in preventing the establishment of a just and comprehensive peace in the region?

The facts, and only the facts, led the conference to condemn the policies and maneuvers of the United States in that region.

When the heads of state or government arrived at the consensus that condemned the Camp David agreement and the Egyptian-Israeli treaty of March 1979, their formulations had been preceded by long hours of detailed study and fruitful exchanges which allowed the conference to consider those treaties not only as a complete abandonment of the cause of the Arab countries, but also as an act of complicity with the continuing occupation of Arab territories.

These words are harsh. But the words are true and just. It is not the Egyptian people who have been subjected to the judgment of the Movement of Nonaligned Countries. The Egyptian people command the respect of each and every one of our countries, and enjoy the solidarity of all our peoples.

The same voices that were raised to denounce the Camp David agreements and the Egyptian-Israeli treaty eulogized Gamal Abdal Nasser, a founder of the movement and an upholder of the fighting traditions of the Arab nation. No one has been unaware and no one will ever be unaware of Egypt's historic role in Arab culture and development or of its merits as a founding nation and a driving force in the Movement of Nonaligned Countries.

The conference also gave its attention to the problems

of Southeast Asia. The growing conflicts and tensions that have been created in the region are a threat to peace that must be avoided.

Similar concern was expressed by the Sixth Summit Conference regarding the situation of the Indian Ocean. The declaration adopted eight years ago by the United Nations General Assembly that the Indian Ocean should be a zone of peace has not been fulfilled. The military presence in the region is not reduced, but rather is growing. Military bases have now reached as far as South Africa, and are also serving as a means for surveillance against the African liberation movements. The talks between the United States and the Soviet Union are still suspended, despite the recent agreement between the two countries to discuss their resumption.

All this led to the Sixth Summit Conference's invitation to all states concerned to work effectively to fulfill the objectives of the declaration of the Indian Ocean as a zone of peace.

The Sixth Conference also analyzed other issues of regional and world interest, such as those touching on European security and cooperation, the problem of the Mediterranean, the tensions that still exist there and that have now been increased as a result of Israel's aggressive policy and the support given it by certain imperialist powers.

The conference also studied the situation in Cyprus, an island still partially occupied by foreign troops, and Korea, still divided despite the Korean people's desire for a unified homeland. This led the Nonaligned states to reaffirm and broaden resolutions of solidarity aimed at fulfilling the aspirations of both peoples.

It would be impossible to refer to all the political decisions of the Sixth Summit Conference. If we were to do so we would be unable to touch upon what we consider to be one of the most fundamental aspects of that Sixth Summit Conference: namely its economic perspectives—the clamor of the people of the developing countries, weary as they are of their backwardness and the suffering it engenders. Cuba as the host country will present to all members of the international community copies of the conference's final declaration and additional resolutions. But before informing you of how the Nonaligned countries view the world economic situation and what demands they make and what hopes they nurture, perhaps you will allow me to take a few more moments to inform you of the final declaration's approach concerning Latin American issues of the moment.

The fact that the Sixth Conference was held in Latin America allowed the heads of state or government meeting there to recall that the peoples of that region began their efforts to obtain independence at the very beginning of the nineteenth century. They also did not forget, as is said in the declaration, that "Latin America is one of the regions of the world that historically has suffered the most from the aggression of imperialism, colonialism, and neocolonialism from the United States and Europe."

The participants in the conference were forced to point out that remnants of colonialism, neocolonialism, and national oppression still remain in that area of struggle. Thus the conference spoke out in favor of the eradication of colonialism and all its forms and manifestations. It condemned the presence of foreign military bases in Latin America and the Caribbean, such as those in Cuba and Puerto Rico, and again demanded that the United States government and the other colonial powers restore to those countries that part of their territory occupied by those bases against the will of their people.

The experience lived through in other areas led the

heads of state or government to reject and condemn any attempt to create in the Caribbean a so-called security force, a neocolonial mechanism which is incompatible with the sovereignty, peace, and security of these countries.

By calling for the restitution of the Malvinas Islands to the Republic of Argentina, by reaffirming its support for the inalienable right of the people of Belize to self-determination, independence, and territorial integrity, the conference once again gave evidence of what its declaration had defined as the very quintessence of nonalignment. It welcomed the fact that as of October 1 [1979] the treaties on the Panama Canal concluded between the Republic of Panama and the United States would enter into force. It gave its full support to those treaties and it called for their being fully respected in both letter and spirit, and called on all the states of the world to adhere to the protocol of the treaty concerning the permanent neutrality of the Panama Canal.

The heads of state and government reiterated their solidarity with the struggle of the Puerto Rican people and their inalienable right to self-determination, independence, and territorial integrity, despite all the pressure, the threats, and the flattery that was brought to bear by the U.S. government, despite the United States government's demand that the issue of Puerto Rico be considered an internal question of the United States. And they called upon the government of the United States of America to refrain from any political or repressive maneuvers tending to perpetuate the colonial status of that country. [*Applause*]

No more appropriate tribute could be paid to the Latin American traditions of freedom and to the heroic people of Puerto Rico, who in recent days have just celebrated another anniversary of the "Cry of Lares," which expressed their indomitable will for freedom some hundred years ago.*

When speaking to the Latin American reality, the heads of state or government, who had already analyzed the significance of the liberating process that took place in Iran, could not fail to refer to the revolutionary upheaval in Grenada and the remarkable victory of the people of Nicaragua and their vanguard, the Sandinista National Liberation Front, [*Applause*] and to emphasize the historic significance of that event for the peoples of Latin America and of the world. The heads of state or government also stressed something new in Latin American relations, something that sets an example for other regions of the world; namely the way in which the governments of Panama, Costa Rica, and Mexico, as well as the member countries of the subregional Andean Pact—Bolivia, Colombia, Ecuador, Peru, and Venezuela—acted in consort and solidarity to achieve a just solution of the Nicaraguan problem, as well as Cuba's traditional solidarity with the cause of that people.

I confess that these considerations on Latin America would alone have justified the Cuban people's efforts and the work of the hundreds of thousands of men and women of our country who were determined to enable Cuba to give a worthy welcome to the fraternal nations of the Movement of Nonaligned Countries at the Havana summit conference. But for Cuba there was much more than this. There is something that, on behalf of our people, we would like to thank you for in this forum of the United Nations. In Havana, the Cuban people's right to choose their political and social system was supported, as was

---

* In 1868, Dr. Ramón Emeterio Betances led a revolt for Puerto Rico's independence in the town of Lares; the uprising was crushed by Spanish troops.

their claim to the territory occupied by the Guantánamo base, and the condemnation of the blockade with which the United States government continues its efforts to isolate the Cuban revolution, seeking to destroy it. [*Applause*]

We appreciate the deep feeling and the universal resonance of the movement's recent denunciation in Havana of the hostile acts, pressures, and threats against Cuba by the United States, declaring them to be a flagrant violation of the charter of the United Nations and of the principles of international law, as a threat to world peace.

Once again, we respond to our brothers, and we assure the international community that Cuba will remain true to the principles of international solidarity.

Mr. President, history has taught us that when a people freeing itself from a colonial or neocolonial system obtains its independence, it is at one and the same time the last act in a lengthy struggle and the first in a new and arduous battle. Because the independence, sovereignty, and freedom of our apparently free peoples are constantly threatened by foreign control over their natural resources, by financial impositions by official international bodies, and by the precarious situation of their economies, all of which reduce the fullness of our sovereignty.

For this reason, at the very beginning of their analysis of the world economic problems, the heads of state or government "once again solemnly emphasized the paramount importance of consolidating political independence through economic emancipation . . . and they therefore reiterated that the existing international economic system runs counter to the basic interests of the developing countries and is profoundly unjust and incompatible with the development of the Nonaligned countries and other developing countries, and does not contribute to the elimination of the economic and social evils that afflict those countries. . . ."

And furthermore, they emphasized "the historic mission that the Movement of Nonaligned Countries should play in the struggle to obtain the economic and political independence of all developing countries and peoples; to exercise their full and permanent sovereignty and control over their natural and all other resources and economic activities; and to promote a fundamental restructuring of the world economy through the establishment of the new international economic order."

And the statement concludes with the following words: "The struggle to eliminate the injustice of the existing international economic system and to establish a new international economic order is an integral part of the people's struggle for political, economic, cultural, and social liberation."

It is not necessary to show here how profoundly unjust and incompatible with the development of the underdeveloped countries the existing international economic system is. The figures are already so well known that it is unnecessary for us to repeat them here.

There are discussions on whether there are only 400 million undernourished people in the world or whether the figure has once again risen to 450 million, as certain international documents stated. Four hundred million hungry men and women already constitute too heavy an accusation.

But nobody doubts that all the hopes that have been raised in the developing countries appear to have been dashed and extinguished at this ending of the second development decade.

The director-general of the Food and Agricultural Organization council has acknowledged that "progress is still disappointingly slow in relation to the long-term development goals contained in the International Development

Strategy, in the Declaration and the Program of Action on the Establishment of the New International Economic Order, and in the Resolution of the World Food Conference and in several subsequent conferences." We are still far from having achieved the modest 4 percent annual average increase in the developing countries' food and agricultural production which was proposed ten years ago to solve some of the most pressing problems of world hunger and to approach still-low consumption levels. As a result of this, food imports by the developing countries, which right now constitute an aggravating factor on their unfavorable balance of payments, will soon, according to FAO figures, reach unmanageable proportions.

In the face of this, official commitments of foreign aid to agriculture in the developing countries are falling off. This panorama cannot be prettied up. At times certain official documents reflect circumstantial increases in the agricultural production of some areas of the underdeveloped world, or stress the cyclical price increases registered by some agricultural items. But these are cases of transitory advances and of short-lived advantages.

The developing countries' agricultural export revenues are still unstable and insufficient to meet their import needs for food, fertilizers, and other items required to raise their own production. Per capita food production in Africa in 1977 was 11 percent below that of ten years earlier.

While backwardness in agriculture is perpetuated, the process of industrialization cannot advance either. And it cannot advance because most of the developed countries view the industrialization of the developing countries as a threat.

In 1975, the Lima World Conference on Industrialization proposed as a goal to the developing countries that we be responsible for 25 percent of the world's manufacturing output by the year 2000. But the progress from the Lima conference to today has been so insignificant that if the measures proposed by the Sixth Summit Conference are not implemented and if a crash program is not put into effect to modify the economic policies of most of the developed countries, that target will never be met. We now account for less than 9 percent of the world's manufactured output.

Our dependency is once again expressed in the fact that the countries of Asia, Africa, and Latin America import 26.1 percent of the manufactured goods that enter into international trade, and we export only 6.3 percent of them.

It may be said that some industrial expansion is taking place. But it does not take place at the necessary pace, nor in the key industries of industrial economy. This was pointed out at the Havana conference. The world redistribution of industry, the so-called industrial redeployment, should not consist of a new confirmation of the deep economic inequalities that emerged in the colonial era of the nineteenth century. At that time we were condemned to be producers of raw materials and cheap agricultural products. Now, an effort is being made to use the abundant labor power and starvation wages in the developing countries to transfer to them the low-technology industries, the industries of lowest productivity, and those that most pollute the environment. We categorically reject this.

The developed market-economy countries today absorb more than 85 percent of the world's manufactured goods, including those whose industrial production requires the highest technology. They also control more than 83 percent of all industrial exports; 26 percent of those exports go to the developing countries, whose markets they monopolize.

The most serious aspect of this dependent structure is

that our imports—that is, consumer items as well as capital goods—are all manufactured according to the demands, needs, and technology of the most developed industrial countries and the patterns of consumer societies, which are thus introduced through the chinks of our trade, contaminating our own societies and in this way adding a new element to the already permanent structural crisis.

The result of all this, as was noted by the heads of state or government in Havana, is that the gap between the developed and developing countries not only persists, but has substantially increased. The relative share of the developing countries in the world output decreased considerably during the last two decades, which has still more disastrous effects on such problems as malnutrition, illiteracy, and poor sanitation and health services.

Some would like to solve the tragic problem of humanity with drastic measures to reduce the population. They remember that wars and epidemics helped to reduce population in other eras. They wish to go even further. They want to blame underdevelopment on the population explosion.

But the population explosion is not the cause, but the result of underdevelopment. Development will bring solutions to the problems of poverty and also, through education and culture, will help our countries to attain rational and adequate rates of growth.

A recent report put out by the World Bank paints an even blacker picture. It is possible—the report says—that by the year 2000 some 600 million people on this earth may still be submerged in absolute poverty.

Mr. President, distinguished representatives, the state of agricultural and industrial backwardness from which the developing countries have still not managed to emerge is, as the Sixth Summit Conference pointed out, undoubtedly the result of unjust and unequal international relations. But, as the Havana declaration also points out, to this is now added the prolonged world economic crisis.

I shall not dwell too long on this aspect. Let us however state that we heads of state or government consider that the crisis of the international economic system is not a phenomenon of a cyclical nature, but is rather a symptom of the underlying structural maladjustments and of a disequilibrium that are part of its very nature; and that that imbalance has been aggravated by the refusal of the developed market-economy countries to control their external imbalances and their high rates of inflation and unemployment. That inflation has precisely been engendered in those developed countries that refuse now to implement the only measures that could eliminate it. And let us further point out, and this is something to which we will return later and which has also been set down in the Havana declaration, that this crisis is also the result of the persisting inequality in international economic relations, so that eliminating the inequality, as we propose, will contribute to reducing and eliminating the crisis itself.

What are the main guidelines formulated in Havana by the representatives of the Movement of Nonaligned Countries?

We condemn the persistent diversion of human and material resources into an arms race which is unproductive, wasteful, and dangerous to humanity. [*Applause*] And we demand that a substantial part of the resources now devoted to arms, particularly by the major powers, be used for economic and social development.

We expressed our grave concern over the negligible progress that has been made in the negotiations for the implementation of the declaration and the program of action on the establishment of a new international economic order. We point out that this was due to the lack of political will on the part of most of the developed countries and we specifically censure the delaying, diversionary, and divisive tactics adopted by those countries. The failure of the fifth UNCTAD [UN Conference on Trade and Development] session highlighted that very situation.

We confirm that the unequal exchange in international economic relations, defined as an essential characteristic of the system, has, if possible, become even more unequal. While the prices of manufactured goods, capital goods, foodstuffs, and services that we import from the developed countries are constantly rising, the prices of the raw materials we export are stagnating and are subject to constant fluctuation. The terms of exchange have worsened. We emphasized that protectionism, one of the factors aggravating the Great Depression of the 1930s, has been reintroduced by some developed countries.

The conference deplored the fact that in the GATT [General Agreement on Tariffs and Trade] negotiations the developed countries belonging to it did not take into account the interests and concerns of the developing countries, especially the least developed among them.

The conference also denounced the way in which certain developed countries are intensifying their use of domestic subsidies for certain products, to the detriment of the products of the developing nations.

The conference further deplored the shortcomings in the scope and operation of the Generalized System of Preferences, and in that spirit condemned the discriminatory restrictions contained in the United States Foreign Trade Act and the inflexible positions adopted by some developed countries, which prevented the adoption of an agreement on these problems at the fifth session of UNCTAD.

We express our concern over the constant deterioration

of the international monetary situation. The instability of the exchange rate of the main reserve currencies, along with inflation, increases the imbalance in the world economic situation, creates additional economic difficulties for the developing countries, lowering the real value of their export earnings and reducing the value of their foreign currency reserves.

We point out that the disorderly growth of international liquidity, mainly through the use of devalued United States dollars and other reserve currencies, is a negative factor. We note that while the inequality of international economic relations is raising the developing countries' accumulated foreign debt to over $300 billion, the international financial bodies and the private banks are raising their interest rates, are imposing shorter terms of loan amortization, and are thus financially strangling the developing countries.

The conference denounced all this as constituting an element of coercion in negotiations which allows them to obtain additional political and economic advantages at the expense of our countries.

The conference took into account the neocolonialist determination to prevent the developing countries from exercising their full, effective, and permanent sovereignty over their natural resources, and it reaffirmed this right. It was for this reason that it supported the efforts of raw-material-producing developing countries to obtain just and remunerative prices for their exports and to improve, in real terms, their export earnings.

Moreover, the conference paid more attention than ever to the strengthening of economic relations and to scientific-technical and technological transfers among the developing countries. The concept of what could be defined as "collective self-reliance," that is, mutual support and collaboration among the developing countries, so that in the first place they will depend on their own collective forces, is given greater emphasis in the Havana declaration than it ever had before.

Cuba, as president of the movement and coordinating country, intends together with the Group of 77 to do everything necessary to promote the program of action outlined by the conference with regard to economic cooperation.

Nevertheless, we cannot conceive of that "collective self-reliance" as anything even remotely resembling self-sufficiency. We rather consider it to be a factor in international relations that will mobilize all the possibilities and resources of that considerable and important part of humanity represented by the developing countries and incorporate them in the general current of resources and economies that can be mobilized in both the capitalist camp and the socialist countries.

Mr. President, the Sixth Summit rejected the attempts of certain developed countries to try to use the question of energy to divide the developing nations.

The energy problem can be examined only in its historic context, by taking into account the fact that the wasteful consumption patterns of some of the developed countries and the role played by transnational oil corporations has led to the squandering of hydrocarbons, and by noting the plundering role of transnational corporations, which have benefited from cheap energy supplies—which they have used irresponsibly—up until only recently. The transnationals have been exploiting both the producers and consumers and reaping unjustified windfall profits, while at the same time falsifying facts by shifting the blame for the present situation onto the developing countries that are exporters of oil.

Permit me to recall that in my opening remarks to the conference I pointed out the desperate situation of the non-oil-producing underdeveloped countries, especially the least developed ones, and at that time I expressed the confidence that the Nonaligned oil-producing countries would devise formulas to help alleviate the unfavorable situation of those countries that had already been hit by the world inflation and by the inequalities of trade relations, and who suffer serious balance-of-payments deficits and sharp increases in their foreign debts. But this does not obviate the principal responsibility of the developed countries, their monopolies, and their transnational corporations.

The heads of state or government, when considering the matter of energy from this standpoint, stressed that this subject should be the main focus of global negotiations within the United Nations, with the participation of all countries and linking the energy question to all the development problems—to financial and monetary reforms, to world trade and raw materials—so as to make a comprehensive and global analysis of the aspects which have a bearing on the establishment of the new international economic order.

In reviewing the main problems confronting the developing countries within the context of the world economy, we could not fail to examine the functioning of the transnational corporations. Once again their policies and practices were declared unacceptable. It was charged that in their search for profits they exhaust the resources, distort the economy, and violate the sovereignty of developing countries. They undermine the rights of people to self-determination. They violate the principles of noninterference in the affairs of states. And they frequently resort to bribery, corruption, and other undesirable practices, through which they seek to subordinate—and they manage to subordinate—the developing countries to the industrialized countries.

In view of the inadequate progress achieved in the work carried out within the United Nations for drawing up a code of conduct to regulate the activities of transnational corporations, the conference reaffirmed the urgency of early completion of this work, in order to provide the international community with a legal instrument with which at least to control and regulate the activities of the transnational corporations in accordance with the objectives and aspirations of the developing countries.

In setting forth all the overwhelming negative aspects in the economic situation of developing countries, the Sixth Summit called special attention to the mounting problems of the least developed, the most disadvantaged, the landlocked countries, and those isolated in the hinterlands, and asked that urgent measures be adopted to alleviate their problems.

That, Mr. President, distinguished representatives, was the far from optimistic, rather somber, and discouraging picture which the members of the Nonaligned movement had in mind when they met in Havana. But the Nonaligned countries did not allow themselves to be swept into positions of prostration or exasperation, however understandable that might have been. While drawing up strategic concepts for advancing and continuing in their struggle, the heads of state or government repeated their demands and defined their positions.

The first and fundamental objective in our struggle consists of reducing and finally eliminating the unequal exchange that prevails today and converts international trade into a very useful and helpful vehicle for the plundering of our wealth. Today, one hour of labor in the developed countries is exchanged for ten hours of labor in the underdeveloped countries.

The Nonaligned countries demand that serious attention be paid to the integrated program for commodities, which up until now has been manipulated and juggled in the so-called North-South negotiations. In the same way, we demand that the Common Fund, which was projected as an instrument of stabilization that would establish a permanent linkage between the prices we receive for our products and those paid for our imports, and which has scarcely begun to have an impact, be given a true impulse and impetus.

As far as the Nonaligned countries are concerned, this linkage—which permanently ties the prices of their export items with the prices of basic equipment, industrial products, raw materials, and technology that they import from the developed countries—constitutes an essential pivot for all future economic negotiations.

The developing countries demand that the countries that have created inflation and have stimulated it through their policies adopt the necessary measures to control it and thus put an end to the aggravation of the unequal exchange between our countries.

The developing countries demand—and will continue their struggle to achieve—access to the markets of the developed countries for the industrial products of their incipient economies; a halt to the vicious protectionism that has been reintroduced in the international economy and that threatens once again to lead us into a murderous economic war; and that nonreciprocal tariff preferences be applied generally and without deceptive falsehoods so that the young industries of the developing countries can be developed without being crushed in the world market by the superior technological resources of the developed countries.

The Nonaligned countries consider that the negotiations which are about to be concluded on the law of the sea should not be used as certain developed countries seek to use them—to ratify and endorse the existing imbalance as regards sea resources—but should serve as a vehicle for equitable redress. The conference on the law of the sea has once again brought out and stressed the arrogance and imperialist determination of some countries which, placing their technological possibilities ahead of the spirit of understanding and accommodation requested by the developing nations, threaten to take unilateral action in carrying out deep-sea mining operations.

The foreign debt of the developing countries has now risen to $335 billion. It is estimated that about $40 billion a year goes to servicing this foreign debt, which represents more than 20 percent of their exports. On the other hand, the average per capita income in the developed countries is now fourteen times that of the underdeveloped countries. This situation is insupportable.

The developing countries need the establishment of a new system of financing, enabling them to obtain the necessary financial resources to ensure continuous and independent development of their economies. These financing methods should be long-range and low-interest. The use of these financial resources should be completely at the disposition of the developing countries. This will enable them to establish a system of priorities for their own economies, in accordance with their own plans for industrial development, and it will help prevent those funds from being absorbed, as they are today, by transnational corporations, which use alleged financial contributions for development to aggravate the distortions of the developing countries' economies and reap maximum profits from the exploitation of these countries' resources.

The developing countries, and on their behalf the Movement of Nonaligned Countries, demand that a substantial portion of the immense resources now being squandered by humanity on the arms race be dedicated to development, which in turn would contribute to reducing the danger of war and to helping improve the international situation.

Expressing the position of all the developing countries, the Nonaligned countries call for the establishment of a new international monetary system, which will put an end to the disastrous fluctuations to which the main currencies used in the international economy, especially the United States dollar, are today subject. The financial disorder also hits the developing countries, which hope that when the outlines of the new international monetary system are drawn up, they, as the majority of the countries in the international community, representing as they do more than 1.5 billion men and women, may be given a voice in the decision-making process.

Summing up, Mr. President, distinguished representatives:

Unequal exchange is ruining our peoples. It must end!

Inflation, which is being exported to us, is crushing our peoples. It must end!

Protectionism is impoverishing our peoples. It must end!

The existing imbalance in the exploitation of the resources of the sea is abusive. It must be abolished!

The financial resources received by the developing countries are insufficient. They must be increased!

Arms expenditures are irrational. They must cease and the funds thus released must be used to finance development!

The international monetary system prevailing today is bankrupt. It must be replaced!

The debts of the least developed countries, and of those

in a disadvantageous position, are burdens impossible to bear, to which no solution can be found. They must be cancelled! [*Applause*]

Indebtedness oppresses the rest of the developing countries economically. There must be relief!

The economic chasm between the developed countries and the countries seeking development is not narrowing but widening. It must be closed!

These are demands of the underdeveloped countries.

Mr. President, distinguished representatives:

Response to these demands, some of which have been systematically presented by the developing countries in international forums through the Group of 77 and by the Movement of Nonaligned Countries, would permit a change of course in the international economic situation that would provide the developing countries with the institutional conditions for organizing programs that would definitely place them on the road to development.

But even if all these measures were implemented, even if all the mistakes and evils of the present system of international relations were rectified, the developing countries would still lack one decisive element: international financing.

All the domestic and internal efforts, all the sacrifices that the peoples of the developing countries are making and are willing to make, and all the opportunities for increasing the economic potential that could be achieved by eliminating the inequality between the prices of their exports and those of imports and by improving the conditions in which their foreign trade is carried out, would not be enough.

In the light of their true financial situation at present, they need further resources to be able both to pay their debts and to make the enormous expenditures required on a global level for the jump into development. Here again, the figures are far too well known to require repeating.

The Sixth Summit Conference was concerned not only because the debts of the underdeveloped countries were practically unbearable, but also because that debt was growing yearly at a rate that could be termed galloping and alarming. The data contained in the recent World Bank report, which came out while we were holding the conference in Havana, confirmed that the situation was growing worse daily. In 1978 alone, the foreign public debt of ninety-six of the developing countries rose by $51 billion. This rate of growth has raised the foreign debt to the astronomical figures already mentioned.

We cannot, Mr. President, resign ourselves to this somber prospect!

The most renowned economists, both Western and those who ascribe to Marxist concepts, admit that the system of international indebtedness of the developing countries is completely irrational and that its persistence could lead to a sudden interruption that might endanger the entire precarious and unstable balance of the world economy.

Some try to explain the surprising economic fact that the international banking centers continue to provide funds to countries that are technically bankrupt by arguing that these are generous contributions to help those countries meet their economic difficulties. But this is not so. In fact, it is an operation for saving the international capitalist order itself. In October 1978, the Commission of European Communities admitted by way of clarification:

"The present balance of the world economy depends to a considerable extent on continuing the flow of private loans to non-oil-producing developing countries . . . on a scale unprecedented prior to 1974, and any obstacle to that flow will endanger that balance."

World financial bankruptcy would be very hard, most of all for the underdeveloped countries and the workers in the developed capitalist countries. It would also affect even the most stable socialist economies. But it is doubtful that the capitalist system would be able to survive such a catastrophe. And it would be difficult for the resulting dreadful economic situation not to inevitably engender a world conflagration. There is already talk of special military forces to occupy the oil fields and the sources of other raw materials.

But if it is the duty of everyone to be concerned over this somber prospect, it is first of all the duty of those who possess the greatest wealth and material abundance.

In any case, the prospect of a world without capitalism is not too frightening to us revolutionaries. [*Laughter and applause*]

It has been proposed that instead of a spirit of confrontation we employ a sense of world economic interdependency that will enable us to call on the resources of all our economies to obtain joint benefits. But the concept of interdependency is acceptable only when you start by admitting the intrinsic and brutal injustice of the present interdependency.

The developing countries will not accept the unjust, arbitrary international division of labor which modern colonialism imposed on them with the English industrial revolution and which was widened and deepened by imperialism as "interdependency."

If we wish to avoid confrontation and struggle, which seem to be the only road open to the developing countries—a road that offers long and arduous battles whose proportions no one today can predict—then we must all seek and find formulas for cooperation to solve the great problems which, while affecting our peoples, cannot be solved without also affecting the most developed countries in one way or another.

Not so many years ago we stated that the irrational squandering of material goods and the subsequent waste of economic resources by developed capitalist society had already become intolerable. Is that not the cause of the dramatic energy crisis that we face right now? Who, if not the non-oil-producing underdeveloped countries, has to bear the main brunt of it?

This sentiment of the necessity of putting an end to the waste of the consumer societies in regard to resources is very widely held. A recent document of the United Nations Industrial Development Organization states, "The present way of life, especially in the industrialized countries, may have to undergo a radical and painful change."

Naturally, the developing countries cannot and do not hope that the transformation they seek and the financing they require will come to them as a gift following mere analyses on international economic problems. In this process, which implies contradictions, struggles, and negotiations, the Nonaligned countries must first of all depend upon their own decisions and their own efforts.

That conviction emerges clearly from the Sixth Summit Conference. In the economic portion of the final declaration, the heads of state or government acknowledge the need to carry out in their countries the necessary economic and social structural changes, considering that this is the only way to eliminate the present vulnerability of their economies and to turn a simple statistical growth into genuine development.

The heads of state and government recognize that only thus will their people be willing to pay the price required of them to become the main protagonists in the process. As I said on that occasion, "If the system is socially just, the possibilities of survival and economic and social development are incomparably greater."

The history of my own country provides irrefutable proof of this.

The emerging and crying need to solve the problem of underdevelopment brings us back, Mr. President, to the problem I mentioned a little while ago, and which is the last one I should like to submit to this Thirty-fourth Session of the General Assembly. I refer specifically to international financing.

One of the most serious phenomena that accompany the accelerated indebtedness of the developing countries, as we have already said, consists of the fact that the majority of the funds received from outside by the developing nations have to cover their trade balances and negative current accounts, renew their debts, and make interest payments.

If we take as an example the non-oil-exporting developing countries, to whose situation I referred at the Havana conference, we note that in the last six years alone they have run up deficits in their balance of payments of over $200 billion.

In view of this, the investments required by the developing countries are enormous and they need them primarily, and with practically no exception, in those branches of production that yield low profits and therefore do not appeal to private foreign lenders or investors.

To increase the production of foodstuffs so as to do away with the malnutrition that afflicts those 450 million persons I mentioned earlier, we must provide many new land and water resources. According to specialized estimates, 76 million more hectares of land in the developing countries would have to be cultivated, and over 10 million more hectares of land irrigated in the next ten years to meet these needs.

Irrigation systems for 45 million hectares of land would have to be repaired. And therefore, even the most modest estimates admit—and I refer to aid and not the total flow of resources—that between $8 billion and $9 billion a year will be required to obtain an agricultural growth rate of from 3.5 to 4 percent in the developing countries.

With regard to industrialization, the estimates are far higher. The United Nations Conference on Industrial Development, when defining the goals for the Lima session, stated that at the heart of international development policy there should stand a target to be achieved in the year 2000 of annual levels of between $450 billion and $500 billion a year, of which a third, that is, from $150 billion to $160 billion, will have to be financed from external sources.

But, Mr. President, distinguished representatives, development includes more than agriculture and industrialization. Development primarily involves attention to human beings, who should be the protagonists and goal of all development efforts.

To cite the example of Cuba alone, I will point out that during the last five years our country has invested an average of nearly $200 million a year in school construction. Investment in medical equipment and construction of public health facilities averages over $40 million a year. And Cuba is only one of nearly 100 developing countries, and one of the smallest in terms of geography and population.

Therefore, it can be deduced that the developing countries will need tens of billions of dollars more invested every year to overcome the results of backwardness in education and in public health services.

This is the big problem that faces us.

And that is not, gentlemen, our problem alone, a

problem solely for the countries victimized by underdevelopment and insufficient development. It is a problem for the international community as a whole.

On more than one occasion it has been said that we were forced into underdevelopment by colonization and imperialist neocolonization. Therefore the task of helping us to emerge from underdevelopment is first and foremost a historic and moral obligation for those who benefited from the plunder of our wealth and the exploitation of our men and women for decades and for centuries. [*Applause*] But it is at the same time the task of humanity as a whole, as was stated at the Sixth Summit Conference.

The socialist countries did not participate in the plunder of the world and they are not responsible for the phenomena of underdevelopment. But even so, because of the nature of their social system, in which international solidarity is a premise, they understand and assume the obligation of helping to overcome it.

Likewise, when the world expects the oil-producing developing countries to contribute to the universal flow of external financing for development, it does not do so as a function of historic obligations and duties that no one can impose, but because of a hope for and a duty of solidarity among underdeveloped countries. The big oil-exporting countries should be aware of their responsibilities.

Even those developing countries that are relatively more advanced should make their contributions. Cuba, which is not speaking here on behalf of its own interests and which is not defending here a national objective, is willing to contribute, in accordance with its means, thousands or tens of thousands of technicians, doctors, teachers, agronomists, hydraulic engineers, mechanical engineers, economists, middle-level technicians, skilled workers, and so on.

The time has therefore come for all of us to join in the task of drawing entire peoples, hundreds of millions of human beings, out of the backwardness, poverty, malnutrition, disease, and illiteracy that keep them from enjoying full human dignity and pride. [*Applause*]

We therefore must mobilize our resources for development, and this is our joint obligation.

Mr. President, there are so many special multilateral funds, both public and private, whose purpose is to contribute to one or another aspect of development, be it agricultural or industrial, or meeting deficits in the balance of payments. Therefore it is not easy for me, on presenting to this Thirty-fourth Session of the General Assembly a report on the economic problems discussed at the Sixth Summit Conference of Nonaligned Countries, to formulate a concrete proposal for the establishment of a new fund.

But there can be no doubt that the problem of financing should be discussed thoroughly and fully in order to find a solution to it. In addition to the resources already mobilized by various banking channels, loan organizations, international bodies, and private finance agencies, we must discuss and decide upon the strategy for the next development decade, so that in the strategy we will include an additional contribution of not less than $300 billion at 1977 real value, to be invested in the underdeveloped countries and to be made in yearly installments of at least $25 billion from the very beginning. [*Applause*] This aid should be in the form of donations and long-term moderate- and low-interest credits.

It is imperative that these additional funds be mobilized as the contribution of the developed world and of other countries with resources to the underdeveloped world over the next ten years.

If we want peace, these resources will be required. If

there are no resources for development there will be no peace. Some may think that we are asking too much, but I think that the figure itself is still modest. According to statistical information, as I stated in the inaugural session of the Sixth Summit Conference of Nonaligned Countries, the world is making an annual investment in military expenditures of more than $300 billion.

With $300 billion you could in one year build 600,000 schools with a capacity for 400 million children; 60 million comfortable homes for 300 million people; 30,000 hospitals with 18 million beds; 20,000 factories with jobs for more than 20 million workers; or you could build irrigation systems to water 150 million hectares of land, which with appropriate technology could feed a billion people. Humanity wastes this much every year on its military spending.

Moreover, consider further the enormous waste of youthful human resources, of technicians, of scientists, of fuel, raw materials, and other items. This is the fabulous price of preventing a true climate of confidence and peace from existing in the world.

The United States alone will in the 1980s spend six times this much on military activities.

We are requesting less for ten years of development than is spent in a single year by the ministries of war, and much less than a tenth of what will be spent for military purposes in ten years.

Some may consider our demand irrational. But where the true irrationality lies is in the world's madness in our era and the peril that threatens humanity. The enormous responsibility of studying, organizing, and distributing these amounts of resources should be entrusted entirely to the United Nations. These funds should be administered by the international community itself on a footing of absolute equality for all countries, whether they be contributors or beneficiaries, without any political conditions, and without the amount of the donations having anything to do with the voting power to decide when and to whom loans are to be granted.

Even though the flow of resources should be measured in financial terms, it should not consist only of money. It may well be made up of equipment, fertilizer, raw materials, fuel, and complete factories valued in the terms of international trade. Aid in the form of technical personnel and the training of cadres should also be considered a contribution and counted as such.

We are convinced, Mr. President, distinguished representatives, that if the secretary-general of the United Nations, with the assistance of the president of the General Assembly, with all the prestige and weight of this organization behind them, and further supported from the very outset by the backing that the developing countries and especially the Group of 77 could and would give that initiative—we are convinced that we would be able to call together the various factors we have mentioned and initiate discussions in which there would be no room for the so-called North-South, East-West antagonisms, joining together instead all forces in a common undertaking, a common duty, a common hope. And that is how this idea that we are now submitting to the General Assembly could be crowned with success.

This is not a project that will benefit only the developing nations. It will benefit all countries.

As revolutionaries we are not afraid of confrontation. We have placed our trust in history and peoples. But as spokesman and interpreter of the feelings of ninety-five nations, I have the duty to struggle to achieve cooperation among people, a cooperation which if obtained on a new and just basis will benefit all countries comprising the international community and will especially improve the prospects for peace.

Development in the short-term view may well be a task entailing apparent sacrifices and even donations which may seem irrecoverable. But the vast world now living submerged in backwardness with no purchasing power and extremely limited consumer capacity will, with its development, add a flood of hundreds of millions of consumers and producers to the international economy. It is only in this way that the international economy can be rehabilitated and help the developing countries emerge from the crisis in which they are submerged.

The history of international trade has shown that development is the most dynamic factor in world trade. A major portion of the trade of today takes place among fully industrialized countries. We can assure you that as industrialization and progress spread throughout the world, so trade will also spread to the benefit of all.

And it is for this reason that on behalf of the developing countries we advocate our cause and we ask you to support it. But this is not a gift which we seek from you. If we do not come up with effective solutions we will all be equal victims of the catastrophe.

Mr. President, distinguished representatives, human rights are very often spoken of, but we must also speak of humanity's rights.

Why should some people go barefoot, so that others may travel in expensive cars?

Why should some live only thirty-five years, so that others may live seventy?

Why should some be miserably poor, so that others be exaggeratedly rich?

I speak on behalf of the children of the world who don't

even have a piece of bread. [*Applause*] I speak on behalf of the sick who lack medicine. I speak on behalf of those who have been denied the right to life and to human dignity.

Some countries are on the sea, others are not. [*Applause*] Some have energy resources, others do not. Some possess abundant land on which to produce food, others do not. Some are so glutted with machinery and factories that even the air cannot be breathed because of the poisoned atmosphere. [*Applause*] And others have only their own emaciated arms with which to earn their daily bread.

In short, some countries possess abundant resources, others have nothing. What is their fate? To starve? To be eternally poor? Why then civilization? Why then the conscience of man? Why then the United Nations? [*Applause*] Why then the world?

You cannot speak of peace on behalf of tens of millions of human beings all over the world who are starving to death or dying of curable diseases. You cannot speak of peace on behalf of 900 million illiterates.

The exploitation of the poor countries by the rich must cease.

I know that in many poor countries there are exploiters and those who are exploited.

I address myself to the rich nations, asking them to contribute. And I address myself to the poor nations, asking them to distribute.

Enough of words! Now to deeds. [*Applause*]

Enough of abstractions! We now want concrete action. Enough of speaking about a speculative new international order, which nobody understands. [*Laughter and applause*] We must now speak of a real, objective order which everybody understands!

I have not come here as a prophet of the revolution. I have not come here to ask or to wish that the world be violently convulsed. I have come to speak of peace and cooperation among the peoples. And I have come to warn that if we do not peacefully and wisely solve and eliminate the present injustices and inequalities, the future will be apocalyptic. [*Applause*]

The noise of weapons, of threatening language, and of overbearing behavior on the international arena must cease. [*Applause*]

Enough of the illusion that the problems of the world can be solved by nuclear weapons. Bombs may kill the hungry, the sick, and the ignorant, but bombs cannot kill hunger, disease, and ignorance. Nor can bombs kill the righteous rebellion of the peoples. And in the holocaust, the rich, who are the ones who have the most to lose in this world, will also die. [*Applause*]

Let us say farewell to arms, and let us in a civilized manner dedicate ourselves to the most pressing problems of our times. This is the responsibility, this is the most sacred duty of the statesmen of all the world. Moreover, this is the basic premise for human survival.

I thank you. [*Ovation*]

PART 6

Dialogue with the Cuban community in the U.S.

Prior to the revolution, a Cuban community of close to 125,000 existed in the U.S., largely as a result of the unemployment and poverty in Cuba. Many of these supported the revolution and some returned to Cuba after its triumph.

At the same time, with the increasingly radical measures of the revolution—land reform, reduction of rents, nationalizations—hundreds of thousands of Cubans went into exile in the U.S. These included Batista's war criminals and torturers; landlords and capitalists; pimps and professional gamblers; many technicians, doctors and lawyers; and some workers and peasants who were influenced by the anticommunist propaganda of the right wing. Among the lies being circulated were that all children were being sent to Russia, that religion was being prohibited, and that the land of small peasants was being expropriated. Significantly, only a relatively small percentage of those leaving were Black.

Cuba's policy was to make emigration unrestricted. To cut across the U.S. government's hesitation to accept emigrés, Cuba opened up the port of Camarioca in 1965 where U.S. ships could pick up those wanting to leave. Following this, flights were established which continued into the early seventies. Hundreds of thousands left during this period. While many of those going were opponents of the revolution, others, lacking a revolutionary consciousness, merely sought a chance to improve their standard of living by going to the richest country in the world.

Inside the U.S., a number of the exiles were organized by the CIA into armed counterrevolutionary units. In addition to the Bay of Pigs invasion of 1961, these groups carried out numerous other anti-Cuba terrorist actions. As a result of these activities, the revolution termed the Cuban exiles gusanos, worms.

With the passage of time, the Cuban community in the U.S. began to change. As the revolution became more entrenched, the terrorist groups, while still exercising influence, came to represent a smaller and smaller minority of the community.

Cubans began to experience the injustice and racism of U.S. society, including the racial discrimination that is directed against Latinos and Spanish-speaking people in general. Although some Cubans became successful in business, the majority entered the working class. Cubans have a lower median income than the U.S. population as a whole and suffer a higher unemployment rate. Among those affected by these factors were those who had been taken out of Cuba as children by their parents. Some became involved in the anti-Vietnam War movement and the radicalization of U.S. society during the sixties and seventies. A number began to take a new look at the Cuban revolution.

Towards the end of 1977, fifty-five young Cubans who had left Cuba with their parents, visited the island as the first Antonio Maceo Brigade, named after the Afro-Cuban leader of the wars of independence from Spain. This tour had a big impact on the population of Cuba and was an emotional experience on both sides. It helped create new attitudes and opened up the possibility of further steps.

In the fall of 1978, a group of leading figures from the Cuban community in the U.S.—the Commission of 75—went to Cuba to meet with Castro and other leaders. Three issues in particular were discussed: visits to Cuba by Cubans in the U.S., reuniting divided families, and the status of the remaining counterrevolutionary prisoners within Cuba. Agreements were reached on all three issues and as a result many families were reunited; the prisoners were released, with most going to the U.S.; and hundreds of thousands of Cuban-Americans were able to visit the island.

While the dialogue was welcomed by the Cuban exile community as a whole, the terrorist groups could only feel more isolated and frustrated, and they sought out targets from among the dialogue participants. Many received threats, and two were assassinated: Carlos Muñiz Varela of the Antonio Maceo Brigade and Eulalio Negrín of the Commission of 75, who was also a prominent member of the Republican Party. In addition, in September 1980, terrorists gunned down a member of the Cuban mission to the United Nations, the only UN diplomat ever to be assassinated.

The following are excerpts from several different events during the late summer and fall of 1978 that present a chronological picture of the development of the dialogue. The first set of excerpts is from a press conference September 6 that announced Cuba's invitation to representatives of the Cuban community in the U.S. and explained Cuba's motivation. The second is from a press conference following the first meeting with the Commission of 75 held November 20–21. Third are excerpts from the December 9 press conference following the signing of the agreements. And finally, Castro's speech at the conclusion of the December 9 meeting.

Dialogue with the Cuban community in the U.S.

1. SEPTEMBER 6, 1978

FIDEL CASTRO: Perhaps it would be convenient to explain that—and this is my opinion—there has been a certain change in attitude within the Cuban community abroad and in the opinion of our own people and the revolution in general as well. I believe that hostility has diminished. Several factors—in fact many factors—have contributed to this. We mentioned some of them. The United States has made some gestures towards Cuba and a certain détente has been brought about between the government of the United States and Cuba. This has created a particular climate. But there is another essential thing. The revolution will be twenty years old soon. From our point of view, it is absolutely consolidated and irreversible. We know it, the government of the United States knows it, and I think that the Cuban community abroad knows it, too. This is an important factor.

I believe that the conditions have been created—conditions which did not exist before—for us to meditate a little on each of these problems. It is quite possible that more years would have passed without us even having given any thought to this, but it must be said that there are many people who have made an effort in this direction. For example, I'd say that something that helped make us conscious of this, and which made a great impact on Cuban public opinion, was the visit of the Antonio Maceo Brigade. Those young people, who had nothing to do with these problems and who are not to be blamed for these problems, who visited Cuba with an attitude of peace, with a friendly attitude, made a great impact on our country. That is one example.

There are people from diverse groups in the United States who have opposed the blockade, who have been in favor of lifting the blockade and of a policy of peace towards our country. I'll give you an example: Reverend Manuel Espinosa.* He's not the only one. For many years, many people have been talking about a change in policy, both on our part and on the part of the community. It seemed as if they were preaching in the desert, and really the conditions did not exist for such a change.

The men and women of the Casa de las Américas in New York have also made efforts for many years.

I've mentioned several examples that helped us realize that we couldn't have a narrow-minded attitude toward the Cuban community abroad, in the United States, in

---

* Espinosa, head of the Christian Evangelical Reformed Church outside of Miami and a proponent of the dialogue, suddenly changed his position in January 1980, claiming that the dialogue advocates were "Cuban spies." His charges were denounced by a number of prominent members of the Cuban community.

Venezuela, in Spain. It seems that in the heat of this long struggle between the United States and Cuba, we had even forgotten that there were many emigrés living in the United States who had, in fact, supported the revolution before its triumph; that there were tens—maybe hundreds—of thousands in the Cuban community who had never taken part in counterrevolutionary activities, who had never carried out hostile actions against Cuba. And yet, we tended to look upon them all as a single group. I would say that time, experience, a number of new factors, and the efforts of many people—including, of course, some figures in the Cuban community who had no connection with counterrevolutionary groups—who talked with us, took an interest in these problems, and made us think over these problems within this new current situation—have made us become aware of these things.

As a result of all these factors, we have come to realize that there are a number of problems of concern to the Cuban community. There are many, but we could name some: the Cuban community has an interest in the question of those prisoners who remain in Cuba; it's interested in the problems that you mentioned concerning the reunion of families; it's concerned with having the same rights as U.S. citizens, that is, the right to visit Cuba, a right that is not shared at present by the members of the Cuban community—whether of Cuban or U.S. nationality—who left Cuba after the revolution. In conclusion, there is a whole series of questions that concern that community. And we've gradually become aware of these problems.

Now then, these problems are internal problems which we are not willing to discuss with the government of the United States because they are matters internal to Cuba, and we do not discuss nor will we ever discuss with the government of the United States questions referring to Cuba's internal affairs or to Cuba's sovereignty.

However, we're willing to discuss these particular problems with the Cubans abroad. In other words, we're willing to discuss, to talk over these questions that concern the Cuban community with the Cuban community—but not with the government of the United States. But the fact remains that these are problems to be analyzed and discussed. I would simply like to express our willingness to discuss them with the Cuban community.

JOURNALIST (WPLG-TV): Before coming here, your government officials informed us that you would be announcing a significant change in policy regarding the exiles. Is there a significant change?

CASTRO: Well, everything is relative in this world, but I think that this change—or rather, these conclusions, or this willingness on our part, obviously implies a change. It doesn't concern spectacular announcements. I only want to explain our present policy regarding this problem. And perhaps there's some significance in the fact that this is the first time in almost twenty years that we're willing to talk with figures in the Cuban community abroad.

It goes without saying that we're not prepared to talk with the counterrevolutionaries. We will never discuss anything with the counterrevolution—even though it's become so weak that nobody knows if it really exists any more. I must say, though, that there are still some signs of counterrevolution; there are still some who make a living out of counterrevolution and want to continue living off it. That's what's left. But, I repeat, we are not prepared, nor will we ever be prepared, to talk or enter into discussion with counterrevolutionary ringleaders. We are, however, prepared to talk and discuss the problems that concern the Cuban community with figures of the Cuban community.

JOURNALIST (AREÍTO): Commander, going back to the policy regarding the emigrés. . . . I'm curious to know what factors led to the decision to approve the Antonio Maceo Brigade. . . . Can you speak a little about what factors led to that decision, how the Brigade is looked upon, and what brought it to Cuba?

CASTRO: Look, there have always been some contacts, relations, groups that have worked. That is, we could single out some people in the United States, and we started to realize that they were not our enemies, that they weren't making war on us, nor were they involved in terrorism. That is why I said there were many factors that had contributed, which helped us to become aware of this. But we had never gone so far as to have here a brigade made up of children of Cuban emigrés. How and when the idea first came up, I couldn't tell you because I don't remember. I recall that one day some comrades told us there was the possibility that a brigade of children of emigrés might come. We might say it was a strange thing. And we even wondered whether such a thing would be understood—that was the first thing we asked ourselves. Some comrades felt they should come. But, would the people understand? How would the people react? Because I want you to know there was a climate of hostility and struggle, a very difficult atmosphere. One of the things we were concerned about was whether the people would understand such a brigade coming following so much hostility and antagonism.

Well, it proved to be a test. We might say it was a test. Later, they went everywhere and met with everyone from the very first moment they arrived. And they met with many leaders as well. I also met with them near the end of their visit. But I had noticed that all the people, the political cadres, and leaders who had met with them, were all very favorably impressed and deeply touched. The meetings were very moving. And just a few days after their arrival they were working well, and their gesture of helping to build a project of value to society helped create a very favorable feeling towards them, very favorable.

Well, at the end, it became an event, and one of the things that has really made an impact on people.

Let me tell you: the World Festival of Youth and Students has just been held. Nearly 20,000 young people from various countries came to Cuba. And representatives of the Brigade also came, returning once again. But they had already won the recognition and sympathy of the people as a whole. I think this was very important for us as well, since we were able to see these problems and realities. Because these young people are in no way to blame for the drama their parents lived through, for the drama of the revolution. When they were children—five, two, or three years old—they were taken to the United States, and not all of them were able to adjust.

There is something else: they have helped us to understand to a certain degree the problems of what we call the community. Some have been struck by the fact that we use this new expression: the community. And yes, we're going to use a new expression. Because we have always used expressions—all of us have used them—that were unjustly generic references to people who had emigrated, unjust generalizations. We generalized and used terms such as traitors and *gusanos* and the like. I was the first, I used them, and I don't deny it. I think they established unjust generalizations. They were in a way based on the idea that all Cubans were involved in counterrevolution and terrorism. I think these expressions resulted from the heat and the passion of the struggle. And I have been the first to use the term "community," and I plan to continue doing so, because I think it makes no sense to continue using a generic term for an entire community, one which is derogatory and overgeneralizes. These young people helped us. If we were to use derogatory terms we would be including the young people of the Brigade, all of them. We would be placing all Cubans in the same bag.

They also helped us become aware of the problems of the community. Because there is something which we have started to realize, the fact that, as I see it, the Cuban community, like all other communities in another environment, in another country, tries to maintain its national identity. They try to hold on to their language, want their children to speak the language; they try to maintain their beliefs, customs, culture, traditions, and celebrations. We realized that among the Cuban community abroad—especially those in the United States, because those in Latin areas speak the same language and don't have this problem—there is an effort to maintain their national identity. Actually, we view this sympathetically. Regardless of what they might be, whether a Cuban millionaire or a worker in the emigré community. Because there are many workers who have emigrated, many Cubans abroad work hard at earning a living in factories, and others gain their livelihood by other means, all kinds of ways. But it is a national and not a class question. We have noticed that the community has tried to maintain its national identity.

This, logically, arouses our solidarity. I mean just that: it arouses our solidarity and appreciation. The fact that they do not support the revolution doesn't matter, but we are pleased to see—we have taken note of and confirmed this—that the Cuban community tries to maintain its language, customs, and Cuban national identity. And, I repeat, this arouses our solidarity and appreciation, even if they don't support the revolution.

Because we support all communities which try to maintain their identity. We support the Puerto Ricans, Mexicans, Latin Americans, Blacks, and Indians as well—in short, all the minorities who struggle for their interests. We support them. Why not view the Cubans in the same light? Why should we only generalize and view them as one hostile, counterrevolutionary bloc?

In our contacts we were able to note this angle of the problem. But our contacts have been made primarily with these young people, because they had a great impact on us. There is even a documentary film about the Brigade, and I know that many people cry when they see it. There is no doubt that national feeling is very strong.

To sum it up, we have seen the Cuban community trying to defend its national identity, and we sympathize with this. It is not something we need, but, logically enough, it has its effect; it makes an impression on us. And these young people made a great impression on all the people.

We had thought there might be criticism of the government and the party as a result of the Brigade's visit, but there was no criticism. The reaction was just the opposite. People were even more pleased when they came for the festival. Everyone welcomed them everywhere.

From then on, other initiatives sprung up, such as the visit organized I believe by a church, which brought fifty people here.

You shouldn't think this is easy. We need the understanding of the people, because we don't do anything behind the backs of the people nor contrary to their feelings. Everything we do must always be in accordance with this. If it is not understood it can't be done. I think these young people have greatly encouraged understanding of these things, and have even helped enable steps to be taken or thought about and for these points to be raised. I think they have played a very important role.

Not only them; they weren't the only factor. There are many other factors.

But what's more, there are new conditions, and I'd say in this context we must take into account the contribution of the U.S. government, because a new climate was created as a result of the points I mentioned earlier. This is the indirect contribution of the U.S. government.

JOURNALIST (MIAMI HERALD): Finally, one last question, which is also very short.

Lourdes Casal [*Areíto*] spoke of the Antonio Maceo Brigade. Does the possibility exist for Cubans who are not sympathizers, Cubans of the emigré community who are not partisans of the Cuban revolution, to come to visit their relatives if they wish to?

CASTRO: That comes under another point I mentioned regarding the concerns of the community. Why? Because we aren't going to ask anyone if they sympathize with the revolution. Moreover, I don't think any of the fifty who came were asked whether or not they were sympathizers. That would be absurd. There would be no point to it.

JOURNALIST (CHANNEL 23, MIAMI): . . . On the same subject, seeing the sympathy that the young people on the Brigade aroused, could that be taken as a model or example of the type of persons who might participate in the group that would discuss these problems?

CASTRO: No, not necessarily, because that seems to me very restrictive. I would like to see, for example, a representative from the Brigade, persons like Espinosa, let's say—we would like that. We would like to see included people who have taken a position, those committed to finding solutions for some time now, and who were apparently preaching in the desert. But it can't be limited exclusively to those people, not exclusively to them. There must be greater breadth and a certain representativeness.

Of course, I said we could not include figures involved with the leadership of counterrevolutionary factions. It must be broader, though. The people we referred to should be there, but it mustn't be exclusively limited to them.

JOURNALIST (CHANNEL 23, MIAMI): Could these people come from the working class in Miami?

CASTRO: From among the working class, businessmen, professionals. The broader, the better. We aren't talking about representation, because if we start talking about that, who has the right to delegate himself? That's why I've referred to figures in the community who would be representative. There must be hundreds of persons—I can't speak with all of them; a talk with fifteen, twenty, twenty-five, thirty—

JOURNALIST (CHANNEL 23, MIAMI): And that conversation could be the beginning of such a dialogue, and those persons. . . .

CASTRO: No, when we talk with those persons we'll already be discussing these problems.

JOURNALIST (CHANNEL 23, MIAMI): Commander, what conditions and requirements must those persons meet in order for the talks to begin immediately?

CASTRO: Look, there are few requirements. I've set the minimum: that they not be linked to the leadership of counterrevolutionary factions, because we've said we won't have discussions with counterrevolutionaries, but rather we'll have discussions with the community. It's enough for us that they be representative without being representatives; representative without representing. Because it would be very difficult to talk of representing the community, since that would only create a tremendous problem, and everyone would be claiming: I represent the community.

Now when we talk of our position on such conversations, we aren't expecting utopia by saying: we're going to talk with those who represent the community. It's enough for us that they be a representative group of figures, or in our judgment in some way representative, not limited to those who you mentioned and who have been mentioned here—the Antonio Maceo Brigade or Espinosa's church, or other groups who have been working for this. I think these people have a legitimate right to be present, but they should not be the only ones. We wouldn't be able to say they were representative then. And I'll tell you, this hasn't been worked out yet. We've spoken with some figures, but this idea hasn't been worked out yet, to a certain extent because of the publicity. So in case you ask me now, we still don't have it elaborated as to how to do this, but the basic idea is as I said: we are willing to discuss with a group of figures from the community. Now they don't have to be famous personalities; let's say persons who are well known, or not so well known, but who represent or stand for something. But not everyone who represents something, because there are hundreds or thousands. A group, that's enough. Then, understanding that these people are going to express the community's concerns, we're willing to discuss these concerns with them, not because they are the community's representatives, but because they are people who are able to express the concerns of the community, who are representative. We will not and are not asking anything of them. They're not going to commit the community to anything. They are simply going to express the problems that concern them. And we're willing to analyze them. But let it be understood that we will be discussing these things with someone who represents a feeling or concern of the community. We'll have discussions with the community or members of the community. We won't discuss this with the United States government. That's our basic position.

CASTRO: . . . It seems to me that it would be absurd to forego a chance like this, because what we are proposing will not harm the community; it will benefit it. It is a gesture to the community, recognition that it exists, recognition for the fact that it has interests and concerns, and that we are prepared to discuss them. It would be absurd, wouldn't it? And some people will be absurd enough to say: no, not that.

We don't stand to gain anything out of it, that is, we aren't looking for any advantage, or anything like that; we are acting on principle. And we say that: we aren't acting according to any plan or seeking any advantage. We are following a policy, and it seems to us that this is the policy that has to be applied at this moment. And I have explained very clearly what we are doing and why we are doing it.

2. NOVEMBER 20–21, 1978

JOURNALIST (SIEMPRE): Well, commander, what can you tell us after two days of talks with members of the Cuban community in exile? What was accomplished? Was agreement reached on the three points? What news do you have for us and the world?

CASTRO: We can say that considerable progress was made on all three points.

Regarding visits, we indicated the willingness of the Cuban government to receive visits by Cuban citizens living abroad starting in January, individually in humanitarian cases and collectively for the rest, with very few exceptions.

JOURNALIST (SIEMPRE): Also starting in January?

CASTRO: Yes, those who left before and after the revolution—and we have even included those who left illegally—can come starting in January. Some of those who had left illegally were here, participating in this dialogue! It is paradoxical. Even in the case of those who have legal proceedings pending, this factor will not be taken into account as far as their visiting here is concerned. Just as any other state, there are exceptions we will make; there will be some excluded. Very few. I myself don't know who they would be, but I imagine it would be the ultraterrorist types who want to wage a holy war, CIA agents, etc. In short, not for having been, but for being now.

JOURNALIST: Commander, what about visits by Cubans who want to go abroad?

CASTRO: That too, though taking into account our limited economic resources; we feel we are ready to make them possible in cases of a humanitarian nature.

The issue of visits depends only on us, and nobody else. The other two issues don't depend only on us; they depend on the attitude the United States adopts.

We are willing to facilitate the departure [of people from Cuba], to give permission for the departure of all cases that can be justified by family reunification. Also the reverse, but in very special, exceptional cases, right? Because we are limited by the availability of housing and other resources. But we express our willingness to facilitate family reunification by authorizing the departure of all those who want to join relatives in the United States, or elsewhere, right? This includes spouses and children and disabled adults with parents there. It also includes cases of those who left, while their sons were unable to do so because they were of military service age; to facilitate their departure—if they want to leave, of course. But this doesn't only depend on us.

We have expressed our willingness on this, our policy and our desire to seek this solution, so long as the United States is willing—because most of the families are in the United States. I don't think other governments would create obstacles. The United States is the key here. Whether or not the United States is willing to facilitate family reunification in cases of Cubans who want to go to the United States to be reunited with their families.

This doesn't depend on us. It is something left pending, depending on what this group of Cubans can work out in the United States.

To wrap up, item one on the agenda [relating to the prisoners] was the one most discussed, the one most debated. Well now, practically all the seventy-five Cubans who were here spoke and gave their views on these and other issues in detail, and our delegation listened with keen interest and attention. Our party, the leadership of our party, has been following the talks, has been kept up to date on the talks, to be able to give a reply to the proposals made.

Naturally, I started by explaining that we were not setting conditions for this group of representatives of the emigrés, or Cuban community abroad, because we were not discussing, nor did we want to discuss, with the United States. Therefore we did not pose conditions. All this results from a new policy, from a constructive policy. We gave an ample explanation of why this had to be discussed to reach a decision.

Regarding the prisoners, the point which was discussed the most, we indicated our willingness to release 3,000 persons imprisoned for crimes against state security, [Applause] for crimes during the era of the dictatorship, always given that the United States was willing to take those who want to go there because they have families or circles of friends in the United States.

Thus, the implementation of this proposal or offer of ours depends in the last analysis on the willingness of the United States to accept the percentage of those prisoners who want to go to the United States.

We have said we could release a minimum of 400 prisoners a month. This is a minimum; it could be more; it won't depend only on us, but on the United States, too. A minimum of 400 a month, of which, to judge from the surveys we have made, about 50 or 60 percent want to go to the United States, because they have their families or circles of friends there. We estimate it is between 50 and 60 percent, so the United States should be prepared to receive between 200 and 250 of each group of 400.

I gave the minimum figure; but that doesn't mean we are setting a minimum. It could be 500, it could be 600, depending on whether or not the United States wants to take them.

On the other hand, I don't think the United States can refuse, because the United States, the U.S. government, because of its policy of hostility, as head of counterrevolution, as inspiration and encouragement for counterrevolution—an activity in which successive U.S. administrations have been involved—is duty-bound to assume this minimum of historical responsibility and to make this elementary gesture toward those who were led into the struggle against the revolution and led into prison by this policy of the United States.

Thus, implementation of this offer depends on the willingness of prisoners who want to go to the United States.

We explained that we were unable to release the prisoners en masse because then they would be here with job problems, adjustment problems, waiting indefinitely to be reunited with their relatives in the United States or to start a new life.

At the same time, we expressed our willingness and repeated it to this group of representatives of the community, asking them to help solve the problem of the ex-prisoners—because we shouldn't confuse those who are now in prison with ex-prisoners.

We have sent a series of lists to the government of the United States which included a large group of ex-prisoners and some who were prisoners—forty-eight in all—who were those we initially offered on September 6 [1978]. Those lists were sent to the State Department several weeks ago; lists have been sent—I don't remember the exact number, but there are several lists—that included some prisoners and the majority of ex-prisoners who, because of employment or adjustment problems, or, above all, because they have their relatives and circles of friends in the United States, wanted to go there. But we have observed that the U.S. government has been reticent, slow; it hasn't shown any special interest in settling the matter; it seems rather to have decided to leave these people's trips to the U.S. up in the air indefinitely.

I really don't understand it, I don't understand it; because at one time the United States wanted to take all our technicians, all our skilled workers, and all our doctors, hundreds of thousands of people. They took half our doctors; yet we accepted the challenge, and now we have many more doctors, more than double—magnificent doctors; we even have many doctors working abroad in technical aid programs.

The United States at a particular moment followed a policy of promoting emigration; so why does it now resist—refuse to solve the problem of these men who ended up in prison chiefly because of U.S. policy?

I don't think any U.S. government can shirk its responsibility, especially not one that talks such rhetoric about human rights.

3. DECEMBER 9, 1978

JOURNALIST (SIEMPRE): There are more people here this time. You said in the last meeting that you recognized the seventy-five members of the group as those doing the negotiating, but I see more people have been invited this time. Why is this and what took place this time?

CASTRO: There were those who had expressed their desire to come the other time but were unable to for various reasons. There were also those who later on expressed their desire to take part in the talks and others whom we invited to take part in the second dialogue because there were no rules as to how many people should attend. Furthermore we thought the more who took part the better. There are times, according to the principle of dialectics, when quantity makes for quality. Therefore, there were more people this time.

We would have liked to have had enough people here to fill the Karl Marx Theater, and had we invited all those who wanted to come we would have packed the theater for sure. But such a thing wasn't practical; it wouldn't have been possible because we really don't have the transportation facilities. We were in favor of the largest number of representatives possible. And that's what happened.

However the Commission of 75 does exist; that's the name they gave it because the number of representatives who came here the first time ran to 75.

Of the original 75, there were some 70 who took part in these talks; 5 couldn't make it, but there were 70 others, which made for a total of 140—more or less the number of countries in the United Nations right now or maybe a little less.

JOURNALIST (WPLG-TV): Commander, I'd like you to be a little more specific as to the outcome of the dialogue. What was it that was signed this morning by the Cuban commission and the Cuban community?

CASTRO: By the Cuban commission and the Cuban community? Nothing, because the commission and the community are the same thing. You mean between the community commission and us. [*Applause*]

Well, I already explained that, about the agreement we had reached in principle and about how we then decided to put on record an act of the agreements and the sessions; the essential things, the matters of greatest interest, which go to confirm what we had said about our proposals last time concerning the release of 3,000 persons imprisoned for crimes against the security of the state and 600 for violating the regulations on emigration—what we call illegal departures—and which we do not consider to be political crimes, counterrevolutionary crimes, but which, in our past, went hand in hand somewhat, and we thought it only logical to include them also.

The solution no longer depended on us alone. We said that some of these people wanted to travel to the United States and that the United States should say whether or not it was willing to receive those prisoners who would like to go to the United States. The Cuban government based its proposal on the responsibility the United States has, as a result of the policy of governments before Carter, which, in our opinion, led many people to engage in counterrevolutionary activities. And, analyzing the problems facing those who have been in prison, the difficulties, the way they are to some extent rejected, we felt that in order to help solve the problems these people had we should facilitate or authorize their leaving our country, if they so wished. Of course, not all of them want to leave Cuba. Many of those who've been in prison have become fully integrated into our society. Many, including many of those still in prison, have no desire to leave the country because, I'd like you to know, they have relatives and friends not only in the United States but also here in Cuba. And it should be said that many of their relatives are fully integrated into the revolution, that many of their relatives are members of the party and that many of their children are members of the Young Communist League. These are realities in our country, and there are many of these people who do not want to leave, who want to be integrated into our society.

Needless to say, this entails quite a lot on our part, because we've gone through twenty years of antagonism and problems, but we're doing everything we can to make it possible for all those who want to stay to get a job and lead a normal life in our country. Of course, that's what we want and what we're fighting for. We may not always succeed but we'll keep on trying just the same.

On the other hand, there are those prisoners whose relatives or circles of friends are in the United States and who wish to travel to the United States.

We thought that the best solution would be to authorize the departure of those who want to leave and, of course, to try to assimilate, to help those who remain in the country become integrated.

The government of the United States gave an answer regarding those who are still in prison. It was a positive answer, saying yes, that it was willing to accept those who want to go to the United States.

However, the government of the United States has not yet given an answer regarding the ex-prisoners, and I think that the government of the United States has the same responsibility toward them as it has toward those still in prison. Thousands were in prison and have already been released, and we said that we were willing to give the same opportunity to those who wanted to leave the country. But the government of the United States has not given a categorical answer to this problem. In other words, it is differentiating between the situation of those still in prison and that of those who are now free, many of whom may have their relatives and their circles of friends in the United States and who may have had some trouble finding employment.

Now, we say that the United States led them into carrying out counterrevolutionary activities; the United States has a moral obligation toward these ex-prisoners, to these people who served time, many of them for many years. Why is the United States so reluctant now? Why does it put obstacles in the path of these people who want to go to the United States? That's what we don't understand and that's the problem that still isn't solved. Or rather, it's solved now, and the situation of the prisoners constitutes a positive step which allows us to put into effect our idea to release 3,000 now in prison for crimes against the security of the state and 600 for illegal departure. And this is why we have formalized our agreement today.

In spite of all the obstacles laid by the government of the United States, we are still willing to authorize the departure of the exprisoners who wish to leave for the United States or any other country.

JOURNALIST (ABC): Given the evident cooperation between your government and the government of the United States, can you tell us where you see relations between Cuba and the United States to be at this point, bearing in mind the cooperation given by my government to this important program?

CASTRO: Well, to tell you the truth, I think that the relations between the United States and us are pretty bad. Moreover, the United States has not discussed this problem with us, nor have we discussed it with them. We didn't want to discuss with the United States anything to do with this problem of the prisoners and family reunification, because these things are exclusively a question of our national sovereignty. This is why we have discussed the problem with persons representing the Cuban community abroad. In other words, we have discussed the problems with the Cubans, with the Cubans! [*Applause*]

All we had to discuss with the United States was whether or not they were willing to take these people. And I think that the United States did the only thing they could do, because I simply couldn't see how, after all Carter's rhetoric about human rights, the United States could refuse this minimum of cooperation, which is to authorize the entry of these persons into the United States.

Of course, the fact that these people are in prison is not Carter's fault. Carter is not at all responsible for the situation of these people. Carter himself, his administration, has made a positive contribution because he at least made some gestures toward Cuba, and for the time being, in our opinion at least, he stopped giving support to the subversive and terrorist plans against Cuba. That's what Carter's contribution consisted of. However, Carter cannot accept some of the responsibilities inherited from the empire—from the great empire of the United States—and reject others. I don't see why he wants to hold onto the Guantánamo base when on the other hand he wants to shirk all responsibilities toward the Cuban prisoners, to the men who were dragged into counterrevolutionary activities by the administrations that preceded Carter's. This is a moral obligation of the U.S. government and therefore Carter must assume this moral responsibility.

This is our opinion. This is our viewpoint. And, to tell the truth, we cannot say that the relations between the United States and Cuba are ideal, nor by any means optimal, because the blockade against Cuba is still in force. And Carter inherited the blockade. He didn't invent it, but he maintains it. Moreover, an attempt is being made to use the blockade as a weapon for putting the pressure on us. And we think that the blockade is a crime, and the attempt to use it to put pressure on us obscene. [*Applause*]

JOURNALIST (L'HUMANITÉ): How would you describe this, say, lack of enthusiasm and reticence on the part of the government of the United States toward the Cuban government's policy regarding the Cuban community abroad and the political prisoners? What are the fundamental reasons for such reticence?

CASTRO: I must be fair. I don't think they displayed great enthusiasm about this. I think they were faced with a given situation, which they were unable to avoid.

I think their response in relation to the prisoners has been positive; I really must say so. We raised the issue in the last interview, and they have answered. I really didn't expect a different response because I don't think they could have evaded their moral responsibility, and the fact is that they have given a positive answer which facilitates the release of the prisoners.

Of course, if they had given a negative answer, we would have found a solution. That I also said in the last interview. Because we were willing to meet again, as quickly as possible, and to discuss what steps could be taken to solve the problem of the prisoners—not only releasing them but making it possible for them to be with their families, to have jobs and a means of making a living. We were willing to pursue the matter even if the answer had been a negative one, but they have actually given a positive answer and I believe we should say so.

Now, they have not given a clear answer and are reticent in the case of the ex-prisoners. I don't know why. I don't know if they have become bored with Cubans, if they don't want any more Cubans there. In short, they have changed their policy and I don't understand this very well, I really don't.

4. CLOSING REMARKS
DECEMBER 9, 1978

So it's all signed, right?

I was saying that you must all excuse me for not making a formal, protocol speech to wind up this meeting.

I would just like to say that we are all aware of how hard, how rigorously we have worked to accomplish what we have achieved. We're also aware that it was no easy task. And we also know perfectly well that you had to face misunderstandings and even risks.

The time before I noted that you had the courage to face these risks. I believe that for every one of you it has been an important test of moral courage. At times I pick up one of those newspapers published there; I've picked up a cassette now and then; and we understand perfectly well how bitter it can be to face such a task as this, in such a climate.

But if it weren't difficult in this sort of way, I don't think what you have done would have merit. I well know how difficult it is and that it takes conviction; it takes determination to defy all these appearances; because it is a question of appearances, all those fireworks set off by the enemies of this effort. And since I know that it is difficult, that it takes courage, I greatly value the merit of all of you.

Of course, we made our proposals on September 6. And we were as determined as you to go ahead with this idea, despite the difficulties.

I think that what we have done is going to benefit a lot of people; but believe us, we've also needed a large dose of moral courage to do it, because twenty years like the ones that have just gone by in the midst of great misunderstandings, great hostilities, and major developments, are not just so much water under the bridge. But above all what we've put to the test has been the conviction, the fortitude of our people on this side, of the community here on the island, which is characterized by the passion, the ardor with which they have struggled throughout these years, the conviction, and the dignified, noble, and courageous way they have faced the threats, the blockades, the aggressions, all of it. It must not be forgotten that this community that is here on the island had to go through such experiences as the October Crisis, which was really a dramatic moment, extraordinarily perilous. And I don't know if you know it, but one of the things that characterized our people in that very difficult moment—possibly one of the most difficult, one of the most perilous, most dangerous the world has lived through, and where our country was the center of the crisis—our people were characterized by their serenity, their composure, their determination to face any peril with truly incredible dignity.

I'm talking about the characteristics that define our people, and it wasn't easy for our people to understand all this either. Still and all, we're confident. We're confident in the first place of their confidence. We're confident of the people's confidence in the revolution, in the certainty they've always had that the leadership of the revolution has acted correctly, honestly, seriously, and in a revolutionary way.

I believe—sincerely—that what we have done and are doing is revolutionary. If we'd let ourselves be carried along by routine, by what's easiest to do, we wouldn't have taken on what we have. I firmly believe that we wouldn't be doing it if we weren't revolutionaries. I believe we're doing it because we are revolutionaries.

To our way of thinking, being a revolutionary means defying routine, turning off the easy road, and many times it means taking the difficult road. But we don't doubt for a moment that what we're doing is highly positive, highly constructive, highly moral, and that it will benefit all Cubans: the Cuban community at home and the Cuban community abroad.

I believe that whatever present misunderstandings and doubts there may be, that the future will bestow recognition on what we're doing here.

I don't want to be too grandiloquent or use too many high-flown phrases, because if one uses them and says—like I said—that, even though we proposed to write, perhaps are writing, a page in history (because some of you said that a page in history was being written, and I agreed with this, because perhaps that's what we were doing), men must not act in order to write pages in history. There's no point to that. But always history will record the things that have some human, social, political value; and we believe that this has value, a high human, social, and political value.

The purpose of this meeting wasn't to make propaganda about ourselves, neither for you nor for us. This meeting wasn't for us to pretend to be one thing or another. In reality, I think that in this meeting you have been yourselves and we have been ourselves. And we have talked, all of us, with absolute sincerity, with absolute integrity, with absolute freedom, with absolute confidence. We believe that if it isn't done like this, there can be no success; and we believe further that if we hadn't always acted like this, the revolution would not exist, the revolution would have been defeated. We believe that what has given strength to our revolution, raised it above the marvel of technology, the riches, the military and political might of our adversaries, has been that profound morality, that honesty that has characterized it. And thus have these meetings been, and thus have been the results. Our uppermost interest, from this moment forward, is that everything we have agreed to be carried out, to the last word, to the last comma, and the last period; and that it cannot be said of us, given that the largest share of the job falls to us now, that we failed to live up to a single agreement, but instead that we live up to our word absolutely.

I believe, in fact I'm sure, that though we have had to work hard, and though you have had to leave your jobs, travel, and spend your scarce resources in order to attain these results, that the results have really been worth it.

Don't be discouraged by anyone's bad faith. Never be discouraged by the campaigns, intrigues, the lies, or insults. Sustain yourselves with the conviction that you have done something absolutely correct, the most correct that it is possible to have done. I am certain that no resentment, no bad faith, no jealousy can cast a stain on what you have done. And I am certain that you yourselves, as much as we, will always feel satisfied with this effort we have made together.

Thank you. [*Prolonged applause*]

PART 7
Cuba and the United States

During the mid 1970s some steps were taken toward an improvement of relations between the United States and Cuba. An airplane hijacking agreement was signed in 1973 and for the first time, foreign subsidiaries of U.S. corporations were permitted to trade with Cuba. This process was cut short in late 1975 and early 1976 following the sending of Cuban troops to aid the Angolan revolution. The hijacking agreement was terminated by Cuba following the bombing of a Cuban airliner in October 1976, killing all seventy-three persons aboard. Four right-wing Cuban and Venezuelan terrorists were arrested and imprisoned in Venezuela for this crime. Castro also pinned the blame for the murders on the U.S. government—because of the terrorists' known CIA training and connections, and the general pattern of CIA activities against Cuba since the revolution. For years it had organized counterrevolutionary terrorist groups, which committed acts of sabotage and murder—in Cuba and around the world. U.S. complicity in these actions was made clear by a document drawn up by members of the State Department in November 1980: "Their [the terrorists] mobility and their links with the US—it seems reasonable to assume—could not be maintained without the tacit consent (or practical incompetence) of at least four agencies: INS, CIA, FBI and US Customs."

In 1977, following Carter's election as president, some new steps were taken: a fishing rights agreement was signed, Washington agreed to suspend spy flights, travel visas to Cuba for U.S. citizens were issued, and charter flights were reestablished. Each country set up an interests section in the other country to handle its affairs—a step short of diplomatic relations. However, this limited progress was halted by the U.S. following Cuba's aid to Ethiopia.

In 1979, coinciding with the approach of the Nonaligned conference in Havana, the U.S. opened a new offensive, ostensibly directed against the existence of a Soviet "combat brigade" in Cuba. Castro promptly labeled this "a fabricated crisis." Although centered on Cuba, this campaign was also directed against Nicaragua, Grenada, and others whom some Washington officials were accusing of being "agents" of Cuban "subversion" in the Caribbean and Central America.

Coming on top of this campaign, the U.S. organized a Caribbean military command, planned military maneuvers at the Guantánamo base, stepped up its recently resumed spy flights, and even scheduled a mock invasion of Cuba. The Cubans answered these threats as they have been accustomed to over the years: by mobilizing the Cuban people in support of the revolution and issuing an appeal for international solidarity.

Eulogy for seventy-three terror victims

October 15, 1976

Speech given at the memorial meeting of one million people in Havana's Revolution Square for the seventy-three victims of the October 6 bombing of a Cubana Airlines plane. The text is from *When an Energetic and Forceful People Cry, Injustice Trembles,* Editorial de Ciencias Sociales, Havana, 1976. (In September 1980, the Venezuelan prosecutor announced that the charges against the four terrorists imprisoned for the crime would be dropped for "lack of evidence." Amid worldwide protest against this move by Venezuela, Cuba recalled its ambassador from that country.)

Relatives of the Cubans assassinated October 6; Compatriots:

In sorrow, mourning, indignation, we meet today in this historic square to bid farewell, however symbolically, to the remains of our comrades assassinated in the brutal act of terrorism perpetrated against a civilian plane in flight with seventy-three persons aboard, fifty-seven of them Cubans. Most of the remains lie in the unfathomable ocean depths, without the tragedy having left the relatives even the consolation of their bodies. It has been possible to retrieve the physical remains of only eight Cubans. They thus become the symbol of all those who died, the sole material remains we will bury in our land of those fifty-seven healthy, vigorous, enthusiastic, selfless, young compatriots. Their average age was barely thirty, although their lives had nevertheless already been immensely rich in terms of their contribution to work, studies, sports, to their family and friends, and the revolution.

When we read each one's biography, we see what a splendid page of service to the country their lives represented. The captain of the plane had been elected National Work Hero this very year. Many had earned the Twentieth Anniversary Medal. A number of crew members had provided various internationalist services, and the athletes had just finished writing a brilliant and unsurpassable page in sports history by winning all the gold medals in the regional fencing competition that had just been held in Caracas. Many were members of the communist youth or the party, all were outstanding in their activities, each one of them had been a lucid example of how devotion to study, achievement, work, and the fulfillment of duty is the essential characteristic in our citizenry today.

They weren't millionaires on a pleasure trip, they weren't tourists with time and money to visit other countries; they were humble workers or students and athletes performing the tasks their country had given them, with modesty and devotion.

Among the passengers were eleven Guyanese youth, six of them selected to study medicine in Cuba—lives lost of men whose destiny was to save lives in their underdeveloped and poor country. Five dedicated citizens of the Democratic People's Republic of Korea also died, representatives of a people who have been victims of United States aggression for so long, who were visiting Latin American countries on a friendship trip.

The plane was destroyed in flight by an explosion a few minutes after it had taken off from the Barbados airport. With indescribable heroism, the brave and expert pilots of the plane made a supreme effort to land, but the burning and almost destroyed craft could remain aloft only a few more minutes. They had enough time and fortitude, however, to explain that there had been an explosion aboard, that the plane was on fire, and that they were trying to make a landing. It is unimaginable what an impact the explosion and fire must have had on the passengers and crew enclosed in an airplane at an altitude of approximately 6,000 meters.

Some imperialist news agency immediately mentioned a possible mechanical failure, but everything the pilot transmitted to the Barbados airport was taped. More evidence was immediately added. Two individuals with Venezuelan documents had boarded the plane in Trinidad and left it in Barbados, before the accident; almost immediately after the plane blew up in the air, they boarded a return flight to Trinidad, where they checked into the most luxurious hotel without any luggage at all. At the request of the Barbados authorities, whose suspicions had been aroused, they were arrested.

The investigations begun by the police of both countries immediately produced evidence strongly indicating that they were the physical perpetrators of the sabotage.

Because of the documents they used, the Venezuelan authorities also quickly became apprised of the events and involved in the investigation. On the following day, October 7, in a cable of condolence to Cuba, the president of Venezuela, Carlos Andrés Pérez, described the deed as an abominable crime. Later, the prime minister of Barbados used similar terms publicly when he spoke at United Nations headquarters. The fact that those governments—whose officials had access to the most immediate and important sources of information, the detainees themselves, the circumstances surrounding their behavior, and their documents—labeled the act as one of terrorism, was already very significant in itself.

Although from the first information, the government of Cuba had not the slightest doubt about what caused the tragedy, it refrained from making any statement, waiting to analyze carefully the news that was being received as well as the background and reports—some public and others confidential—that were in its hands.

At first, the real identity of the detainees was not precisely known. It was said that perhaps the documents were false. The names Freddy Lugo and José Velázquez were released and it was said that the latter also called himself José García, and that he held more than one passport. Later the press also reported that the Venezuelan consul had talked with the detainees for five hours and that the United States ambassador in Barbados had hurriedly left for Washington. Nevertheless, news surrounding the detainees and other details and circumstances of interests were fairly tightly guarded.

On October 9, the government of Venezuela stated that Freddy Lugo was a Venezuelan citizen and that investigations were proceeding to identify José Velázquez or José García.

On October 10, several absolutely reliable sources in Venezuelan press circles, indignant at the monstrous crime, sent Cuba highly important reports. They revealed that a photographer from the newspaper *El Mundo* named

Hernán Ricardo had been seen two weeks earlier with Félix Martínez Suárez, well-known enemy of the Cuban revolution, and two other individuals; that this Hernán Ricardo was inseparable from Freddy Lugo; that two days after the explosion of a bomb in the Cubana Airlines office in Panama, Hernán Ricardo had arrived at Marquetía airport on a flight from that country; that they had proof that said person held three passports, one of them in the name of José Velázquez. It was added that, in the very editorial offices of *El Mundo* newspaper, he had bragged that he knew a Cuban plane would be blown up in Barbados.

But the most essential and important point these well-informed Venezuelan sources communicated to us is that it was widely known that Hernán Ricardo was a CIA agent, that he often handled reports from the agency, and that, earning a relatively modest salary of 1,600 *bolívares*, he had a car that cost 40,000 and an apartment that cost 100,000. Some people had also heard him talking with Freddy Lugo about courses in explosives they were receiving. And because of all these antecedents, they suspected that the other person arrested, who claimed to be José Velázquez, was Hernán Ricardo.

Two days later, on October 12, the government of Venezuela officially announced that the second detainee, José Velázquez, was really Hernán Ricardo.

This explains everything.

To the reports from Venezuela we must add that, according to data in our hands, Félix Martínez Suárez, is a well-known CIA agent.

News reports from Venezuela speak about fabulous amounts of money given to the physical perpetrators of the deed.

Venezuelan territory was unquestionably used to work out the final phase of the sabotage and citizens of that country were undoubtedly the physical perpetrators of the horrible crime. But this in no way leads us to confuse the issue.

It is true that there is a group of well-known Cuban counterrevolutionaries in Venezuela, who have a degree of access to specific political circles, who are implicated in imperialism's terrorist plans against our country; and it is very likely that some of them had a hand in the events. But we don't harbor the slightest doubt that the government of Venezuela had absolutely nothing to do with the United States' aggressive plans against Cuba; that its attitude toward our country has been honest; that just as President Carlos Andrés Pérez himself has promised, it will make an exhaustive investigation concerning the involvement of Venezuelan citizens or residents of the country in the repugnant events, and will demand that responsibility for the use of Venezuelan territory as a base for terrorist acts of aggression be placed where it belongs.

The recruitment of citizens and the use of territory of other countries to carry out acts of that nature are methods typical of the CIA.

At the beginning we had doubts as to whether the CIA had directly organized the sabotage or had carefully elaborated it through its cover organizations made up of Cuban counterrevolutionaries; we are now decidedly inclined toward the first theory. The CIA participated directly in the destruction of the Cubana Airlines plane in Barbados.

The most repugnant aspect of this case is the use of mercenaries who, for money, are capable of cutting off in a few seconds the precious lives of seventy-three defenseless persons, people who had been their fellow passengers in the plane a few minutes earlier.

In recent months, the government of the United States, resentful at Cuba's contribution to the defeat the imperialists and racists suffered in Africa, has unleashed a series of terrorist actions against Cuba, accompanied by brutal threats of aggression. That campaign has been intensified day by day and has been directed chiefly against our diplomatic headquarters and our airlines.

On July 9 of this year, in Kingston, Jamaica, only a few weeks before the plane sabotage in Barbados, a powerful bomb exploded in a cart carrying the luggage to the Cubana Airlines flight leaving for Cuba. The bomb did not explode while the plane was in flight because its arrival had been delayed.

On October 2 of this year, four days before the plane sabotage in Barbados, the counterrevolutionary journalist Llano Montes, who has reason to be well informed about those events, wrote in the Caracas *El Mundo* that a plastic dynamite bomb had been fastened under the wing of a Cubana Airlines plane in Barbados and had been loosened by a little stream of gasoline when the plane went down the runway to start its flight. He added that an airport security employee found the plastic dynamite on the ground, deactivated it, and took it to the office, where it disappeared without his superiors being informed of the fact.

Not only have all the Caribbean and Central American states that maintain relations with our country been used in the terrorist acts perpetrated against Cuba—Mexico, Panama, Colombia, Jamaica, Barbados, Trinidad and Tobago, Venezuela—but also other neighboring states such as Santo Domingo and Costa Rica, where the terrorists live, move, and organize, without of course excluding the United States, Puerto Rico, Nicaragua, and Chile where they are based and act openly with official support. In expanding these activities, imperialism has shamelessly violated the sovereignty and the laws of many countries in the region.

The perpetrators of these crimes move everywhere with impunity; they have inexhaustible funds; they carry United States passports as naturalized citizens of that country, or real or false documents from other countries, and they use the most sophisticated methods of terror and crime.

Who, if not the CIA, with the sanctuary of established imperialist domination and impunity in this hemisphere, is capable of such deeds?

An important aspect is the Central Intelligence Agency's close association with the tyrannies of Nicaragua and Chile in order to carry out these plans.

While the territories of Nicaragua and Guatemala served as a base for armed aggressions against Cuba even at the time of the mercenary attack on Playa Girón, and later pirate attacks were made from bases in Miami, Puerto Rico, Santo Domingo, and Costa Rica, today the same groups of counterrevolutionary types are being used by Somoza and Pinochet as well, according to the specific purposes of each, not only against Cuba but also against Panama, Jamaica, Guyana, the Chilean popular movement, and other Latin American progressive movements.

It is a well-known fact that every time the CIA has concocted a plan of action against Cuba, at the time of Girón or later, to perpetrate the interminable chain of pirate attacks, subversive actions, and arms deliveries it organized and directed, it has always, on every occasion, disguised its activities under the cloak of various Cuban counterrevolutionary organizations. It is impossible to recall the number of names and initials this shady Yankee institution has created.

Last June a group of terrorist counterrevolutionary organizations, all of them located inside the United States—the so-called National Liberation Front of Cuba, Cuban Action, Cuban Nationalist Movement, Brigade 2506, and

F-14, chiefly composed of individuals who have worked for the CIA for a number of years and have received training from it—met in Costa Rica to create the so-called United Revolutionary Organizations' Command (CORU).

These groups not only act freely and with impunity from United States territory, but through CORU, their main heads are closely linked to CIA activities against Cuba.

The actions are not always carried out by members of these cover groups. Many times the CIA does the dirty work by other means, and the events are then attributed to the organizations that have been created.

In the United States these groups publicly proclaim their crimes and announce new acts of vandalism.

In the month of August 1976, an alleged war communiqué was printed in a counterrevolutionary newspaper published in Miami, which, after describing how they blew up an automobile in front of the Cuban embassy in Colombia and destroyed the Air Panama offices, states at the end: "Very soon we will attack airplanes in flight. . . ." and it is signed by the five previously mentioned terrorist organizations located in Miami.

In another Miami newspaper on September 19 of this year, we read a detailed description by CORU of the attempt to kidnap the Cuban consul in Mérida and the assassination of the fishing technician Artagnán Díaz Díaz together with the plan to dynamite the Cuban embassy in Mexico. Two of the assassins had flown from Miami to Mexico with United States passports to do the work, and were arrested in that country following the crime. A third returned to the United States to escape the action of Mexican justice.

In another of the malicious articles published in Miami, on September 9, 1976, there is a picture spread of a so-called congress of the terrorist organization Brigade 2506 held in that city. The same publication includes the photo of the tyrant Somoza making the closing speech and with him, a Yankee congressman, Claude Pepper.

Another publication printed the photo of an assembly of those counterrevolutionary groups presided over, according to the picture caption, by Julio Durán, Chilean ambassador to the United Nations; the mayor of Miami, Maurice Ferre; Col. Eduardo Sepúlveda, Chilean consul general in Miami; and U.S. Congressman Tom Gallagher.

What is strange about the fact that now CORU claims responsibility, through the news agency AP, for that repugnant feat of having dynamited a passenger plane in flight with seventy-three people aboard?

Why should it be strange for these same groups to have assassinated the former Chilean minister Orlando Letelier, whose death infuriated Latin American and world opinion?

Reviewing the terrorist acts perpetrated against Cuba since the United States government launched its insolent threats against our country, we have the following:

April 6, 1976. Two fishing boats, *Ferro 119* and *Ferro 123*, are attacked by pirate launches proceeding from Florida, causing the death of the fisherman Bienvenido Mauriz and serious damage to the boats.

April 22. A bomb is placed in the Cuban embassy in Portugal, causing the death of two comrades and seriously wounding several others, completely destroying the premises.

July 5. The Cuban mission to the United Nations is the object of an explosives attack, causing important material damage.

July 9. A bomb explodes in the cart carrying luggage to the Cubana Airlines flight, in the Jamaican airport, moments before boarding time.

July 10. A bomb explodes in the British West Indies

Airways office in Barbados, which represents Cubana Airlines interests in that country.

July 23. A technician from the National Fishing Institute, Artagnán Díaz Díaz, is assassinated in an attempt to kidnap the Cuban consul in Mérida.

August 9. Two officials of the Cuban embassy in Argentina are kidnapped, and have disappeared without a trace.

August 18. A bomb explodes in the Cubana Airlines' office in Panama, causing considerable damage.

October 6. The Cubana Airlines plane is destroyed in flight with seventy-three persons aboard.

As is evident, in just two months, two extraordinarily serious sabotages, one of which was fatal, were organized against Cuban planes on international flights filled with passengers.

Behind these deeds stands the CIA. And almost without exception, on all occasions, the terrorist organizations located inside the United States and acting with impunity in that country's territory, essentially the five that form the so-called CORU, claimed responsibility for them.

I wish to recall that the CIA has been the instigator of criminal methods that have increasingly affected the international community in recent years. The CIA plotted and encouraged skyjacking in order to use it against Cuba during the early years of the revolution; the CIA plotted pirate attacks from foreign bases in its aggressive policy against Cuba; the CIA plotted the destabilization of foreign governments; the CIA revived for modern times the deplorable policy of plotting and committing assassinations of leaders of other countries; the CIA has now plotted the ominous scheme to blow up civilian airplanes in flight. The world community must be aware of the gravity of these events.

Even after the United States Senate investigated and

publicly acknowledged the countless CIA plots to assassinate leaders of the Cuban revolution and its dedication to that end for a number of years, the United States government has given the Cuban government no explanation of those events, nor has it in any way apologized.

We suspect that the United States government has not given up such practices. On October 9, only three days after the criminal sabotage in Barbados, a message sent by the CIA to an agent in Havana was intercepted. That message, transmitted from the CIA's central headquarters in Langley, Virginia, says in part: "Please inform at earliest opportunity any data concerning Fidel's attendance at the ceremony for the first anniversary of Angola's independence, November 11. If he's going, try to get complete itinerary for Fidel's visit to other countries on the same trip."

Another order, dated earlier, says: "What is the official and specific reaction concerning bomb attacks against Cuban offices abroad? What are they going to do to avoid them and prevent them? Whom do they suspect is responsible? Will there be reprisals?"

We hope the United States government does not dare deny the truth of these instructions from the CIA's main office, and many others sent to the same person, in flagrant acts of espionage. We have the code, the ciphers, and every proof of authenticity for these messages. In this particular case, the presumed agent recruited by the CIA has kept the Cuban government informed [*Applause*] from the very beginning and for ten years of all details of every contact he had with it, the equipment and instructions he received. The CIA thought the agent had succeeded in placing a modern electronic microtransmitter given to him for that purpose in no less a place than the office of Comrade Osmany Cienfuegos, secretary to the Executive

Committee of the Council of Ministers. Hence the CIA's certainty in assuming it would receive, in plenty of time, the pertinent information on any trip abroad made by the Cuban prime minister.

Those who believe the CIA has changed one iota because of the denunciations its hair-raising actions have caused within United States society itself are deeply mistaken. Its methods will simply become more subtle and more perfidious.

Why did the CIA want to know the exact itinerary of the prime minister's possible trip to Angola and other African countries in honor of November 11? Why did it want to know what measures would be taken to avoid and prevent terrorist acts?

Considering the importance of this fact and the enlightening value it has in terms of the CIA's conduct and activities, we have considered it appropriate to reveal it publicly, although this implies the sacrifice of a valuable source of information. [*Applause*]

Three years ago the Cuban government signed an agreement with the United States government on air and maritime piracy and other crimes. This was an important contribution on the part of our country to the solution of the serious world problem of skyjacking. The Cuban government demanded no conditions whatsoever for signing that agreement, not even the end of the criminal economic blockade the United States government has maintained against our country. Moreover, without any legal obligation whatsoever, Cuba returned to a United States enterprise the two million dollars some skyjackers had brought with them and which was confiscated by our authorities.

On one occasion, Cuban authorities at the Rancho Boyeros airport saved the lives of a number of United States citizens proceeding from Florida when the plane had to make an emergency landing after United States police had shot up the tires in a futile attempt to keep it on the ground. We would have behaved in precisely the same way under any similar circumstances, strictly for humanitarian reasons.

How different from the brutal conduct of those who armed the assassins and inspired the destruction of our plane in Barbados!

Cuba has never and will never propagandize in favor of skyjackers, and is prepared to collaborate realistically with any responsible government in the struggle against air piracy and terrorism.

But the United States government has been incapable of fulfilling the spirit and letter of the agreement signed with Cuba in February 1973.

After the unpunished assassination of a Cuban fisherman and the destruction of two boats by a pirate attack off the Florida coast, we warned the United States government that if events such as those were repeated and their perpetrators were not properly punished, the agreement would no longer be valid. [*Applause*] There was no reply. The crime was neither investigated nor punished.

The events that have occurred since then are much more serious, because the terrorist action unleashed by United States hostility and its policy toward Cuba has culminated in the incredible barbarity of destroying Cuban passenger planes in flight.

The agreement signed between the governments of the United States and Cuba on February 15, 1973, cannot survive this brutal crime. [*Applause and shouts of "For sure, Fidel, give the Yankees hell!"*]

The Cuban government finds it necessary to cancel it and will, therefore, so inform the United States government this afternoon. [*Applause*] According to the textual terms of that agreement, at any time during the period of its validity and by written renunciation made six months beforehand, one of the parties can communicate to the other its decision to end the agreement. Strictly adhering to the agreement and proceeding to notification of its renunciation today, October 15, 1976, said agreement will have validity only up to April 15, 1977, and we will not again sign any such agreement with the United States [*Applause*] until the terrorist campaign unleashed against Cuba is definitively terminated, effective guarantees against these actions are made to our people, and there is a final end to United States acts of hostility and aggression against Cuba. [*Applause*] There can be no collaboration of any kind between an aggressor country and a country under attack.

If after April 15, 1977, when the validity of the agreement ends, any U.S. commercial plane should be detoured to Cuba, the plane as well as the crew and passengers will be given every facility to return immediately to their country. [*Applause*]

Cuba will never encourage skyjacking nor will it be tolerant with its perpetrators, but Cuba cannot maintain virtually unilateral commitments to return or punish such perpetrators with a government that bears the basic responsibility for this infamous terrorist offensive against our country.

The agreements of a similar nature signed with Canada, Mexico, Colombia, and Venezuela will remain fully valid.

Cuba is also prepared to collaborate with Mexico, Panama, Venezuela, Colombia, Jamaica, Trinidad and Tobago, Guyana, Barbados, and other countries of the Caribbean and Central America capable of acting in good faith, in any joint measures considered appropriate in combating these crimes.

Cuba is even ready to discuss with the United States, whichever government is elected in November, a solution to these problems; but I repeat, on the basis of the definitive halting of all acts of hostility and aggression against our country. [*Applause*]

We might ask ourselves what is the purpose of these crimes? To destroy the revolution? [*Exclamations of "No!"*] That is impossible. The revolution emerges more vigorous in the face of every blow and every aggression; it becomes more profound, more aware, stronger. [*Applause*] To intimidate the people? [*Exclamations of "No!"*] That is impossible. Faced with the cowardice and monstrosity of such crimes, the people are inflamed, and every man and woman becomes a fervent and heroic soldier prepared to die. [*Applause*]

The revolution has taught us all the idea of human fraternity and solidarity. It has made us all the most profound brothers, among whom the blood of one belongs to all and the blood of all belongs to each of the others. [*Applause*] So it is that the sorrow is everyone's, the mourning is everyone's, but the invincible strength of millions of people is our strength. And our strength is not only the strength of one people, it is the strength of all the peoples who have now freed themselves from slavery and of all those in the world who struggle to eliminate exploitation, injustice, and crime from human society. [*Applause*]

In short, our strength is the strength of patriotism and the strength of internationalism. The ideas we fight for are the banner for the world's most honest and worthy men and women and the certain and victorious emblem of the world of tomorrow.

Imperialism, capitalism, fascism, neocolonialism, racism, man's brutal exploitation of man in all its forms and manifestations, is approaching its end in humanity's history, and their maddened lackeys know it; that is why their reactions are ever more desperate, more hysterical, more cynical, more impotent. Only that can explain such repugnant and absurd crimes as the one in Barbados.

For more than 100 years, the shooting of the medical students in 1871 has been recalled and condemned with inextinguishable indignation.* For thousands of years our people will recall, will condemn, and will abhor in their deepest souls this horrible assassination.

Our athletes sacrificed in the flower of their life and intelligence will be eternal champions in our hearts; [*Applause*] their gold medals will not lie on the ocean floor but will rise like unblemished suns and symbols in the Cuban firmament; they will not win the honor of the Olympics but they have ascended for all time to the beautiful Olympus of martyrs of the homeland!

Our crew members, our heroic aviation workers, and all our selfless compatriots sacrificed under cowardly circumstances that day, will live eternally in the memory, the affection, and the admiration of the people! [*Applause*] A homeland ever more revolutionary, more worthy, more socialist, and more internationalist [*Applause*] will be the grandiose monument our people will erect to their memory and that of all those who have died or will die for the revolution! [*Applause*]

To our Guyanese and Korean brothers immolated that day goes our most fervent recollection at this time also. They remind us that imperialism's crimes have no borders, that we all belong to the same human family, and that our struggle is universal. [*Applause*] We cannot say that

---

* On November 27, 1871, eight medical students at the University of Havana were executed, charged with desecrating the graves of Spanish colonial representatives.

the sorrow is shared. The sorrow is multiplied. Millions of Cubans shed their tears today together with the dear ones of the victims of the abominable crime. And when an energetic and forceful people cry, injustice trembles!

Patria o muerte!

Venceremos! [*Ovation*]

We do not negotiate principles

December 24, 1977

Excerpt from a speech given to the National Assembly of People's Power in Havana. The text is from *Granma,* January 1, 1978.

How are our relations with the United States coming along? Well, they're progressing somewhat. Naturally, first of all, imperialism has been dealt a great number of blows of all kinds, such as Vietnam, Watergate, and others. Its economic blockade and its attacks against us have been discredited and are untenable before the eyes of the world. The imperialists have no moral basis from which to defend that kind of policy against us.

Truthfully speaking, we've emerged victorious from this struggle.

Soon, very soon, the revolution will be nineteen, and we could well say that it is still attending kindergarten—kindergarten! [*Applause*] It is still of kindergarten age. All the imperialists' efforts to destroy the revolution crashed ignominiously against the firm resolve of our people, the revolutionary spirit of our people, the dignity of our people, the heroism of our people. They underestimated the Cuban people and thought they could easily toy with, threaten, destroy, and demoralize them. All the Yankee might—to put it bluntly—wasn't enough to achieve their aims. Five administrations maneuvered against us: Eisenhower's, Kennedy's, Johnson's, Nixon's, and Ford's. Five presidents came and went, but the revolution kept standing! [*Applause*]

There's a new administration in power. As we've said before, there've been some positive gestures. It was not characterized by a hostile policy toward our country, it didn't commit itself during the electoral campaign to follow an aggressive policy against Cuba. It has made some gestures, and we, on our part, have made some small gestures as well. Ours have been small gestures, for what other kind can we make?

For instance, we've made it possible for some criminals, U.S. marijuana traffickers jailed here, to go back to the United States, plus one or two of the few others we held here for counterrevolutionary activities.

They extended their territorial waters to 200 miles, so we had no choice but to extend ours also to 200 miles. So we then had to talk about the question of the 200 miles. Since traditionally we fished in waters that were included in the 200 miles claimed by them, we had to talk, and some agreements were reached.

They authorized U.S. citizens to visit Cuba. Very good, we praised the reestablishment of U.S. citizens' right to travel because that's one of their rights. They were allowed to make use of their right once again. As a gesture, we didn't raise any objections. If they want to come to visit Cuba they can come.

They proposed to set up an interests office. After some

analysis we agreed with them: they have an interests office here and we have one in Washington.

This is part of the progress that has been made.

But let's look at the essentials: what's the essential thing? The blockade. The blockade is still on. What's immoral about this United States policy is that they're trying to use the blockade as a weapon for negotiation to deal with us.

And speaking of gestures, we have leveled no blockade on the United States, so we can't reciprocate by lifting a blockade against the United States that is nonexistent, and we hope that this National Assembly will not level an economic blockade on the United States. There's none. They're the ones who must make the gesture of lifting the blockade!

We can't make the gesture of giving back a piece of the territory of Florida because no piece of Florida is occupied by our soldiers. However, there's a piece of our territory occupied by their soldiers. [*Applause*] What gesture is there for us to make? A few old CIA agents are still in jail here. Well, they'll remain in jail as long as necessary. We've made all the gestures possible.

I was telling you that what's immoral about the United States' policy is that they want to use the blockade as a weapon for negotiation: I hold you in a stranglehold and we talk; one of us in a stranglehold and the two of us talking. That's profoundly immoral on the part of the United States government.

The blockade even extends to medicines; no medicines, absolutely none, and no medical equipment can be acquired in the United States.

They talk about compensation. The corporations that exploited this country claim that their properties were worth $2 billion and with the interest, $4 billion. We've told them that all their crimes, acts of sabotage, mercenary invasions, subversion, and blockade against our nation have come to $4 billion and with interest, they come to $6 billion, [*Applause*] that we are ready to acknowledge the losses sustained by their corporations if they acknowledge the damages to Cuba, that they should pay us compensation and we'll pay compensation to the U.S. corporations affected by the revolutionary laws.

Now then, there'd be a lot of things to talk about, but what has happened now? What has happened? They used to talk about Latin America being subverted, but they no longer talk about that. Now they're talking about other things, for instance, the problem of Puerto Rico and the independence of Puerto Rico, a right which we have always defended. And while they elaborate their own theories, we elaborate ours. But above all, we've said that what is involved here is a question of principles. We're not promoting violence in Puerto Rico. Yet when the Cuban Revolutionary Party was founded it sought Cuban and Puerto Rican independence. [*Applause*] We have sacred historical, moral, and spiritual bonds with Puerto Rico. And we've told them that as long as there's one Puerto Rican who defends the idea of independence, as long as there's even one, we have the moral and political duty of defending the idea of Puerto Rico's independence. [*Applause*] We will honor our moral and political duty. There's no need for three or four million Puerto Ricans to be defending their independence, one is enough for us, and we've made this very clear to them, that this is a matter of principle, and to us, principles are not to be negotiated!

Now a new question about Cuban troops in Angola and in other parts of Africa has come up, that is, Cuba's solidarity with the African peoples. We have made it very clear to them that Cuba's solidarity with the African peoples is not negotiable! [*Applause*]

This doesn't mean at all that we reject the possibility of improving the relations between Cuba and the United States; for us this is also based on a matter of principle, as we sincerely believe that the efforts of everybody are required to bring about international détente and peace. We believe that war is not the answer for the world since it would mean the virtual extermination of humanity. We talked about this at the congress of the party, it is on record in the theses of the congress, and it is our growing, deep-rooted conviction that the struggle for international détente and peace is the duty of all peoples and aware persons in the world.

So our first reason, the fundamental one, for being willing to try to improve relations with the United States is on account of that principle. We know about the world, we're familiar with world problems, we're familiar with the problems of the underdeveloped world. We anticipate the terrible problems to be faced by humanity in the future, by the generation made up by our junior high school students and those that are now attending our day-care centers. We know what problems are in store for these generations in future years as part of humanity. We know about the problems to be faced by the world of the future: food, uncontrolled population growth, pollution, power shortages, lack of natural resources, development problems. We believe that in the absence of a true atmosphere of peace in the world we couldn't even start to solve any of these problems.

This means that whenever there's a possibility for improvement we're simply following a principle when we think we should go to work on that connection. But, apparently, the United States government doesn't understand that. Perhaps they think we're impatient or feeling anxious. It could be they have an illusion that somehow we need them; it could be they have the illusion that we can't live without such relations.

It could be that they believe we want to improve relations on account of economic and material interests. Naturally, economically speaking, it would be good for the country; materially speaking, it would be good for the country; good in a relative way, not in a decisive way—let this be well understood—not in a decisive way. Decisive are our relations with the socialist community and with the USSR, these are indeed decisive! [*Applause*] And these relations could never be replaced by relations with the United States because the nature of imperialism prevents it.

What are they doing now with sugar? They've levied enormous import tariffs on sugar, now tremendously undervalued; and a tariff of three or four cents is levied by them on sugar that is sold for seven or eight cents a pound on the world market in order to protect their own sugar production, thus affecting over sixty countries, some of which, to be honest, more than deserve it.

We're watching from the sidelines how events are unfolding. Many of those that, like voracious wild beasts, went after the sugar quotas that Cuba used to have in the U.S. market, who sold their souls to imperialism to get a share of our quotas and who cooperated with the maneuvering and crimes against Cuba to get a share of our quota, who mercilessly and selfishly went after our quotas, are now getting what they had coming. There are no longer any U.S. quotas but very high customs tariffs instead. It boils down to selfishness under capitalism, protectionist laws to save themselves even if it means the sinking of the rest of the world. That's what they're doing to sugar. Will they do like the USSR does, pay excellent prices for sugar, increase the sugar price proportionally to the price rises on their products exported to us, buy practically all the sugar that we can produce and on which we have set up magnificent trade relations?

The most important thing in life and, above all, in revolutionary life, is to be clear about things, and it must be made absolutely clear to the United States government that no improvement in relations between Cuba and the United States can ever alter in the least the close ties of our people and our revolution with the Soviet Union. [*Applause*] The United States government must not fool itself about this; no strategy to counter this will ever succeed. Ours is not one of those governments that can be bought or sold.

As you all know—I don't want to mention names, although I could perhaps mention several—imperialism has toyed with some phony revolutions and their leaders, and has forced them to move away from the socialist camp, has driven them into treason, and has bought them. But there's one government of this underdeveloped world, of this hemisphere, that the imperialists will never be able to buy or manipulate, and that is the government of Cuba! [*Prolonged applause*]

And what's the point of the United States talking about the Cuban troops in Angola and Cuba's solidarity with Africa? What has that got to do with relations between Cuba and the United States? What's this about the United States talking about troops being in another country and turning the presence of our troops in Angola or in any other country of Africa into an obstacle for such relations? That's why I say that apparently the United States has failed to understand our principled policy; they don't understand it nor do they understand principles. And it seems to us like an act of bad faith that the president of the United States was dragged into by some of his advisers, the fact that the U.S. press recently launched a noisy campaign concerning the presence of Cuban advisers in several African countries. Their information was false at that, since advisers were reported to be in places where there weren't any; others were reported in places where there were some but the figures given were exaggerated. They did this, in our opinion, with a clear intent to blackmail.

What moral basis can the United States have to speak about Cuban troops in Africa? What moral basis can a country have whose troops are on every continent, that has, for instance, over twenty military bases in the Philippines, dozens of bases in Okinawa, in Japan, in Asia, in Turkey, in Greece, in the FRG [Federal Republic of Germany], in Europe, in Spain, in Italy, and everywhere else? What moral basis can the United States have to use the argument of our troops being in Africa when their own troops are stationed by force on Panamanian territory, occupying a portion of that country? What moral basis can the United States have to speak about our troops in Africa when their own troops are stationed right here on our own national territory, at the Guantánamo naval base? [*Applause*]

If we're going to talk about troops stationed where they shouldn't be, and that indeed has a lot to do with the bilateral relations between Cuba and the United States, the only troops that should be talked about are those now stationed at the Guantánamo naval base. It's the only point regarding troops stationed in other countries that we can talk about.

It would be ridiculous for us to tell the United States government that, in order for relations between Cuba and the United States to be resumed or improved, it would have to withdraw its troops from the Philippines, or Turkey, or Greece, or Okinawa, or South Korea. Whenever they feel like withdrawing their troops from those countries, let them do it; but it'd be ridiculous for us to tell them now, you must first withdraw your troops from the FRG for otherwise there can't be relations between us, or else say to them, we're disgusted at your having troops stationed in the FRG, so there can't be any relations between us. They then would say, those guys are crazy. Therefore, how come they have the right to say it? Because they don't start out from a logical premise, one of equity, of equality. It's a case of imperial arrogance. Imperial arrogance! It's all right for the imperialists to have troops and advisers everywhere in the world, but we can't have them anywhere. That's a fine concept the United States government has of logic, equity, and equality!

We're supporting African governments that have requested our cooperation; they are duly constituted governments, and revolutionary and progressive governments at that. Our military advisers are not lending their services to any fascist government anywhere in the world, our advisers are not lending their services to any reactionary government anywhere in the world. Our military advisers are assisting governments that help their own peoples, support their own peoples and are either revolutionary or progressive governments. [*Applause*]

We have no military advisers in countries like Chile—to give one example—in fascist countries. Apart from all its bases all over the world, the United States has military instructors and advisers in dozens of countries—and, in some places, like in Iran, Saudi Arabia, and countries like that, thousands of them. The United States has military advisers in nearly all the Latin American countries; the United States has sent military advisers to and has trained the armies of the most repressive, reactionary, and bloodthirsty governments of this hemisphere.

The fundamental difference between the advice given

by the United States and Cuba is that the United States will never advise a revolutionary or progressive people and it will, generally speaking, always advise reactionary and fascist governments. Revolutionary Cuba advises revolutionary and progressive governments.

What right has the United States got to oppose such advice given by our people? What's more, what are they complaining about? They tried to isolate our revolution and destroy it. The revolution developed its ties with the Third World; these are solid ties and we'll be firm and loyal to such ties. We will not forsake such ties for a smile from the United States, we will not exchange such ties for any concession that the United States might make. Such ties are not negotiable!

Our revolution has many soldiers, and very good soldiers at that. There are tens of thousands of officers among the regular and reserve troops and hundreds of thousands of fighters among the regular and reserve troops. The Yankee imperialists are to blame for that; the blame falls on them for they forced us, with their attacks and their blockade, to adopt these elementary measures to survive.

We don't deny it: we support and have sent military advisers to many countries in Africa, that's clear, very clear, and on this we do not negotiate. [*Applause*] This has nothing to do with the new U.S. administration; this is the traditional policy of our revolution. We're now helping and we'll go on helping Angola! [*Applause*] We're now helping and we'll go on helping Mozambique! [*Applause*] We're now helping and we'll go on helping the Ethiopian revolution! If that's why the United States is blockading us, let them go on blockading us.

Why doesn't the United States blockade South Africa, a racist, fascist country whose troops are committing crimes in Africa and whose minority is oppressing 20 million

Blacks? Why doesn't it blockade Rhodesia, where 300,000 white fascists are oppressing 6 million Africans, a country whose troops are perpetrating indescribable massacres of men, women, and children in Mozambique? We've seen photos showing the bodies of children, women, and old people murdered and thrown in a heap like Hitler's fascists used to do. Why don't they blockade them? Why don't the Yankee imperialists blockade Pinochet? They blockade Cuba instead. What is understood by the peoples, what is understood by the African peoples is that while the Yankee imperialists have sided with South Africa, Rhodesia, the repressive and reactionary African governments, we've sided with the revolutionary and progressive peoples of Africa. We're fighting against fascism in Africa, we're fighting against racism in Africa.

Historically, it'll always be on record that while our role is a highly honorable role, the role played by imperialism is a shameful one. Since the African peoples trust us, they have requested our cooperation. And not only are we helping the governments of Angola, Mozambique, Ethiopia, and other governments in Africa, but we're also helping the liberation movements in Namibia, Zimbabwe, and South Africa. [*Applause*] We're helping them now and we'll go on helping them! [*Applause*] And no matter what they do, the imperialists have already lost the battle in southern Africa.

Ours is a transparent, clear policy. We do not negotiate principles; we can't be intimidated by any campaigns or any pressure whatsoever.

For the reasons stated this evening, we're sincere advocates of peace, and to us struggling to improve relations among all countries on a just basis is a principle. No material benefit, regardless of its nature or magnitude, would make us betray the trust placed in us by Angola, Mozambique, Ethiopia, or the heroic peoples struggling against fascism and racism in Africa. And all these things must be very clear to the United States.

Every positive gesture made by the present administration has been met by positive gestures by us, according to the best of our ability. Yet if the U.S. government were to embark on a policy of blackmail and pressure against us, an immoral policy and conduct against our nation, maintaining its blockade as an ignoble and criminal weapon against our people; if the U.S. government believes that in order for relations to improve our people must give up their principles, then in the same manner that in the past we fought against five presidents of the United States, we will now fight against the sixth. [*Applause*] If they persist in blockading us, it'll be worse for them. For the longer their blockade is on, the greater the number of soldiers trained by us will be! [*Applause*] The more attacks that are launched against our country, the larger the number of brave and experienced soldiers our country will be able to count on!

The confidence that revolutionaries all over the world have in our people constitutes an immense honor for Cuba. It's not for nothing that our country will be the site of the Eleventh Festival [of Youth] next year and that it will be the site of the conference of Nonaligned countries in 1979. [*Applause*] Revolutionary life assigned these tasks to our country and we, in turn, will abide by our principles and our obligations. If the blockade lasts, it doesn't matter. If the U.S. government discards the possibility of improving relations with us, that's its own responsibility.

At times they even enjoy meddling in the internal affairs of other countries. They talk about counterrevolutionary prisoners in Cuba. Naturally, they are responsible for such prisoners existing since they encouraged them just as they encouraged hijackings and terrorist acts, just as they encouraged and made plans to murder leaders of the Cuban revolution. After all the crimes the United States has committed against our country, it has no moral basis to look our country in the face.

Later on, the piracy turned against them, terrorism turned against them, and there you are: now, U.S. trained counterrevolutionary terrorists of Cuban origin want to govern the United States, they want to plant bombs in U.S. companies that might have relations with Cuba or in airline companies that might want to fly to Cuba. They bred ravens and now the ravens are plucking their eyes out!

In the same way, they promoted banditry and counterrevolution in our country. The counterrevolutionary *gusanos*, the counterrevolutionary delinquents, believed that some day the imperialists would get them out of jail, but the imperialists did not get them out of jail. We were the ones who, through rehabilitation programs of a voluntary nature and through remunerated work, through the really humane methods of the revolution, released thousands and thousands of counterrevolutionaries. Let's point out that of the counterrevolutionaries in prison twelve years ago, not even 20 percent remain! And there was a time when there were over 15,000. We admit it, yes.

Our revolution has always been very transparent and very clean. In our revolution, torture was never allowed; our revolution never committed crimes; in our revolution no one ever disappeared; in our country there never was a state of emergency, etc. No battalion was ever moved into the street here to battle against workers, peasants, or students. The people were always in the streets, yes, they were always in the streets, but with the revolution! [*Applause*]

U.S.-allied governments in this hemisphere have made thousands of persons vanish, they torture and murder, but that doesn't deter the United States from trading with them, giving them credits, selling them arms, and sending military advisers to them.

We had revolutionary laws and they were rigorous, but in this country no man has ever been punished without appearing before a court and in accordance with the dictates of revolutionary laws. In its methods and procedures, the conduct of our revolution has been irreproachable.

From time to time, U.S. politicians like to remember notorious counterrevolutionary prisoners. They're concerned about Cuban counterrevolutionary prisoners. However, they don't say a word about Puerto Ricans like Lolita Lebrón and others who have been imprisoned for more than twenty-five years in filthy U.S. jails. [*Applause*] They talk about counterrevolutionary prisoners who, instigated by the imperialists, committed crimes against our country, but they don't talk about the tens upon tens of thousands of Blacks who, plagued by unemployment and hunger, have landed in U.S. jails. They like to tell us that we must release Cuban counterrevolutionary prisoners. Our answer is this: all right, you free an equal number of U.S. Blacks who had to go to jail because of the regime of exploitation, the hunger, the poverty, the discrimination, and the unemployment that the United States reserves for a large part of the Black population, and we'll release all the counterrevolutionary prisoners who are left in Cuba. [*Applause*]

What do they mean by imposing conditions on anybody, by telling a country what to do or what not to do, they whose system of government has nothing to teach anyone? The curious thing is that many of those who are so concerned about those counterrevolutionaries were responsible for the war in Vietnam and for the murder of millions of Vietnamese, and they were the accomplices of dozens of repressive and reactionary governments in the world that have murdered hundreds of thousands of revolutionaries. On what moral basis can they talk about counterrevolutionary prisoners in Cuba? On what moral basis can they talk about human rights?

We are aware, educated revolutionaries, and therefore, we don't let ourselves be duped by empty words and ridiculous watchwords.

Carter talks about human rights. The supreme test of a minimum of sincerity of his words is the question of the blockade of Cuba. Can any government that maintains a criminal blockade, that attempts to starve millions of human beings to death, speak of human rights? Let him prove his assertions with facts. I repeat, the question of the blockade of Cuba is the test of a minimum of sincerity of his statements. Subjectively speaking, there may be a minimum of sincerity but, objectively speaking, there can't be in a political and social system like that of the United States.

How can a capitalist society par excellence, an exploiting society par excellence, a society where millions and millions of persons of Mexican descent are discriminated against, where Puerto Ricans who also number millions in the United States—are discriminated against and held in contempt, where Latin people are scorned, where the Indians were exterminated, where millions and millions of Blacks are discriminated against, talk about human rights? How can anyone in that country raise that flag on an objective footing?

Absolutely no one will confuse us with that kind of talk. The imperialists have nothing left, not even a message they can spread to the peoples of the world. The only thing they have left is empty words to see what gullible persons in the world they can deceive. Let's not talk nonsense.

If we speak to one another, we know that we have very different social regimes, that we are very different. If we are ever going to have relations, these relations must be based on mutual respect and equality, and we are ready to have them, knowing full well that we have and will continue to have two radically different regimes.

Aside from this, we learned what human rights are when we eradicated crimes and economic and social injustice committed every hour, minute, and second; when we eradicated gambling, prostitution, discrimination, begging, and unemployment; when we created the people's power, the true power of the people; when we laid the foundations of this beautiful revolution, in which there has been complete identification between the masses, the party, and its leadership. This indeed is democracy; this assembly, indeed, represents democracy; these discussions, indeed, are democratic. [*Applause*] What they have in the United States is a government of the oligarchy, by the oligarchy, and for the oligarchy, whereas our government is a government of the people, by the people, and for the people, the government Lincoln spoke of. In the United States they have a government of the bourgeoisie, by the bourgeoisie, and for the bourgeoisie, whereas in our country we have a government of the workers, by the workers, and for the workers. [*Applause*]

Regarding political matters, the United States would have much to learn from us. We, however, have nothing to learn, politically, from the United States. They belong to a class society, to the political prehistory of humanity, and we to the new history of humanity, for, as Marx stated, when the regime of exploitation of man by man disappears, the real history of human society will begin. [*Applause*]

We are, socially and politically, a century ahead of them.

That is the truth. Late in the eighteenth century they began to secure their independence, when we still were a Spanish colony. They began before we did, but we have advanced more quickly. Capitalist trash cannot be compared with the really human and really fraternal essence of socialism. [*Applause*] Imperialism is ideologically very weak and economically it is undergoing an insurmountable crisis.

A while ago I referred to what should be, in our opinion, our country's economic policy, the policy we should follow in the next seven or eight years. It should be a policy of development, of changing our structures, and not a policy for consumption. That's how we shall be building a secure future.

If the blockade goes on for ten more years, it doesn't matter. If the blockade continues for fifty years, it doesn't matter; it just doesn't matter. [*Applause*] The U.S. government should understand this very clearly, and when these things are sufficiently clear to the U.S. government and to its advisers, then we will have real and objective bases on which to discuss, negotiate, trade, and have diplomatic relations.

From the international viewpoint, these are the basic issues I wanted to put before you today.

Very soon our revolution will be nineteen years old. We have not been much inclined to solemn celebrations of great dates; we would have too many to commemorate. The triumph of the revolution was an extraordinary event, but we are in the habit of celebrating it without ceremony and in the innermost part of our conscience. On the eve of the nineteenth anniversary, we can feel proud and satisfied with the work of our revolution. [*Applause*] I have never contemplated the future with such clarity and optimism as on the eve of the nineteenth anniversary.

I wanted to share with you these feelings of satisfaction, pride, and optimism today, and I'm sure that we will continue to march ahead on the road we have determined, struggling bravely, with integrity, with heroism; consolidating what we have done and enhancing our revolutionary work so that future generations may be proud of us.

Patria o muerte!

Venceremos! [*Ovation*]

Interview with CBS

September 30, 1979

Interview with Dan Rather for CBS-TV's "Sixty Minutes." The text is from *Granma,* October 7, 1979.

DAN RATHER (CBS-TV): Mr. President, President Carter last Tuesday called you and Cuba a puppet of the Soviet Union. And last Friday you said President Carter was dishonest. Less than two years ago now, you said that President Carter was an ethical man.

Now, what's happened in these recent weeks to make you change your mind?

FIDEL CASTRO: I did say I had the impression that Carter was a man with a religious ethic, a Christian ethic.

My feeling is that on this specific issue we are discussing, Carter has not been honest; Carter has not been moral; Carter has not been sincere. That is what I am saying. I'm not going to pass final judgment on him. I'm referring to this specific issue.

It's true Carter made some statements recently, that he

called us puppets and things of that sort. A bit strange, because he had not used that sort of language in relation to Cuba before. Anyway, out of an elementary sense of dignity, I'm not going to answer that ridiculous charge.

What I will do is ask a question: Why, if we are a satellite, is so much attention paid to Cuba? It's clear that in the political sphere the U.S. government is practically paying more attention to Cuba than to the Soviet Union. Thus, we are clearly faced with a strange sort of satellite.

RATHER: Mr. President, regardless of who is right and who is wrong on the facts, when you describe a president of the United States as dishonest and the headline reads: "Castro says Carter is a liar...."

CASTRO: I didn't want to use the word liar. I spoke of dishonesty.

RATHER: You said dishonest, but the headline reads: "Castro says Carter is a liar...."

CASTRO: I didn't want to use that word.

RATHER: Dishonest. But regardless of who is right or wrong on the facts, when you describe a president of the United States as dishonest, are you not contributing to world tension? Taunting Mr. Carter that way?

CASTRO: That really was not my intention, nor do I desire such a thing. But how am I expected to describe the policy he has adopted towards Cuba on this issue? I have a way of seeing things, and I at least follow a principled line in politics. Now we are faced with a case in which a crisis has been created artificially and dishonest methods have been used. That's what I maintain.

RATHER: But you say it has been artificially created. President Carter's official spokesman said again, and in the past twenty-four hours, that this is not an artificial crisis. They say it's a real problem. That there's something new in Cuba. A Soviet combat brigade.

CASTRO: That is precisely where the falsehood lies. Do you understand?

I'm not going to argue, and I already said on Friday that I was not going to stoop to giving the United States explanations about the nature of our military installations. I'm not even going to explain if it's simply a case of advisers or if these advisers can fight or not. That's not the point since that isn't the main issue.

We are a sovereign country. The United States has no rights, privilege, or jurisdiction over Cuba. Cuba is not the property of the United States; Latin America is not the property of the United States. We consider ourselves to be a free country, and we have the right to think like a free country. If I were to stoop to giving an explanation about the nature of these military installations, I would be calling into question Cuba's right to adopt the defensive measures it deems necessary. Besides, we are no less than Japan, England, the FRG, no less than Spain or any other country which has felt it even has the right to station troops of another country on its soil for its defense. So I do not accept questioning Cuba's right to do likewise and I'm not going to give any explanations on that score.

That's not the problem, it really isn't. Why has the crisis been created? I have the following to say: That Soviet military personnel, which the U.S. government calls a brigade and we call Training Center Number 12, is a military installation which has been in Cuba for seventeen years—seventeen years! Their number and nature are similar to what they were seventeen years ago. This installation was set up after the October Crisis, in keeping with the spirit of the solution of the October Crisis and in line with the status quo created during the October Crisis. That is, it isn't anything new.

RATHER: This is October 1962?

CASTRO: October 1962. Seventeen years ago.

RATHER: Has there been any change in the nature of the Soviet troops in this country since that time?

CASTRO: There has been no change in the nature nor in the functions of the Soviet personnel in Cuba in the last seventeen years. That is the key to the matter.

Kennedy, Johnson, Nixon, and Ford were perfectly aware of the existence of this installation, and Carter had to know about it. It's impossible for them to have been unaware of it given that it's an installation which has existed for seventeen years in a country over which they have carried out hundreds of flights, where they have sent hundreds of espionage agents, a country in which the United States has used all its electronic means to discover what's going on. Who do they think is going to believe that they were unaware of the existence of this installation for seventeen years? Who do they expect to believe this? That's why I challenge Carter to explain the truth to the people of the United States and to world opinion and to say since when this alleged brigade has been here. Since when? He should say if it was set up under his own administration, during the Ford administration in 1976, during the Nixon administration in 1970, during the Johnson administration in 1965, or whether it has been here since October 1962. I think this is the key to the matter, and this is where the falsehood lies; in trying to make world opinion and U.S. opinion believe that the Soviet Union and Cuba have taken steps of a military nature to create a problem and create a crisis. That is the key to the issue.

RATHER: I agree that that's the key, and I can assure you that I believe President Carter tomorrow night is going to say to the American people that the nature of the Soviet presence in Cuba has changed. That for the first time in his knowledge there is a Soviet combat brigade in Cuba—not a training brigade, but a combat brigade.

CASTRO: Well, if President Carter says tomorrow that there has been a change in the number, nature, or functions of the Soviet military personnel in Cuba since 1962, he will be telling a big lie to U.S. public opinion and to world opinion. Because I assert that there has been no change in their number, nature, or functions in the last seventeen years.

RATHER: Mr. President, we have only a limited amount of time and I want to quickly move on. There are reports circulating in Washington tonight about possible American military movements, strengthening U.S. forces in Key West, Puerto Rico, even sending a contingent of U.S. marines to Guantánamo, and the possibility of sending a U.S. aircraft carrier to the Caribbean Sea. This may be what President Carter will announce tomorrow night. Now, do you have any intelligence information indicating this is true?

CASTRO: My information is what has appeared in newspapers, in dispatches. We haven't detected military movements with our means for some time.

RATHER: What is your reaction to that kind of attitude?

CASTRO: First of all, I think that what the United States should do, what Carter should do, is not create a crisis with no legal basis—with no legal basis!—and with no moral basis. I think the only thing the U.S. government should do is refrain from doing that, refrain from doing it because it means heading for conflicts and crises.

I think it would be much more constructive for Carter to announce the contrary: the willingness of the U.S. government to respect Cuba's sovereign rights; to end the economic blockade, which includes medicine, that it has maintained for twenty years; and to express its willingness to dismantle the Guantánamo base and withdraw its ships and troops from our waters and territory.

Now, what's our reaction? We aren't frightened by any of this, we aren't intimidated. We've been subjected to this hostility on the United States' part for twenty years. They're going to send soldiers to Puerto Rico? I don't think Puerto Ricans will like that. They're going to send soldiers to Key West? The tourists won't like that. They're going to send soldiers to Guantánamo? That will cost U.S. taxpayers more money. None of that will affect us; we won't let ourselves be intimidated and we aren't going to get nervous about the situation.

RATHER: Mr. President, if President Carter should suggest a meeting with you, are you willing to agree?

CASTRO: I wouldn't propose it; but if he were to propose it, I wouldn't have any objection to coming in contact with President Carter or with someone he designated, if he thought it appropriate. We wouldn't reject such a proposal.

RATHER: And the same would apply if Secretary of State Vance were willing to meet with your foreign minister?

CASTRO: We wouldn't object to that either. They've met with top Cuban officials on other occasions.

RATHER: But not on this subject.

CASTRO: No, not on this issue.

RATHER: Mr. President, do you plan to go to the United Nations before the end of this year?

CASTRO: It's possible, but a final decision has not been made yet.

RATHER: Mr. President, I want to make very clear: you have flatly denied that there is a Soviet combat brigade in Cuba?

CASTRO: I'm not denying that there are Soviet military personnel in our country. What I'm saying is that it is exactly the same personnel, organized in the same way, as seventeen years ago. That is what I'm stating clearly and categorically. You call that Soviet personnel, or part of that Soviet personnel, a brigade and we call it a training center.

RATHER: Mr. President, how is the situation right now different from the October Crisis of 1962, if it is different?

CASTRO: It's different in every sense.

First, during the 1962 crisis there was a real and objective danger of nuclear conflict: and that's not the case now.

The October Crisis was a real crisis; this is a fabricated crisis. The October Crisis could have been a tragedy; this is a comedy.

Now then, during the October Crisis there were dozens of nuclear missiles here; there were more than forty thousand Soviet soldiers in Cuba, there were squadrons of IL-28 bombers. That's not the case now.

When a settlement of the October Crisis was reached, an agreement between the USSR and the United States—an agreement in which we did not participate and therefore to which we do not feel committed—when that agreement was reached, by virtue of which the Soviet Union decided to withdraw all those weapons in exchange for a guarantee that Cuba would not be invaded, the situation was different from what it is now. None of these problems exist now.

When Kennedy reached those agreements with Khrushchev, he was satisfied with the withdrawal of those weapons. It isn't that he was right or that he had any right! Those are two different things. We didn't agree then, but it was a different problem: there was a real threat to peace at that time. Kennedy was satisfied, Kennedy wasn't concerned about the 2,000 or 3,000 Soviet military personnel left behind. Do you understand? He didn't attach any importance to that.

I ask myself why Carter has revived the issue, why he has created a crisis. Why has Carter staged this comedy over 2,000 or 3,000 Soviet military personnel in Cuba? I want him to explain why, if Kennedy didn't do so, nor Johnson, nor Nixon, nor Ford, why has Carter done so? How can he explain this? What's the reason? What's the justification?

He won't get the people of the United States to believe that no U.S. president was aware of this. That's like saying that the CIA doesn't exist, that the government of the United States is absolutely misinformed about all problems.

There are two factors that explain this. First, the attempt to sabotage the Sixth [Nonaligned] Summit. Second, the effort to improve Carter's image and overcome the problems he is facing to be reelected. That, in my opinion, is the only explanation of why Carter has created this problem.

RATHER: Mr. President, our twenty minutes are up. I want to pause for one second. I have tried to stay within the time limit and finish this part, but I am so interested in what you are saying that I wonder if you could give us a few more minutes.

CASTRO: Yes, with pleasure.

RATHER: Thank you. Mr. President, if you ask the Soviet troops to leave Cuba—all the troops—would they leave?

CASTRO: You talk of troops, I speak of Soviet military personnel. You speak of brigades and I of a training center, of a military installation.

Now that I've made this point, what is your question?

RATHER: If you asked all the Russians on this island to leave—whatever you want to call them, military trainers—if you asked them to leave, would they leave?

CASTRO: Of course, there's no doubt about it.

RATHER: You see, so many people in the United States question that.

CASTRO: But why?

RATHER: For one thing, President Carter has said that it isn't true, that you're a Soviet puppet, a satellite.

CASTRO: And in order to prove we're not we have to ask the Soviet personnel to leave?

I think this is absurd. That statement is completely absurd. We have no intention of asking the Soviet personnel to leave Cuba, but it would be absurd to think that if we were to ask them to leave, they would want to stay.

That's absurd. That's inconceivable.

RATHER: Let me ask you a question about what I'm sure is perhaps . . .

CASTRO: What I am sure of though, is that we have told the U.S. forces to leave Guantánamo and they haven't. They are the only ones who are capable of staying in the territory of another country against the will of the people.

RATHER: Let me ask you a question I believe is possibly the most asked question about Cuba in the United States. What is Fidel Castro doing in Africa if he isn't just being a mercenary army for the Soviets?

CASTRO: Mercenary armies never defend a just cause. The causes we have defended all over the world have been just causes.

You can ask the Africans, the Angolans, the Ethiopians, and the fighters in Namibia and Zimbabwe; you can ask all the really progressive and honorable movements.

You can ask the most prestigious governments in Africa; they can answer that question.

RATHER: Are you doing the Soviets' work in Africa, or your own?

CASTRO: Do I have to answer that question?

Twenty years ago we had relations with the MPLA, with the African revolutionary movements. How can we do the work of others?

Besides, it is repugnant to me to stoop to answering that.

When I explain what our policy is, the peoples we have helped understand and acknowledge it.

The Sixth Summit and the tremendous support our country received at the Sixth Summit is the clearest indication that the peoples know that Cuba has its own policy.

RATHER: Separate from the Soviet Union?

CASTRO: At times we coincide. We don't always coincide.

RATHER: Can you think of a time when you've not coincided with Soviet policy?

CASTRO: I gave an example, the October Crisis in 1962.

RATHER: Another question. This is a quote from a newspaper. I quote: "The Soviets have assumed that the presence of their troops in Cuba will discourage the United States from stopping any of Fidel Castro's military adventures in this hemisphere."

CASTRO: And what are Fidel Castro's adventures in Latin America?

RATHER: Nicaragua.

CASTRO: What is it that makes Nicaragua Castro's adventure? It was an adventure of the United States. It was the United States that intervened in Nicaragua, that set up the National Guard and installed Somoza in power and kept him there for over forty years. It was the United States' big adventure, not Cuba's.

It wasn't Cuba nor was it Cuban soldiers that overthrew the government of Nicaragua, that is, the Somoza dictatorship. It was the Sandinistas, the people of Nicaragua. And the United States itself recognizes this: President Carter recently met with representatives of the Nicaraguan government.

RATHER: Were you the principal arms supplier for the Nicaraguan rebels?

CASTRO: There is absolutely no proof of that. But I have no intention of answering that question.

RATHER: You asked what are Fidel Castro's adventures in the Western Hemisphere referred to here. El Salvador?

CASTRO: I ask myself what they are referring to. What's happening in El Salvador? There is a corrupt, tyrannical, genocidal government, and the people are no longer willing to tolerate the regime. Why must we be blamed for that?

RATHER: Because you were training the people, you are supplying the arms, the money . . .

CASTRO: I think that the United States is the one that has trained all those armies—the one in Chile that murders the people, the one in Uruguay that has killed thousands of Uruguayans, Somoza's army, and that of El Salvador—the United States has trained and equipped all the genocidal governments in this hemisphere, not Cuba.

If we were to help the revolutionaries we would have the right to do so, but I'm not going to say here that we are doing so.

That is our affair and not a matter to be discussed on television.

RATHER: But you don't deny it?

CASTRO: I neither confirm it nor deny it. I proclaim it as a right; furthermore, as a duty.

RATHER: So many Americans—set aside the government—not President Carter, not Mr. Brzezinski, but American people, rank-and-file people, believe, many of them believe, that Cuba is a nuclear pistol pointed at their heads.

CASTRO: A nuclear pistol?

RATHER: Pointed at their heads.

CASTRO: I think the people of the United States are too intelligent to believe such a thing. Who could have convinced the people to believe such a thing?

We have no nuclear weapons. I said that on Friday. It's not that we don't have the right to; we don't relinquish that right. We'll relinquish that right when all countries of the world renounce nuclear weapons.

But the only country that could supply us with nuclear weapons is the Soviet Union, and on this issue the Soviet Union worked out an agreement with the United States. As a result, we have no possibility of having nuclear weapons.

RATHER: Within the last week a United States senator, at least one, and I think more than one, Senator Helms of North Carolina, said that he had evidence that Soviet MIG-23s in Cuba were going to be equipped with nuclear devices. Are there any Soviet nuclear weapons on this island?

CASTRO: Let me say the following: I've already made a statement on this, and I said that we didn't have any nuclear weapons. Furthermore, everyone knows this.

As for that senator, I think the best thing his constituents could do is not vote for him again, because he is simply a big liar.

RATHER: Now you used the word "liar."

CASTRO: Yes.

RATHER: In regards to him?

CASTRO: Exactly.

RATHER: I'll give you a chance to withdraw that.

CASTRO: What?

RATHER: Do you want to retract that?

CASTRO: No, no, I don't retract the statement.

RATHER: Mr. Brzezinski, as you know, is President Carter's National Security Council adviser. Mr. Brzezinski has said this weekend that the problem of what he calls the Soviet combat brigade is a political problem similar to the problem of the Berlin Wall. Now, is that true? For the United States he says it's the same kind of problem.

CASTRO: Well, I think Brzezinski says a lot of foolish things. I don't understand what has come over U.S. presidents. They always have some brain behind them. Nixon had Kissinger, Ford had Kissinger, and when everyone was hoping that these powers behind the throne would disappear, Carter chose Brzezinski. There is always some sinister type behind the throne in the United States, someone who is believed to be very intelligent, very wise.

Now, I really think that Brzezinski is one of the most erratic and stupid advisers in the U.S. government. I think he is precisely the person who is responsible for the present situation. I say this because in the United States and in the U.S. government there are realistic people, honest people, and intelligent people.

But it is Brzezinski who has set the style for this problem and other problems having to do with Cuba and with questions of world peace. He is very dangerous for world peace.

RATHER: Mr. President, you have been very generous with your time. And let me ask you one last question: Is there any question that I should have asked you that I didn't ask you?

CASTRO: There may be quite a few, but I won't choose any right now.

I wanted to ask—I'm the one who would like to ask a question—would President Carter be willing to have a journalist from Cuban television interview him? To allow for some parity in the situation, so that he could answer our journalists' questions.

In any case I would like to thank you and U.S. television for this opportunity to address the people of the United States. And likewise, if Carter should so desire, we will put all the television channels in Cuba at his disposal so that he can say whatever he wants to the Cuban people.

RATHER: First of all, I appreciate your kindness to us. As you know I can't speak for President Carter. I can only say that I will assure you I will make him aware of your offer. Thank you for your time today. Thank you.

Speech to the fighting people
May 1, 1980

Speech given to Havana rally of 1.5 million people. The text is from *Granma*, May 11, 1980.

Compatriots:

I know you've been standing in this square for a long time. [*Shouts of "No!"*] I ask you to be patient a little longer. [*Applause and shouts of "Fidel, our friend, we're with you to the end!"*]

Well then, let's have another show of discipline. Let's keep quiet.

I was saying—or trying to say—that on the way to this meeting this afternoon, I could see once again the incredible sight of absolutely empty streets. How could I have imagined the size of this meeting? I thought it would be very big. I thought it would be the biggest in all the twenty-one years of the revolution; but it was really impossible to imagine its magnitude. Perhaps only from the tower here, or from the air; perhaps only graphically—in the movies, on television, or in a photograph—can you really appreciate the size of this meeting. [*Shouts of "The people love you!" and applause*]

I don't say this or view it in terms of its significance as support for me. I say it and view it in terms of its significance as support for our noble and true revolutionary ideas, for our revolutionary cause. [*Applause*]

It was a question of showing our strength, but not just for the show. We have been waging a mass battle whose scope and depth is unique in the annals of the revolution. The reasons for it are known. This had to be done. [*Applause and shouts of "Good riddance, good riddance!" and "Down with the gusanos!"*] The enemy had to be shown, the enemy had to be taught that he couldn't mess with the people. [*Shouts of "No messing!" and applause*] The enemy had to be shown that he couldn't mess with the revolution. [*Applause and shouts*] The enemy had to be shown that he couldn't offend the people with impunity; [*Applause and shouts of "No!"*] that he couldn't threaten the people with impunity. [*Shouts of "No!"*] And this image we see here is what they dreamed of destroying; the image of the people—the real, revolutionary people—the proletariat, the farmers, the students—the fighting people! [*Applause and shouts of "The people united will never be defeated!"*]

Perhaps they thought the revolution had weakened; [*Shouts of "No!"*] but look what a "weak" revolution they've found! [*Shouts of "No!" and "Good riddance!"*] Just look at the kind of revolution they've found! That's why this battle had to be waged.

As you know, in the last few months our party and people have been fighting tenaciously and unselfishly to raise standards, eliminate inefficiencies, and overcome difficulties; this important work has been progressing quietly, consistently, for months. You could say that our revolution, our people, and our party have all been dedicated to this task and to productive work—especially in the sugar harvest and the new planting; confronting the problems of blights in tobacco and sugarcane and swine fever and which mysteriously—mysteriously!—appeared almost simultaneously in our country; confronting various problems in our revolutionary process; struggling for development; trying—within our material possibilities—to advance; and preparing for our party congress. This is what we were doing.

Why did this situation arise? It didn't just happen by chance. Every time they've messed with us before, they've come out on the short end of the stick; every time they've provoked us, they've been the losers. And this time is no different.

You know the facts; if foreign journalists weren't present, it wouldn't be necessary to go into the background. The situation was escalated by the acts of provocation at the Peruvian and Venezuelan embassies.

The whole world knows that for a long time now, imperialism has been using various schemes to try to damage the relations between Cuba and Venezuela and between Cuba and Peru.

We can't forget that it was in Venezuela, with the participation of Venezuelans, that the monstrous crime of Barbados—one of the most outrageous events in the entire revolutionary period—was planned, prepared, and executed. We all know that the perpetrators still haven't been convicted and it's even claimed they're going to be released, because, some of them have long-time relations with the ruling party in Venezuela.

We can't forget that the Peruvian navy—we know it was the navy, and I don't think they'll contest it—that agents of that country's navy sank two of our fishing boats, the

Río Jobabo and the *Río Damují*. That was an incredible act of provocation. Nor can we forget that the fishing agreement between Cuba and Peru—which had been working perfectly well for some time and was useful, very useful, to the Peruvians, because it helped produce food for them, and also helped produce food for us—was unilaterally cancelled at the behest of the navy, in a scheme to introduce private agreements whereby an individual became a millionaire overnight, just by signing his name. Nor can we forget that the Peruvian government failed to fulfill the contract it had with us to build twenty tuna-fishing ships, a contract that led our country to spend tens of millions of dollars on a fish-processing plant. When the contract wasn't honored and the tuna-fishing ships weren't built, we were left with the processing plant and no boats.

There's a history and a background to all this. Naturally, these matters led to a cooling off of the warm, close relations we had had with the revolutionary government of Velasco Alvarado,* [*Applause*] relations that were established during those difficult days of the earthquake in Peru, when our people responded to an appeal from the revolution and—even though the two countries had no diplomatic relations—made a hundred thousand blood donations for Peru in ten days, and our doctors, nurses, and construction workers, all our people, volunteered to help the fraternal people of Peru. [*Applause*] The "fraternal people of Peru," yes, because we refer and will always refer to the people of Peru and the people of Venezuela as fraternal peoples. [*Applause*]

We willingly donated our blood to the people, because

---

* Gen. Juan Velasco Alvarado was president of Peru, 1968–75. Although his regime nationalized Peru's oilfields and instituted some reforms, it continued to defend capitalist rule.

the people are the ones who usually die in these catastrophes. It's their houses that fall; the houses of the rich, of the bourgeoisie, are earthquake-proof. If we had to do the same thing again for the Peruvian people, we would do it—just as we would again donate a part of our rationed sugar to Chile if circumstances there made it necessary for us to do so. Just yesterday Laura Allende recalled those circumstances in her beautiful letter.

These are our people; the people who are here; these workers and soldiers; [*Applause*] the internationalists who took part in glorious battles in Angola and Ethiopia; the people whose armed forces have more than 100,000 internationalist soldiers (active and reserve) in their ranks; [*Applause*] the people who, when asked to send teachers to Nicaragua, came forth with 29,500 volunteers. These are the people, not the lumpen, not the scum that went into the Peruvian embassy—as they would try to make it seem. [*Applause and shouts of "Good riddance!" "Down with the scum!" "Good riddance to all those who don't want to work!" "Down with the gusanos!"*] That was what most offended the people.

Some dust here and there became a pile of dirt; a few light breezes blew up into storms. And then a strange thing occurred, something that had never happened in any other embassy. Thugs, criminals, and lumpen went there who, if they had peaceably asked for visas would have been denied them out of hand. They would have been refused. But when they forced their way in by driving a truck or a bus into the gate were received with honor, supported, sheltered, given free passage, and welcomed as heroes. That couldn't fail to incite lumpen; it couldn't have any other result.

It didn't do us any good to be patient for years, explaining that this wasn't right, that it was going to have negative results, that it was going to encourage violence against diplomatic missions, that such a policy should not be pursued. Time and again, we solved their problems when they said they didn't want to live with that kind of people inside their embassies. Of course, we could have told them all along: "Let them stay there forever." However, since they said they didn't want to live with such people, when problems arose, we authorized their departure. We did it on numerous occasions, and what we predicted always happened: as soon as one group left, another entered. That's how it went.

Why did they go to the Venezuelan and Peruvian embassies? Why didn't the same thing happen at the Mexican embassy, for example, or the Guyanese or Panamanian or Jamaican embassies—not to mention the Nicaraguan and Grenadian embassies, since not even a madman would think of crashing them in a tank or a truck? Simply because the lumpen know the governments almost as well as we do; they know that Mexico has a friendly attitude toward Cuba and wouldn't stand for such riffraff or irregularities; they know that Panama, Guyana, and Jamaica wouldn't stand for it either. Why did these things happen specifically at the Venezuelan and Peruvian embassies?

It is apparent that behind all this—the monstrous crime of Barbados, the sinking of the fishing ships in Peru, the cancellation of the fishing agreement, the breaking of the contract for the twenty tuna-fishing ships—behind all these acts of provocation was the CIA.

Then came the killing of embassy guard Ortiz Cabrera,* [*Applause*] and that's where we lost our patience. That

---

* Pedro Ortiz Cabrera, a twenty-seven-year-old policeman guarding the Peruvian embassy, was killed April 1, 1980, by a group of Cubans seeking entry in order to leave the country.

was when we couldn't stand for any more and decided that no matter what the price—understand this clearly: no matter what the price—we had to put an end to these acts of provocation. And when the revolution says it is ready to put an end to something no matter what the price, everyone can be sure it will be done. [*Applause and shouts of "For sure!"*]

We simply withdrew our guards from the embassy, knowing what would happen. Imperialism and its lackeys couldn't continue encouraging the lumpen for so long, promising them streets paved with gold, paradise, everything, filling them with illusions, while at the same time not letting them into their countries. It's a strange thing: they encourage them to enter forcibly, to leave illegally; but they don't let them in if they request a visa in a normal, peaceful way.

We knew that when the guard was withdrawn, when the lumpen learned there was no guard, the embassy would be filled with lumpen—and that's just what happened. You might say that the lumpen did what they were expected to do.

Then provisional custody had to be restored—and the custody of that embassy is provisional. I want to make this clear, because we still haven't decided what to do with those who enter embassies by force. [*Shouts of "Withdraw the guard!"*] The withdrawal of the embassy guard isn't very important now, because we've withdrawn the custody over the Florida peninsula, which is much bigger. [*Applause*] We've had to withdraw the guard from the peninsula of Florida, and now they have an easier way to go to the United States. [*Applause*]

Through the bourgeois and right-wing press in this hemisphere and in the world, imperialism immediately used this problem to launch a propaganda campaign to slander Cuba. We expected this. However, this battle is being won and is going to be won completely, because we are defying not only Yankee military threats but also the imperialist news monopolies; we are defying their barrage, their campaign, with absolute calm.

If we aren't prepared to defy all dangers—both of military aggression and of propaganda—we can't respond adequately to the enemy; if we are intimidated by propaganda, it's like being intimidated by enemy guns. It's the same thing. There's nothing to be afraid of: we've learned this very well in twenty-one years.

Our enemies launched this international campaign with the idea that the people wanted to leave, that there were lots of dissidents. That, in particular, was the idea: dissidents. Some of the lumpen in that embassy—as you could see in the documentary film—don't even understand what the word *dissident* means. [*Laughter*]

They orchestrated their campaign around this, naturally, using the imperialist, reactionary, right-wing press of the hemisphere and the world that is directed against socialism, communism, and the Cuban revolution.

Meanwhile, the Yankees had been doing exactly what was being done in the Venezuelan and Peruvian embassies. In recent months, illegal departures from Cuba had increased. Individuals hijacked boats, often taking their crews along as hostages, and were welcomed in Florida as heroes, dissidents, patriots, etc. We warned them—repeatedly—through diplomatic channels. We also warned them publicly, because I spoke of this on March 8 [1980], International Women's Day, in the final session of the [Federation of Cuban] Women's congress. We used every means to warn them of the consequences this could have and of the fact that Camarioca could be reopened.

On March 8, the revolution's past, present, and future

policy was outlined: we set forth the ideas of the revolution, including one of our basic concepts: that the work of a revolution and the building of socialism were tasks for free men and women acting completely voluntarily. [*Applause*] In our country, we don't need those who don't have revolutionary genes, revolutionary blood, minds adapted to the idea of a revolution, and hearts adapted to the effort and heroism of a revolution. [*Shouts of "Good riddance!"*] After all, those who lack these qualities are an insignificant part of the people. There are certain truths that the imperialists try to hide, because it hurts them to admit them—for example, the fact that no other revolution has the militant mass strength of the Cuban revolution. [*Applause*]

It isn't a good idea and it's never pleasant to make comparisons, but certainly the mass strength, the moral, political, and ideological strength of the revolution is tremendous; and, when it's put to the test, you get the people's march of April 19 and this rally today—measured not only by the numbers of people but also, basically, by their quality and spirit. [*Applause and shouts of "Good riddance to the scum, Fidel!"*]

This is the image imperialism tries to hide, because it doesn't suit its purposes. It wants to make people lose faith in Cuba and be discouraged by its example. Yet, in the entire hemisphere—we'll leave out Nicaragua and Grenada, but they might agree—in spite of everything, in spite of the fact that, unfortunately, we still have lumpen and some declassed and other antisocial elements, we have fewer of them than any other country in the American hemisphere; we have fewer robberies—although there are thieves—a lower crime rate; almost no drugs; no prostitution; a strict ban on gambling. The Nicaraguans and Grenadians haven't yet been able to overcome these problems, and it will take them some time to do so; we weren't able to manage this, either, in the first or second years of the revolution.

No society in the entire hemisphere has a healthier moral atmosphere than ours; [*Applause*] no society has higher moral values than those our society has achieved in the twenty-one years of the revolution; a sense of justice; honor; dignity; regard and admiration for merit, work, and self-sacrifice. This is shown every time it's put to the test. And, as I've said on other occasions, at the time of the wars in Ethiopia and Angola, hundreds of thousands of Cubans volunteered to participate in those struggles. It is shown by the fact that fifty thousand of our compatriots—military personnel and civilians—are working abroad; it is shown by the fact that Cuban technicians are working in thirty-five countries. [*Applause*]

Imperialism has no allies here. At the beginning, it had the bourgeoisie, the landowners, it had the vacillating elements of the middle class including among the petty bourgeoisie; now, however, where can it find allies? Among the workers? [*Shouts of "No!"*] Among the farmers? [*Shouts of "No!"*] Among the students? [*Shouts of "No!"*] Among our honest manual and intellectual workers? [*Shouts of "No!"*] No. At first, it sought out those classes because they existed as exploiting classes in our country and were its natural allies. Now, only the lumpen remain; they and those few who have a lumpen mentality or are like lumpen, are the only potential allies of imperialism, that's all. They are the only potential allies imperialism has—and, therefore, the group in which it had to start dreaming up refugees, asylum seekers, and dissidents.

As I said, along with this, the United States was encouraging illegal departures from the country, which is the basic reason why the port of Mariel was opened up—Mariel, which is a considerable improvement over Camarioca. Camarioca was nothing compared to Mariel. [*Someone shouts "From Mariel to the Florida shore, we have opened a festering sore!"*] You say, "From Mariel to the Florida shore, we have opened a festering sore!" [*Laughter*] Look though, it was a self-inflicted sore, and I'm going to explain why.

The strange thing is that, this time, we weren't the ones who took the initiative in opening Mariel; no, the initiative was taken over there. As a result of the situation and of the campaign launched inside the United States about what was happening in the Peruvian embassy, the idea of sending boats to pick the lumpen up arose spontaneously in Florida. Then all we had to do was tell them that we wouldn't shoot at them because they weren't coming to make war, and that we would show them every courtesy. So that's how this thing, which might be described as a self-inflicted sore, hara-kiri, or whatever, was opened. Now let's see how it closes, how it can be closed down; [*Laughter*] this is what we have to see now. They're performing a tremendous sanitary service, [*Laughter*] tremendous. And now they're complaining.

They say there are criminals—as if it were a sudden discovery, as if they were astounded that they should find some criminals. Who did they think went to the Peruvian embassy? Did they think they were intellectuals, artists, technicians, engineers? Who did they think took haven in the Peruvian embassy? They thought it was propaganda on our part, thought we were being unfair in calling their "poor little dissidents" lumpen—but that was what most of those who went to the Peruvian embassy were. Of course, some of them took their families; we aren't going to call a child a lumpen. It's a shame when a child has lumpen parents; it's a terrible shame. But the vast majority of the people there were just that: lumpen.

A few weaklings, as someone said, [*Laughter*] a few hypocrites—but you know them; the committees know them very well, better than anyone. They know that some of those people slipped in, too—and, of course, these who pretend are the most irritating.

In any case, Mariel was opened, and we were rigorously, strictly complying with our watchword that anyone who wanted to go to any other country that would accept them could do so [*Shouts of "Good riddance!"*] and that the building of socialism, the work of the revolution, was a task for free men and women. Don't forget this principle; don't forget this principle; which has tremendous moral value. [*Applause*]

We didn't limit safe conducts and passports to the lumpen who went to the embassy; no. All the lumpen who requested them got exit papers. Of course, now the lumpen say, "This is International Lumpen Day." [*Laughter*] When they heard that, many of the lumpen wanted passports and safe conducts. What could we do? Why should we refuse? As *Granma* put it, "That would be unjust and unconstitutional."

What do they think they're going to get there? Of course, at the beginning, ah! they took the refined bourgeoisie, the well-dressed landowners. Then they took the doctors and other professionals. Remember, they took half of all the doctors we had at that time: we had 6,000, and they took 3,000. Now it's very hard for them to get a doctor, very hard, because our doctors have a different quality. In the first place, the ones who stayed here were the best. Then there are the doctors who are trained in a different spirit of solidarity and humanity, doctors who are not commercialized. And we have quite a few. The fact that some 1,500 doctors are now on internationalist missions shows this. Our engineers, architects, and teachers are no longer the same kind that existed at the beginning of the revolution. [*Applause*]

It must be said that this battle has had many interesting aspects. I might begin by mentioning the incredible participation of the youth, the militancy and enthusiasm of our young people, because this has been the first great battle for a whole generation of young people. [*Applause*] The massive participation of women has also been notable, as has the attitude of our intellectuals, our intellectual workers—journalists, writers, artists, technicians, doctors, and other professionals. They've maintained a magnificent attitude. Our intellectual workers have also been in the front line in this battle, along with the students.

Of course, imperialism used to make a selection. Well, how is it going to select now? As Nuez* says, they have no alternative but to swallow the sword right down to the hilt. [*Shouts*] That's the situation.

But this wasn't the whole problem—only a part of it. Coinciding with this and the great campaign, there was the announcement of military maneuvers in the Caribbean—which was more serious—with air and sea landings at the Guantánamo base. This was more serious, much more serious, especially in view of the world situation: more serious if we analyze imperialism's ever more aggressive policy toward us.

In the early days of the present administration some things occurred that could be considered positive, but later on the more reactionary elements, the "hawks" in the U.S. government, started calling the shots, imposing a line that was ever more aggressive against Cuba.

This didn't begin just now; it began at the time of the Sixth Summit Conference of Nonaligned Countries. The

---

* René de la Nuez is a well-known Cuban political cartoonist.

United States was irritated by Cuba's strength and prestige, by Cuba's positions and its victories in the Movement of Nonaligned Countries. In the midst of the summit conference, it unleashed that monstrous, hypocritical campaign about the Soviet personnel in Cuba—the same number of Soviet military personnel that had been in Cuba for seventeen years, since the October Crisis, which had nothing to do with the October Crisis agreements: Soviet military personnel. The Yankees knew this; they knew it. They'd known it ever since then; all their presidents knew it, but suddenly they "discovered" the Soviet military personnel. They said it was a brigade. We didn't feel like calling it a brigade; we called it something else—I think it was called Training Center Number 12. It doesn't matter; the name isn't important. We don't deny that this personnel was here; they are here, and we are very happy that they have been here for seventeen years. We're just sorry that there aren't more training centers, that there isn't a Center 13, a Center 14, a Center 15! [*Applause*] We would be even more pleased if we had several more study centers of this kind, because they are magnificent study centers. Let's make this clear.

They knew this. That shows imperialism's self-righteous hypocrisy. In the midst of the conference, however, it kicked up a big ruckus about this, launching a huge campaign—that then boomeranged against the prestige of the U.S. government, because the "discovery" at this late date forced it to take some measures.

Simultaneously with this—simultaneously, and using it as a pretext—it set up a troop command for the Caribbean over there in Florida, in Key West, and established a multiforce operational command.

Its main concern was over the revolutionary triumph in Nicaragua and the growing upsurge in the revolutionary movement in Central America. It began to prepare a mechanism for intervention. Naturally, it used the pretext of the Soviet military personnel in Cuba to pressure and threaten Cuba, and it carried out small-scale maneuvers at the Guantánamo base at the end of last year. These maneuvers, however, are much larger, on a much greater scale, with more equipment and more soldiers—and something strange about them. And we said, No, no, no; this cannot be. We are not going to sit by passively while the Yankees organize maneuvers like that.

As has already been said, they are a flagrant rehearsal for an invasion of our country, a shameless invasion rehearsal on our own soil. This, really, is what is intolerable, unacceptable: maneuvers for invading Cuba—held on our own soil.

The maneuvers became a serious problem, and we weren't about to sit by with arms crossed. Measures were immediately taken to mobilize the Eastern Army and, with reinforcements from other provinces, to hold maneuvers of the Cuban armed forces to confront the Yankee maneuvers. [*Applause and shouts of "For sure, Fidel, give the Yankees hell!"*]

It was only logical that the hurricane should double back on the United States, and that is exactly what it did.

The United States has imposed a blockade against Cuba for more than twenty years, a tight economic blockade that even prohibits the sale of foodstuffs and medicines—even medicines! It has been a brutal thing, for twenty-one years.

The United States occupies a part of our territory by means of force, against the will of our people. What doctrine, what principles, what law, and what legality justify its maintenance of a naval base in the territory of another country, against the will of its people? This has no legal, juridical, or moral basis, absolutely no basis in principles; it is simply an act of force.

The United States sends modern SR-71 planes over Cuba's territory. They fly between 25,000 and 30,000 meters up, at very high speeds. They are what cause those unusual explosions that can be heard every so often throughout our country, as they break the sound barrier, shaking the walls, the glass, and the windows whenever they fly past. [*Someone shouts "Shoot them down!"*] It isn't easy to bring down an SR-71; it isn't very easy, technically.

Now, is it legal for them to do that? Is it legal to blockade our country? Is it legal to have a naval base on our soil? Is it legal to violate our airspace? [*Shouts of "No!"*] They do these things. And then, there are the maneuvers.

And that isn't all imperialism has done over the years. Many of the comrades who have spoken here have mentioned it and also referred to *La Coubre*, Playa Girón, the Escambray,* the acts of sabotage, the plans for subversion, the attempts to introduce and the introduction of agricultural blights, the plans to assassinate the leaders of the revolution, the sabotage of the Cubana plane off Barbados—many things, not just the maneuvers, as the United States should realize.

We didn't turn the hurricane that began with the Peruvian embassy toward the United States out of any caprice; rather, the natural course of that hurricane was toward the United States, just as the natural course of the struggle against those violations and that blackmail was to lift exit restrictions by sea and withdraw our custody over Florida. That was the natural course of events, and it must

---

* *La Coubre,* a French merchant ship carrying ammunition from Belgium, was blown up in Havana Harbor in March 1960, killing 100; CIA involvement has long been suspected. In the early 1960s, the CIA supported armed counterrevolutionary bands in the Escambray mountains of central Cuba.

not have been so surprising for them, because they knew this was going to happen. As I said, formally, we weren't the ones who opened up Mariel; Mariel was opened up from over there, and we don't have any policemen over there. That's their affair, their job, over there—if nobody wants to obey their orders, that's their headache. We, however, have a legal right to do what we want within our own territory, and we may authorize the exit of all those antisocial elements who wish to leave. We aren't forcing anyone to go, not anyone at all! Let's make that clear. We have never deported anyone! Ah, but we have the right to authorize the exit of the antisocial elements, and this is what we are doing. And this battle is getting very interesting.

Today, this morning, dispatches and news items began coming in to the effect that the Yankees had suspended the naval landing at Guantánamo. Listen to this. One U.S. radio station even said early this morning that the naval operation—but not the air one—had been suspended. By this afternoon, we had the official report, and it was confirmed by both the U.S. Interests Section in Havana and the Cuban Interests Section in Washington, that sent this uncoded dispatch. It says: "We have just spoken with Mr. Myles Frechette, head of the Cuban Affairs Bureau of the State Department, who confirmed that the military maneuvers planned for Guantánamo have been completely cancelled." [*Applause and shouts of "Fidel, give them hell; let's make 'em respect us well!"*] "Frechette commented that the Voice of America had been requested to correct an erroneous report that the parachutists' part of the maneuvers would be maintained."

It seems that now they're saying they'll restrict the maneuvers to the Florida coast and the East Coast of the United States. We know that these maneuvers are directed against us, Central America, and the Caribbean, but we aren't going to contest their right to hold maneuvers there in U.S. territory. What we do contest is their right to hold maneuvers on Cuban soil.

Doubtless, this is a noteworthy victory for our people's struggle and international solidarity. [*Applause*] Therefore the Cuban government will suspend the special maneuvers that the Eastern Army was going to hold under the name of Girón 19, which were to have begun on May 7. [*Applause*]

But the March of the Fighting People is still on; the March of the Fighting People is still on! [*Applause*] The March of the Fighting People was to be not only against the maneuvers but also against the blockade, against the Guantánamo base, and against the SR-71 spy flights. [*Applause*] We aren't going to let the Yankees get an advantage by demobilizing the people in the middle of the battle. [*Shouts of "Never!"*] The March of the Fighting People must go on, and it has to be even stronger than the march of April 19. [*Applause*] It is a people's mobilization against the blockade; against the Guantánamo base; and against the violation of our airspace. Rather than sit back quietly, we should show world public opinion our rejection of and our militant opposition to all that.

If the U.S. government announces that it has lifted the blockade against Cuba, that it is going to return our occupied territory at Guantánamo, and that it is going to suspend the SR-71 flights—then, very well, we will be pleased to call off the March of the Fighting People. [*Applause*] They aren't going to do that, no; but they are going to respect us a little more. They are going to learn a little bit more about Cuba and learn to respect Cuba more. [*Applause and shouts of "Fidel, give them hell; let's make 'em respect us well!"*] They have suspended the maneuvers, but they haven't renounced their self-assigned prerogative to hold them three, four, or five months from now, when they think the international or other circumstances are more propitious. They must renounce their presence in that part of our national territory.

Therefore, we will hold fast to these three goals, and we will organize the march. They say that I am organizing it. They say, "That was organized by Castro." It was really the mass organizations that organized it. Of course, the masses have their political leaders and their party; we don't engage in hypocrisy of any kind. Just as the political leaders are participating today, we take part in everything. [*Applause*] We don't go in for tales; we don't go around making things up! We are united, and we have a party and a leadership. Naturally, however, the party can't organize the march; it simply can't. The march can be organized only by the mass organizations, this rally can be organized only by the mass organizations, and the enthusiasm of a rally such as this can be created only through the miracle of a revolution. These are the facts.

The truth is that all the people have participated in this—all the people have participated, just as we are participating in this rally.

So the march will be held on Saturday, May 17—the seventeenth, not the eighth. The maneuvers were going to begin on the eighth, but that wasn't the exact day they set for the amphibious troop landing. So the March of the Fighting People will be held on Saturday, May 17, throughout the country. This time it won't be a million people; I think it will be around five million people who will march in all parts of our home land on that day. [*Applause*]

Naturally—and this is why I'm saying this—we shouldn't boast about our success. This is not a time for boasting. The enemy still exists and is strong; it harasses, blockades, and threatens us much more because of the new world situation, in which we are on the brink of—or already fully in—an arms race and a cold-war situation. Therefore, we cannot be careless and lower our guard.

The party has issued instructions to the armed forces to create the Territorial Troop Militia as an additional force. [*Applause*] This militia will be composed of men and women, workers, farmers, students—everyone who is able to fight—to be organized and united so they can defend every bit of our national territory. [*Applause*] Everyone who can fight and isn't already a member of the reserve units of the regular troops can belong to the Territorial Troop Militia.

Let our enemies see clearly that, in Cuba—as in Nicaragua, though, logically, Cuba has a much stronger army than Nicaragua, because Cuba has had much more time and has a larger population—let them see that if they attack Cuba they will have to face not only a regular war but also a people's war. This means two things: resistance by the regular units and resistance by all the people.

Do you know what makes us really strong—us, Nicaragua, and Grenada? The fact that ours are people's revolutions, revolutions with deep roots and great support among the people. Any enemy realizes that it is crazy to invade a country like this—crazy, because the same thing could happen that happened to Napoleon's troops in Spain, that went in and then couldn't get out; or Napoleon's troops in old Russia, that also went in and couldn't get out. The enemy could come in, all right, but then it would come up against the people, and if it comes up against this people, it will have a very hard time getting out. That is the problem. [*Applause*]

That is, we have to prepare for both types of war: conventional and people's. Two kinds of war. This will make the imperialists think several times before committing the mistake of invading our country.

There are risks, because some of them have already begun to speak in more aggressive terms. Some of them have suggested flaunting the 1962 agreements—that is, they are beginning again to proclaim their right to invade us. Others have said, cynically, that, if a conflict arises in another part of the world, they will take action wherever it best suits their interests—in other words, in Cuba, since Cuba is a long way from the Soviet Union and the rest of the socialist camp.

Thus, we have to be realistic. We have to be realistic, because these dangers arise out of imperialism's growing aggressiveness and its theories and the other things it is saying. However, the imperialists should be advised of what they are going to find. This is why we said that this rally was so important, because it shows imperialism that the people are here—and what quality people!

I would say that this is a battle waged in defense of the integrity of our homeland. [*Applause*] Your being here—your being here in this square—is a battle, an important battle in defense of Cuba's integrity and security. It would be dangerous for the enemy to be mistaken about this; it would be dangerous for the enemy to deceive himself.

We are going to do something else, as well: work has already begun on drawing up plans concerning what our country should do to survive and resist in case of a total blockade, what each one of us should do in order to survive and resist if no foodstuffs and no fuel enter our country.

Our enemies also speak of these things. They say, "OK, we won't carry out any military actions in the territory; we'll just mine the ports." One of the objectives of the maneuvers was to study how to mine the ports. They speak of naval blockades, figuring out how difficult it would be for a country with no oil to survive a naval blockade. So, we have to draw up plans for coping with such a situation. Raygan, Rayagan, or Reagan—I don't know how it's pronounced—who is the shoo-in Republican presidential candidate, has said that he is in favor of imposing a naval blockade of Cuba. It goes without saying, however—and I should warn him of this—that it won't be easy. However, as revolutionaries, as a realistic people, we should have our plans made for meeting each of these problems. What they have no grounds for thinking is that Cuba would ever surrender, because that we will never do—never! [*Prolonged applause*]

We are not to blame for the lack of a climate of peace in the Caribbean; they are. Let them lift their blockade, dismantle their base at Guantánamo, stop making flights over Cuba, respect Nicaragua, and respect Grenada. If, in addition, they stop interfering in the internal affairs of other peoples in Latin America, then it might be possible to create a climate of peace and détente. Now, we should struggle to develop peace and cooperation among the peoples—but we will never get down on our knees at the feet of imperialism to beg it for peace. [*Shouts of "No!" and "Carter, CIA: the same old garbage!"*]

The international situation is getting more complicated. Now, I would like to speak about the situation in Iran.

We are all interested in these problems, because a conflict over there or in some other place could trigger certain actions by them in other places, as they have cynically said. That is, what happens anywhere in the world interests us; it interests us as revolutionaries, as aware people, and also for ourselves. What happens in the world interests us.

You know that the shah's dynasty in Iran lasted for more than thirty years. The people were subjected to a bloody tyranny for dozens of years. The people had overthrown the shah once, but the CIA—just as it did in Guatemala, exactly the same—reinstated him. This is known; it is history. There are all kinds of documents and evidence to prove this. He assassinated hundreds of thousands of Iranians, imprisoning and torturing them and committing all kinds of other horrors. The Iranian people, who had tremendous courage and patriotism but very few arms, overthrew the shah, even though he had the most powerful army in the area. Naturally, there was also irritation and widespread rejection of U.S. policy, especially when the United States made the mistake of bringing the shah into that country—which led to an explosion of the people's indignation and the subsequent events in the U.S. embassy in Iran: the seizing of the embassy and the capture of a group of its officials.

The United States' arrogant reply to actions of this kind is to use force. It was the CIA's action of installing the shah there that aroused the masses' hatred, the United States' support for the shah that produced the hatred against the United States, and the shah's arrival in the United States that triggered the masses' explosion.

We have always held that this problem of the embassy and the "hostages" should be solved by political and diplomatic means—not force.

The United States, however, committed a series of errors. The first one was to practically confiscate, or seize, billions of dollars that the Iranian state had in U.S. banks. This illegal measure of force, of prepotency, naturally increased the Iranians' irritation, and each successive action by the U.S. government has only made things worse. It has mobilized enormous forces—aircraft carriers and dozens of naval units—near Iran, threatening it; naturally this irritates the Iranians even more. In addition, it goes around saying that it will carry out military actions before July, and it has carried some out already—such as the attempted commando attack, which tried to solve the problem in Iran by means of a surprise move by force.

The U.S. government has only complicated the situation. Now the students have separated the "hostages." Certainly, any act of force against the people of Iran would have very serious consequences.

Moreover, the United States has now banned all trade with Iran and has set up a kind of blockade. It is also threatening to take new measures, trying to bring Western Europe and Japan into its economic blockade of Iran—that is, its attempt to starve Iran into submission, somewhat as it tried with us. A real people's revolution has taken place in Iran—that is unquestionable—and it has tremendous strength. Our duty is to support and express our solidarity with Iran, because everything that is happening there reminds us of what happened in our own country. [*Applause*]

In addition, we should work to resolve the conflicts between our Iraqi and Iranian brothers and sisters. We should work to help solve these problems by diplomatic means, because such conflicts only play into imperialism's hands.

Now, what will happen if the United States manages to impose this blockade on Iran? Will it try to starve it into submission? Iran is a country that belongs to the Third World, the Movement of Nonaligned Countries, and OPEC—that is, the Organization of Petroleum Exporting Countries.

OPEC can prevent the economic blockade of Iran. It can do so simply by announcing that oil supplies to the countries that join the blockade will be suspended. [*Applause*] The West can't apply an economic blockade against Iran if OPEC doesn't want it to and if OPEC resists—if OPEC, with all the right in the world, warns what consequences this will entail; if it says, "OK, if you want to starve 35 million human beings, we won't send you the fuel for your Sunday drives." This is the time for OPEC to show what it is made of, to show that it wasn't created just to raise prices and amass huge fortunes. This is the moment of truth for OPEC, the Nonaligned countries, and the countries of the Third World.

Therefore, it will be very interesting to see what OPEC does. We hope that OPEC won't do what the OAS did when the imperialists set up their blockade and made their aggressive plans against Cuba. This is a problem that we should watch closely, and we should mobilize our friends all over the world to support Iran.

Iran is far away, but here, very close to us, we have the case of El Salvador, where genocide is being committed, with thousands of patriots being assassinated.

In order to see just how inconsistent the policies of some states are, look at what the Andean Pact did concerning this and other problems. We aren't opposed to the integration of Latin America and the Caribbean; to the contrary, we support it. Along with Mexico, Cuba was a founding member of SELA, the Latin American Economic System. What we do oppose are the political Mafias in this hemisphere, because they don't lead to anything. We would have liked a progressive Andean Pact—and even more, a revolutionary one. As one sign carried on the day of the March of the Fighting People said, the Andean Pact should make itself worthy of Bolívar and Sandino.

But what did it do? What has it done, for example, concerning these provoking, menacing maneuvers that the Yankees were preparing? It didn't even issue a statement. What has it done concerning the blockade of Cuba, which is a crime? It has issued no statement denouncing the blockade. What has it done concerning the base at Guantánamo? Not even issued a statement demanding that the territory be returned to us. What has it done concerning the spy flights over Cuba, which are a shameless violation of our sovereignty? Not even issued a statement denouncing them. What has it done concerning the fraternal people of Puerto Rico, which U.S. imperialism wants to swallow up and annex? It hasn't opened its mouth. What has it said about Iran and the blockade of Iran? As far as I know, it hasn't said a word. What has it said about the genocide that is being committed in El Salvador, where thousands of people are dying or have died in the last few months? Not a word.

It let loose a flood of propaganda against us concerning the events in the Peruvian embassy—where nobody was even injured.

But there in El Salvador, where thousands of patriots are dying, the Andean Pact hasn't said a word. Naturally. The ruling party in Venezuela, one of the members of the Andean Pact, supports the genocidal government of El Salvador—as it also supports "Christian Democracy," a rightist, reactionary group that is conspiring against the progressive government in Panama.

These are the facts. With regard to this problem, it adopted a demagogic policy against Cuba. It acted like a Mafia. I'm not going to say that all its members acted in the same way; there were differences among them. But that is all the Andean Pact did.

Returning to the situation in El Salvador, I repeat that the broadest possible international support is required to stay the hands of the imperialists.

These demonstrations of ours are a part of the struggle—not only to defend our own integrity but also to defend the integrity of Grenada and Nicaragua and the sovereignty of the other Caribbean and Central American countries. This is all a part of our struggle.

This is why this rally has had a singular character. It has really been an international workers' rally. For us, it has been cause for great honor and satisfaction; we have felt very stimulated and strengthened by the presence here of Comrade Bishop—who had a rally in Grenada in the morning and this rally in Havana this afternoon—[*Applause*] and Comrade Daniel Ortega—[*Applause*] you already know both of these leaders, from the Sixth Summit Conference; Comrade Chandra, president of the World Peace Council; [*Applause*] and Comrade Pastorino, leader of the world organization of workers. [*Applause*] We have also been honored by the presence of what we might describe as a representation of the best of the intellectuals of Latin America: Comrade Juan Bosch [*Applause*] and Comrade Gabriel García Márquez. [*Applause*]

All this has meant much to us, for it has given a really historic tone to this, the largest rally ever held by the revolution.

Aside from maintaining the mobilization and preparations for the May 17 march, we must turn this energy into not only a political and military, but also a productive, force. As [Confederation of Cuban Workers leader Roberto] Veiga said, the next few weeks will be decisive, both for finishing the sugarcane harvest and for preparing and planting a tremendous area of land to cane. We should turn this energy into a productive force. We should turn this tremendous force, derived from this colossal mass battle; derived from this revolutionary definition of the people; derived from this hatred of loafers, parasites, lumpen, and other antisocial elements, into a tool for struggling to achieve a demanding approach, to rectify our deficiencies and to overcome all difficulties. It will be very important if we can make this incredible, huge force a tool in our struggle against our own deficiencies and weaknesses.

This has been a moving, stimulating day in many ways. The most essential, basic thing has been the people. I believe that this afternoon will leave a lasting, indelible impression on all of us.

Without demagogy or flattery, but rather as an expression of the deepest, most sincere, and most deeply felt spirit of justice, I would venture to say that a people such as this deserves a place in history, a place of glory. A people such as this deserves victory!

Patria o muerte!

Venceremos! [*Shouts of "Venceremos!"*] [*Ovation*]

PART 8

Nicaragua: The Sandinista revolution

On July 19, 1979, the Nicaraguan people threw out the tyranny of the Somoza family, which had ruled the country for forty-six years. To Cubans, this event had special meaning. In looking at Nicaragua's history, they saw their own struggle against imperialist domination. U.S. marines occupied Nicaragua in 1910–26 and 1927–32, installed Anastasio Somoza García in power and built him an army, the National Guard. To consolidate his power, Somoza organized the assassination of Augusto César Sandino in 1934, who, since 1927, had been leading a peasant army against the marines and the Nicaraguan ruling class for independence and social justice. After Somoza was assassinated in 1956, his son Luis took over, and later his other son, Anastasio Somoza Debayle, who was also supported and maintained in power by the United States government.

In 1961, drawing inspiration from the Cuban revolution, a movement was organized to carry on Sandino's tradition—the Sandinista National Liberation Front (FSLN) led by Carlos Fonseca Amador, who was killed in 1976. From the beginning the Cubans supported the FSLN, many of whose leaders spent time in exile in Cuba.

When the Sandinistas toppled the Somoza dynasty in 1979, Cuba was one of the first countries to come to its aid. Closely studying the Cuban experience, the Nicaraguan revolution carried out widespread social reforms: a massive literacy campaign; agrarian reform; greatly expanded health care; formation of a popular militia; and the building of trade unions and mass organizations of women, youth, and agricultural workers. It began laying the foundations for a new social and political order, where the workers and peasants run society.

On the first anniversary of the Sandinista triumph, a massive rally of half a million was held in Managua. Besides Castro, the other heads of state attending were Maurice Bishop of Grenada and George Price of Belize. Castro's address was one of the high points of the event. Afterwards, he was given a tour of the country, visiting cities where he talked to workers and peasants, spoke at rallies, and met with Nicaragua's leaders.

On his return to Cuba, Castro described his impressions of Nicaragua and what its revolution meant for the Cuban people. Recognizing its historic importance and significance for all Latin America and the Caribbean, Castro's message to the Cuban people was: Cuba is no longer alone.

The triumph of Nicaraguan independence

July 26, 1979

Speech given at the Moncada anniversary rally in Holguín, Cuba, one week after the Sandinista victory in Nicaragua. The text is from *Granma* Weekly Review August 5, 1979, and also appears in *The Nicaraguan Revolution,* Camejo and Murphy, eds., Pathfinder Press, 1979.

Heroic Sandinista fighters; [*Applause*]
Comrades of the party and government leadership; [*Applause*]
People of Holguín; [*Applause*]
Compatriots: [*Applause*]

Two weeks ago we thought that in this rally various topics would be discussed, among them the successes and the merits of this province; the enormous transformation to be seen throughout the province and the city; its tremendous march forward and its progress, its new buildings, its new factories, its work spirit, its production successes.

The great merit of having produced 764,000 tons of sugar in this year's harvest: [*Applause*] 150,000 tons more than last year, bringing this year's national sugar production to 7,992,000 tons, 96 base, [Applause] only 8,000 tons short of the 8 million mark [Applause] and surpassing last year's production figure by more than half a million tons. [Applause] And all this under adverse weather conditions and working the sugar mills right up until yesterday, which was when the last one stopped.

This is what we were thinking. But when we learned less than forty-eight hours ago that our people were to receive an extraordinary honor, that a large contingent of fighters, of heroic and self-sacrificing leaders, leaders of the sister people of Nicaragua, wished to be with us on this July 26, [Applause] I realized that today's rally would inevitably turn into a Sandinista rally. [Applause and shouts of "Cuba, Nicaragua, united we will win!"]

What should we talk about, what else could we talk about, what more extraordinary event of our times, what act of greater historical importance, of greater significance and implications has taken place in recent times than the victory of the Sandinistas in Nicaragua? What has touched us more deeply, what has captured our attention more during these weeks, what could have excited or inspired us more than this popular and heroic victory?

And what greater honor could we have received, what greater splendor for this revolutionary day of ours, what greater honor for this city and this province than the warm, fraternal visit of solidarity from this contingent of heroic, valiant, intelligent, and capable commanders and fighters of the Sandinista National Liberation Front of Nicaragua? [Applause]

I say solidarity, because we too need solidarity; I say stimulating, because we also need that stimulation. Solidarity, stimulation, because for a long time it was almost a crime to visit Cuba; for a long time imperialism tried to cut the ties with our sister peoples of Latin America and the Caribbean, and for a long time blockaded us, prohibited and thwarted the coming together and development of the natural, historical, and logical ties between the Nicaraguan and the Cuban peoples.

For so many years we have remembered and mourned those brothers of ours who died fighting at Playa Girón, because of the invasion that left precisely from Nicaraguan territory, in one of the most infamous services which the tyrant offered imperialism, given that this same Somoza—now but a shadow of his former self—was the head of the General Staff of the Nicaraguan army at the time of Girón, when the B-26 bombers left from there to bomb our homes, to kill peasant families, women and children, to drop tons of bombs on our militia and soldiers.

How can we fail to see in this gesture of the Sandinistas, in this spontaneous gesture—because it was not our initiative, since we know the tremendous amount of work they have at this moment, the enormous job they have to do, the great need for their presence in the country, especially in these early days. We would not have been able to ask them for this honor, this immense, infinite honor that came entirely from them. [*Prolonged applause*]

This is proof of the political valor of Sandinism, proof of revolutionary valor, because we know this world of ours and we know that political and revolutionary valor do not always abound.

They were not prejudiced, they were not afraid. They didn't have to ask anyone for permission to come to Cuba. They did not have to explain themselves to anyone, nor worry about what anyone would think. [*Applause*]

This is proof of political honesty, because they don't go about pretending; they don't go about denying that they are friends of Cuba, that they feel respect for Cuba, that they are in solidarity with Cuba. They are open, they don't harbor fears.

For this reason, I believe that they inspire confidence not only in our people but in all peoples and in world political opinion. They are not prejudiced, in spite of the gossip, the intrigues, the fact that now the campaigns will begin, that now the accusations will begin, once the victory honeymoon has ended.

They do not harbor prejudices, because they are not afraid of the Nicaraguan and Cuban revolutions being confused, because they are way beyond those prejudices.

Yet they themselves will by no means say that the two revolutions are exactly alike. [*Applause*] They are both profound revolutions, alike in many ways and in many ways different, as all true revolutions must be. [*Applause*]

This is important for our people, important also for world opinion. Every country has its own road, its own problems, its own style, methods, objectives. We have our own; they have theirs. We did things one way, our way; they will do things their way. Similarities: they achieved victory by means similar to ours; we both achieved victory by the only means by which we could free ourselves from imperialist tyranny and domination: gun in hand, [*Applause*] fighting fiercely, heroically.

And we should say, we should stress, that the Nicaraguan revolution was noted for its heroism, for its perseverance, for the tenacity of its fighters, because it is not the victory of one day; it is the victory of twenty years of struggle—twenty years of struggle! [*Applause*]

Because in the same year that our revolution triumphed, there were already groups of fighters led by that extraordinary and marvelous fighter Carlos Fonseca Amador, follower of Sandino [*Applause*] and founder of the Sandinista National Liberation Front, the people's guide in those terrible days when victory was so far away, leader fallen in the struggle, as so many fell in our own land; like Martí, Maceo, Agramonte; like Abel [Santamaría] and Frank País from our generation, who fell without being able to see the victory but certain that victory would be achieved!

The young fighters took up Fonseca's struggle. Yes, it was said that the average age of the fighters was twenty years; but the leaders, what's their average age? Some of the oldest are in their thirties—those who began to fight when they were only fifteen, sixteen, seventeen years old, and who faced the difficulties and obstacles for twenty years. Twenty years to gather the fruits of the seed sown, cultivated, and irrigated with blood for such a long time, to achieve victory in the midst of a truly popular epic.

Who among us has not seen at the movies, on television, in books and magazines, pictures of the incredibly brutal repression, the ruthless, genocidal, unscrupulous war unleashed against the people of Nicaragua by the Somoza dictatorship?

Who has not seen pictures of mothers weeping for their children, for their loved ones; pictures of children crying for their parents, of homes that have been destroyed, of piles of corpses, of torture, murders, bombings of the cities?

Where else has such barbarism been seen? Where else has there been an air force dedicated to dropping tons and tons of bombs on the cities of its own country? On Managua, Masaya, León, Estelí, on this group of martyred cities.

They did not hesitate to give orders to drop 500-pound bombs on populated and even overpopulated areas, acts that really filled the world with anger and amazement and that, in their own way, contributed to creating the huge campaign and the unshakable feeling of solidarity with the Nicaraguan people and the Sandinista fighters.

These are the fruits of imperialist intervention in

Nicaragua. These were the fruits of intervention, the bitter fruits of imperialist policy in our hemisphere. Because they were the ones who shaped, aided, and abetted those sanguinary, repressive, reactionary, tyrannical, fascist regimes in this hemisphere. And it is said, it has been said—and I think even Somoza himself said it—that in the United Nations the government of Somoza never once failed to vote with the government of the United States.

Throughout the world, U.S. policy was to create this type of political regime, throughout the entire world! Not only in our America, but in each and every continent!

As for the bombings, we see similar cases: the bombings of the Namibian camps by the racist South Africans, the Rhodesian racists' bombings of the refugee camps of the people of Zimbabwe, using the most modern planes, the most deadly weapons, sophisticated bombs that spread thousands of pellets that are often not even made of steel, but of rubber, so that surgeons can't spot them in X-rays.

Examples of this kind are the genocidal acts perpetrated against the Palestinian people in the Middle East, the constant bombings against the Palestinian camps in Lebanon, against Lebanese communities in Lebanon, bombed practically every day by Israeli planes, symbols of crime.

But it was not only the Israeli bombs falling on the Palestinians, the Lebanese, the imperialist bombs falling on the Namibians and the Zimbabweans; it was also the imperialist bombs, Israeli bombs, falling on the Nicaraguans.

When the imperialists wanted to pretend that they were not furnishing arms, they furnished them through their allies. And who is going to believe that the Israeli state would have sent Somoza those arms, those Galil guns, those bombs, those planes without the consent of and approval of the government of the United States? And with those bombs and guns tens of thousands of people in that country were murdered; we were told that 40,000 people died, that is to say, twice the number of people attending the rally this afternoon.

These are the fruits of the conspiracy that led to the cowardly murder of Sandino, to the implantation of that disgraceful regime that governed the country for almost fifty years and has disappeared thanks to the heroic struggle of the Nicaraguan people and the Sandinista fighters.

From now on, the people of Nicaragua will also be able to meet together as we have done since our revolution; I also think that one day, in squares such as this one, the portraits and images of the heroes mentioned here by Commander Humberto Ortega will appear alongside the people, ennobling and dignifying revolutionary rallies, and depicted there will undoubtedly be Sandino, Fonseca, and all the patriots that over 150 years—as has been said here—fought for the independence of Nicaragua. [*Applause*]

The Sandinista victory is not only a victory over 45 years of Somozaism; it is a victory over 150 years of foreign domination in the country, [*Applause*] it is a victory over many centuries of conquest, exploitation, and foreign domination. If anything is certain it is that for the first time, for the first time in all their history, the Nicaraguan people became completely free and independent on July 19, when the columns of hardened Sandinista forces entered Managua, [*Applause*] because our peoples—and especially Central America, which became a hunting ground for pirates, filibusters, and interventionists—passed from Spanish to Yankee domination.

So that day marks not only the day of the victory of the revolution, but also the triumph of Nicaraguan independence, [*Applause*] two great and important historical objectives achieved in one battle. It is in this that we see the importance and the significance of the victorious conclusion of the struggle led by the Sandinista National Liberation Front.

But this Sandinista victory, this struggle, means even more. A great degree of international solidarity developed around this struggle, and a great degree of unity in all the Central American and Latin American left; around the Sandinista struggle what we could call a great democratic, pro-independence, and anti-interventionist front developed tacitly in Latin America, something of historic significance and enormous importance.

In Latin America and the Caribbean, in this hemisphere, the Sandinista movement encouraged the pro-independence and anti-interventionist feelings of Latin American peoples. This reached its high point, its moment of culmination, at the last meeting of the Organization of American States. Let's refer to this organization for the first time without adding any epithets, because for the first time, for the first time, there was outright insubordination on the part of the Latin American states.

This is very symptomatic, since the most reactionary and aggressive sectors in the United States advised the present U.S. administration to pursue a policy of intervention in Nicaragua, and at this meeting the United States advocated an inter-American peace-keeping force, supposedly to bring peace to Nicaragua, when peace in Nicaragua, the peace imposed by imperialism since it began its many interventions and set up that reactionary regime was the peace of the grave. In reality this was the kind of peace they wanted to continue upholding in order to prevent revolutionary peace, to prevent the Sandinista victory, to deprive the people of their victory.

We know what these inter-American peace-keeping forces amount to, who supplies the weapons, who leads them, who supplies them, and who makes up their forces.

We have seen these so-called inter-American forces more than once before.

The imperialist aim was really a sinister one: it was to intervene in Nicaragua. The imperialists were used to having all the Latin American governments say yes, but this time a sufficient number of Latin American governments said no! [*Applause*]

And as always, the pretexts were very noble: "to bring peace to the suffering people of Nicaragua." They did not want this moment to come, they did not want the nineteenth of July to come. A month later the Sandinistas brought real peace, the peace of a happy and victorious people; a people that had suffered to the full, true, but a people that was also full of hope and optimism in the future.

We, our people, cannot help noting the full magnitude and significance of this historic event: the defeat of the U.S. interventionist scheme in the heart of the Latin American states. There was a majority which resolutely opposed intervention and defended the principle of non-intervention, of sovereignty, of absolute respect for the sovereignty of our peoples, as something sacred.

It must be said that the U.S. proposal was isolated. In the end they adopted an intelligent position. If they had voted in favor of their own proposal, that is, in favor of the proposal for intervention, they would have ended up in the company of Paraguay and Somoza, because the only one who advocated intervention, who openly voted for intervention, was Somoza, and I think Paraguay as well.

Of course, intervention was in Somoza's interest, for the time being at least. Such a course would have preserved the National Guard and would have preserved his interests, along with those of the monopolies. If the United States had abstained, it would have found itself together with Chile, Uruguay, El Salvador, and Guatemala, and they did not think it was very honorable to be seen in that kind of company. And so they too voted with the majority. An interesting phenomenon.

In our opinion the decision, the result of the meeting, constituted a great victory for the people of our America and it helped develop the spirit of solidarity with Nicaragua. And in the position maintained at the OAS, we must stress the role of Panama, Costa Rica, Venezuela, and the other Andean Pact countries, [*Applause*] and that of Mexico, Jamaica, Grenada, and others. [*Applause*] In the creation of this democratic, anti-interventionist front which has formed, we must mention the names of people as well as countries: the names of Torrijos, [*Applause*] Carazo, [*Applause*] López Portillo, [*Applause*] Manley, [*Applause*] and Bishop. [*Applause*] And it is also only fair to recall the name of a person who, though he is no longer president of his country, contributed a great deal to the development of this solidarity with the Sandinista struggle: the former president of Venezuela, Carlos Andrés Pérez. [*Applause*]

And let me stress that there was not a single party or organization of the left in Latin America that did not express its willingness to struggle; not a single one failed to express its solidarity with the struggle of the Sandinista people. [*Applause*]

It is very important for all the peoples still suffering from fascism and the bloodiest tyrannies that this climate, this front, and this spirit should be maintained. This is a duty—in our opinion—of the Sandinistas as well; it will be their contribution, the contribution of the victorious people of Nicaragua, toward maintaining that spirit and that broad front.

Many questions are now being raised, and there are many people wanting to establish similarities between what happened in Cuba and what has happened in Nicaragua.

Some of these questions are not being posed in good faith, but are inspired by the wish to start creating justifications and seeking pretexts to apply aggressive measures against the people of Nicaragua as well: blockades against the people of Nicaragua, aggression against the people of Nicaragua—all those filthy measures and all those crimes they committed against us—and we must be careful about this.

The Nicaraguans have given a magnificent answer for those people with this sort of aim in mind who have made assertions or expressed fears to the effect that Nicaragua would become a new Cuba. The Nicaraguans have replied: No, Nicaragua will become a new Nicaragua! [*Applause*] And this is something quite different.

They do not see themselves in us, as if they were looking in a mirror. Rather, it is we who today see ourselves mirrored in them, because nothing reminds us more of our own struggles, our sacrifices, and our own image in those early days of the revolution.

There are no two revolutions the same. There can't be. There are many similarities—as I said—as to spirit, heroism, combat. But our problems are not exactly the same as their problems; the conditions under which our revolution took place are not exactly the same as the conditions under which their revolution is taking place, including the fact that in our case this front I mentioned did not exist and that the imperialists launched their campaigns and their aggressions immediately.

The imperialists knew less then, and now even the imperialists have managed to learn something. Not much, but something.

The conditions under which their struggle was fought, its characteristics, were different. For instance, the unity of the entire people, which was an essential condition for victory, the participation of all social strata, the organization of various popular movements, which joined ranks, reaching certain compromises, creating certain circumstances that differed from ours. In other words, in Nicaragua and Cuba things are not going to be exactly the same—quite the contrary.

Some of the characteristics we have noted in our Nicaraguan revolutionary comrades are worthy of mention. Firstly, the people's militant spirit, their heroism, their bravery. They have distinguished themselves as great fighters, but they have also distinguished themselves as great political tacticians and strategists. They have displayed great wisdom, great ability to unite, great ability to act in difficult, complex circumstances.

They fought heroically, but they have also been able to be flexible, and when they needed to negotiate in a certain way to avoid the risks of intervention, they were not afraid to negotiate. And they showed great ability, great talent both in military and political strategy. Needless to say, had it been otherwise their victory would have been inexplicable.

Even during the final stage, when the Somoza regime was in its death throes, they discussed how the end would be, the graveside protocol, as it were, Somoza's funeral. Several countries took part in these talks—the Government of National Reconstruction took part, the Sandinista leadership took part, and even the United States took part.

And as *Granma* briefly explained, Somoza's demise was supposed to occur at four in the morning; then somebody called Urcuyo—at first I found it hard to remember the name, even now I do not remember it very well, and I daresay in a couple of weeks I will have forgotten it again—[*Laughter and applause*] then somebody called Urcuyo was supposed to take over at eight in the morning and finally hand over the government to the Junta of National Reconstruction at one in the afternoon. In the interim period I believe that someone was to be appointed head of the National Guard, something like that.

The Sandinistas made some concessions. And it was wise of them to make these concessions, those they thought they should make. At the same time they were firm and did not make concessions they should not have made.

It was assumed, of course, that there would be a new army. The country could not remain in the hands of those genocidal maniacs. Basically, the new army would be made up of the Sandinista fighters and, it is said, also some National Guard members who were not guilty of corruption, repression, and crimes.

Now, this may be all right in principle, in theory, but it is hard to imagine there could be even one of them who was not guilty of corruption, repression, and crimes. However the Sandinista attitude was a generous one.

We were too, in our own struggle. We repeatedly appealed to the army. At the end we even held talks with them, and they said to us: "We've lost the war, how do we bring it to an end?"

We gave them our opinion on how to proceed. We told them that the forces in Santiago should surrender and that they should neither discuss things with the U.S. embassy, nor stage a coup d'etat in the capital, nor help Batista escape. And so we came to an agreement. We waited for the thirty-first [of December, 1958] and we did not attack the Santiago garrison, waiting for the agreement to be honored.

But they did the exact opposite; they staged a coup in Havana, they came to an agreement with the U.S. embassy, and they saw Batista off at the airport. So that was the end of the agreement and we had no choice but to disarm the army, which we did in forty-eight hours, as you all know perfectly well, so there is no need to repeat it here.

Well, something similar happened in Nicaragua; when this Urcuyo character had been appointed president, he said no, he intended to stay there until 1981. [*Laughter*] So the Sandinistas gave the order to attack, and in less than seventy-two hours they disarmed the National Guard, and now there is no National Guard. [*Applause*] It turned out that the U.S. government could not even honor its own part in the agreements.

Nonetheless, the Government of National Reconstruction and the Sandinista leadership have done a very correct thing, in our opinion, in maintaining the generous attitude they displayed in these talks. Of course, the U.S. government was not concerned about the tens of thousands of people killed by the bombings; but they were very concerned about the lives of Somoza's thugs, his poor little thugs. But the magnanimity and generosity displayed by the Sandinistas has been extraordinary, exemplary, exemplary! Needless to say all this was just to pave the way for launching a campaign against the Sandinista movement, which has won so much solidarity and sympathy all over the world.

And so the Sandinistas have not only been heroic and efficient in war and flexible in politics; they have also been extraordinarily magnanimous in victory! I am sure that this will earn the broadest sympathy and will strengthen feelings of solidarity throughout the world. It will deprive the reactionaries of arguments, it will deprive them of weapons, it will deprive them of fuel for slander and defamation.

It also shows the enormous influence the Sandinista commanders and the Government of National Reconstruction have over the masses, because the masses have not forgotten—nor will they ever forget—the crimes, torture, and bombings. They will not forget. But they have also given proof of their great trust in the leadership by holding back when it was necessary for them to hold back.

We hope that in Nicaragua's case the imperialists will not repeat their interventionist ventures or try fostering counterrevolution. Of course, we are not going to deceive ourselves. We're not going to imagine that the reactionaries will leave the Nicaraguan revolution in peace, despite its magnanimity, generous attitude, and democratic aims.

They have said that if an election is needed it's fine with them to have an election. In any election held in Nicaragua, no matter how many resources are supplied to the reactionary bands, the Sandinistas will win with an enormous majority. [*Applause*]

In any kind of election, under any kind of constitution that allows a citizen the right to vote and the citizen does vote, the Sandinistas would win. [*Applause*]

This is why—and this is what I'm explaining to our people—it's the circumstances in which the Nicaraguan victory was won that determine that the ways they adopt differ from ours. Furthermore, the fact that right now Nicaragua is in ruins, completely destroyed, calls for a national reconstruction program with the participation of every sector of Nicaraguan society.

The Sandinistas are revolutionaries. We don't deny it, nobody denies it, they don't deny it. But they are not extremists, they are realists. And it is realists who make the best revolutions, [*Applause*] the best and most profound revolutions.

I predict that they will go far because they are taking their time, because they're not extremists, because they're taking things slowly. They know what to aim for at each stage of a political and revolutionary process, and the means that correspond to these aims. I'm sure of that.

They used their heads, too, the Sandinistas, because they closed ranks at just the right moment and the result was victory, fruit of the wisdom with which they acted. And our greatest hope is that this unity becomes ever more solid and closer as an essential requisite for the future. The people, weapons, unity. That's all they need to go as far as they want for as long as they want.

They are now faced with a tremendous job, tremendous, much worse than the one that faced us when we won; because our war, and the development of the columns and the guerrilla fronts, was different. They combined the development of the columns and the guerrilla fronts with insurrection in the cities, an infallible system that neither Somoza nor the National Guard could beat.

The enemy had no qualms at all in shelling and bombing the rebellious cities with every available weapon, mercilessly destroying entire cities and facilities of all kinds and leaving behind an enormous wake of destruction, the country's finances bankrupt with not a single reserve left.

Engineer Alfonso Robelo was telling me that there were some $3 million left in the treasury, with an immediate debt of $250 million and an overall foreign debt of $1.2 billion. There wasn't a single cent left. Therefore one of the first things they had to do was nationalize the banks, among other things, as a measure to protect depositors from ruin, because the banks were bankrupt and nobody could guarantee the savings held in them.

So that's one of the first measures they've had to take. There's much hunger in Nicaragua. I believe that Nicaragua needs help from everybody. In the past few weeks, a large number of leaders have expressed their readiness to help Nicaragua.

I think that's very good.

Governments of different hues, of different ideologies,

of different political systems have expressed their readiness to assist the people of Nicaragua on a large scale. And Nicaragua certainly needs this help.

Even the United States has stated that it's ready to send food and organize other kinds of help. We're glad to hear it. They said they were going to start an airlift and send 300 tons of food a day. We think that's a very good idea.

Martí said that heaven wanted tyrants to be wise only once. Needless to say, Somoza wasn't wise even once; the government of the United States, however, has been wise at least on this one occasion, because it's much better in every sense, more productive, and makes for better relations among the peoples and for a climate of peace all over the world, to send food instead of sending bombs and marines, like they did in Vietnam and so many other places.

Naturally—since I mentioned Vietnam—if the United States had intervened in Nicaragua it would have been an act of suicide for United States policy in this hemisphere, because we haven't the slightest doubt that the Sandinistas would have continued fighting in spite of U.S. intervention. There's no question about that.

We're extremely happy that it didn't happen—who knows how many lives have been spared for that very reason—but we are also convinced that had there been an intervention it would have met with tremendous resistance on the part of Sandino's people. And not only that, but also that a gigantic Vietnam might have developed throughout Central America and in the rest of Latin America, a gigantic Vietnam. [*Applause*]

Intervention would have been an act of sheer stupidity, but also an act that would have meant a great deal of bloodshed for our peoples.

So an intervention in Nicaragua wouldn't have gone unpunished, of course—we must be quite clear about that—but we are glad that the firm struggle waged by the people of Nicaragua, international solidarity, the support given by the Latin American peoples, and the realism and flexibility of the Sandinistas prevented the perpetration of one of the most mistaken acts imaginable, and which was a real possibility.

We are glad to know the United States is sending food to Nicaragua. We are glad to know that everybody is sending food and giving aid of all kinds to the people of Nicaragua.

We are not rich; we cannot compete with the United States in numbers of planes and tons of food. But we will send something, because even though we are poor we can always spare some of what we have. [*Applause*]

And something very important: we may not have great financial or material resources, but we do have human resources. [*Applause*]

Engineer Robelo said here that they need doctors, that they need campaigns to wipe out illiteracy. And we know our doctors and teachers. [*Applause*] They'll go wherever they're needed. If they have to go to the mountains, they go to the mountains; if to the countryside, the countryside. In Cuba and in Ethiopia, in Vietnam, in Yemen, in Angola, anywhere.

Nicaragua is much nearer, right nearby. There's practically the same distance between Cape San Antonio and Managua as between Cape San Antonio and Maisí Point. So it's really close.

Therefore, I believe that we are expressing the feelings of our party and of our people when we say to our Nicaraguan brothers and sisters that, if they plan to put into effect a broad health and medical care program and there aren't enough Nicaraguan doctors, we are ready to send all the doctors they need to support this health program. [*Applause*]

Of course, we do have more than 1,000 doctors working abroad, but we still have some to spare. We have our commitments and we can meet them.

How would we be able to do it? By asking our hospitals and our doctors for their collaboration. We have done it on other occasions—for example, in the matter of time off following guard duty. We've said wait for the future, a splendid future because some 4,000 students are already entering medical school every year and we are building medical schools in practically every province. We would need the collaboration of the hospitals, People's Power, the public health sector, and especially the doctors themselves, to cover the work of those who go.

We've already sent the first medical brigade of sixty people, forty of them doctors. It was done quickly, in a matter of hours. [*Applause*]

We sent a large medical brigade when Nicaragua was hit by an earthquake, even though Somoza was still there. And I remember that the colonel they mentioned today, who wasn't yet a colonel at the time, that son of Somoza's who they say was the head of the EBI [Basic Infantry Training School], was waiting at the airport to steal the shipments that came in. [*Laughter*]

So they stole the medicines we sent. They couldn't steal our doctors, however, [*Laughter*] and our doctors did a good job, offered their services to the people, and the people were very friendly toward them. If we did it when Somoza was there, we can certainly do it now.

We have doctors now and we'll have more in the future. But we're not going to wait for those. The ones we send will come from those we have now.

If our doctors collaborate—and of course I'm sure they will—if our hospitals, the heads of hospitals, the health sectors, everybody collaborates, we can find all the doctors we need to tell the people of Nicaragua that we will send them all they need if they haven't enough themselves.

This means that if they need 100, we'll send them 100. If they need 200, we'll send them 200. And if they need as many as 500, we'll send them 500. No trouble at all. [*Applause*]

The need for a large-scale education campaign has also been mentioned here. And it looks as if there are some teachers here who are quite enthusiastic at the idea. A great educational campaign. [*Applause*]

Only a revolutionary government can carry out a great health and education campaign. Who knows how many lives they will save, especially how many children's lives they will save, with campaigns against polio, tetanus, and tuberculosis.

Many lives will be saved in just a few years. In fact, many lives will be saved in but a few weeks. I know how much people appreciate a health campaign; I know how much people appreciate an educational campaign.

Even in the midst of destruction and ruins, a revolutionary government can wage a great campaign in these fields, and since our country has plenty of experience in these things we can offer some advice in both the health and the education campaigns. And, I repeat, if they don't have enough teachers in Nicaragua to put this education campaign into effect, we are ready to send them as many as they need. [*Applause*]

It's not for nothing that we have more than 30,000 students in our primary education teacher training schools, and tens of thousands—50,000 I think—training as teachers in the pedagogical institutions. We're doing all right. [*Applause*]

We also know that our teachers go wherever they are

sent—to the most remote places, to the farthest mountains, to the most forgotten little town. [*Applause*]

They're not interested in being in the capital. We know our teachers and our doctors and we know how much they can do. This is why our country can make quite a valuable contribution in these two fields.

Needless to say, we are also ready to collaborate, within the scope of our modest resources, in any other field.

It is not a case of our going to engage in politics in Nicaragua—and there will certainly be some who will say that we are.

Who's going to engage in politics, who's going to influence the Sandinistas? On the contrary, our teachers and our doctors will be influenced by the Sandinista spirit, and we are very pleased and happy about this. [*Applause*] The revolutionary spirit of the Sandinistas will have a great effect on them. Everyone knows our technicians' dedication to their work.

I repeat that we're glad that the United States and other countries are to help Nicaragua. What's more, we're ready to enter an emulation campaign with the United States, an emulation campaign [*Applause*] to see who can do the most for Nicaragua. We invite the United States, we invite all the countries of Latin America, we invite all the countries of Europe, the countries of the Third World, our sister socialist nations, everybody, to take part in an emulation campaign to help Nicaragua. [*Applause*] This is our position, in order to make a really human, really constructive effort based on a spirit of emulation.

Of course, when I mentioned who could do the most you all stood up. What do you think? What do you think? [*Shouts of "Yes!"*] And that we're willing and ready to do it? [*Shouts of "Yes!"*] Then, we ask you to raise your hands, on behalf of all our people, as an expression of this feeling of solidarity with the people of Nicaragua. [*All hands go up. Applause*] Our feelings, our response couldn't be otherwise. [*Applause and shouts of "For whatever and however it may be necessary, commander in chief, we await your orders!"*]

The Sandinistas have set a further example of how much a revolutionary spirit can accomplish. Weak men never achieve any goals; timid souls never get anywhere. But a revolutionary spirit can achieve even the most incredible goals.

We thank the Sandinistas not only for their beautiful gesture, their unforgettable gesture, for the great honor they have conferred on us with their presence and their affectionate and fraternal words. We also thank them for stimulating us in our own efforts, in our own struggle, because they help us to improve, to overcome our own shortcomings.

They stimulate us in our task of perfecting our work, perfecting our revolution, in the uncompromising struggle against weaknesses, against errors, against things badly done; this struggle is not a temporary campaign, a matter of one day, one week, one month, or one year, but rather a struggle that we must go on waging for many years.

Now they are faced by the problem that all those who begin a process on the ruins of their country must face, while here, with twenty years of revolution behind us, the conditions are different, the circumstances are different.

What better way to celebrate this July 26, to pay tribute to our martyrs, what better way to honor our visitors than for every one of us to promise and commit ourselves to make more effort, to struggle harder, to work harder, to become better!

Long live the revolutionary victory in Nicaragua! [*Applause and shouts of "Long live!"*]

Long live Sandino! [*Applause and shouts of "Long live!"*]

Long live the FSLN! [*Applause and shouts of "Long live!"*]

Long live the Government of National Reconstruction of Nicaragua! [*Applause and shouts of "Long live!"*]

Long live the friendship and solidarity between the peoples of Nicaragua and Cuba! [*Applause and shouts of "Long live!"*]

Patria o muerte!

Venceremos! [*Ovation*]

In Nicaragua

July 19, 1980

Speech given to mass rally in Managua, Nicaragua to celebrate the first anniversary of the Sandinista revolution. The Spanish text was printed in the July 20 Managua daily newspaper *Barricada* and the translation is by the editor.

Compañero leaders of the FSLN and of the Government of National Reconstruction;
Distinguished delegations and invited guests;
Valiant Sandinista soldiers and militia members;
Dear Nicaraguan brothers and sisters:
Some may think that I'm going to give a lengthy speech. Others perhaps think my words will be polemical. And there will no doubt be some who anticipate a fiery, revolutionary harangue. [*Applause*]
However, I'm not going to be long-winded, nor am I going to introduce polemics into this rally, nor am I going to give a fiery harangue.
It would not be fitting for me to fail to consider what

ex-President Carlos Andrés Pérez [of Venezuela] has already pointed out—the presence on this platform of delegations and individuals who come from the most diverse and varied systems, outlooks, and political shadings. There is something, however, that unites all of us today—even, I would say, the North Americans and ourselves: [*Applause*] this rally, this tribute, this recognition of the heroic people of Nicaragua and their historic victory of July 19, 1979.

I would like to say that I cherish the hope that all of us might understand that our presence here implies a commitment of solidarity, support, and aid to Nicaragua. [*Applause*]

I am not going to hide the fact that I was overcome with deep emotion when I arrived in this country at noon yesterday. I was struck by the warmth and enthusiasm of the children, by the beauty of your natural surroundings. The magnitude of this rally today is astonishing—the martial demeanor of the troops; the organization, discipline, and impressive silence in this plaza, where not even the buzzing of a mosquito can be heard; the attentiveness of the people as they listen to the speakers amid the scorching noonday heat.

Nor can we forget our arrival in Nicaragua, right in the territory of Puerto Cabezas, from where the mercenary invasion of Girón was launched. It is said that the tyrant Somoza, on bidding farewell to the troops, asked them to bring back at least one hair from Castro's beard. I have come with my entire beard, to offer it, if only symbolically, to the victorious people of Nicaragua. [*Applause*]

The embraces our delegation exchanged yesterday with the leaders of the FSLN and the government are fully symbolic of these times and of the changes that have taken place.

As I look at you here, I confess that I am reminded of

our own people, our own rallies, our own masses. Because you are a profoundly revolutionary people, we Cuban visitors have the impression that we are in our own homeland.

But this historic miracle was not the work of chance or accident. The days of struggle are still too recent. Only a year ago the last shots of that long struggle, that long conflict, were still being fired. It is impossible to forget the feelings of admiration with which we listened to the news of the people's struggle, of a people practically without arms—the people who rose up in Managua with only a few weapons, the people who rose up in León and took it with only a few weapons, the people who rose up in Estelí, in Masaya, and in other cities, and took them [*Applause*] with only a few weapons.

We also recall with admiration the heroic fighters on the southern front, and the anguish felt by all the friends and sympathizers of the FSLN as they wondered what was to be the fate of the revolutionaries rising up in Managua. We recall our happiness upon receiving the news that after many days of heroic struggle, the organized and concentrated mass of fighters of Managua had been able to retreat toward Masaya—from the military point of view a retreat, but really one of the greatest feats and one of the greatest victories of the Nicaraguan people.

The pages of heroism you have written will go down in history. But that spirit, that heroism, was not the product of chance either. For many years, Sandino fought to defend the independence of the homeland, and he blazed a trail for you.

For twenty years, the Sandinistas fought to bring down the tyranny and free their people. Twenty years! So on a day such as this the heroes cannot be forgotten; the outstanding ones cannot be forgotten; [*Applause*] the extraordinary merit of that indefatigable fighter who was Fonseca Amador [*Applause*] can never be forgotten. There were men who saw things from far off and prepared the way.

The Somoza dynasty tyrannized this country for nearly fifty years. But when the hour of freedom seemed most distant, there were men who thought, organized, and elaborated a strategy of struggle. Those men were the Sandinistas, the Sandinista National Liberation Front.

They elaborated a strategy, they elaborated tactics of struggle, and they went on perfecting them. They succeeded in pulling the entire people behind them. They are not the vanguard because they want to give themselves the title of vanguard. They are the vanguard because they learned how to win for themselves the place of the vanguard in the history and struggle of their people. [*Applause*]

And they were wise—we have them right here—they were wise, very wise indeed. They were wise in the struggle, and at the decisive moment they had the supreme wisdom to unite, achieving a unity that today appears to be stronger than ever. [*Applause*] They were wise in the struggle and they were wise in victory. And they have continued being wise throughout this entire first year. Because as we see it the plan developed by the FSLN for the national reconstruction period—appealing to the entire people, appealing to the different social sectors to reconstruct the country, thereby allowing for a multiparty system and opposition—is one of the wisest things that any political movement in these circumstances could have done. [*Applause*]

And we are not just saying this here today. We said it almost a year ago, when on July 26, 1979—a few days after the victory—we received a large and prestigious Sandinista delegation on the date of our own anniversary. We wished them all of our sympathy and gave all our support to that plan, to that conception.

There are many who were afraid and who still harbor fears about the Sandinista revolution. There are those who seek to teach the Sandinistas what to do. We will never seek to tell the Sandinistas what they should do, or give or offer them free advice.

We are ready to give you all our support, all the solidarity of our people without conditions—without conditions and without advice. We did not come here to teach or to influence. We came humbly to learn and to be influenced. [*Applause*] We are sure that the Sandinista revolution will teach us a great deal and that the Sandinista revolution will have a great influence on us, just as we are certain that your example will have an extraordinary influence on the rest of Latin America. [*Applause*]

I have deliberately refrained from mentioning points of conflict. I have refrained from mentioning names that both you and we Cubans carry deeply in our hearts. We haven't wanted to mention points of conflict for reasons that I outlined at the beginning—so that no one will try to impute that we have come to Nicaragua to try to set fire to Central America or to try to put the torch to Latin America.

Besides, it is impossible to set fire to our peoples, it is impossible to carry such a torch. As some of you said recently, the best, most fundamental, and most decisive aid you can bring to the revolutionary movement is your example—because peoples are like volcanoes: no one sets fire to them; they explode by themselves. [*Applause*]

And Central America and the Andean Range are volcanic.

It is impressive, dear Nicaraguan brothers and sisters, what you have done in a year's time. What you have done in all fields, including in the difficult area of the economy. Yesterday we saw the excellent way in which the countryside has been sown and cultivated for kilometers and kilometers around.

We have seen the factories that are recovering. We know that the literacy campaign is going forward successfully, and that 108,000 Nicaraguans who have just learned how to read and write saluted the revolution today. [*Applause*] And that half a million more Nicaraguans will be able to receive their literacy certificates in the next few weeks. [*Applause*]

What country has done the same in so short a period of time, in the first year?

What other country has been able to organize a disciplined and combative army like this one in just the first year? We also know what an effort the Nicaraguan revolution has made to bring health care and well-being to the family.

Such achievements, such miracles, can only be the work of revolutions. Only popular revolutions are capable of such feats.

You have a country with great natural resources. It is almost impossible to imagine how far you will be able to go down this road, despite the great international difficulties, despite the difficulties of the world economy. But of course, no one must think I'm telling you that the fruits are just around the corner. Achieving the fruits of revolutionary labor—the work the people can accomplish when they get tired of so much poverty, so much underdevelopment, so much exploitation—requires a very long road. Whoever tells you that you will see material fruits the very next day is lying to you. That is a demagogue. But whoever talks to you about the long road to be traversed, that is an honest leader. [*Applause*]

In spite of all these impressive things, what is most striking is the barbarous and brutal way in which the cities of Nicaragua were destroyed—the overwhelming human sacrifice that the people of Nicaragua had to give for their liberation. I recall the final days of the war and the first days of the triumph, the enormous sympathy that the Nicaraguan revolution evoked everywhere.

So much was said then of the help the Nicaraguan people needed. Billions of dollars were being talked about—billions, not only to rebuild the country but also to deal with the gigantic debt left by Somozaism. Facing up to all that required tremendous international aid. It is painful to affirm that today, one year later, the actual amount of aid received by Nicaragua up to now is only a few tens of millions of dollars.

Almost a year ago, we suggested the need to launch an emulation campaign among all countries to see who could aid Nicaragua the most. Let us take advantage of this anniversary to reiterate that challenge—to appeal for such emulation in aiding Nicaragua. [*Applause*]

This noble people needs such help. It deserves such help. We hail collaboration with Nicaragua wherever it may come from. We even salute the aid that the government of the United States is reportedly going to provide. [*Applause*] I only lament, really and sincerely, that it is so little, given the wealth of the United States. It is little, for the richest country in the world. It is little, for a country that spends $170 billion [a year] for military purposes. It is little, for a country that according to projections is going to spend a trillion dollars in the next five years on the military. [*Applause*]

How much more fruitful and beneficial those and other expenditures on the arms race would be if they were devoted to helping the world's underdeveloped countries—countries like Nicaragua that need it so much. [*Applause*]

The specialists, the statesmen, the economists, the analysts all know what the world's real problem is at this moment—the dangers that threaten universally, dangers of further arms races, of cold wars, and even of hot war. Concern is very deep among the most serious and sensible people the world over; above all, after hearing of the platform of the Republican Party of the United States. A horrible platform, threatening to peace. A horrible program that threatens to apply the big stick to Latin America once again. A horrible platform that speaks of reneging as much as possible on the Panama Canal agreements. One that also speaks of annexing the fraternal people of Puerto Rico, that speaks of supporting the genocidal governments of this hemisphere, that speaks of cutting off all aid to Nicaragua.

There is great concern in the world, and thus it is everyone's duty to do whatever is in our power to confront those policies and to fight to safeguard peace. We are in such a situation that one must practically fight to safeguard peace.

That is the situation in the world today. But we revolutionaries cannot be pessimists; revolutionaries are and always will be optimists. Nor will we let ourselves be intimidated. Our peoples have demonstrated throughout history their capacity for struggle. Our peoples must not be underestimated. Our peoples must not be deprecated.

And if an example of this is called for, here then is the example: the people of Nicaragua. [*Applause*] We are the descendants of Indians, of Blacks; we have some Spanish blood as well. From those three races we have inherited what is best—valor.

It is my duty to come to an end. Excuse me, dear Nicaraguan brothers and sisters, if I have been lengthy. [*Applause*]

Long live Sandino!
Long live the Sandinista revolution!
Long live the heroic people of Nicaragua!
Patria o muerte!
Venceremos! [*Ovation*]

There is only one road to liberation: That of Cuba, that of Grenada, that of Nicaragua

July 26, 1980

Speech given at the rally in Ciego de Avila, Cuba, on the twenty-seventh anniversary of the Moncada attack. The text is from *Granma* Weekly Review August 3, 1980.

Distinguished guests;
People of Ciego de Avila;
Compatriots: [*Applause*]

New things are in the air. Last year, we celebrated our July 26 one week after the great Sandinista victory, and a large number of Nicaraguan guerrilla commanders attended the festivities. As a result, our July 26 celebration of 1979 turned into a Sandinista celebration. [*Applause*]

And again this year, a close relationship was established between the Nicaraguan people and the Cuban people, [*Applause*] because, as fate would have it, and as a result of the struggle of the peoples, both dates are in the same month. But something else. Since there is a seven-day difference between the two dates, not only do we always have in July a nineteenth and a twenty-sixth, it also happens that if the nineteenth is a Saturday, so is the twenty-sixth [*Applause*] and if the nineteenth is a Monday, so is the twenty-sixth, [*Applause*] and we have just come back from Nicaragua.

It is inevitable that we say something about Nicaragua. It is of interest to us, all of us. Not only we Cubans, but all Latin Americans.

I'm sure you all realize what it means, the impression, the happiness, the enthusiasm, the optimism, the emotion involved in arriving at the second Latin American country to free itself from imperialism. [*Applause*] In this hemisphere, there are now not two but three of us, because Grenada also has to be included.

Naturally, Nicaragua, Cuba, and Grenada are not the only progressive countries. There are other progressive governments, friendly with Cuba. We could mention, for example, the government of Mexico, [*Applause*] and we will soon have the great honor of welcoming the president of the sister republic of Mexico. [*Applause*] There are governments like that of our dear friend Manley, in Jamaica. [*Applause*] There are governments like that of Panama. [*Applause*] But three of us have shaken the yoke of imperialism in the last twenty years in a radical way, once and for all, [*Applause*] and it is a historical imperative that one day we'll all be free. [*Applause*] We'll either be free or we will cease to exist [*Applause*] because one day the battle cries of "Patria libre o morir" and "Patria o muerte" will be the battle cries of all the peoples of Latin America and the Caribbean. [*Applause*]

What we saw in Nicaragua was really stimulating and encouraging. We visited practically the entire country in only a few days, on a series of tours lasting as much as sixteen and a half hours nonstop. We were in Estelí, León,

Matagalpa, Masaya, Granada, Rivas, and the southern front. First of all, Managua and also Bluefields, on the Atlantic coast. You're probably wondering why it's called Bluefields. This is because the English were there at a time when the English and the Yankees were vying for the territory and wanted to have control over the area where they could build a canal. So the English built a sort of empire there among the Indian communities and for a time controlled practically the entire Nicaraguan Atlantic coast.

Nicaragua's land area is larger than Cuba's. The most developed area is the central and the western part, the Pacific side, that is. The Atlantic side, while more than half the country, is practically undeveloped.

Nicaragua is a country that, we might say, has more natural resources than Cuba. It has great water resources, which means vast possibilities to produce all the electric power it needs. They also have geothermal energy, which can be obtained from the volcanoes. They have large forests and large tracts of very fertile land. They have large lakes capable of producing food for the population. They have a large source of marine products all along their coast, a large shelf rich in every species of seafood and fish fit for human consumption. Therefore, the population, which is quite small—approximately one-fourth that of Cuba—has sufficient natural resources for great development in the future.

Needless to say, Somoza ran Nicaragua like a sort of private hacienda. Somoza owned the largest estates, most industry and production, so simply by confiscating the property of Somoza and his followers, the Sandinistas got control of a large percentage of the country's industry and agriculture.

Nicaragua does not have a socialist system. What it has is a mixed economy. There's even a multiparty system. There's the Sandinista Front and left-wing groups, and—why not?—there are also several right-wing parties. Therefore, we can't imagine Nicaragua's situation as exactly like Cuba's.

In Nicaragua there's a new revolutionary project, in the sense that what they have in mind at this stage is national reconstruction with the cooperation of everybody. As they announced on July 19, they aim to put into effect an agrarian reform covering lands standing idle, but they're also trying to stimulate private industrialists who have remained in the country and middle-level farmers—who were capitalist farmers—to contribute the utmost to national reconstruction. This in itself is a new experience in Latin America.

From our point of view and in the light of the international situation and the Nicaraguan reality, this project they have worked out is the best, the wisest at this moment.

We met with the people in many parts, in many places. We could see they are a very radical people, a very revolutionary people, a people who, in spite of illiteracy there, are extremely courteous and educated. They're a very hospitable, very warm, very enthusiastic, very disciplined, very intelligent, very aware, and very revolutionary people. [*Applause*] It is impressive to see what the people of Nicaragua are like one year after their victory.

Of course, everywhere you go you see the signs of the struggle that was waged there, particularly the last battles for the liberation of the cities. All that destruction, the damage caused by the artillery shells, by the bombs, the marks left by the bullets, must be seen to have a clear idea of the intensity of the struggle there.

The sight of Managua in ruins is also most impressive. The downtown section was completely destroyed by the earthquake. Therefore, Managua was rebuilt and goes on developing around the section that was destroyed by the earthquake.

However, in Nicaragua there were two earthquakes: the one that destroyed Managua, and Somozaism, which destroyed the country. And whereas the quake that devastated Managua had its toll of 10,000 dead, the earthquake of Somozaism had 50,000 dead. It is difficult to find a family in Nicaragua that hasn't lost a son, a brother, or some other close relative.

What the Sandinistas have been able to do in the reconstruction of the country in the first year of revolution is really impressive. They even have things that we didn't have in our first year. For example, they have the masses already organized: the trade unions, the Sandinista Defense Committees, the women, the young people, the Sandinista Children's Associations, somewhat like our Pioneers, and they have the Sandinista National Liberation Front, well organized throughout the country and which is like the revolutionary party and the vanguard of Nicaragua. [*Applause*] They have a collective leadership composed of a group of guerrilla fighters, with a long record, with great prestige and a lot of experience, who, in spite of the long years of struggle, are still a very young group, but with the advantage of being both experienced and mature.

They have a Government of National Reconstruction composed of experienced, capable men. There's a close relationship between the Sandinista Front and the Government of National Reconstruction; there's great unity among the Sandinistas, in the Sandinista ranks, and in the Sandinista leadership. Therefore, all the conditions exist for the revolutionary process to continue successfully.

The Sandinista struggle earned great sympathy and great international solidarity not only in Latin America but throughout the world. The broad form of government they have set up is without a doubt very favorable for continuing to have the broadest international support.

Last year we challenged the Western world to show who would help the Nicaraguan people the most, a sort of emulation in assistance. We stated our willingness to cooperate to the best of our possibilities, and we asked all other countries—capitalist, oil-producing, and socialist countries alike—to give the Nicaraguan revolution their utmost support, because it really needed it.

Now then, is there a revolution in Nicaragua or not? [*Shouts of "Yes!"*] There is a real revolution in Nicaragua. [*Applause*] And does the existence of the bourgeoisie, of private property in Nicaragua mean that there's a bourgeois revolution there? [*Shouts of "No!"*] No! There's no such thing as a bourgeois revolution in Nicaragua. In Nicaragua there is, in the first place, a people's revolution whose main strength is found in the workers, the peasants, the students, and the middle strata of the population. That people's revolution conducts the process, plans the process, so that the right thing is done at the right moment.

The fundamental thing in a revolution, the fundamental thing to be able to speak of a revolution, a people's revolution, is to have the people and the weapons.

What happened in Chile can never happen in Nicaragua, under any circumstances, because the people have the power, [*Applause*] because the people have the weapons. [*Applause*] Therefore, the revolution is guaranteed. And the revolution plans its development according to the country's real and objective conditions.

My meetings were not limited to the people. I also met with almost 400 trade union leaders, explaining our experiences in every field. I also met with a large number of priests and progressive religious leaders who are on the side of the revolution and give it their full support. [*Applause*]

Nicaragua is a country where religious feelings go far deeper than they did in Cuba; therefore, the support given to the revolution by those religious sectors is very important.

In Chile once, and also in Jamaica, we spoke of the strategic alliance between Christians and Marxist-Leninists. [*Applause*] If the revolution in Latin America were to take on an antireligious character, it would split the people. In our country, the Church was, generally speaking, the Church of the bourgeoisie, of the wealthy, of the landowners. This is not the case in many countries in Latin America, where religion and the Church have deep roots among the people. The reactionary classes have tried to use religion against progress, against revolution, and, in effect, they achieved their objective for quite a long time. However, times change, and imperialism, the oligarchy, and reaction are finding it more and more difficult to use the Church against revolution.

Many religious leaders have stopped talking exclusively about rewards in the other world and happiness in the other world and are talking about the needs of this world and happiness in this world. [*Applause*] For they see the hunger of the people, the poverty, the unhealthy conditions, the ignorance, suffering, and pain.

If we bear in mind that Christianity was, in the beginning, the religion of the poor, that in the days of the Roman Empire it was the religion of the slaves, because it was based on profound human precepts, there is no doubt that the revolutionary movement, the socialist movement, the communist movement, the Marxist-Leninist movement, would benefit a great deal from honest leaders of the Catholic Church and other religions returning to the Christian spirit of the days of the Roman slaves. [*Applause*]

What's more, Christianity would also benefit, along with socialism and communism. [*Applause*]

And some religious leaders in Nicaragua asked us why strategic alliance, why only strategic alliance; why not speak of unity between Marxist-Leninists and Christians? [*Applause*]

I don't know what the imperialists think about this. But I'm absolutely convinced the formula is highly explosive. [*Applause*] It exists not only in Nicaragua but also in El Salvador, where the revolutionary forces and the Christian forces are closely united.

Look how reaction and fascism are constantly murdering priests, how the archbishop of El Salvador was brutally assassinated. This is because reactionaries and fascists—many of whom go to church every Sunday—when they see their interests affected, endangered, do not hesitate to plant bombs in churches and to assassinate priests and bishops. They'd murder the pope if they could. [*Applause*]

But not only in El Salvador; there's Guatemala, where there's also constant repression and murder, including that of priests. There are numerous priests who are on the side of the revolution.

I'm telling you this so you'll have an idea of how situations change, how different they are in each country, and therefore we cannot be thinking of a strictly Cuban formula, because that formula is specifically for us. Of course, many of the other formulas have many of the ingredients that ours has, [*Applause*] but they'll never be completely alike.

We also met with the leaders of the Sandinista Front, about a hundred of them. They requested this meeting, and we explained our experiences to them. And I want to tell you that in those meetings I was very critical of our revolution, because I believe that honesty is worth more than anything else in the world, and we cannot be arrogant, or vain, or consider ourselves as savants. I do believe we are wise; but we are wise because we know how to recognize our own shortcomings, [*Applause*] because we know how to learn from our mistakes, [*Applause*] and we are wise because we are self-critical, [*Applause*] because we are modest. [*Applause*] And we sincerely believe that extraordinary lessons can be drawn from our revolution.

If you were to ask us what we'd do if we were to start all over again, I would tell you that we'd do exactly the same thing and we would arrive at this point where we are today exactly the same way. [*Applause*] Except that there's no doubt that we'd do it much better! [*Applause*]

When I spoke in Revolution Square in Managua, I wasn't there to give advice. I said I wasn't there to teach, but to learn; that I wasn't going to influence anybody, that I was there to be influenced. Any student of history who is really interested in politico-revolutionary processes will learn a great deal from every new revolution. [*Applause*]

There were some people who were worried about Fidel visiting Nicaragua and were wondering if the visit might not be harmful to the Nicaraguans. The Nicaraguans knew full well that I never mentioned visiting Nicaragua and that I never invited myself to go there. They knew full well that I was ready to visit Nicaragua the day and the time that suited them, [*Applause*] be it the first year, the second, the third, or the next ten or twenty years, or never. Because we have no use for any vanity, [*Applause*] for any kind of chauvinism, [*Applause*] or for any kind of hegemonism. [*Applause*] Our revolution wants to be an example; it does not want to be hegemonic. [*Applause*] Our revolution is not interested in appearing as the leader or leading the peoples. We'd be very glad to bring up the rear—the very rear—of a whole revolutionary Latin America and Caribbean. [*Applause*] What we're interested in is the revolution, the liberation of our peoples. And this is why, when we went to Nicaragua it wasn't because the Sandinistas invited us but because they demanded that we visit Nicaragua. [*Applause*]

I'm saying this as a warning to those who think we are conceited and that we are trying to make a big show of ourselves. Our friendship with the Sandinistas wasn't born yesterday, or a year back, but twenty years ago. [*Applause*] And we have very close relations, but based on mutual respect and confidence.

The imperialists and the reactionaries are alarmed over what may happen in Guatemala and El Salvador and all the other places. We are not alarmed. The imperialists are alarmed when there are Marxist-Leninists; they are horrified. To them, the sight of a Marxist is like seeing a ghost, like seeing the Devil himself; they lose sleep over it. But we are not alarmed when we see the bourgeoisie, [*Applause*] we laugh. When the reactionaries see a socialist, a communist, a Marxist-Leninist, they think that's the end of the bourgeoisie; but when we see a member of the bourgeoisie we never think that socialism and communism are coming to an end. [*Applause*] This is because bourgeois society already belongs to the past, as do slave society and feudal society. The time will come when people will ask, "What was that madness called capitalism?" "What was it good for?" Capitalism will then be a past stage, here and elsewhere.

I'm explaining all these things so that nobody will be confused and in order to express our confidence in the Sandinista revolution, to express our opinion that what they are doing they are doing exceptionally well, in a very correct fashion. [*Applause*] They have power in their hands, and they can plan their future. No two-bit coup d'état is ever going to liquidate the Sandinista revolution. There won't be any coups d'état there, because the people are in power and they have the weapons. [*Applause*] What happened in Chile can't happen there; what happened in Bolivia can't happen there.

This shows what the reactionaries, the capitalists, and the imperialists are capable of doing. They talk of parliament, constitutions, and democracy. What kind of lousy democracy is it [*Applause*] when the people don't count, when an election is held, the people vote and elect a progressive government, and then there's a fascist coup d'état and the repression starts? The same thing happened in El Salvador. As soon as the revolutionary movement grew in strength, there was a coup d'état. In El Salvador the fascist military, allied with Christian Democracy—which has nothing left of democracy and is certainly not Christian—have established a genocidal regime. An average of fifty people a day are murdered in El Salvador.

I would like to ask those governments that raised such a hue and cry over the scum why they don't say a single word about the dozens of crimes that are being committed against the people every day in El Salvador. [*Applause*] They got very concerned over some odd lumpen here, [*Shouts of "For sure, Fidel, give the Yankees hell!" and applause*] over common criminals, loafers, and parasites who were never once harmed, hadn't a single hair on their head touched. Well, to tell the truth, they had to be protected so their hair wouldn't be mussed [*Laughter*] and we had to call on our people several times to refrain from liquidating the lumpen; but what counts is that they weren't harmed. They all wanted to go to the Yankee paradise, to the paradise of prostitution, narcotics, gambling, etc. In a nutshell, scum! Those governments became very concerned over that lot and started all kinds of campaigns, and now here we are in the presence of a monstrous genocide—monstrous! The fascists' plans are to assassinate 200,000 Salvadorans in an attempt to crush the revolution; and they are murdering men, women, and children, innocent people, in order to sow terror.

Why aren't there democratic voices speaking up to defend this heroic people's most elementary right to live? And what are they speaking of? Aha, possible interventions!

I don't want to mention governments, although I know full well which they are. I don't want to mention them because sometimes it's better not to stir things up, given the special situation that exists on the continent at the moment; given the fact that a coup has just taken place in Bolivia, a coup which has been widely condemned. But some of those who condemn the coup in Bolivia, where they have unleashed fierce repression against the workers, peasants, and students, in turn support the genocidal government of the fascist Christian Democratic junta in El Salvador. [*Applause*] And the United States sends instructors, sends arms, and offers economic aid to the fascist Christian Democratic junta. And they speak about intervention; let's see what happens if they intervene in El Salvador. The people of El Salvador should not be underestimated. The imperialists should not underestimate the people of El Salvador, nor should they underestimate feelings throughout Latin America with respect to El Salvador. [*Applause*]

We saw the unanimous, total solidarity the Nicaraguan people have for El Salvador. I am convinced that if the imperialists are stupid enough to intervene in El Salvador, they will create a Vietnam in Central America. [*Applause*]

Moreover, the Yankee imperialists supported Somoza, because they were the ones that put him there. I didn't want to talk about these things when I spoke at the main rally there, because there was a U.S. delegation present, and I was a visitor and didn't think I had the right to speak on such a subject, but here I think I have some right to bring it up. [*Applause*] The imperialists put Somoza there; they intervened directly in Nicaragua for many years; they created the Somoza National Guard, which brought Somoza to power, the first Somoza dynasty, because there have been at least three monarchs there. They are the ones responsible for the death of Sandino; they are the ones responsible for fifty years of tyranny that took the lives of over 100,000 Nicaraguans; and they supported that tyranny to the very end. They also created the idea of an inter-American peace-keeping force, with the objective of intervening to snatch victory from the Sandinistas. They failed, because even the OAS, the famous OAS, rebelled when they tried to put this plan into effect; otherwise, they would have tried to do what they did in Santo Domingo.

Well, the Sandinistas triumphed and the U.S. declared itself ready to cooperate, to be friendly. We were pleased about that, because a policy of cooperation seems much more sensible than a policy of hostility; a policy of cooperation and not a policy of aggression.

Of course, the imperialists have already learned something from the Cuban revolution, and from their plans of aggression, their blockade, and their hostility against Cuba. They apparently didn't want to take two doses of the same medicine.

Well, we are glad they don't put a blockade on Nicaragua, that there is no economic or any other kind of aggression against Nicaragua, that there are no subversive plans against Nicaragua; this is what we demand of imperialism. And it's the imperialists' basic moral obligation to cooperate economically, since they exploited the Nicaraguan people and were responsible for the fifty years of tyranny they suffered. We are by no means opposed, but happy to see the imperialists cooperate economically with Nicaragua. But they have spent a year debating a $75 million credit. Finally, after much discussion, which was at times humiliating for the receiving country, the credit was approved. Of course, the major part of it goes to private enterprise and is not at the free disposal of the Government of National Reconstruction.

That is, the imperialists, after the triumph of the Sandinistas, want to build, support, and stimulate capitalism in Nicaragua. Their intentions are clear, but we are happy, very happy, that they have granted credit and are cooperating economically with Nicaragua.

We have very eloquent proof of the ties between Somozaism and imperialism: the mercenary invasion at Playa Girón. Because the mercenaries trained in Guatemala were sent to Puerto Cabezas in Nicaragua, and from Puerto Cabezas—as if it were CIA property—they were sent to Cuba. The B-26 bombers that attacked our air bases, that attacked our people, left from Puerto Cabezas. All the ships and the entire mercenary expedition left from Puerto Cabezas. These were the kind of ties between Somoza and imperialism.

Genocide is not only being committed in El Salvador, but in Guatemala as well. Corpses of workers, students, professionals, even priests, appear daily. It is a repressive, genocidal regime. Here with us is our friend Toriello, who was foreign minister during the time of Arbenz.* [*Applause*] He witnessed the Yankee intervention, an expedition like

---

* The government of Jacobo Arbenz Guzmán in Guatemala (1951–54) carried out labor and agrarian reform and expropriated some U.S. properties, including that of the United Fruit Company. The government was overthrown by a CIA-organized coup.

that of Girón, which overthrew the democratic government of Guatemala more than twenty years ago to establish a mercenary government, a mercenary government that has cost Guatemala 60,000 lives in the past twenty years. And I ask myself if the peoples can go on accepting this state of affairs.

The Guatemalan experience, the Salvadoran experience, the Chilean experience, the Bolivian experience, what have they taught us? That there is only one path: revolution! [*Applause*] That there is only one way: revolutionary armed struggle! [*Applause*] That is the thesis Cuba defended when it said to the people: they're deceiving you.

The oligarchy, reaction, and imperialism use all these so-called constitutional mechanisms, the so-called representative democracy, to deceive the peoples. Even when the overwhelming majority of people through the democratic, or so-called democratic mechanisms, vote against a reactionary government and in favor of a progressive government, or even a democratic one, there's a coup d'état. Like in Chile, in Bolivia. And the peoples learned their lessons and saw that there was only one road to liberation: that of Cuba, that of Grenada, that of Nicaragua. There is no other formula.

Now then, the imperialists are threatening us with intervention. Should we lose our sleep over that? Have we not lived under constant threats for the past twenty-one years? The peoples will not give up fighting. The example of Nicaragua is eloquent proof of what a people can do, for they liquidated the Somoza army almost unarmed. The peoples already know that there are possibilities for fighting not only in the mountains, not only in the rural areas, but also in the cities. [*Applause*] They know how to dig tunnels, tear down walls, connect some houses with others on the same block, and turn rebellious cities into fortresses. And when one sees the image of how it happened in Nicaragua, one realizes that no army could have countered that action. The peoples already know that the myth, the old myth dating back to the times of Mussolini, to the effect that the revolution can be made with or without the army but never against the army, is a lie. For we already have here in our own hemisphere three revolutions against three armies! [*Applause*]

We are living through truly dangerous international moments that affect our region and affect the whole world. Analysts, statesmen, men given to calm thinking, understand and realize how somber the world's prospects are in the next few years: the energy problems facing the world, particularly the underdeveloped world; the food problems; the problems of uncontrolled population growth; the educational problems, the health problems; the ecological problems, that is, not only the destruction of the landscape, but also the gradual poisoning of the water and the atmosphere. Even if you can prevent war from breaking out, the effort that must be made to tackle these problems is truly impressive, and they could not be solved at all without international collaboration—we need not only a climate of peace but one of collaboration.

Now the world finds itself anew on the brink of cold war, of the arms race, at a time when the underdeveloped countries of the world are shouldering a debt of $300 billion and it is estimated that it will be $700 billion by 1985. This means that the world is on the verge of an unprecedented economic and financial catastrophe. And faced with this situation that undoubtedly calls for a supreme effort for peace, coexistence, and collaboration among all nations of the world, we find ourselves with the present situation of the United States, its warmongering policy, its plans to deploy over 500 medium-range nuclear missiles in Europe, its plans to rearm NATO, its plans to set up military bases in the Persian Gulf and the Indian Ocean, set up bases in the Middle East, etc. For all this, the current U.S. administration is responsible.

Now then, the Republican Party convention was recently held in the United States, and its candidate has drawn up and approved a political platform of an extremely dangerous and extremely reactionary nature. At times one gets the impression that we are living through days similar to those that preceded Hitler's election as chancellor of Germany.

I do not mean to say that both situations are exactly the same. Back then a lunatic like Hitler could start a war with the hope of winning it and without the risk of humanity being wiped out. I think that lunatics nowadays have a different straitjacket, which are the changes that have taken place in the world, the current world balance of forces; and we still hope that these lunatics will use some common sense.

But at this moment there's a real possibility of the party that approved such a platform winning the U.S. elections. And of course, its views on Latin America couldn't be more gloomy. It is in favor of cutting all aid to Nicaragua and getting rid of revolution there much as one would get rid of a cyst, blocking all progressive change in Central America, practically helping fascist governments, repudiating the Panama Canal accords, annexing Puerto Rico. Mention has even been made of a naval blockade against Cuba; there is the most reactionary talk of aggressive policies in Southeast Asia and in the Middle East, of a rearmament policy, of a policy to achieve military superiority over the socialist camp.

I know that there are some in the United States who would prefer us Cubans not to attack that platform. They say that owing to certain U.S. public opinion trends to the right, any criticism leveled at that program may help its authors, since we are looked upon as enemies and it might be considered a merit if Cuba should attack that program. Very well, I can understand that point of view. But what's in the cards here is not a U.S. presidential election; what's in the cards may be the fate of humanity, the fate of the world, maybe peace and war. [*Applause*]

That platform must be denounced and world opinion has to be aware of this. It is essential that world opinion react to such a political program. Names are not important to us; we don't care who becomes the president of the United States; we do not intend to get mixed up in that. But we are interested in a situation that derives from the existence of a U.S. party program that threatens the world with war. [*Applause*] What is involved here is not just a national but an international question. What is involved here is not just concern for our country but concern for humanity.

As a revolutionary country, we are aware of the risks we have run ever since we decided to make a revolution. We have lived through twenty-one years of such risks, we have had to endure everything: economic blockade, subversion, sabotage, counterrevolutionary bands, plans to murder us all. The fact that we are still alive evidences how inefficient imperialism is, for everybody knows about the plans they made; and in all fairness it also evidences how efficient our state security organs are. [*Applause*] Mercenary invasions, pirate attacks, plans for direct aggression. Wasn't all that what led to nuclear missiles being stationed in Cuba? Why did we agree to that? Simply to counter U.S. plans of direct aggression against Cuba.

Many of us lived through that experience, a great many

people who are here—perhaps not the boys and girls who won first place among the junior high schools—but there were times here when we had nuclear missiles, and when there were many nuclear weapons also pointed against us. And everybody will recall that during those critical October days no one here was intimidated, or frightened, or lost any sleep. A time even came when we were willing to disappear from the map rather than yield one iota to the imperialists' demands. [*Applause*]

Subsequently I explained to the First Congress of the party our current appreciation of the solution given to the crisis that ensued, and I said, in all frankness and all honesty, that in the light of history, in the light of the nearly twenty years that have elapsed since then, the solution seems to us to have been a correct one.

But if I bring this up today, when there are new threats looming on the horizon, I do so to make it quite clear to the Republican clique, to Mr. Reagan, or Regan, or however you pronounce it—and to his advisers, that threats against Cuba will be of no avail, [*Shouts of "For sure, Fidel, give the Yankees hell!" and "Fidel, give them hell; let's make 'em respect us well!"*] to warn the imperialists that we are not going to lose any sleep over it. Our people are a tempered, veteran people and are sufficiently brave as not to be intimidated by anyone.

We don't know what's going to happen. It also often happens that the electoral platform is one thing and what the presumed lunatics do when they're in power is something else. Maybe all that is just demagogic waffle, but in our opinion it is dangerous, because we think that they are saying what they feel, that they are saying what they think.

We should analyze these problems and our people must be warned. I think it is one more reason for us to improve our work, develop our strength, develop our defenses, and, above all, develop our awareness.

If a platform of this nature is carried into practice, there will be war between the United States and the Latin American peoples, because it is impossible to take this continent back to the times of the big stick. And our people—a highly educated and politically aware people—must be kept posted of these realities, must be conscious of these realities.

We are not pessimists, we have never been pessimists: on the contrary, we have been and still are optimists. That's why we attach so much importance to international public opinion and the people's opinion, because there's no possible way, there are no ways to bring the world, or to attempt to bring the world, under the yoke of fascism, the yoke of colonialism, the yoke of neocolonialism, the yoke of oppression, without first wiping out humanity. In other words, we do not believe that there's anything or anybody in the world capable of turning the clock back historically. But we would be naive, very naive, we would be unrealistic, not to be aware of the dangers.

I think there are a lot of people in the world—not only socialists, not only Marxist-Leninists, but also democrats, liberals, bourgeois, bourgeois intellectuals, religious sectors, statesmen, even from the capitalist world, even from the industrialized capitalist world, who are aware, must be aware, of these dangers. We know that there are many people warning of this, and these sensible, fundamentally sensible opinions must surely prevail.

That's why our duty is to struggle for peace while at the same time being ready for anything. [*Applause*] That should be our stand: to struggle for peace, work for peace, defend peace, and, at the same time, be ready for anything. [*Applause*]

It was decided that this year's July 26 celebrations be held in the new province of Ciego de Avila. [*Applause*] This was our party's recognition for the province's enthusiastic, efficient, brilliant work. [*Applause*] I know how happy this decision made you, I know how hard you worked since the decision was announced fifty-four days ago; how all of you have created in just a few weeks: this square, these avenues, the bypass, the works you have completed—even a movie theater scheduled for December was completed in nearly forty-five days; [*Applause*] how you have repaired the city, painted everything, all you have done so that Ciego de Avila could host the July 26 celebrations, be host to all the delegations that have arrived here. [*Applause*] For we are now commemorating July 26 precisely in our country's smallest provincial capital. [*Applause*]

This rally, its organization, its size, is all very impressive. We also know how long you have been mobilizing for this, how long it took you to get here, the hours you have waited in this square. We know about the huge effort which has been made in agriculture, in the planting and weeding of cane. [*Applause*]

From the standpoint of sugar, Ciego de Avila is one of the country's most important provinces. In years past, this province needed tens of thousands of workers from Havana Province and the eastern provinces—manpower from other provinces—to make the harvest. I do not mean the province, for it didn't exist then as such; I mean the region. Your greatest merit, being a province with a population of 315,000—possibly Cuba's smallest province—and large sugar areas, lies in the fact that you were capable, relying almost totally on your own forces, to complete the province's productive tasks, to plant and harvest the cane and do other agricultural work, finish construction projects, and maintain services. [*Applause*]

This is a province with a high productivity index. We can quote some figures to show how productivity has been boosted during the revolution in agriculture and the sugar industry. For instance, back in 1952 a canecutter used to cut an average of 1.74 tons, as compared with 3.68 tons in 1979. In 1952, 30,836 canecutters were needed for the harvest; in 1979 only 6,949 were needed. This gives you an idea how much mechanization has progressed; that is, we now need 23,887 canecutters less than in 1952, the year of the capitalists' largest harvest.

To cut, load, and haul the cane, 35,315 workers were required in 1952 as against 11,341 today.

Sugar production per agricultural worker in 1952 was 26.5 tons; in 1979, the figure was 77.4, nearly three times as much. In 1979, sugar production per inhabitant was 2.74 tons, Cuba's highest. [*Applause*] This means that 2.74 tons were produced for every Ciego de Avila inhabitant, and the province's total sugar production amounted to nearly 900,000 tons. This means that at prevailing prices—averaging the Western market and the socialist market prices—it can be said that every Ciego de Avila inhabitant has produced nearly one thousand pesos in sugar. [*Applause*]

But other indexes are not as favorable. Although the cane yield is now higher per hectare of land, it should be much higher still if we bear in mind the irrigation areas and the amount of fertilizers we are using. There is still room for growth in cane yield. The sugar recovery was under par; that is, it was an unfavorable index. You people here have still a long way to go, in spite of what you have achieved. Efforts to mechanize cane cutting will continue. Cane loading is now mechanized 100 percent. Fifty-six percent of the last harvest was mechanized. In the future there will be more machines, fewer canecutters. In the future, you can raise the sugar recovery indexes. The nation selected and dispatched to the province's sugar mills a few dozen engineers and young technicians—there were some mills which had very few technicians or none at all. We must have all the technicians and qualified personnel necessary for sugar production.

I believe you will be capable of achieving higher sugar recovery indexes, I believe you will be capable of boosting production considerably, just as you have done, for instance, in bananas, for there are areas in the province where up to approximately thirty-four tons of bananas are produced per hectare. In other areas, a substantial increase has been reached in potato growing. But the spirit prevailing of late in Ciego de Avila to boost work productivity by all means is essential, since a province with a small population, with large agricultural areas, important industrial areas, and important service areas, must make a special effort by applying all factors needed to increase work productivity.

On a national level, an extraordinary effort was made this spring to take care of cane planting. As you all know, we were afflicted with plagues that were very damaging, three plagues.

The blue mold nearly wiped out the tobacco plantations. Yet we think that by next crop we will restore tobacco production to what it used to be with the use of proven chemical products which are highly efficient against the blue mold.

We also had a bout of African swine fever and for the second time succeeded in eradicating that disease.

We are now confronting sugar cane smut, which mainly affected the 4362 variety, the Barbados 4362, and we are now eradicating it. This year, practically half of this cane was uprooted and those areas were planted with other varieties, and we think that by next year the disease will be eradicated in the remaining 200,000 hectares. But some 200,000 hectares will be affected in next year's harvest. Instead of yielding between around 51–60 tons of sugar, it is estimated we will only get some 17 tons per hectare. This boils down to hundreds and hundreds of thousands of tons of sugar; hence the special importance attached to planting and weeding the cane. An appeal was made to the people, and the people, as always, came through. And it can be said that our country has just witnessed a true March of the Fighting People in production. [*Applause*]

This spring, 274,100 hectares of cane were planted, the largest planting done in the five-year period; 1,033,970 hectares of land planted with ratoon cane were fertilized with a balanced formula, the highest figure of the five-year period; [*Applause*] 204,024 hectares of new cane were fertilized with a balanced formula, the highest of the five-year period; [*Applause*] nitrogenized fertilization was applied on 1,306,118 hectares, the highest of the five-year period; [*Applause*] 1,781,398 hectares of ratoon cane were grown, the highest of the five-year period; [*Applause*] 378,229 hectares of new cane were grown, the highest of the five-year period; [*Applause*] 185,907 hectares of land were replanted, the highest of the five-year period; [*Applause*] 668,349 hectares were irrigated, the highest; [*Applause*] herbicides were used on 1,510,340 hectares, the highest; [*Applause*] 1,720,578 hectares had been weeded by hand by July 24—the plan called for 1,510,958 hectares by July 31. [*Applause*] Compared with last year, more than twice the number of hectares were weeded by this date—on July 20, 1979, the figure was 698,256 hectares. This means that compared with this time last year, much more than twice the number of hectares were weeded by hand this year. [*Applause*] There were days when more than 400,000 workers were mobilized to do the weeding.

What now remains is the unpredictable factor of the weather, how much rain we will have in the rest of July, how much in August. But from a human standpoint, everything possible was done and will continue to be done.

We now have ahead of us the schedule for late planting, involving over 174,460 hectares. This is very important since the late cane will be the one with the highest sugar yield in the 1982 harvest.

The program for building new sugar factories and boosting sugar production will go on being developed. Work is already pressing ahead on getting the next harvest ready; we are at a considerably more advanced stage than last year in having all the materials available and repairing the mills. Repair work on the machinery and harvesters is underway. After thoroughly analyzing all the details that affected the last harvest, steps are being taken so that our next harvest will be really efficient.

Not only has a big effort been made in cane growing but also in construction, transportation, unloading in the ports, where last month an all-time record was registered. Owing to the simultaneous arrival of a great number of vessels, a special effort was required and the port and transportation workers really came through in response to an appeal that was made; in July they surpassed the unloading plan in spite of the difficulties they ran into in some places like, for instance, the City of Havana, where it was carnival month.

Our capital's passenger transport workers also made a great effort and considerably improved the service. They are intent on making 29,000 daily trips, which is seen as the figure necessary to provide adequate bus service in the capital.

I am also aware of the effort made by the doctors and other health personnel to improve the quality of services; the effort made by teachers to improve the quality of education.

The appeal made by the revolution to be more disciplined and more demanding is beginning to bear fruit. It is our sworn duty and should be our commitment for this July 26 to continue resolutely along the road of struggle against all that is badly done, [*Applause*] against the weaknesses, against the deficiencies, and to insist on being demanding and disciplined! [*Applause*]

When we talk about the efforts of our workers in recent months, it is important on a day like this to remember and praise the tens of thousands of our countrymen who are working as workers, technicians, teachers, doctors, and fighters in diverse parts of the world. [*Applause*]

Right now there are Cuban doctors and technical personnel in more than thirty countries. Thus, we do not feel ashamed of still having a little bit of scum left, which we are certainly sweeping up and sending to the perfect garbage dump, [*Applause and shouts*] when more than 50,000 self-sacrificing and magnificent Cubans elevate the name of our homeland and do exemplary work in scores of our sister countries. [*Applause*] These and other examples demonstrate what our homeland is, what our revolution has forged!

When Nicaragua asked us for teachers, teachers with years of experience, 29,500 volunteered; [*Applause*] during the internationalist missions to Angola and Ethiopia, hundreds of thousands of members of our armed forces and reserves volunteered. [*Applause*] When we send a group of construction workers, no matter to what part of the world, there are always more than enough Cubans ready to go on the mission. [*Applause*]

I had the opportunity in Nicaragua to see the work being done by Cuban doctors, nurses, and health workers. In less than a year, they have done thousands and thousands of surgical operations and have seen more than a million patients. More than a million! [*Applause*] That gives an idea of what a handful of our compatriots, a handful of revolutionary technicians can accomplish. I could also evaluate the work of the teachers, through all the information that I collected, how they have taught tens upon tens of thousands of Nicaraguan children and adults to read and write. [*Applause*] Of course, I forgot to mention that the literacy campaign is a great success, and in one year—in one year!—they will almost eradicate illiteracy, which was running at about 60 percent. [*Applause*]

Over there, in very remote areas, I found many young Nicaraguan literacy brigade members working with a spirit that reminded us of the members of our literacy brigades in 1961. [*Applause*] Our teachers have gone to some of the most remote parts of the jungle and the mountains. That contingent returns to Nicaragua in September; but this time, instead of 1,200 Cuban teachers in Nicaragua, there will be 2,000. [*Applause*] And that will not leave us short of teachers.

When I entered this area this afternoon, I saw the dazzling building of the primary teachers' school in Ciego de Avila. We now have schools for primary teachers in every province, with more than 30,000 students. We have students in different stages to become teachers, and we have a large number studying for degrees in primary education. Altogether there are 152,000 education workers studying at the various levels. We will not lack teachers, we will not lack teachers! [*Applause*] Do you remember when 70 percent of our primary school teachers were not accredited? Now 100 percent of our teachers are accredited. [*Applause*]

And we asked the comrades in the Sandinista leadership, "Are there still children not going to school?" "Well, we estimate about 25 percent," they answered. I say, "We are ready to send them even more teachers." [*Applause*]

And doctors? Do you remember when 3,000 out of 6,000 doctors left the country? Well, now we have more than 15,000 doctors, and good doctors! [*Applause*] More than 4,000 students entering the universities each year to study medicine, and we are building medical schools in all the provinces. Besides having the highest level of health of all the underdeveloped countries in the world, or the countries known as the Third World; we also have the highest level of education.

Now we are reaping the benefits of our efforts in these last few years. It is a satisfaction to think that we have one doctor for every 750 residents, and we do not just take care of our own medical needs. There are countries in the world that have a doctor for every 300,000 people; for example, Ethiopia has 125 doctors for 34 million inhabitants; but we have sent doctors to Ethiopia, about 150 doctors. [*Applause*] More than 1,500 Cuban doctors and dentists are working in other countries. Thus, we are not only able to care for our own health and maintain the highest level of health in the Third World, but we are able to help other countries.

And we must think about when the revolutions in El Salvador and Guatemala and other countries are victorious, because eventually they will triumph and no one and nothing can stop that, [*Applause*] and they will need more internationalist doctors and more internationalist teachers, and more internationalist technicians. [*Applause*]

I believe I reflect the sentiments of our people when I say that that should be our consciousness and that should be our conduct, [*Applause*] without any chauvinism, without any national egoism.

It is right that we work and continue to work for our

welfare, it is right that we work and continue to work for better standards of living, to solve many of the problems that we still have; but we can share some of the fruits of our efforts and our revolution.

As I once said, to be an internationalist is to pay our own debt to humanity, [*Applause*] because other countries, other peoples, helped and continue to help us a great deal. [*Applause*] The Soviet worker who grows wheat in the Ukraine or extracts oil in Siberia and ships it to the ports and from the ports to Cuba has helped us tremendously. [*Applause*] So have the technicians from the Soviet Union and other socialist countries, and the arms we've received to defend ourselves so that we can today feel secure and not be afraid of anyone—including Reagan, or King Kong, if he were president of the United States. [*Laughter and applause*]

Thanks to internationalism, our country is secure, our energy needs and many raw materials are guaranteed, and we are assured of steady, fair trade. [*Applause*]

We don't have great material resources, but we do have great human resources—our doctors are our human resources, our teachers are our human resources, [*Applause*] our technicians, our construction workers are our human resources. This we have, and of extraordinary quality! [*Applause*]

Universities with more than 150,000 students, tens of thousands of workers studying in higher education, tens of thousands of workers already completing ninth grade, almost all our workers having completed the minimum of sixth grade—these are truly impressive advances. And I think we will go even further, since the workers' organizations have already proposed making ninth grade the minimum for all workers. [*Applause*] And the two Latin American peoples to eradicate illiteracy are Cuba first, and now Nicaragua [*Applause*]—this is what the revolution means, what the revolution is capable of doing.

So we must continue to prepare ourselves and continue working to develop our country and contribute as much as we can to the development and progress of other peoples.

Speaking of this date, of the men who died on this date, of the martyrs of the revolution, of those who shed their blood on a day like today which is a symbol of other dates, a symbol of those who died later, in the clandestine struggle, a symbol of those who died in the landing of the *Granma* or in the eastern or Escambray mountains or fighting the saboteurs and counterrevolutionaries on any front, or completing internationalist missions—I think that all these men and women would be happy with this country as it is today, with this dignity, with this people. Nothing could have made them prouder than the idea that the people who twenty-seven years ago lived under the darkest, most infamous oppression are what they are today; [*Applause*] that this revolution is what it is today. [*Applause*] That is why I said at the beginning that we were wiser, because we have learned a great deal in these twenty-seven years. We have learned from experience, we have learned from mistakes, we have always been open and honest, ready to correct ourselves whenever necessary. Whoever says he was born wise is a liar; whoever says he knows everything is an egoist who knows nothing. There is no better teacher than the revolution itself, [*Applause*] and we correct our mistakes as soon as we recognize them.

I sincerely believe that our revolutionary process today is strong, very strong, stronger than ever! [*Prolonged applause and shouts of "For sure, Fidel, give the Yankees hell!"*]

What have we gained today in comparison with that twenty-sixth of July, twenty-seven years ago? First of all, a great party, [*Applause*] with hundreds of thousands of communist members coming from the heart of our people. [*Applause*] We have powerful mass organizations, to which the immense majority of our population belong [*Applause*]—the unions, the CDRs, the Federation of Cuban Women, the peasant associations, the student and Pioneer associations. [*Applause*] Forging new party members, we have the powerful organization of our Young Communist League. [*Applause*] We have the socialist state and People's Power. [*Applause*] We have our glorious Revolutionary Armed Forces [*Applause*] and our members of the Ministry of the Interior. [*Applause*] We have tens of thousands of veterans and experienced cadres everywhere—in the party, the mass organizations, and the state. [*Applause*]

We should not be afraid to face the future, no matter what the prospects. We continue to hope for a world of peace, a world of cooperation between the peoples, regardless of political systems. We are prepared to take on the task of development, to work for long-term plans, [*Applause*] to think of the year '85, the year '90, and the year 2000. We are already working on the next five-year plan, and on the plans for the year 2000. We hope to considerably improve our economic efficiency, with the help of the economic management and planning system; [*Applause*] that is, we are applying the experience accumulated by socialist revolutions, applying science to economic planning and management.

We will not achieve victory and success only by applying a system, applying an experience, applying science to planning and management. Behind all this there must be the people. [*Applause*] We will unite science, experience, and consciousness. [*Applause*] We will not abandon voluntary work, [*Applause*] because, although we are in the phase of the construction of socialism and it is necessary to apply the principle of distribution according to work, we are and aspire to be communists. [*Applause*] Other generations will live in communism, but from now on we must begin to forge not only socialist men and women, but communist men and women. [*Applause*]

When I ask myself what is a communist, I think of a doctor in Bluefields, a woman who is both wife and mother, capable of leaving her family to save lives thousands of miles from home. [*Applause*] I think of a teacher in a remote area of the world; I think of a Cuban fighter ready to die in another country to defend a just cause thousands of miles from home. [*Applause*] And I say to myself, these are communist men and women. I think of one of these Heroes of Labor; [*Applause*] I think of one of these canecutters who, for months at a time, work ten, twelve, even fourteen hours a day to complete our harvests; [*Applause*] I think of the hundreds of thousands of devoted compatriots—manual and intellectual workers—who dedicate their lives to their work and duty, and thanks to whom there is a homeland and a revolution. [*Applause*] Not only does our party have hundreds of thousands of members, but in the heart of our people there are millions of communists. [*Applause*]

I think we have ample reason to be optimistic, we have ample reason to proudly celebrate this July 26, [*Applause*] as an affirmation that the blood shed twenty-seven years ago and the blood shed throughout these twenty-seven years has not been in vain! [*Applause*]

Patria o muerte!

Venceremos! [*Shouts of "Venceremos!"*] [*Ovation*]

Appendix A

Cuba in Angola: Operation Carlota

by Gabriel García Márquez

This article by one of Latin America's most famous writers is the most complete account yet written about the Cuban role in Angola. It is copyright © 1977 by Gabriel García Márquez and is reprinted by permission of the author. The translation is by Prensa Latina.

Officially, the United States first announced the presence of Cuban troops in Angola on November 24, 1975. In February the following year, during a brief visit to Caracas, Henry Kissinger privately said to President Carlos Andrés Pérez: "Our intelligence services must be deteriorating because we found out that the Cubans were going to Angola after they were already there." At that moment, many Cuban soldiers, military specialists, and civilian technicians were in Angola, many more than Henry Kissinger knew about. There were so many Cuban ships anchored in the Bay of Luanda that President Agostinho Neto, counting them from his window, was overcome with remorse, a characteristic trait of his: "It's not fair," he told an official, "at this rate Cuba will ruin itself."

Possibly, the Cubans themselves had not foreseen that their solidaric aid to the people of Angola would acquire such proportions. But they clearly understood from the start that their aid had to be decisive and swift, and that they had to win.

Contacts between the Cuban revolution and the MPLA (Popular Movement for the Liberation of Angola) were established for the first time—on a very intense level—in August 1965, when Che Guevara was working with the guerrillas of the Congo. The following year, Agostinho Neto visited Cuba accompanied by Endo, commander in chief of the MPLA, who would later be killed in the war. At the time, both met with Fidel Castro. Later, and because of the peculiar conditions of the war in Angola, those contacts became sporadic. In May 1975, when the Portuguese were preparing to move out of their African colonies, Cuban Commander Flavio Bravo met Agostinho Neto in Brazzaville. Neto asked Bravo for assistance in transporting an arms shipment and consulted him on the possibility of receiving larger and more specific aid. As a result of this meeting, Commander Raúl Díaz Argüelles went to Luanda three months later, at the head of a delegation of Cuban civilians. Agostinho Neto was then more precise but not more ambitious; he asked for a group of Cuban instructors to set up and run four military training centers.

Only a superficial knowledge of the situation in Angola was enough to see that Neto's request was extremely modest. Although the MPLA, founded in 1956, was the oldest liberation movement in Angola and the only one that had a broad popular base and a social, political, and economic program to fit the conditions of the country; it was, nevertheless, the organization in the worst military situation. It had Soviet arms but no trained personnel to use them. On the other hand, the regular troops of Zaïre—who were well trained and well equipped—had been penetrating Angola since March 25, and had proclaimed a de facto government in Carmona headed by Holden Roberto, leader of the FNLA and Mobutu's brother-in-law. Roberto's contacts with the CIA were then in the public domain. Meanwhile, under the protection of Zambia, UNITA was operating in the west under the leadership of Jonas Savimbi, an unscrupulous adventurer who had collaborated constantly with the Portuguese military and with the foreign companies. Finally, the regular troops of South Africa had crossed Angola's border in the south, across the occupied territory of Namibia, on August 5, under the pretext of protecting the dams of the hydroelectric complex of Raucana-Caluaqua.

All those forces with their enormous economic and military resources were ready to close in on Luanda, to encircle it tightly on the eve of November 11, when the Portuguese army would abandon the vast, rich, and beautiful territory where it had been so happy for 500 years. Therefore, when the Cuban leaders heard Neto's request, they did not limit themselves to a strict interpretation of its terms, but decided immediately to send a contingent of 480 specialists, who, in a period of six months, were to set up four training centers and train sixteen infantry battalions. They also sent 25 mortar batteries and antiaircraft machine guns, a team of doctors, 115 vehicles, and communications equipment.

That first contingent was transported in three hurriedly improvised ships. *Heroic Vietnam*, which was the only passenger ship used, had been purchased by dictator Fulgencio Batista from a Dutch company in 1956 and was converted into a school ship. The other two—*Coral Island* and *La Plata*—were merchantmen which were quickly outfitted for the emergency. However, the way in which they were loaded is an excellent example of the foresight and audacity with which the Cubans fulfilled their commitment to Angola.

Incredibly, they carried with them their own fuel for the vehicles. Angola is an oil producer and the Cubans have to bring in their own fuel halfway across the world from the Soviet Union. However, the Cubans preferred to take no risks and in that very first voyage they took 1,000 tons of gasoline distributed in the three ships. *Heroic Vietnam* carried 200 tons in 55-gallon tanks and sailed with its holds open to eliminate the gases. *La Plata* carried its gasoline on deck. The night the Cubans finished loading them coincided with a popular Cuban fiesta celebrated with fireworks right from the docks of Havana, where a spark could have converted those three floating arsenals into ashes. Fidel Castro himself came to see the ships off, as he would do with all the contingents sent to Angola. After seeing the conditions in which they would travel, he uttered a phrase typical of his spontaneity: "Anyway," he said, "you'll be more comfortable than the expeditionaries on the *Granma* were."

There was no certainty that the Portuguese military would let the Cuban instructors land. On July 26 of that year, when Cuba had received the MPLA's first request for aid, Fidel Castro asked Col. Otelo Saraiva de Carvalho then in Havana, to obtain permission from the Portuguese government for the landing of Cuban aid in Angola. Saraiva de Carvalho promised he would, but his reply had still not arrived. So that when the *Heroic Vietnam* arrived in Puerto Amboim on October 4 at 6:30 in the morning, and when the *Coral Island* arrived on the seventh, and *La Plata* on the eleventh at Punta Negra, they did so without authorization from anyone, but also without opposition.

As was planned, Cuban instructors were received by the MPLA and immediately began to set up the four training schools: one in Delatando, which the Portuguese called Salazar, 300 km. east of Luanda; another in the Atlantic port of Benguela; another in Saurimo, formerly Enrique de Carvalho, in the remote desert province of eastern Luanda, where the Portuguese had built a military base which they destroyed when they left; and the fourth in the enclave of Cabinda. By that time, the troops of Holden Roberto were so near Luanda that a Cuban artillery instructor, giving his first lesson to the students at Delatando, could actually see the armored vehicles of the mercenaries advancing forward.

On October 23, the regular troops of South Africa penetrated Angola from Namibia with a mechanized brigade, and three days later they had taken, without resistance, the cities of Sa de Bandeira and Mocamedes. They were on a holiday excursion. The South Africans were listening to tape recordings of popular music in their tanks. In the north, the chief of a mercenary column directed operations from aboard a Honda sports car, sitting next to a blonde movie actress. He advanced as if on holiday and ordered no scout parties out, so he probably never knew from what direction the rocket came that blew his car to bits. The woman's travel bag contained only an evening dress, a bikini, and a printed invitation for the victory party that Holden Roberto was preparing to celebrate in Luanda.

By the end of that week, the South Africans had penetrated more than 600 km. into Angola, advancing on Luanda some 70 km. a day. On November 3, they had attacked the few soldiers at the training center for recruits in Benguela. Thus, Cuban instructors had to abandon their schools to fight the invaders alongside their apprentice-soldiers, and they could be heard giving them instructions during pauses in the battle. Even the Cuban doctors had to recall their militia training and take to the trenches. The leaders of the MPLA, prepared for guerrilla actions but not for a large-scale war, saw that the conspiracy mounted by their neighbors, and supported by imperialism's most rapacious and devastating resources, could not be defeated without an urgent recourse to international solidarity.

The internationalist spirit of Cubans is a historic virtue. Although the revolution has defined and magnified it in keeping with the principles of Marxism, its essence was very well established in the conduct and works of José Martí. This vocation has been evident—and conflict provoking—in Latin America, Africa, and Asia. In Algeria, even before the Cuban revolution had proclaimed its socialist character, Cuba had already given considerable aid to the combatants of the NLF in their war against French colonialism, so much so that the government of General de Gaulle took reprisal and prohibited Cuban flights over France. Later, while Cuba was being devastated by Hurricane Flora, a battalion of Cuban internationalist combatants sailed off to defend Algeria against Morocco. It can be said that there has been no African liberation movement of our times that has not received Cuban solidarity, in the form of either materiel and arms or the training of military and civilian technicians and specialists: Mozambique since 1963 and Guinea-Bissau since 1965. Cameroon and Sierra Leone asked for and obtained the solidaric aid of Cuba. Sékou Touré, president of the Republic of Guinea, routed a mercenary landing with the help of a Cuban unit. Commander Pedro Rodríguez Peralta, today a member of the Central Committee of the Cuban Communist Party, was captured and imprisoned for several years by the Portuguese in Guinea-Bissau. When Agostinho Neto called upon Angolan students in Portugal to study in the socialist countries, many of them went to Cuba. At present, all of them are helping to build socialism in Angola, and some of them are in very high posts. This is the case of Minga, an economist and present minister of finances of Angola; Enrique Dos Santos, a geologist, commander, and member of the CC of the MPLA, who is married to a Cuban; Mantos, agronomist and present head of the Military Academy; and N'Dalo, who, as a student, was the best football player in Cuba—today he is the second chief of the First Brigade of Angola.

However, nothing illustrates the antiquity and intensity of Cuba's involvement in Africa as well as the fact that Che Guevara himself, in the prime of his fame and life, went to fight with the guerrillas of the Congo, on April 25, 1965, the date of his farewell letter to Fidel Castro in which he renounced his rank of commander and everything that had legally tied him to the Cuban government. He went off by himself, in a commercial airliner, under a false name and passport, with his physical appearance scarcely altered by two master strokes, and a suitcase full of literary books and inhalers for his insatiable asthma. He would spend the interminable hours of solitude in hotel rooms playing chess. Three months later, he was joined in the Congo by 200 Cuban soldiers who had come from Havana in a ship carrying armaments. Che's specific mission was to train guerrillas for the National Council of the Revolution of the Congo, to fight against Moise Tshombe, an instrument of the former Belgian colonialists and of the transnational mining companies. Lumumba had already been assassinated. The head of the National Council of the Revolution was Gaston Soumaliot, but the person who directed the military operations was Laurent Kabila, from his hideaway in Kigona, on the opposite shore of Lake Tanganyika. That, of course, helped to preserve the real identity of Che Guevara, who, for greater security, did not figure as the principal head of the mission. That was why he was known under the pseudonym of Tatú, which means Number Two in Swahili.

Che Guevara remained in the Congo from April to December 1965. He not only trained guerrillas but also led them in combat and fought alongside them. His personal ties with Fidel Castro, the subject of so much speculation, were never weakened at any time. Their contacts were regular and cordial and held through very efficient communication systems.

When Moise Tshombe was defeated, the Congolese asked the Cubans to withdraw as a measure to facilitate the signing of an armistice. Che Guevara left as he had arrived: silently. He left through the airport in Dar es-Salaam, capital of Tanzania, in a commercial airliner, reading a book on chess problems from cover to cover to keep his face hidden during the six hours of flight; while in the adjacent seat, his Cuban aide tried to entertain the political commissar of the Zanzibar army, an old admirer of Che's who spoke of him constantly throughout the trip, trying to obtain news of him and reiterating his desire to meet him again.

Che Guevara's swift and anonymous passage through Africa left behind a seed that no one would be able to stamp out. Some of his men went to Brazzaville and there trained guerrilla units for the PAIGC, led by Amilcar Cabral, and especially for the MPLA. One of the columns trained by them entered Angola clandestinely through Kinshasa and joined the struggle against the Portuguese under the name of the "Camilo Cienfuegos Column." Another infiltrated into Cabinda and later crossed the Congo River and established itself in the zone of Dembo, where Agostinho Neto was born and where the struggle against the Portuguese was 500 years old. Cuba's solidaric action in Angola, therefore, was not an impulsive or casual act but the logical result of the Cuban revolution's policy in Africa. Only, this time there had been a new and dramatic element in the making of that delicate decision. This time it was not a matter of simply sending in all possible aid, but of waging a regular large-scale war 10,000 km. away from their country, at an incalculable economic and human cost and with unpredictable political consequences.

The possibility that the United States would openly intervene—and not through mercenaries or South Africa, as they had done until then—was, without doubt, one of the most disquieting enigmas. However, a rapid analysis showed that the U.S. would at least think about such a move at length since it had just emerged from the Vietnam quagmire and the Watergate scandal. It had a president that no one had elected; Congress was attacking the CIA, which was fast losing public prestige; it could not openly appear as an ally of racist South Africa, not only in the eyes of the majority of the African countries but also in the eyes of the Black population in the United States; and it was in the middle of an electoral campaign and the flamboyant year of the Bicentennial. On the other hand, the Cubans were certain to receive moral and material aid from the Soviet Union and other socialist countries, but they were also aware of the implications their action could cause in regard to the policy of peaceful coexistence and international détente. It was a decision of irreversible consequences and a problem too big and too complicated to be solved in twenty-four hours. However, the leadership of the Cuban Communist Party did not have more than twenty-four hours to make the decision, which it did, without vacillation, on November 5, in a long and serene meeting. To the contrary of what has been said, that decision was an independent and sovereign act of Cuba and it was only after it was taken, and not before, that Cuba notified the Soviet Union. On another November 5, this one in 1843, a slave from the Triumvirate sugar mill in

Matanzas, called Black Carlota, had risen up, machete in hand, at the head of a slave rebellion, and was killed in the act. In homage, the solidarity action in Angola was named after her: Operation Carlota.

Operation Carlota began with the shipment of a battalion of special forces, composed of 650 men. They were transported by plane during thirteen days of successive flights from the military section of the José Martí Airport in Havana to the Luanda airport, still occupied by Portuguese troops. Their specific mission was to stop the offensive and keep the capital of Angola from falling into the hands of the enemy before the departure of the Portuguese, and later to keep up resistance until the arrival of reinforcements by sea. But the men who were sent on the two initial flights were convinced that it was too late and they hoped only to save Cabinda.

The first contingent left on November 7, at four in the afternoon, in a special Cubana Airlines flight, aboard one of the legendary Bristol Britannia BB 218 turboprops, which had been discontinued by its British manufacturers and retired from all the air fleets of the world. The passengers, who recall that they numbered eighty-two because that was the number of expeditionaries who had sailed in the *Granma*, had the healthy appearance of tourists tanned by the sun of the Caribbean. All were in summer sportswear, with no military insignia, traveling with briefcases and normal passports bearing their real names. The members of the battalion of special forces, which does not belong to the Revolutionary Armed Forces but to the Ministry of the Interior, are expertly trained fighters, with a high ideological and political level; some of them even have university degrees. They are habitual readers and are constantly concerned about their intellectual betterment. Therefore, that fiction of civilians on a holiday was not difficult to keep up. But in their briefcases they carried machine guns; and in the cargo hold of the plane there was no luggage, but rather a large shipment of light artillery, sidearms, three 75 mm. cannons, and three 82 mm. mortars. The only change that had been made on the airplane, staffed by two stewardesses, was a trapdoor in the floor for the removal of armaments through the passenger cabin in case of emergency.

The flight from Havana to Luanda was made with a stopover in Barbados to take on fuel, in the middle of a tropical storm, and with another stopover of five hours in Guinea-Bissau to wait for nightfall, and from there to fly in secrecy to Brazzaville. The Cubans used those five hours to sleep and that was their most horrible nap, since the holds of the airplane were so full of mosquitos that the sheets on the cots were completely bloodstained.

Mobutu, with his proverbial arrogance, had once said that Brazzaville lights itself with the glare of Kinshasa, the modern, busy capital of Zaïre. And he was not completely wrong. The two cities are located in front of each other with only the Congo River in between, and their respective airports are so near that the first Cuban pilots had to study the maps well so as not to land on the enemy's airstrip. They landed without problems, with their lights off so as not to be seen from the other shore, and stayed in Brazzaville just long enough to ask for information by radio on the situation in Angola. Angolan Commander Xieto, who had good relations with the Portuguese commissioner, had obtained the latter's authorization for the Cubans to land in Luanda. The plane landed at ten in the evening on November 8, with no aid from the tower and under a torrential rain. The second plane landed fifteen minutes later. At that moment leaving Cuba were three ships carrying an artillery regiment, a battalion of motorized troops, and artillery personnel, who would land in Angola starting on November 27. Meanwhile, Holden Roberto's columns were so near that hours before, one of their cannons had killed an old woman in an attempt to hit the Gran Farni Fortress, where the Cubans were now gathered. The Cubans, therefore, had no time to rest. They hurriedly donned their olive-green uniforms, formed ranks with the MPLA soldiers, and marched off to battle.

The Cuban press, for security reasons, did not publish the news of Cuba's involvement in Angola. But, as usually happens in Cuba, even with military matters as delicate as this one, the operation was a secret zealously guarded by eight million persons. The First Congress of the Communist Party, which was to be held a few weeks later and which became a national obsession during the entire year, then acquired a new dimension.

The procedure used to organize the volunteer units was a citation delivered privately to members of the first reserve units, which include all males between seventeen and twenty-five years of age, and those who had already served in the armed forces. They were called in by telegram to their regular military committees, but no mention was made of why they were being called. However, the reason was so evident that everyone who believed himself to have some military capacity reported to his military committee, even though he had not received a telegram. It took a lot of work to keep that mass-scale volunteer movement from turning into a national riot.

As far as the urgency of the situation allowed, the selection was quite strict. Taken into account were military qualifications, physical and moral conditions, work history, and political training. Despite this rigor, there were innumerable cases of volunteers who sneaked past the selective filters. There is the case of an engineer who said he was a truck driver, a high official who said he was a mechanic, and a woman who was almost admitted as a rank-and-file soldier. There is also the case of the youngster who went without his father's permission and who later met his father in Angola, because he also had volunteered without telling his family. Then there was the twenty-year-old sergeant who, despite his efforts, was turned down, and had to nurse his wounded male ego when his mother, a journalist, and his fiancée, a doctor, were sent to Angola. Some common criminals in prison also asked to be sent, but they were all flatly refused. The first woman that was sent, early in December, had been turned down several times with the argument that "it would be too rough for a woman." She was all set to go as a stowaway on a ship and had already hidden her clothes in the hold with the help of a photographer, when she found out she had been finally chosen to go legally, and by plane. Her name is Esther Lilia Díaz Rodríguez, twenty-three, a former school teacher who joined the armed forces in 1969, and an excellent markswoman. With her but separately, went three of her brothers: César, Rubén, and Erineldo. Each one individually and without letting anyone else know, had told their mother the same story: they were going off to military maneuvers in Camagüey in honor of the party congress. All returned safe and sound, and their mother is very proud that they went to Angola, but she still hasn't forgiven them for the lie about the maneuvers in Camagüey.

Conversations with those who returned showed that the Cubans wanted to go to Angola for very different personal reasons. At least one person went with the purpose of deserting, and after hijacking a Portuguese airplane, asked for asylum in Lisbon. None were forced to go; before leaving each person had to sign a volunteer's declaration. Some refused to go after having been chosen and were victims of public mockery and private scorn. But there is no doubt that the immense majority went to Angola in the full conviction that they were carrying out an act of political solidarity, with the same consciousness and courage with which fifteen years earlier they had defeated the Bay of Pigs invasion. That is why Operation Carlota was not a simple expedition of professional soldiers, but a popular war.

For nine months, the mobilization of human and material resources was a veritable epic of temerity. Almost incredibly, the decrepit Britannias, patched up with brakes from Soviet Ilyushin 18s, maintained constant traffic. Although their normal take-off weight is 185,000 pounds, many times they took off weighing 194,000 pounds, violating all the rules. The pilots, with a normal flight time of 75 hours a month, flew more than 200 hours. In general, each of the three Britannias in service carried two complete crews who took turns during the flight. But one pilot recalls that he was in his seat up to fifty hours in a round-trip flight, with forty-three hours of actual flying time: "There are moments when you're so tired that you can't possibly get more tired," he said with no pretensions of heroism. In those conditions, and because of the time differences, the pilots and stewardesses lost all track of time, and their only guidelines were the needs of their own bodies: they ate when they were hungry and slept when they were sleepy.

The route from Havana to Luanda is bleak and desertic. The Britannia's cruising altitude is between 18,000 and 20,000 feet, but information on winds is nonexistent in this era of the jet. The pilots took off in every direction, without knowing the conditions of the route, flying at incorrect altitudes to economize on fuel, and without the slightest idea of what landing conditions would be. The route between Brazzaville and Luanda, the most dangerous, had no alternate airport. In addition, the soldiers traveled with loaded weapons, uncrated explosives, and unprotected projectiles in order to reduce cargo weight.

The United States aimed against the weakest point of the Britannias: their lack of air-staying power. When they succeeded in persuading the government of Barbados to stop the fueling stopovers, the Cubans established a transatlantic route from Holguín, in the easternmost part of Cuba, to the Isla de Sal in Cape Verde. It was a daring trapeze act with no safety nets; on the flight out the airplanes would arrive with fuel for only two more hours, and on the return flight, because of adverse winds, they would arrive with fuel for only one hour more of flight. Finally, that roundabout route was stopped to avoid creating an unfavorable situation for defenseless Cape Verde. It was then that four additional tanks of gasoline were placed in the cabins to permit the airplanes to fly nonstop, but with thirty passengers less, from Holguín to Brazzaville. The other solution of stopping over in Guyana was not implemented because, first of all, the airstrip there was too short, and, second of all, Texaco, which exploits petroleum in Guyana, refused to sell Cuba the fuel. Cuba tried to solve this problem by sending a ship loaded with gasoline to Guyana, but, because of a freak accident, the cargo became contaminated with earth and water. In the middle of so many bitter adversities, the Guyanese government maintained firm solidarity with the Cubans, so much so that the U.S. ambassador, in person, threatened to bomb and destroy the Georgetown airport. Plane maintenance work was done in less than half the normal time, and one pilot recalls that he flew several times without radar, but no one recalls an instrument failure. In those incredible conditions, 101 flights were made until the end of the war.

Maritime transport experienced a no less dramatic situation. Cuba's only two passenger ships, 4,000 tons each, were fitted out with cots in all free spaces; latrines were set up in the cabaret, the bars, and the corridors. Normal capacity, 226 passengers, was tripled in some trips. The cargo ships, with a capacity for 80 crewmembers, began to sail with as many as 1,000 passengers in addition to armored cars, armaments, and explosives. It was necessary to set up field kitchens in the cargo holds and the salons. To economize on water, paper plates were used, and plastic yogurt containers served as glasses. The ballast tanks were used for bathing and toilet purposes, with the decks full of some fifty latrines which flushed overboard into the sea. The weary engines of these old ships began to complain after six months of this arduous situation. This was the only motive for exasperation on the part of the first returnees, whose much-awaited trip back home was delayed for several days because the filters aboard the *Heroic Vietnam* did not work. Other units of the convoy were obliged to wait for it, and some of their passengers then understood Che Guevara's statement that the march of a guerrilla band is determined by the slowest man. Those obstacles loomed great in that period, because Cuban ships were then the objects of all sorts of provocation by U.S. destroyers that harassed them for days on end, and by U.S. warplanes that photographed them and buzzed over them at low altitudes.

Despite the difficult conditions of those trips, which lasted for almost twenty days, no serious sanitary problem came up. In the forty-two trips that were made during the six months of the war, shipboard medical services handled only one appendectomy, one hernia operation, and one outbreak of diarrhea caused by some canned meat. However, there was a more difficult epidemic to control: that of the crew members who wanted to stay and fight in Angola. One of them, a reserve officer, managed to obtain an olive-green uniform, landed with the troops, and succeeded in staying on shore. He became one of the best information officers of the war.

On the other hand, Soviet material aid, which entered through different channels, required the constant inflow of skilled personnel to handle—and to teach the handling of—those new arms and complex equipment, then unknown to the Angolans. The chief of the Cuban general staff himself went to Angola at the end of November. Everything then seemed tolerable, except losing the war.

Nevertheless, the historic truth is that it was about to be lost. In the first week of December, the situation was so desperate that Cubans and Angolans were thinking of holding up in Cabinda and establishing at least a beachhead around Luanda to initiate evacuation of the city. And to top things off, that somber prospect appeared at the worst possible moment for both Cubans and Angolans. The Cubans were preparing to hold their First Party Congress December 17 to 24, and the Cuban leaders knew that a military defeat in Angola would be a mortal political blow. On the other hand, the Angolans were preparing for the OAU conference and wanted to go there with a military position favorable enough to turn the majority of African countries in their favor.

The adversities of December were due, in the first place, to the tremendous firepower of the enemy, who, by that date, had already received more than $50 million in military aid from the United States. In the second place, it was due to the delay with which Angola had asked for Cuban aid, and the inevitable slowness of transporting that aid.

And finally, it was due to the conditions of misery and cultural backwardness left in Angola by 500 years of pitiless colonialism.

More than the first two reasons, it was this last point that created the biggest difficulties for the decisive integration of Cuban combatants with the armed population of Angola.

In reality, Cubans found the same climate they knew in their own country, the same vegetation, the same apocalyptic showers, and the same afternoons fragrant with molasses and alligators. Some Cubans resembled Angolans so much that a joke soon made the rounds to the effect that it was possible to distinguish them only by touching the point of their noses, because the Africans have soft nose cartilage from the way they were carried as babies, with their faces pressed against their mother's back.

The Portuguese colonizers, perhaps the most insatiable and cruelest in history, built modern and beautiful cities to spend their entire lives, with air-conditioned glass buildings and stores with enormous neon signs. But the cities were for whites, like the ones the *gringos* had built around Old Havana and which the peasants looked at with astonishment when they came down from the Sierra for the first time, with their rifles slung over their shoulders.

Underneath that shell of civilization was a vast and wealthy country full of poverty. The living standards of the native population were the lowest in the world, with an illiteracy rate of more than 90 percent and cultural conditions much like those of the Stone Age. Even in the cities of the interior, only the men spoke Portuguese, and many times they kept as many as seven wives in the same house. Atavistic superstitions not only obstructed everyday life but also the war. The Angolans were convinced that bullets could not harm a white man, they had a superstitious fear of airplanes, and refused to fight inside the trenches because they said that tombs were only for the dead. In the Congo, Che Guevara had seen the soldiers donning bead necklaces to protect themselves from cannon fire, and bracelets to protect themselves from machine-gun fire. They would also sear their faces with smoldering embers of charcoal to ward off the risks of war. He became so interested in these cultural absurdities that he began to study African idiosyncrasies and learned Swahili in an attempt to change those habits from the inside, conscious of a deep and pernicious force in the hearts of men, a force that bullets could not stop: colonization of the mind.

Sanitary conditions, of course, were atrocious. In San Pedro de Cota, the Cubans had to forcibly bring in a child for medical treatment: his entire body had been burned with boiling water, and his family had already laid him out funeral-fashion, believing he would die at any moment. Cuban doctors also treated diseases they never saw before. Under Portuguese rule, Angola had only ninety doctors for six million inhabitants, and most of the doctors were concentrated in the capital. When the Portuguese left, only thirty doctors stayed behind. On the very day he arrived in Puerto Amboim, a Cuban pediatrician saw five children die for lack of medical resources. That was an unforgettable experience for a doctor, thirty-five, trained in a country with one of the lowest infant mortality rates in the world.

The MPLA had made great progress against primitivism in its long and silent years of struggle against Portuguese rule, and in this way had created the conditions for final victory. In the liberated areas, the political and cultural level of the population was raised, tribalism and racism were fought, and free education and medical services made available. It was the seed of a new society.

However, those meritorious and ambitious efforts paled when guerrilla warfare turned into a big, modern war and it became necessary to call upon not only the people with military and political training, but also the entire population. It was an atrocious war where one had to be careful of both mercenaries and serpents, cannons and cannibals. A Cuban commander, in the middle of a battle, fell into an elephant trap. The Black Africans, conditioned by their age-old resentment of the Portuguese, were initially hostile to the white Cubans. Many times, even in Cabinda, Cuban scouts felt they had been betrayed by the primitive telegraph of the drums, which could be heard up to 35 km. around. The white soldiers of South Africa, who fired on ambulances with 140 mm. cannons, threw up smoke screens in the battlefield to pick up their white dead, but left their Black dead to the vultures. In the home of a UNITA minister who lived in the comfort appropriate to his rank, the men of the MPLA found in his refrigerator jars of viscera and bottles of frozen blood taken from the war prisoners he had eaten.

Meanwhile, Cuba was receiving only bad news. On December 11 in Hengo, where the FAPLA were launching a strong offensive against the invaders from South Africa, an armored car with four Cuban commanders aboard ventured upon a mined road. Although four cars had safely crossed the road before, the sappers had warned the Cubans not to take that route, since its only advantage was to gain a few unnecessary minutes. The car had scarcely entered the road when it was blown into the air by an explosion. Two commanders of the battalion of special forces were seriously wounded. Commander Raúl Argüello, commander-general of the internationalist operations in

Angola, hero of the struggle against Batista, and a well-loved figure in Cuba, was killed instantly. That was very bitter news for the Cubans, but it was not the last in that long streak of bad luck. The next day brought the disaster of Catofe, perhaps the biggest defeat of the entire war. A South African column had repaired a bridge over the Nhia River with incredible rapidity, they had crossed the river under the cover of the dawn mist, and had surprised the Cubans in the tactical rearguard. An analysis of this setback showed that it had been due to an error of the Cubans. A European military man, with much experience in World War II, considered that analysis too severe and said later to a high Cuban leader: "You don't know what an error in war is." But for the Cubans, it was a very serious error, only five days before the party congress.

Fidel Castro personally kept up with the smallest details of the war. He saw off all the ships, and before each departure he gave a pep talk to the soldiers in the La Cabaña Theater. He personally had picked up the commanders of the battalion of special forces that left in the first flight and had driven them himself in his Soviet jeep to the foot of the plane ramp. It is probable that during each of the send-offs, Fidel Castro had to repress a deep sentiment of envy for those going off to a war that he could not participate in. There was no spot on the map of Angola that he couldn't identify or a physical feature that he hadn't memorized. His concentration on the war was so intense and meticulous that he could quote any figure on Angola as if it were Cuba, and he spoke of Angolan cities, customs, and people as if he had lived there his entire life.

At the beginning of the war, when the situation was bad, Fidel Castro remained up to fourteen hours straight in the operations room of the general staff, at times without eating or sleeping, as if he were in the battlefield himself. He followed the details of every battle with colored pins on the detailed maps which covered the walls, and remained in constant communication with the top commands of the MPLA in a battlefield with a six-hour time difference. Some of his reactions during those uncertain days revealed his confidence in victory.

A combat unit of the MPLA was forced to blow up a bridge to delay the advance of armored columns of South Africa. Fidel Castro sent them a message, suggesting: "Don't blow up any more bridges; you won't be able to pursue them later." And he was right. Only a few weeks later, brigades of Cuban and Angolan engineers had to repair thirteen bridges in twenty days to reach the invaders, then in flight.

On December 22, at the closing session of the party congress, Cuba officially announced for the first time that Cuban troops were fighting in Angola. The war situation continued to be uncertain. In his final speech, Fidel Castro revealed that the invaders of Cabinda had been crushed in seventy-two hours, that on the northern front, the troops of Holden Roberto, only 25 km. from Luanda on November 10, had had to retreat more than 100 km., and that the armored columns of South Africa, which had advanced 700 km. in less than twenty days, had been stopped at more than 200 km. from Luanda and had not been able to continue their march. This was comforting and accurate news, but victory was still not in sight.

The Angolans had better luck on January 14 when they went to the OAU conference in Addis Ababa. A few days earlier, the troops under Cuban Commander Victor Schueg Colas, an enormous and cordial Black man who had been an auto mechanic before the revolution, threw out Holden Roberto from his illusory capital of Carmona, occupied the city, and a few hours later took the Negage military base. Cuban aid then was so intense that in the beginning of January there were fifteen Cuban ships sailing simultaneously to Luanda. The uncontainable offensive of the MPLA on all fronts definitively turned the tide. Offensive operations originally scheduled for April began in the middle of January on the southern front. South Africa was using Camberra airplanes and Zaïre was flying Mirages and Fiats. Angola had no air force, because the Portuguese had destroyed the bases before leaving. It had only a few old DC-3s, which Cuban pilots had put back into service, and at times those planes, carrying the wounded, had to land at night on air strips lit with improvised lamps, arriving at their destination with lianas of jungle foliage wrapped around their wheels. At one time, Angola had a fleet of MIG-17s staffed by Cuban pilots, but they were considered the reserve of the top military command and were used only in the defense of Luanda.

In the beginning of March, the northern front was liberated with the defeat of the British and American mercenaries whom the CIA had recruited at the last moment in a desperate effort. All the troops, with their full general staffs, were concentrated in the south. The Benguela railroad had been liberated, and UNITA was disintegrating in such disorder that an MPLA rocket in Gago Cutinho destroyed the house which Jonas Savimbi had occupied only an hour before.

In the middle of March, South African troops began their retreat, which must have been ordered from the very top, for fear that the MPLA's pursuit would continue into occupied Namibia and carry the war right up to South African territory. That eventuality would have had, without doubt, the support of all Black Africa and the great majority of the United Nations countries that opposed racial discrimination. Cuban combatants had no doubt of it when they were ordered to mass up in the southern front. But, on March 27, when the fleeing South Africans crossed the border and took refuge in Namibia, the only order the MPLA received was to occupy the abandoned dams and guarantee the safety of the workers of all nationalities. On April 1, at 9:15 in the morning, the MPLA vanguard under Cuban Commander Leopoldo Cintras Frías reached the Raucana Dam, on the very edge of the chicken-wire fence of the border. One hour and fifteen minutes later, the South African governor of Namibia, General Ewefp, accompanied by other officers of his army, asked for authorization to cross the border and hold conversations with the MPLA. Commander Cintras Frías received them in a wooden barracks built on a neutral stretch of ground ten meters wide separating both countries, and the delegates of both sides with their respective interpreters sat down to talk at a long dining-room table. General Ewefp, fiftyish, fat, and bald, did his best to give an image of a jovial man with much experience in the world, and unconditionally accepted the MPLA's terms. The agreement took two hours, but the meeting took much longer because General Ewefp ordered a succulent lunch brought in from the Namibian side. And while everyone was eating and making toasts with beer, he told his adversaries how he had lost the little finger of his right hand in a traffic accident.

At the end of May, Henry Kissinger visited Prime Minister Olaf Palme in Stockholm, and upon emerging from the meeting jubilantly declared to the world press that Cuban troops were being evacuated from Angola. The news, he said, came in a personal letter which Fidel Castro had sent to Olaf Palme. Kissinger's joy was understandable because the withdrawal of Cuban troops eliminated a thorny issue from the electoral campaign in the United States.

The truth is that Fidel Castro had sent no letter to Olaf

Palme. However, the information was correct although incomplete. In reality, the program for the withdrawal of Cuban troops from Angola had been drawn up by Fidel Castro and Agostinho Neto on March 14 in Konenry, when victory was already a fact. They decided that withdrawal would be gradual, but that as many Cuban troops would remain in Angola as were necessary—and for the time it took—to organize a modern and strong army capable of guaranteeing in the future the country's internal security and independence without aid from anyone.

So that when Henry Kissinger committed that indiscretion in Stockholm, more than 3,000 Cuban troops had already returned from Angola and many others were on their way back. The return of the soldiers was also kept secret for security reasons. But Esther Lilia Díaz Rodríguez, the first woman who went to Angola and one of the first who returned by plane, had occasion to rediscover Cuban ingenuity in unearthing secrets. Esther had been put in the Naval Hospital of Havana for the obligatory medical checkup before her family was notified of her return. After forty-eight hours she was authorized to leave the hospital. She took a taxi on the corner and the driver took her to her home without any comments, but he refused to take the fare because she had just returned from Angola. "How do you know?" Esther asked him, perplexed. The driver answered: "Because I saw you yesterday on the terrace of the hospital, and that terrace is reserved for those who return from Angola."

I arrived in Havana in those days and even in the airport I had the definite impression that something very profound had been happening in Cuban life since I was there last. There was an undefinable but notable change not only in the spirit of the people but also in the very nature of things, the animals, the sea, and in the very essence of Cuban life. There was a new male fashion of suits made of light cloth with short-sleeved jackets. Portuguese words had penetrated the language heard in the streets. There were new accents in the old African musical rhythms. There were discussions noisier than usual in the lines in front of the stores and in the overcrowded buses, between those who had been resolute partisans of the action in Angola and those who were just beginning to understand it. However, the most interesting experience, and strangest, was that the returnees seemed conscious of having contributed to changing the history of the world, but they conducted themselves so naturally and so simply, like people who had merely done their duty.

On the other hand, perhaps they themselves were not conscious of the fact that on another level, perhaps less generous but also more human, even the Cubans without too many passions felt compensated for so many years of unjust setbacks. In 1970, when the ten-million-ton sugar harvest failed, Fidel Castro asked the people to turn defeat into victory. In reality, Cubans had been doing that for too long a time with a tenacious political consciousness and a moral strength that resisted all. Since the victory at the Bay of Pigs more than fifteen years ago, Cubans had to absorb, with their teeth gritted, the assassination of Che Guevara in Bolivia and of President Salvador Allende in the catastrophe of Chile; they had suffered the extermination of the guerrillas in Latin America, the endless night of the blockade, and the implacable and deep-rooted corrosion of so many internal errors of the past which kept them at all times on the brink of disaster. All this, apart from the irreversible but slow and arduous victories of the revolution, created in Cubans an accumulated sensation of unmerited penances. Angola, at last, gave them the gratification of the big victory they needed so much.

Appendix B

Resolution on international policy

This resolution was adopted by the Second Congress of the Communist Party of Cuba, held in Havana, December 17–20, 1980.

I. Having reviewed the last five years' achievements in implementing the foreign policy agreements adopted by the First Congress and the basic guidelines set forth in the party's Programmatic Platform, and having listened to the thoroughgoing report on this subject made by Comrade Fidel Castro, first secretary of the Central Committee, the Second Congress expresses its wholehearted approval of the Cuban revolution's international activity during this period, viewing it as a major advance and the basis for significant progress in the coming years.

The congress notes that the key aim of Cuba's international policy has been and is its contribution to the cause of socialism, the liberation of the peoples, progress, and peace. The Cuban revolution's foreign policy is based on Marxist-Leninist principles; proletarian internationalism; friendship and cooperation with the Soviet Union and the other countries of the socialist community; close bonds of solidarity with the communist, workers', and revolutionary movements everywhere; and militant support of the national liberation movements and all peoples that are struggling to develop and defend their vital historic interests. From this platform, on behalf of all Communists and the Cuban people as a whole, the congress reaffirms the validity of this policy, to which we have always been, and will remain loyal.

Our experience during these years confirms the need for firmly adhering to revolutionary principles. Aware that the Cuban people's historic goals are the same as those of other peoples, our free and sovereign homeland subordinates its national interests to the higher objectives of socialist and communist progress; the peoples' liberation; the defeat of imperialism; and the eradication of colonialism, neocolonialism, and all other forms of oppression and discrimination of individuals and peoples.

The Second Congress considers the struggle for peace to be the most vital, decisive international task, and urges the party, state, and all other organized forces to redouble their efforts in this sphere.

The basis of our party's foreign policy is its historic, lasting alliance with the Soviet Union, based on our common ideology and goals. The importance of this unity in stimulating proletarian internationalism, backing the Cuban people's heroic determination to defend their independence and their revolution at whatever price may be required, and as a solid basis for our socioeconomic development efforts, has been dramatically confirmed during the past five years. The congress notes the exemplary nature of these relations and reaffirms the determination of the party and the people as a whole to work steadily to improve and strengthen them.

Our Communist Party and the revolutionary state it directs will also continue working to strengthen their fraternal ties with the parties, governments, and peoples of the rest of the socialist community. The Communist Party of Cuba will spare no efforts to help achieve unity among all the forces of the international communist movement on a principled basis.

The Second Congress specially stresses the need to continue working unreservedly for unity of action by the three great forces of the modern revolutionary process: socialism, the international workers' movement, and the national liberation movement. We Communists and all other Cubans will firmly continue our struggle against the imperialist strategy of breaking up the revolutionary movement, opposing all efforts to divide these forces as they merge in a single torrent struggling for socialism, communism, social progress, and peace.

The congress once again confirms the indestructible ties that make the Cuban revolution a part of the great family of Latin American and Caribbean peoples—whose problems, concerns, and destiny our people share.

II. The Second Congress of the Communist Party of Cuba salutes the great victories the peoples have won since the First Congress.

We greet the Nicaraguan people's triumph with deep revolutionary joy. In staunch, heroic struggle, led by the Sandinista National Liberation Front, the Nicaraguan people overthrew and wiped out Somoza's brutal tyranny—which U.S. imperialism had installed and kept in power—making way for a genuine, deep, popular, antioligarchic, and anti-imperialist revolution.

Under the leadership of the New Jewel party, the people of Grenada won a resounding victory which has given life and energy to the struggles being waged by the former European colonies in the Caribbean.

At the same time of the First Congress, Angola was battling against the attacks launched by the racist regime of South Africa and its reactionary allies, supported by imperialism. Under the leadership of the People's Movement for the Liberation of Angola (MPLA) and the late President Agostinho Neto, the Angolan people won a victory that marked a turning point in African politics in favor of independence and revolution.

The Ethiopian people's extraordinary triumph in overthrowing the semifeudal monarchy allied with imperialism was consolidated when a genuinely revolutionary leadership assumed power, mobilized the masses, and drove out the traitorous Somalian invaders.

The Second Congress proudly acknowledges the modest, truly internationalist role that Cubans, fighting bravely alongside heroic Angolans and Ethiopians, played in Angola's second war of liberation and in socialist Ethiopia's victory over the aggressors on the eastern and southern fronts. Thousands of members of our party and other representatives of our glorious Revolutionary Armed Forces participated in these noble missions, and their exemplary attitude fills us with pride and satisfaction and does us honor.

We also express our joy over the important victory won by the patriotic forces of Zimbabwe in defeating the maneuvers of imperialism and the reaction. The Zimbabwean people's victory is eloquent testimony to the justice and invincible strength of the cause of independence and people's liberation. It marks an important step toward the final elimination of colonialism and racism in the African continent and throughout the world.

In one of the most far-reaching political and human events in recent years, the people of Kampuchea, backed by Vietnam's solidarity and support, wiped out the genocidal regime that the Peking rulers had maintained in their country. A new people's revolutionary Kampuchea is rising from the ruins.

In another important victory which we greet with joy, the heroic Vietnamese people firmly beat back the expansionist, hegemonic Peking clique's craven, criminal attack on them—thus preserving Vietnam's independence, defending the territorial integrity of the other countries of Southeast Asia, and helping to preserve world peace. By attacking Vietnam, China's leadership revealed its true essence and the collaboration and support provided by its Yankee imperialist allies for its criminal actions. Even now, the Vietnamese people are constantly threatened and attacked all along their border with China; we must maintain our vigilance and solidarity with Vietnam.

The reactionary monarchic regime of the shah of Iran, U.S. imperialism's ally and special gendarme in the Middle East, was toppled by the sweeping upsurge of the Iranian people, paving the way for significant anti-imperialist changes that knocked imperialism's entire system of influence and action off balance, forcing it to readjust its positions in that vital region.

We are pleased to salute the revolutionary victory of the Afghan people, who overthrew the despotic, semifeudal regime in their country, and we denounce the maneuvers by imperialism and its reactionary allies aimed at undermining the revolutionary process that was initiated in that country in April 1978.

These great victories of the peoples of Asia, Africa, and Latin America confirm the course of events predicted in the agreements adopted by the First Congress. Socialism, which emerged with the triumph of the great October revolution, is now a reality in four continents. New revolutionary processes are opting to build socialist societies on the basis of the universal principles of Marxism-Leninism; working-class struggles in the industrialized capitalist countries are on the rise; the national liberation movement is extending its scope and deepening its content; the role of internationalist solidarity carries greater weight; and socialist ideas are becoming more attractive and influential all the time.

These factors show that the characteristic feature of our period is the revolutionary transition from capitalism to socialism and the deepening of all aspects of the general crisis of capitalism. These victories also reaffirm the First Congress's position that any people that decides to struggle for its freedom today can overcome even the most difficult obstacles and the most aggressive imperialist powers if it has wise political leaders who can mobilize the masses, and are supported by the forces of socialism and international solidarity.

III. Recent events in the period 1975–80 have confirmed the First Congress's predictions as to how the international situation would develop. Every international event that has occurred during this five-year period proves that the world correlation of forces decidedly favors socialism, the international workers' movement, and the national liberation movement.

In the new, perturbing international atmosphere in which this Second Congress is taking place, the most reactionary imperialist sectors' threats against the process of détente—threats which our party congress denounced five years ago—have now stalemated that process, bringing the world to the brink of a new cold-war period, with the real possibility of world war.

The decisive influence of the Soviet Union's foreign policy of peace made possible an incipient, difficult process of relaxing international tensions, a process that humanity found both encouraging and hopeful. Imperialism—especially U.S. imperialism—is wholly responsible for its paralysis.

Because of the strong pressure that the United States brought to bear on its European allies, NATO decided to install intermediate-range nuclear missiles in Western Europe, with the obviously dangerous aim of qualitatively tipping the military balance in its favor by directly threatening the Soviet Union and the European socialist countries. Meanwhile, imperialism has deployed its military strength, creating rapid deployment forces; modernizing and extending its network of bases throughout the world; stepping up its aggressive naval presence in the Arab Gulf and the Indian Ocean; escalating its military activities in the Caribbean; trying to rebuild its military alliances in southeast, central, and southwest Asia; and indefinitely postponing its ratification of SALT II. All these expressions of military superiority are designed to impose its world domination, dust off its cold-war tactics, and block the upsurge of the people's revolutionary movement to win true and definitive independence.

In spite of the prevailing situation, the Second Congress of the Communist Party of Cuba believes that détente can be saved mainly because of the firm and consistent peace policy practiced by the Soviet Union and the other countries of the socialist community, with the support of all other progressive forces. An essential factor is that this policy is based not on weak military positions but on the full capacity to defeat any attack. Not even the most aggressive imperialists can deny that a nuclear adventure launched against the Soviet Union would bring about their own destruction.

The capitalist regime is bogged down in a prolonged crisis that is undermining its economy and exacerbating its sociopolitical contradictions. The effects of this are felt most acutely in the countries of the so-called Third World. This is a complex situation in which millions of people are faced with the terrifying prospect of hunger and uncertainty, and the most backward, warmongering sectors of imperialism are stepping up their activities. It is incumbent on us to halt these reactionary forces.

The battle for peace is one of the basic objectives of the Second Congress. The struggle to keep imperialism from pushing humanity into a nuclear holocaust has greater significance and immediacy than ever before. Our country has worked hard for a just and universal peace, defended the creation of an atmosphere of détente, and supported disarmament and an end to the arms race. We will continue working along these lines. Our party gives great priority to the efforts to establish a broad world front of all those who defend peace and peaceful coexistence in order to actively oppose the resurgence of warmongering policies, imperialist and reactionary blackmail, and interventionism. We will continue to devote our most active efforts to this vital priority task.

We Cuban Communists denounce the Chinese leaders' treasonous policy, which has done great harm to the world revolutionary movement. China's policy is a serious threat to world peace and a stimulus to warmongering adventurism in international life. China's rapprochement with U.S. imperialism has gone beyond occasional points of agreement and now constitutes an alliance that includes very specific military agreements. The lamentable example of China shows the tragic consequences of supernationalism and betrayal of socialist and internationalist principles.

A review of the present world situation shows the persistence of serious focal points of conflict that threaten world peace.

The Second Congress agrees that U.S. imperialism will not accept the democratic social changes that some of the peoples of Latin America and the Caribbean are making, following the kind of independent policy that imperialism brutally opposed before the advent of the Cuban revolution. In answer to the victorious revolutions in Nicaragua and Grenada and to the people's revolutionary uprising in El Salvador, imperialism has arrogantly attempted to reimpose its control over Central America and the Caribbean, the subregion it considers to be of "special interest." The U.S. military presence in the Caribbean has been increased considerably; spy flights have been stepped up, especially over Cuba; and military maneuvers have been staged in an unsuccessful attempt to intimidate our people and others that are struggling for their liberation.

This imperialist policy, a new version of the big-stick and gunboat approaches, is creating a tense and dangerous situation in Central America and the Caribbean, where the peoples are threatened with direct U.S. military intervention that seeks to destroy the revolutionary process. The Second Congress alerts all progressive, peace-loving forces to this dangerous situation and its unpredictable consequences.

U.S. policy on the Middle East has sought to subject this region to its total domination by trying to wipe out the Palestinian resistance and undermine the consistent efforts of Algeria, Libya, Syria, Democratic Yemen, and the Palestine Liberation Organization (in the Steadfastness and Confrontation Front), and other progressive countries in the area. Through the Camp David Agreements—which have been roundly denounced by the international community—U.S. imperialism fosters the establishment of an aggressive, reactionary alliance with Israel and the Egyptian regime.

We condemn Zionism and its expansionist practices, which inflict enormous suffering on the Palestinian people and are a permanent threat to all Arab peoples in that region. We Cuban Communists reaffirm our solidarity with the just cause of the Arab peoples, especially the Arab people of Palestine, and express our conviction that a just and lasting peace in the Middle East must be based on recognition of the legitimate rights of the Palestinian people, including their right to a sovereign state led by the PLO, and on Israel's withdrawal from the occupied Arab territories.

Imperialist attempts to take over the energy resources of the Arab Gulf states and establish new military bases there have made the situation in that region particularly explosive, with the concentration of a dangerous military force that seriously threatens international peace and security.

The congress stresses its concern over the continuing armed conflict between Iran and Iraq, two progressive Nonaligned countries. This conflict weakens the united front of struggle against imperialism and Zionism and may further exacerbate the already problematical economic situation of the non-oil-producing countries of the so-called Third World and the international situation in general. The congress hopes that a solution will soon be found to this war, which has already taken a high toll in lives and material goods.

Reviewing the situation in the Southern Cone of Africa, the congress noted the persistence of a dangerous focal point of conflict emanating from Pretoria's aggressive policy, and reaffirmed its staunch solidarity with Angola, Mozambique, and other front-line countries under constant pressure and attack. The crisis of white racist minority rule has become more acute in South Africa as the patriotic forces are stepping up their struggle for full rights, freedom, equality, and social progress.

The people of Namibia are continuing their struggle for independence, opposing the maneuvers to apply neocolonial solutions contrary to their legitimate aspirations and rights.

As the African revolutionary struggle advances, the imperialists continue their economic and military—including nuclear—collaboration with the criminal, reactionary South African regime so it can continue to act as an imperialist gendarme in the area.

The Second Congress reaffirms its most energetic condemnation of the ignominious apartheid regime and the Cuban party's and people's militant solidarity with the struggles of the peoples of Namibia and South Africa and with their respective legitimate representatives, the South West Africa People's Organisation (SWAPO) and the African National Congress (ANC).

The situation in the Horn of Africa is still tense, because Somalia refuses to renounce its expansionist aims and persists in attacking Ethiopia. Recently, it signed an agreement with the United States for the establishment of U.S. military bases in its territory. The delegates to the Second Congress strongly denounce this agreement as a further threat to peace.

The increased imperialist military presence in the Indian Ocean is a provocation and a serious threat to world peace and to the independence and sovereignty of the surrounding states. We express our support for the proposal made by Madagascar and other countries to hold a conference that will contribute to making the Indian Ocean a zone of peace.

IV. In the five years since the First Congress the statement in the Programmatic Platform on the importance of the Movement of Nonaligned Countries in international relations has been confirmed.

The Sixth Conference of Heads of State and Government, held in Havana in September 1979, made a valuable contribution to peace and promoted efforts to wipe out injustice, inequality, and oppression, and to attain real socioeconomic development in the developing countries.

As a member of the movement and its current chairman, Cuba has worked hard to implement the decisions and resolutions of the Havana summit conference and will continue to do so.

Fulfilling the mandate of the Sixth Summit Conference, Comrade Fidel Castro, chairman of the movement, addressed the United Nations General Assembly presenting the summit conference's main agreements and the view of the international situation contained in its final declaration.

In discussing the economic plight of the underdeveloped countries, he presented the basic points of a proposal for alleviating this situation through the provision of at least $300 billion in additional resources to finance development. This important proposal has been given broad support by these countries in international organizations and has forcefully emphasized the essential link between the problems of development and the struggle for peace.

Aware of the movement's need for internal unity in order to bring all its strength to bear in international policy, Cuba is anxious to find a just and harmonious solution to the differences that sometimes arise among its members and may even lead them to oppose each other. With this in mind, Chairman Fidel Castro has made every effort to lead Iraq and Iran to work out their contradictions by means of peaceful negotiations.

V. The Second Congress reaffirms this historic significance of the democratic, popular, anti-imperialist, and revolutionary struggles that the peoples of our America are waging for national liberation, socialism, and the definitive defeat of imperialism.

The experience of the past five years has also confirmed, beyond the shadow of a doubt, the crisis that exists in U.S. foreign policy and the insoluble contradictions between the interests of U.S. imperialism and those of the countries of Latin America and the Caribbean. In this regard the continuation of the international economic crisis of capitalism has made it increasingly evident that the United States is no longer able to lull the countries in the region with reformist promises.

It is also clear that Latin America's serious problems of underdevelopment cannot be solved as long as the transnational corporations and the U.S. financial system exist, for they offer only great economic deformation, an unbearable economic structure, the sacrifice of nonrenewable natural resources wasted by the U.S. consumer economy, discrimination in trade, and enormous foreign debts. These are the factors that have widened the gap between U.S. interests and those of a considerable number of governments that refuse to be manipulated like puppets any longer.

The Cuban revolution's historic defeat of U.S. imperialism, its internal consolidation, its hemispheric relations, and its influence are constant factors in the new reality in our continent.

The congress notes with satisfaction that the 1979 revolutionary victories in Nicaragua and Grenada constitute the most important gains for the revolutionary struggle in Latin America and the Caribbean since the triumph of the Cuban revolution in 1959. These victories show that our revolution was no exception and confirm the historic need for social revolution and the possibilities for decisive action by revolutionary forces to overcome imperialist domination in this hemisphere.

In addition to the resounding peoples' victories in Nicaragua and Grenada, the Second Congress also considers other situations in Latin America and the Caribbean to be very important.

The development of the revolutionary national and social liberation movements is accompanied by an upsurge or revival of the mass movement in a number of countries. Both phenomena are expressions of the economic and political crisis of the system of imperialist and bourgeois domination in the region, and they also show the maturity of the workers, peasants, young people, women, and other sectors that are fighting alongside their vanguards.

Mass militancy in our region has reached a high point not only in some Central American countries but also in Bolivia, where the people have put up firm resistance against the military assault. In Chile and Uruguay, patriots are giving increasing signs of their repudiation of the neofascist tyrannies' attempts to hold on to power by means of deceitful pseudodemocratic maneuvers.

The Latin American working class has also revealed its fighting spirit since the First Congress. Huge strikes in Peru, Ecuador, and Colombia, and the ongoing workers' struggles in Argentina indicate what the Latin American proletariat can do when it combines national unity with correct leadership.

Unity of the revolutionary forces in some countries and steps toward unity in others have been decisive factors in the evolution of the Latin American revolutionary national and social liberation movements. The tremendous importance of the solidarity and fighting unity among Communist parties and other revolutionary groups was brought out with the support that a number of organizations gave the Nicaraguan people's struggle.

The role of Social Democracy and other political and ideological trends must also be taken into consideration in describing the situation in Latin America in this period. Without ignoring Social Democracy's reformist policy, its activity in the region and democratic, antidictatorial positions that provided points of contact for joint actions with the people's revolutionary movement should be noted.

At the same time, most of the leaders of the parties aligned with Christian Democracy maintained a stance against the people, in line with U.S. policy in the continent, thereby losing the support of broad sectors of honest, progressive Christian Democrats.

Significant leadership sectors of the Catholic Church and its clergy not only proved more realistic in approaching our people's main political, economic, and social problems but also showed an encouraging understanding of how to solve them. This trend offers very positive prospects for unity between Marxists and Christians, an essential in the revolutionary struggle for national and social liberation.

The struggles in Latin America and the Caribbean have reached a crucial stage. In spite of the revolutionary movement's different characteristics, forms, and levels of the struggles and proportions of the working class and progressive sectors that are involved—all of them have the same historic goal of anti-imperialist national liberation.

Meanwhile, the United States has shown that it intends to use all the means necessary to try to maintain its hegemony over the region. In those countries where it can't keep reactionary regimes in power, it does everything possible to turn aside the most advanced ideas and positions of the people's revolutionary movement, to divide its forces, present pseudoreformist approaches, and corrupt the sectors that are the least committed to the cause of their peoples.

The congress reaffirms that the struggle against imperialism in our continent will not be simple or easy in the years to come. Latin America and the Caribbean are sure to be an area of singular confrontation in the world struggle against the capitalist system and for peace and social progress.

The Second Congress once again sends a message of solidarity to the Salvadoran and Guatemalan people, who are fighting for full freedom; to the Nicaraguan and Grenadian people, struggling to overcome the difficulties involved in building a new society; to the Bolivian, Chilean, Haitian, Uruguayan, and Paraguayan people, opposing their countries' bestial military dictatorships; to the Argentines, who are struggling to have their democratic rights respected; and to all Latin American revolutionaries seeking national and social liberation for their peoples.

The Second Congress of the Communist Party of Cuba reaffirms its staunch support for the Puerto Rican people's struggle for national independence. It also reiterates its firm backing for the Panamanian people's historic struggle for full sovereignty over the Panama Canal and for the Belizean people's just aspirations for independence and territorial integrity.

In the coming years, Cuba will express its continuing solidarity with all patriotic, anti-imperialist governments that have decided to oppose Washington's domination with dignity. In this regard, we especially esteem the firm, progressive positions that Mexico has taken on such important matters as peace, energy, development, and opposition to U.S. interference in our countries. Cuba will maintain its strategic guideline of seeking the broadest possible unity for national independence, progress, and democracy in the region. Our party encourages and supports all sovereign actions and attitudes by Latin American and Caribbean governments and political forces protecting their legitimate national interests and promoting more just and equitable economic relations.

VI. As part of its foreign policy, the Communist Party

of Cuba places priority on participating in the international communist movement, and the alliance with all other progressive, anti-imperialist forces that support national liberation, peace, and social progress.

The Second Congress ratifies what Comrade Fidel Castro said in his report to the First Congress: "The Communist Party of Cuba considers itself a modest but reliable detachment of the international communist movement. Proletarian internationalism is expressed, above all, in the essential unity, cohesion, and determination of those all over the world who have taken up the banners of Marx, Engels, and Lenin and are giving their efforts and even their lives to implement the revolutionary program they proposed for humanity. Our party participates in this with its own independent views but, at the same time, with complete loyalty to the cause of communists the world over."

On the basis of these principles, our party is devoting and will continue to devote special attention to strengthening its ties of friendship and solidarity with the other Communist parties, national liberation movements, and people's revolutionary parties throughout the world.

The congress notes with satisfaction that our longstanding, close ties of friendship with parties, organizations, and movements have been extended and strengthened, and relations have been established with a large group of progressive political forces and parties all over the world.

Our contacts with Socialist and Social-Democratic parties—especially in Western Europe and Latin America—have also been greatly extended.

On examining Cuba's participation in the international democratic and progressive movement, the congress places great value on the contributions that the World Federation of Trade Unions, the World Federation of Democratic Youth, the World Peace Council, the International Union of Students, the Women's International Democratic Federation, the Permanent Congress of Latin American Workers' Trade Union Unity, the Latin American Continental Students' Organization, and other international organizations have made to the struggles for national liberation, social progress, and world peace. Therefore, the Communist Party of Cuba promotes the most active participation in these bodies by all our political, mass, and social organizations.

VII. The Second Congress confirms that the state agencies charged with developing and implementing the foreign policy principles set forth in the Programmatic Platform and in the resolution on foreign policy adopted by the First Congress have done so correctly. Cuba's foreign policy has been and will remain a true reflection of the positions and principles of the Communist Party of Cuba.

Cuba's permanent ties with the other countries of the socialist community and especially its relations of deep fraternity with the Soviet Union are of the greatest importance. The Second Congress of Cuban Communists emphasizes the importance of the protocols for coordinating plans for 1981–85 that were signed with the USSR and other socialist countries, and the stability they give our country's economy, and urges that we continue to integrate our economy with those of other members of the Council for Mutual Economic Assistance, consolidating and extending our forms of economic cooperation and giving a new boost to the development of trade with those countries.

In our state relations, the ties of friendship and cooperation that unite our homeland with the countries that are building socialism in Asia and Africa or that have decided, after defeating their oppressors, to advance toward this goal, following the principles of Marxism-Leninism, are especially meaningful.

Our party places great value on the strengthening of the fraternal relations between Cuba and the progressive and revolutionary countries of Asia, Africa, and Latin America. Because of our common struggle against colonialism, neocolonialism, imperialist rule, and the reactionary tyrannies, we are linked to these governments by historic ties of solidarity and friendship and by our united efforts to achieve progress within the international community.

In close and permanent union with the other members of the Movement of Nonaligned Countries and other developing countries, Cuba has been very active in all forums—especially the United Nations and its agencies—supporting the just causes of these countries, their true independence and economic and social development. Our country has hosted several international meetings in this period, and it will continue working hard in this direction.

The promotion of the widest international cooperation and Cuba's active participation in the most important regional and world events and conferences are also part of the permanent work of our state agencies. Programs of economic and scientific-technical cooperation with countries in Africa, the Middle East, and Latin America have been considerably increased in the last few years and constitute a basic element in Cuba's foreign relations.

Since the First Congress, Cuba has extended its state relations to a large number of countries, mainly members of the Nonaligned movement, in spite of U.S. imperialist pressure and harassment and some former metropolises' hostile reactions to our policy of solidarity with the struggles of the peoples of Africa, Asia, Latin America, and the Caribbean. Diplomatic relations were either established or renewed with Botswana, Burma, Chad, the Comoros,

Ecuador, Gambia, Ghana, Grenada, Iran, Jordan, Lesotho, Libya, the Maldives, Malta, Mauritius, Nicaragua, Niger, Rwanda, the Democratic Sahraoui Arab Republic, St. Lucia, São Tomé, the Seychelles, the Sudan, Surinam, Togo, Upper Volta, Zaïre, and Zimbabwe, and relations were renewed with Costa Rica at the consular level.

As exceptions to this tendency, both Somalia and Morocco decided to break off diplomatic relations with Cuba in response to actions carried out in fulfillment of our internationalist duty—in the first case, because of our cooperation with Ethiopia in its victory over the Somalian invasion, and in the second, because of Cuba's support for the just cause of the people of Western Sahara and recognition of the Democratic Sahraoui Arab Republic.

Latin America continues to be the scene of continuous political battles, expressed in the relations between Cuba and her neighbors. Even though the Cuban government has reiterated its readiness to establish normal relations with all countries that are willing to respect our sovereignty, the problem of diplomatic relations with Cuba continues to be, for some, a political and ideological problem, and for others, a matter of political cowardice and subjection to imperialism. The most reactionary forces in Latin America refuse to admit the possibility of diplomatic ties based on the principles of ideological pluralism. This explains why, in addition to our known and firm rejection of the regimes in Chile, Uruguay, Paraguay, Haiti, Guatemala, and El Salvador, there are still other countries with which we do not have diplomatic relations—a situation for which the governments of those countries are entirely responsible.

Recently, the improper, illegal use of the right of asylum by antisocial elements seeking to leave Cuba illegally, who were encouraged by the protection given them by some governments in the area, triggered an energetic response by the Cuban government, which repudiated the use of such tactics to stir up trouble and make propaganda against our revolution, in connivance with U.S. imperialism.

This strained our relations with certain governments—especially the government of Venezuela, which was more interested in protecting criminals than in reaching agreements guaranteeing reciprocal respect. The situation between our two governments deteriorated even more with the monstrous attempt to exonerate those responsible for blowing up a Cuban plane off the coast of Barbados.

The Second Congress of the Communist Party of Cuba again stresses that one of the aims of the Cuban people and their Communist Party is to achieve Latin American and Caribbean unity, as the best means of attaining our historic continental goals and the democratic and independent consolidation of each of our countries. Cuba will continue to work actively in the Latin American Economic System (SELA) and other regional economic agencies that uphold a progressive line representing the interests of the countries in the area.

The results obtained in the last five years in Cuba's state relations with the developed capitalist countries, based on equality, mutual respect, and reciprocal benefits, have corroborated the justice of the party's policy in this sphere.

Even though successive U.S. administrations have continued to exert pressure to extend the blockade of our country, the contradictions between the United States and the other capitalist countries—especially their economic contradictions—have hindered the effectiveness of these attempts and have enabled our state agencies to work to raise the level of our economic and political ties with other countries.

The Second Congress reaffirms the course of this policy, which is aimed at extending and developing Cuba's relations of friendship and cooperation with all countries in the world, regardless of their social regimes and political orientations, as a contribution to the establishment of a climate of world peace and understanding.

VIII. The Second Congress has devoted special attention to analyzing the relations between Cuba and the United States. An examination of this problem shows that, at first, the Carter administration indicated its interest in reducing the tensions with our country and took some steps in that direction. However, with the failure of its attempt to negotiate Cuba-U.S. differences from positions of force and to make the eventual lifting of the blockade conditional on modifications of our revolution's principled policy toward the revolutionary movement, the U.S. administration adopted a hard line in political statements and hostile actions against our country.

Anti-Cuban policy was mainly manifested in the various artificial crises the Carter administration provoked to counter Cuba's growing influence in the international arena and meet the needs of its domestic policy: Cuba's supposed participation in the Shaba events, the presence of MIG-23 planes in Cuba (an alleged danger to U.S. security and an attempt to deny Cuba's right to adequate defense equipment), and more recently the presence of Soviet military personnel—who have been in our country since 1962.

Meanwhile, the aggressive international policy the U.S. government developed to generate a cold-war climate was expressed in a hard line on Latin America—especially following the revolutionary triumphs in Grenada and Nicaragua—basically characterized by the constant exacerbation of tensions in the Caribbean. The U.S. military presence in the area became more visible with the establishment of the Caribbean Joint Operational Contingency Force, whose general staff is located in Key West; and interventionist activities in Central America were stepped up to neutralize the peoples' revolutionary upsurge; and especially to harass the Cuban revolution by renewing spy flights over our territory and planning maneuvers against our country, including landings at the Guantánamo naval base—a crude exercise in invading our country.

The Second Congress reaffirms that Cuba is and will continue to be an internationalist country that practices militant solidarity with the peoples struggling for liberation and national independence, and that this principle of our international conduct is not negotiable under any circumstances.

We Cuban Communists believe that there is a historic need for normal relations among all countries in the world, based on mutual respect and recognition of international law and the sovereign rights of states.

The Second Congress reiterates that the normalization of relations between Cuba and the United States will contribute to a healthier political climate in Latin America and the Caribbean and to world détente. Therefore, it expresses Cuba's serious, responsible desire to solve the historic disagreement created by the United States's hostility toward the Cuban revolution.

At the same time, the congress reiterates that the adoption of steps leading to the normalization of relations with the United States is dependent on the U.S. government's willingness to lift the blockade, return the territory occupied by the Guantánamo naval base, and refrain from violating Cuban sovereignty.

IX. During the five years since the First Congress, Cuba has upheld the internationalist focus of its foreign policy.

The imperialists make every effort to slander and distort the true nature of this modest, disinterested aid that Cuba offers its brothers and sisters in other parts of the world. The peoples know the truth, however. They know that, although Cuba has occasionally provided significant military aid in exceptional situations of foreign aggression and in response to the request of sovereign, legitimate governments, this is not the only—nor even the main—form of Cuba's cooperation with the fraternal peoples of Asia, Africa, Latin America, and the Caribbean.

This policy of solidarity is implemented by all our people—in the services that thousands of Cuban technicians and specialists in many different fields provide wherever their technical assistance is required: in the most remote parts of Angola, Mozambique, Tanzania, and Guinea; the forests of Nicaragua; and hospitals in Kampuchea. This cooperation has acquired tremendous prestige.

What most concerns imperialism is precisely the impact of this example of relations that are truly based on friendship, respect, and solidarity. It is not easy to combat this, because, even with their enormous resources, the imperialists have nothing like it to offer the peoples—which is why they resort to lies, threats, and compromises.

The Second Congress reaffirms that neither threats nor flattery can make Cuba surrender. The Cuban people and their leaders are not frightened by the fact that aggressive mobile forces equipped with the most modern arms are stationed a few kilometers from our coasts, nor are they intimidated by military maneuvers. Rather, they reject them energetically, defending their firmly held principles of sovereignty and territorial integrity. The threat of a total blockade will only lead Cuba to increase its preparations to confront this or any other action.

Cuba's internationalist policy serves only one interest:

the defense of the peoples' freedom and self-determination. It is based on universally recognized international principles; does not threaten the sovereignty of any other state; and constitutes an effective aid to the economic, cultural, and social development of the poorest, most needy countries in the world. It is a source of pride for the Cuban people to practice this policy—either while risking their lives or while making the daily sacrifices inherent in being away from their homeland and families, living in the most difficult conditions.

Our solidarity is directed toward all the peoples of the world, but it especially responds to a historic pledge dating from the time of our struggle for independence—a pledge to stand by our sister peoples of Latin America and the Caribbean against any exploitative imperialist country or oppressive tyrannical regime. It implies absolute respect for those who respect our sovereign rights. It is never tarnished by betrayal of loyally offered friendship. It is and will continue to be the greatest pride of our people and of their Communist Party.

The Second Congress, expressing the deep feeling of Cuban Communists and the people as a whole, proclaims its determination to continue applying this noble, generous, and unselfish policy of internationalist solidarity, a harbinger of the relations that will exist in the liberated, socialist society of the future.

Finally, the Second Congress wishes to express its great appreciation to Comrade Fidel Castro, our first secretary, for his activities in leading and implementing the international policy of the party and state. The fruitful development of our close ties with the Soviet Union and the other sister socialist countries; our homeland's active role in the worldwide revolutionary, communist, and national liberation movement; our country's activity to solve the serious economic problems that affect the underdeveloped countries and its constructive unifying work within the Movement of Nonaligned Countries; the establishment of fruitful relations with a growing number of states, based on mutual respect; Cuba's prestige and influence in the most important international organizations—are achievements in which the tireless work and attention of Comrade Fidel Castro were essential. The congress salutes that effort, which has meant so much for our revolution, and expresses the party's and all the people's desire to advance—solidly united around Fidel, the Political Bureau, and the Central Committee—toward new victories for socialism and proletarian internationalism.

The Second Congress of the Communist Party of Cuba entrusts the Central Committee with carrying out, guiding, and controlling the implementation of the present resolution.

Appendix C

Cuba's view of the revolution in Latin America and the Caribbean

The following article was printed in *Granma,* November 2, 1980. We are reprinting it because it offers a succinct view of Cuba's analysis of the dynamics of the revolutionary upsurge in Latin America and the Caribbean.

BERLIN, October 21—Jesús Montané Oropesa, member of the Central Committee of the Communist Party of Cuba, said here today that the revolutionary victories in Nicaragua and Grenada were the most important events in Latin America since 1959.

Speaking at the International Scientific Conference on the Struggle of the Working Class Against Imperialism, the Cuban leader added that these victories took place amidst a U.S. imperialist counterrevolutionary offensive against the peoples of the hemisphere.

In his paper, Montané, the third speaker during the morning session held at the Palace of the Republic, discussed the movement for national and social liberation in Latin America and the Caribbean. He said that the victories of Grenada and Nicaragua were an expression of the upsurge of the popular and revolutionary movement in the area.

The head of the General Department of Foreign Relations of the Central Committee of the Communist Party of Cuba said these new gains should be viewed in the framework of the historical stage which opened up in the hemisphere following the victory of the Cuban revolution. These new victories did away with the myth that other revolutions in the hemisphere were impossible, he added.

Montané said the Nicaraguan process showed that the United States is unable to resort to fascist or reformist measures when faced by a genuine revolution grounded in the armed and united masses.

The enemies of the revolution will be much less successful than they were in 1959 if they try to have people believe that the victories in Nicaragua and Grenada are isolated and unique cases which do not reflect the realities of the peoples' struggle for genuine liberation in Latin America, he said.

The Cuban leader stated that Nicaragua's victory confirmed the effectiveness and viability of armed struggle as the decisive means to take power in countries where all other paths are closed and the vanguard relies on the masses and achieves firm unity.

He stressed that these countries had shown that the only guarantee for the development of a program of radical anti-imperialist change is the elimination of the bourgeois state apparatus and the creation of a new army recruited from the people.

On referring to the situation in Latin America and the Caribbean, Montané said a great historic shift is underway there. He explained that, although the revolutionary movements have different features, take different forms, and advance in varying degrees, they are all part of the historic trend toward anti-imperialist national liberation.

He said the shift in the balance of forces in favor of socialism and the development of the popular and revolutionary movement in Latin America has transformed what was formerly the backyard of U.S. imperialism into an area that the imperialists are finding increasingly difficult to control and to impose political decisions on. "The United States has no structural or intermediate solutions to ease the economic and social crisis in underdeveloped Latin America. It is having increasing differences with many governments which it is no longer able to manipulate like puppets."

Montané said that the strategic military, economic, and political value which Washington attaches to Latin America and the Caribbean poses a challenge to the revolutionary movements for national and social liberation in the area.

He added that, following the victory of the Cuban revolution, the U.S. ideologues realized that the popular and revolutionary parties and movements in Latin America based their actions on profound ideological and political factors.

This led the imperialist ideologues to chart a course of action aimed at carrying out provocations to discredit the socialist model as the only alternative which could pave the way for liberation and economic development. They also tried to split the revolutionary forces, he added.

In spite of the Alliance for Progress, the Peace Corps, coups, and reformist pipe dreams, he said, they were unable to stop the advance of revolution initiated by Cuba in 1959.

Regarding the forms of struggle in Latin America, he said that at times a false alternative has been posed between armed and other forms of struggle.

"The revolutionary content of any form of struggle is determined by its results, that is, whether or not it leads to an advance or retreat of the masses vis-à-vis their ultimate objectives."

The Cuban leader said experience in his country showed that dividing political and military functions adversely affects both.

"Only an integral political-military concept makes it possible to pass at the right time from one main form of struggle to another depending on the stages and circumstances of each process."

In his speech to the conference, which he entitled "The Common Struggle of the Workers and National Liberation Movements against Imperialism and for Social Progress," Montané said that with the advent of the eighties new political, economic, and social factors have developed, while the revolution ripens and added possibilities for liberation exist.

In the contemporary revolutionary situation in Latin America, one of the unique features is the growing participation of Christian sectors in the popular and revolutionary struggles, he remarked.

He said it was very important to grasp the features common to the area, focused on united efforts to destroy the common enemy, a view shared by the Communist parties and revolutionary movements in Latin America.

Montané praised the watchful attitude displayed by Latin American revolutionaries toward the Maoist groups, which are bankrupt, he said, adding that they are insignificant in terms of size but damaging because of their provocative actions, which benefit imperialism.

On summarizing the revolutionary upsurge in the region, he said that Latin America is witnessing a merging of class and national liberation struggles, an original combination of democratic tasks linked to socialist objectives and the struggle for anti-imperialist liberation of the workers and peasants from capitalist domination.

The Cuban delegate praised the opening speech by Erich Honecker, general secretary of the Socialist United Party of Germany, which, he said, would provide guidelines for discussion at the conference.

Montané hailed the participation of delegations from the socialist camp and the national and social liberation movements and parties in Asia, Africa, and Latin America.

The conference, organized by the Central Committee of the SUPG and the international magazine *World Marxist Review,* was attended by representatives of 116 Communist and workers' parties and national liberation movements.

Index

Afghanistan, 186–87, 234, 515
Africa
  conditions in, 32–33, 35–37
  Cuba's solidarity with, 113–14, 184–85, 360, 365–67, 383, 489–94
  liberation struggles in, 181–84, 263
  See also Angola; Cuban aid; Ethiopia; Racism; South Africa; United States
African National Congress, 521
Agramonte, Ignacio, 58
Agricultural development, 291–92
Albania, 79
Algeria, 40–41, 519
  Cuba's aid to, 76, 113, 117–18, 490
Allende, Salvador, 18, 220
Alliances, 459, 526–28
Alliance for Progress, 128
Almeida, Juan, 100
Almeyda, Clodomiro, 220
Andean Pact, 413–14, 430
Angola, 487–90
  colonial heritage of, 89, 148–49, 154, 156, 502–3
  Cuban aid to, 19, 76, 90–91, 115–18, 130–32, 150–58, 166, 366–67, 485–510
  significance of victory in, 75, 129–30, 183–84, 186–87,

Angola
  significance of victory in *(continued)*, 221–22, 240, 513–14
  1975–76 war in, 89–91, 129–33, 486–87, 503–10
  See also South Africa; United States
Anti-imperialism, 215–16
Anti-imperialist front, 14–15, 215–17
Anti-interventionist front, 428–29
Antiwar movement, U.S., 193, 251, 304
Antonio Maceo Brigade, 304–5, 308, 311–15, 317
Arafat, Yasir, 93
Argentina, 271, 524, 526
Armed struggle, 467, 538–39
Arms race, 68–69, 225, 249–52, 278, 286, 295, 451–52, 468, 517

Barbados, 341–43, 353, 499
Batista, Fulgencio, 433
Bay of Pigs. *See* Girón
Belize, 248, 271, 526
Bishop, Maurice, 218, 415, 430
Blacks, U.S., 370, 493
Blockade, 60, 248–49, 308, 328, 357, 371, 379–80, 409–10, 534

543

Blockade *(continued)*
  effects of, 14, 373, 404
  and negotiations, 136–37, 359
  and Nonaligned, 215, 273
  See also United States, relations with Cuba
Bolivia
  1980 coup in, 464, 467, 524
  Cuban solidarity with, 526
  guerrilla struggle in, 17, 76
  and Nicaragua, 272
  and Nonaligned, 234, 248
Bolsheviks, 44–45
Bosch, Juan, 415
Boumedienne, Houari, 40, 233
Bravo, Flavio, 486
Brigade 2506, 346–47
Brzezinski, Zbigniew, 204, 386–87

Caamaño Deñó, Francisco, 124
Cabral, Amilcar, 492
Camacho Aguilera, Julio, 144–45
Camarioca, 303, 396, 399
Cambodia. *See* Kampuchea
Cameroon, 490
Camp David agreements, 185, 242, 268, 519
Canada, 353
Cape Verde, 183, 240, 499
Capitalism, 30–31, 34–36, 371
  crisis of, 225–26, 516
  See also Economic crisis
Carazo, Rodrigo, 430
Caribbean, 270–71, 414
  upsurge in, 20, 518–19, 523–26

Carter, Jimmy
  and China, 195–96, 204–5
  and Cuba, 10, 327–28, 337, 376–77, 379–87
  and human rights, 72–73, 371
Carvajal, Ladislao González, 110
Carvalho, Otelo Saraiva de, 488
Casa de las Américas, U.S., 308
Castro, Fidel, 21–22, 27, 39–40, 102–4, 218, 461–62, 486, 488, 505–6, 510
Castro, Raúl, 101, 107
Castro, Reinaldo, 97
Catholic Church, 459, 525
CENTO, 234, 240
Central America, 20, 403, 414, 427–28, 437, 449, 519
  See also Latin America; United States
Céspedes, Carlos Manuel de, 55–56, 58
Chauvinism, 73–74, 168–69, 461
Chile, 128
  1973 coup in, 123–24, 220–21, 458, 467
  dictatorship in, 346, 365, 385, 429–30
  and Popular Unity, 18, 37, 393
  struggle in, 524, 526
China
  betrayal by, 74–79, 126, 187–88, 245–46
  and Cuba, 203–4
  Cultural Revolution in, 77

China *(continued)*
  and U.S., 194–95, 200, 202–5, 518
  and Vietnam, 195–96, 198–211, 514–15
Christian Democracy, 414, 463, 525
Christians, 459–60, 540
CIA, 71–72, 114, 124, 220, 343–44, 410–11
  in Angola, 89–90, 130, 132–33, 493
  and assassination attempts, 61, 124, 347–50
  and terrorists, 303, 337, 344–51, 394
  See also Cubana Airlines bombing
Ciego de Avila, 473–77, 479–80
Cienfuegos, Camilo, 83
Class society, 56–57, 372
Class struggle, 540
Cold war, 225, 468–69, 516
Colombia, 272, 353, 524
Colonialism, 34–35, 40–41, 154–55, 182–83, 270
Commission of 75, 304–5, 324
Comoros, 266
Communism, 51–53, 484
Communist Party, Chinese, 77–78, 204
Communist Party of Cuba, 97, 100–101, 121, 127, 482–83, 493, 526–28
  Central Committee of, 94–102, 107
  First Congress of, 110–12, 496
  Political Bureau of, 98–100

Congo, 486, 491–92
  See also Zaïre
Consumerism, 64–65, 249–50, 277
Corvalán, Luis, 94
Costa Rica, 272, 345
CORU (United Revolutionary Organizations' Command), 347–48
Counterrevolutionary propaganda, 303
  See also United States, relations with Cuba
Crime, 397–98
Cuba
  African heritage of, 129, 151
  agriculture in, 10, 141–44, 146, 256, 473–77
  defense of, 66–69, 407–10
  economic development of, 11, 66–67
  education in, 10, 67, 140–43, 292, 478–82
  emigration from, 21, 303, 322, 393–95, 399–400
  health care in, 10, 140–41, 292, 480
  history of, 55–58, 140–41
  imperialist allies in, 397–98, 482
  mass organizations in, 11, 13, 407, 483
  political principles of, 62–63, 82–84, 103, 116–17, 236–39, 511–13, 534–36
  See also Cuban aid; Cuban revolution; United States, relations with Cuba
Cuban Action, 346–47
Cuban aid, 12–13, 17–18,

Cuban aid *(continued)*, 37–39,
    83–84, 236–37, 293, 384–85,
    392–93, 398, 400, 489–91,
    533–35
  to Africa, 113–14, 489–94
  versus U.S. aid, 76–77,
    135–36
  See also Angola; Ethiopia;
    Grenada; Nicaragua;
    Vietnam; other countries
Cuban exile community,
    303–5, 307–10, 312–14,
    318–27
Cuban missile crisis. *See*
    October Crisis
Cuban Nationalist Movement,
    346
Cuban revolution, 61–63, 307,
    372
  example of, 460–61, 538–40
  humane character of, 110,
    354, 369–70
  mass strength of, 397
  voluntary character of, 397
  and war versus Batista, 144,
    433
Cuban Revolutionary Party,
    360
Cubana Airlines bombing,
    337, 339–44, 391, 404, 531
Cyprus, 222–23, 245, 269

de Gaulle, Charles, 490
de los Santos, Asela, 101
Deng Xiaoping, 195, 199,
    203–5
Democracy, 372, 463, 467
Détente, 262, 361, 410, 493
  See also Peace

Development fund, 215,
    229–31, 285–86, 290–96,
    522
Dialogue, 19, 304–5, 313–19,
    323–24
Díaz Argüelles, Raúl, 486,
    504–5
Diaz, Julito, 146
Díaz Rodríguez, Esther Lilia,
    497, 509
Diplomatic relations, 530
Disease, 35–36
Domínguez, Orlando, 110
Dominican Republic, 124
Dos Santos, Enrique, 491
Drugs, 397
Durán, Julio, 348

Economic crisis, 16, 74, 225–26,
    253, 277–78, 517, 522–23
Economic development,
    296–97
Ecuador, 272, 524
Egypt, 241–42, 247, 268, 519
  See also Camp David
    agreements
Eisenhower, Dwight, 135
El Mundo, 342–43, 345
El Salvador, 20, 414, 429, 460,
    463–64, 466, 526
Energy crisis, 254, 256, 281
Engels, Frederick, 33, 39, 58–59,
    84, 105
Eritrea, 164, 224
Escambray, 404
Espín, Vilma, 101
Espinosa, Manuel, 308, 317
Ethiopia
  Cuba's aid to, 19, 76, 163–64,
    166–67, 172–75, 178, 367

INDEX / 547

Ethiopia *(continued)*
revolution in, 163–64, 169–71, 173, 183, 186–89, 223–24, 234, 514
See also United States
European Economic Community, 255
Exchange rates, 280

F-14, 347
Fascism, 69–70, 128, 168, 186
Fernández, José R., 101
Fernández, Pilar, 97
Ferre, Maurice, 348
Fishing agreements, 358
FNLA, 89–91, 114–15, 130, 154, 487
Fonseca Amador, Carlos, 419, 424–25
Ford, Gerald, 112, 120–21, 129–30, 132–33, 135, 378, 382, 387
France, 41, 113, 490
Frechette, Myles, 405

Gairy, Eric, 240
Gallagher, Tom, 348
Gambling, 14, 397
García Márquez, Gabriel, 415
Geneva negotiations, 185
Genocide, 201–2, 466
German Democratic Republic, 42
Germany, Federal Republic of, 364
Germany, Nazi, 168, 199, 205–6, 241, 244, 267, 469
Ghana, 182
Giap, Vo Nguyen, 108

Girón, 9, 75, 123–28, 346, 423, 446, 466
Gómez, Máximo, 58
Great Britain, 185, 265
Greece, 222
Grenada, 19–20, 397, 408, 430, 453–54, 467, 513, 523, 537–38
and Cuba, 414–15, 526
and Nonaligned, 218, 234, 240, 272
Grobart, Fabio, 102, 110
Guantánamo, 14, 60, 328, 379–80, 383
U.S. maneuvers at, 338, 403–7
Nonaligned position on, 215, 272–73
Guatemala, 248, 429, 460, 466–67, 526
Guerrilla warfare, 17
Guevara, Che, 13, 17, 90, 486, 491–92
Guillén, Nicolás, 97
Guinea, 182, 490
Guinea-Bissau, 76, 96, 113, 490
Cuban aid to, 76, 96, 113, 490
Gusano, 304, 312–13
Guyana, 346, 353
and Cuba, 394, 499

Haiti, 526
Hart, Armando, 100
Haile Selassie, 163–64
Helms, Jesse, 386
Heng Samrin, 195
Hijacking, 337, 349, 351–54
History, 39–40, 56–57, 354–55, 372–73

Hitler, Adolf, 199, 469
Ho Chi Minh, 79
Holguín, 421
Honecker, Erich, 540
Human rights, 70–73, 202, 323, 371–72
Hunger, 253–54, 260, 274–75, 277, 291–92

Ideological struggle, 61, 397–401
Illiteracy, 10, 253–54, 260, 277
Imperialism, 14–15, 60–61, 229–30, 238–39, 293, 344–45, 355, 357, 464–66
and Africa, 182–84, 186–87, 216–17
effects of, 14–15, 35–36, 293
tactics of, 220–21, 255
See also Capitalism; Colonialism; Nonaligned movement; Underdeveloped countries
Indebtedness, 215, 253–54, 280, 285–88, 291
Indian Ocean, 269, 521
Individual, in history, 102–9
Industrial redeployment, 276
Industrialization, 274–76, 292
Inflation, 279–80, 286
Institutionalization, 106
Interdependency, 289
International balance of forces, 514–17, 538
International economic order, 215–30, 256–57, 260, 274, 278–79

International Monetary Fund, 74, 253
International monetary system, 280, 286
Internationalism, 11–13, 38–39, 41, 52–53, 75–77, 189, 480–81, 527
Iran
and Iraq, 224, 412, 520, 522
revolution in, 187, 234, 272, 410–13, 515
under shah, 49, 171, 255
and U.S., 365, 410–12
Iraq, 224, 412, 520, 522
Israel, 242, 266–69, 426, 519–20
See also Palestinians; Zionism
Italy, 170

Jamaica, 346, 353, 394, 430, 454
Jayawardene, Junius, 233
Johnson, Lyndon, 135, 378, 382

Kabila, Laurent, 491
Kampuchea, 78, 224
liberation of, 195, 246, 514
and Nonaligned, 246–47
Pol Pot regime in, 194–95, 200–202, 204
See also Vietnam
Kennedy, John, 135, 378, 381–82
Khmer Rouge, 193–94
Khrushchev, Nikita, 381
Kissinger, Henry, 129–30, 132–35, 387, 485, 508–9
Korea, 232, 247, 269

La Coubre, 404
Laos, 246
Latin America, 270–72
  and Cuba, 61, 134, 530–31
  oligarchies in, 37, 365
  struggle in, 185–86, 523–26, 537–40
  and underdevelopment, 523
  See also United States
Lebanon, 244
Lebrón, Lolita, 72–73, 370
Lenin, V.I., 33, 35, 58, 68
Letelier, Orlando, 348
Libya, 519
López Portillo, José, 430
Lugo, Freddy, 342–43
Lumpen, 393–400, 463, 530–31
Lumumba, Patrice, 182, 491

Maceo, Antonio, 58, 138
Machado Ventura, José, 99–100
Madagascar, 266
Malagasy Islands, 266
Malvinas Islands, 271
Manley, Michael, 430, 454
Maoism, 77–79, 201, 540
March of the Fighting People, 21–22, 406–7
Marinello, Zoilo, 97
Mariel, 398–99, 405
Martí, José, 56, 58, 109, 148–49, 437, 490
Martínez Suárez, Felix, 343
Martínez Vaillant, Facundo, 97
Marx, Karl, 33–35, 39–40, 58, 84, 105, 372
Marxism-Leninism, 34, 39–40, 43–44, 52, 57–58
Mauritania, 244, 266

Mayotte, 266
Mella, Julio Antonio, 102
Mengistu Haile Mariam, 163, 170, 181, 186
Mercenaries, 344, 383
Mexico, 353
  and Cuba, 216, 394
  and Nicaragua, 272, 430
  and U.S., 216, 526
Middle East, 36–37, 181–82, 221, 241–42, 519–20
  See also United States
Milián, Arnaldo, 100
Miret, Pedro, 99
Mobutu Sese Seko, 495
Moncada attack, 27, 60, 101–2
Montané Oropesa, Jesús, 537–41
Montes, Llano, 345
Morocco, 244, 266
Mozambique, 183, 186, 221, 240, 366–67, 520
  Cuban support to, 366–68, 490
MPLA, 89–90, 114, 119–20, 383, 486, 503
Muñiz Varela, Carlos, 305
Muzorewa, Abel, 242–43

Namibia, 36, 90–91, 115, 183, 185, 187, 243, 263–64, 367, 426, 507–8, 520–21
Napoleon, 408
Nasser, Gamal Abdal, 81, 241, 268
National egoism, 30, 39, 44, 52–53, 480
National independence, 182–83

National liberation movement, 513, 515, 524–25, 540
Nationalism, 52
National Liberation Front of Cuba, 346
NATO, 171–72, 176, 222–23, 234, 243
Negrín, Eulalio, 305
Nehru, Jawaharlal, 81
Neocolonialism, 36–37, 182–83, 270–71, 280
Neto, Agostinho, 147–51, 153, 485–86, 490, 509
Neutron bomb, 71
New Jewel Movement, 19
Nixon, Richard, 135, 378, 382, 386
Nicaragua, 419–20, 454–56
 and Cuba, 414, 422–24, 430–32, 448–49, 460–62
 Cuban aid to, 12, 20, 385, 419, 438–41, 478–80
 example of, 467
 and imperialism, 431, 435, 525
 international solidarity with, 428, 430, 446, 451, 457–58
 and lumpen, 397
 National Guard in, 419, 429, 433–34, 465
 and Nonaligned, 234
 reconstruction of, 435, 448–50
 revolutionary policies of, 419, 456–59
 revolutionary war in, 424–25, 436, 447, 456–57, 467–68

Nicaragua *(continued)*
 significance of revolution in, 186, 272, 422, 424–28, 513, 523
 strength of revolution in, 408, 462–63
 under Somoza, 345–46, 448, 455
 See also United States
Nkrumah, Kwame, 81
Nonaligned movement, 81–82, 215–16, 224–27, 235–36, 241, 259–60, 521–22
 Cuba's role in, 9, 19, 215–17, 230–32, 238–40, 338
 Sixth Summit of, 216–18, 235–36, 259, 384
 See also United States
Nuclear power, 50
Nuclear weapons, 385–86
 See also Arms race; Nuclear power
Nuez, René de la, 401

October Crisis, 9, 135, 203, 210, 330–31, 377–78, 381, 471
October 1973 war, 221
Ogaden war, 163–64, 173–77
 See also Ethiopia; Somalia
Oil, 31–32, 46–50, 227–30
Oil-producing countries, 229–31, 254–55, 293
OPEC, 31, 224, 227, 230–31, 412–13
Operation Carlota, 494
 See also Angola
Opportunism, 81, 238
Organization of African Unity (OAU), 506

Organization of American
  States (OAS), 81, 125,
  428–30, 465
Organization of Latin
  American Solidarity
  (OLAS), 17
Ortega, Daniel, 415
Ortiz Cabrera, Pedro, 394

País, Frank, 83
Pakistan, 234
Palestinians, 185, 221, 241–42,
  266–68, 426, 519–20
  See also Zionism
Palestine Liberation Front,
  519
Palme, Olaf, 508–9
Panama, 346
  Canal, 186, 232, 248, 271,
    452, 526
  and Cuba, 394
  and Nicaragua, 272, 430
  and U.S., 77, 124
Paraguay, 429, 526
Patriotic Front, 185, 234, 264
Peace, 136–37, 298–99
  need for, 84–85, 249, 260–
    62, 294–95, 298–99, 361,
    451–52
  struggle for, 41, 68–70,
    409–10, 472, 512, 517–18
Peaceful coexistence. *See*
  Peace
People's Power, 11, 146
Pepper, Claude, 348
Pérez, Carlos Andrés, 342,
  430, 446, 485
Peru, 232, 272, 391–92, 524
Peruvian embassy, 393–95
Petty bourgeois radicals, 103–4

Pinar del Río, 139–47
Pinochet, Augusto, 78, 346
Pioneers, 13
Polisario Front, 245, 266
Pol Pot, 194–95
Pollution, 51, 298
Population control, 50–51, 277
Portugal
  colonial empire of, 40, 89,
    183, 221–22, 486–87, 492,
    502
  1974–75 upsurge in, 16, 89,
    221–22
Poverty, 253, 260
Prisoners, 320–28
Professionals, 400–401
Prostitution, 14, 63, 397
Protectionism, 279, 284, 286
Public opinion, 472
Puerto Rico
  Cuban solidarity with,
    112–13, 248, 360, 526
  international support for,
    186, 232, 270–71
  and U.S., 271, 371, 379–80,
    414, 452

Racism
  in Africa, 36–37, 232, 238,
    242–43
  in Cuba, 10–11
  in U.S., 304, 370–71
Reagan, Ronald, 129, 410, 471
Redondo, Ciro, 146
Refugees, 245–46
Religion, 458–60
Republican Party, 452, 469
Revolution, 21–22, 126,
  458–59, 467–68
  export of, 69, 134

Revolutionary, 331
Revolutionary Armed Forces, 514
Revolutionary consciousness, 21, 157–58
Revolutionary leadership, 93–107, 407
Revolutionary movement, 84
Revolutionary strategy, 17–18, 459–60, 467, 539–40
Revolutionary war, 209
Rhodesia. *See* Zimbabwe
Ricardo, Hernán, 343
Robelo, Alfonso, 436, 438
Roberto, Holden, 486–87, 489
Roca, Blas, 99, 110
Rodríguez, Carlos Rafael, 99, 110
Rodríguez Peralta, Pedro, 96–97, 113, 490

SALT II, 251, 262, 517
Sandinistas, 384, 419, 422–25, 428–29, 434–36, 441–42
 strategy of, 433–36, 448
 and unity, 430, 432, 436, 448
 See also Nicaragua
Sandino, Augusto César, 124, 419, 427, 447
Santamaría, Abel, 83
São Tomé and Príncipe, 240
Saudi Arabia, 49, 171, 365
Savimbi, Jonas, 487
Sea resources, 285–86
SELA (Latin American Economic System), 413, 531
Self-determination, 134, 261, 535

Senegal, 182
Sepúlveda, Eduardo, 348
77, Group of, 225, 281
Shah of Iran, 171, 410–11, 515
Siad Barre, 163
Sierra Leone, 490
Sihanouk, Norodom, 246
Socialism, 44–45, 252, 513, 515–16
 need for, 51–53, 57
 and underdeveloped countries, 33–38
Social Democracy, 524–25, 527
Solidarity, 184, 206, 422, 515–16
 See also Cuban aid; Internationalism
Somalia, 167–68, 175–78
 and Ethiopia, 19, 163–64, 169–73, 521
Somoza Debayle, Anastasio, 240, 346, 348, 419, 423, 425–26, 429, 436, 446
Somoza García, Anastasio, 384, 419, 464–65
Soumaliot, Gaston, 491
South Africa, 119–20, 263–65, 366–67, 426, 520–21
 in Angola, 89–91, 114–15, 119–20, 129–33, 183, 487, 489
 Black struggle in, 183, 187
 and racism, 36, 72, 243–44
Soviet Union, 43, 69, 217, 516–17
 aid to Cuba by, 75, 117, 237
 Cuban relations with, 21, 132, 362–63, 375–76,

Soviet Union
  Cuban relations with
    (continued), 381–83, 493,
    511–12, 528
  and October Crisis, 381, 386
  Soviet "combat brigade," 338,
    376–81, 386, 402, 532
Spain, 234
Sri Lanka, 48
Sugar quota, 362
Surinam, 234
SWAPO, 185, 264–65, 521
Syria, 519
  Cuban aid to, 18, 76, 117

Tanzania, 31–32, 47–48, 183,
  247, 492
Tariffs, 284
Technology, 45
Territorial Troop Militia, 408
Terrorism, 137, 304–5, 311,
  321, 337, 344–50, 368–69
  See also CIA; Cubana
    Airlines bombing; United
    States, relations with Cuba
Thailand, 195
Torrijos, Omar, 430
Touré, Sékou, 490
Trade, unequal relations of,
  32, 47–49, 228–31, 254–56,
  279–80
Trade restrictions, 279
Transnational corporations,
  281–83, 285
Tribalism, 52–53
Trinidad and Tobago, 353
Tshombe, Moise, 491–92
Turkey, 222

Uganda, 247
Underdeveloped countries,
  226–30

Underdeveloped countries
  (continued)
  impact of economic crisis
    on, 16–17, 225–29
  problems of, 30–33, 273–98
  widening gap with
    imperialism, 15, 32, 254,
    277, 285
Unemployment, 10, 254
Unequal exchange, 284, 286
UNITA, 89–91, 130, 154, 487
United Nations, 9, 185–86,
  218, 242, 265–66, 295–96
United States
  and Africa, 132–35, 184–85,
    264
  and Angola, 114–16, 485,
    493, 499, 508–9
  and China, 194–96, 200,
    202–5, 518
  and Ethiopia, 170–73,
    175–76
  and Indochina, 194–96,
    202–5
  and Latin America and
    Caribbean, 123–24, 127–
    28, 220, 463–65, 518–19,
    523–26, 538–39
  and Mideast, 268, 519–20
  and Nicaragua, 419, 425–30,
    434–35, 437–38, 441, 451,
    464–66
  and Puerto Rico, 270–71,
    371, 379–80, 414, 452
  as capitalist oligarchy, 372
  foreign policy of, 125–26,
    468–72
  history of, 372–73
  military bases of, 125–26,
    135–36, 364–65

United States *(continued)*
  and Nonaligned, 81–82, 217–18, 235–36, 382, 401–2
  politics in, 193, 452, 469–72, 493
  racism in, 304, 313–14, 370–71
  and underdeveloped, 215–16, 230–31
  See also Arms race; Imperialism
United States, relations with Cuba, 9–10, 13–14, 236, 307, 315, 326–29, 357–65, 368–69, 469–70, 531–33
  and Angola, 90, 112, 115–16, 119, 136, 337
  and compensation, 359–60
  and dialogue, 309–10, 318, 322, 324–26
  and Ethiopia, 337
  and hijacking, 351–52
  and military threats, 21, 129, 135, 273, 401–6, 467, 532–33
  and propaganda, 395–96
  and spy flights, 337–38, 404
  and terrorists, 321–29
  See also CIA; Girón; Guantánamo
Unity
  against imperialism, 187, 227, 522
  of revolutionaries, 431–32, 436, 512–13, 524–25
Urcuyo, Francisco, 432–34
Uruguay, 385, 429, 524, 526
USSR. *See* Soviet Union

Vance, Cyrus, 380
Veiga, Roberto, 415

Velasco Alvarado, Juan, 392
Venezuela, 232, 341–44, 353, 414, 430
  and Cuba, 391–92, 531
Vietnam
  and China, 78–79, 194–211, 245–46, 514–15
  Cuban solidarity with, 79, 118, 193
  and Kampuchea, 195–96, 201–2, 204–5, 514
  significance of victory by, 16, 75, 207–10, 357, 493
  U.S. war against, 72, 125–26, 193, 224, 232, 370
  See also China; Kampuchea
Visiting rights, 319, 358

War, 252
Watergate, 16, 357, 493
Western Sahara, 244–45, 265–66
Wilmington Ten, 73
Workers' movement, 513, 515
Working class, 44, 57, 524–25
World opinion, 472
World War II, 69

Yemen, Democratic, 519

Zaïre, 90, 130, 486
  See also Congo
Zambia, 183
Zanzibar, 32, 47–48
Zimbabwe, 36, 91, 183, 185, 187, 242–43, 263–65, 367, 426, 514
Zionism, 72, 185, 241, 519–20
  See also Palestinians

BUILDING A PROLETARIAN PARTY

The Low Point of Labor Resistance Is Behind Us
The Socialist Workers Party Looks Forward

JACK BARNES, MARY-ALICE WATERS STEVE CLARK

The global order imposed by Washington is shattering. A long retreat by the working class and unions has come to an end. The bosses and their government are stepping up attacks on our wages, conditions, and constitutional rights. This book highlights opportunities for building a mass proletarian party able to lead the struggle to end capitalist rule, opening a socialist future for humanity. $10. Also in Spanish, French, Greek.

The Turn to Industry
Forging a Proletarian Party

JACK BARNES

A book about the working-class program, composition, and course of the only kind of party in the imperialist epoch worthy of the name "revolutionary." A party that can recognize the most revolutionary fact of this epoch—the worth of working people, and our capacity to change society when we organize and act to win power from the capitalist class. $15. Also in Spanish, French, Farsi, Greek.

Our Politics Start with the World

JACK BARNES

The huge economic and cultural inequalities between imperialist and semicolonial countries, and among classes within them, are perpetuated by the workings of capitalism. To build parties able to lead the revolutionary struggle for power in our own countries, vanguard workers must be guided by a strategy to close this gap. In *New International* no. 13. $14. Also in Spanish, French, Farsi, Greek.

PATHFINDERPRESS.COM

THE CUBAN REVOLUTION AND ITS IMPACT FROM AFRICA TO THE US

New!
Revolution and the Road to Peace in Colombia
The Example of the Cuban Revolution

FIDEL CASTRO

"No crime can be committed in the name of revolution," Fidel Castro declares, drawing from the example set by working people of Cuba as they took state power out of the hands of its capitalist rulers. In 2008, as part of efforts to end six decades of armed conflict in Colombia, he shared the exemplary record of Cuba's revolutionary struggle with the Revolutionary Armed Forces of Colombia (FARC) and the world. $10. Also in Spanish and French.

How Far We Slaves Have Come!
South Africa and Cuba in Today's World

NELSON MANDELA, FIDEL CASTRO

Speaking together in Cuba in 1991, Mandela and Castro discuss the role of Cuba in the history of Africa and Angola's victory over the invading US-backed South African army. That victory accelerated the fight to bring down the racist apartheid system. $7. Also in Spanish and Farsi.

From the Escambray to the Congo
In the Whirlwind of the Cuban Revolution

VÍCTOR DREKE

Dreke was second in command of the internationalist column in the Congo led in 1965 by Che Guevara. He recounts the creative joy with which working people have defended their revolutionary course—from Cuba's Escambray mountains to Africa and beyond. $15. Also in Spanish.

Cuba and Angola: The War for Freedom
HARRY VILLEGAS ("POMBO")

Cuba and Angola
Fighting for Africa's Freedom and Our Own

FIDEL CASTRO, RAÚL CASTRO NELSON MANDELA

Two books that tell the story of Cuba's unparalleled contribution to the fight to free Africa from the scourge of apartheid. And how, in the doing, Cuba's socialist revolution was also strengthened. $10 and $12. Also in Spanish. *Cuba and Angola: The War for Freedom* is also available in Farsi and Greek.

Cuba and the Coming American Revolution
JACK BARNES

This is a book about the example set by the Cuban people that socialist revolution is not only necessary—it can be made. A book about the struggles of workers and other exploited producers in the imperialist heartland, and the youth attracted to them. About the class struggle in the US, where the revolutionary capacities of working people are as utterly discounted by the ruling powers as were those of the Cuban toilers. $10. Also in Spanish, French, Farsi.

The Bolivian Diary of Ernesto Che Guevara

Guevara's day-by-day chronicle of the 1966–67 guerrilla campaign in Bolivia, an effort to forge a continent-wide revolutionary movement of workers and peasants and extend the socialist revolution to South America. $23. Also in Spanish.

PATHFINDERPRESS.COM

REVOLUTIONARY LEADERS IN THEIR OWN WORDS

Speeches for Socialism
JAMES P. CANNON

In speeches given over 40 years, a founder of the communist movement in the US explains the living legacy of the 1917 Russian Revolution; proletarian internationalism and the fight for power; Stalinism's rise and decline; the class-struggle road in the battle against national oppression and imperialist war; and the fight to transform the unions into instruments of revolutionary struggle. "The greatest satisfaction a person can possibly have," Cannon tells young revolutionists, is to live "the life of a rebel against capitalism," the life of a proletarian revolutionist. $20

Che Guevara Speaks

In twenty speeches, interviews, and letters, Guevara dissects the workings of the imperialist system with scientific clarity, truthfulness, and biting humor. Cuba has shown by its example, he says, that "a people can liberate themselves and keep themselves free." $15. Also in Farsi.

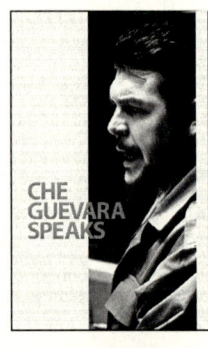

Maurice Bishop Speaks
The Grenada Revolution
and Its Overthrow, 1979–83

The triumph of the 1979 revolution in the Caribbean island of Grenada under the leadership of Maurice Bishop gave hope to millions throughout the Americas. Invaluable lessons from the workers and farmers government destroyed by a Stalinist-led counterrevolution in 1983. $20

Thomas Sankara Speaks
The Burkina Faso Revolution, 1983–87

Under Sankara's guidance, Burkina Faso's revolutionary government led peasants, workers, women, and youth to expand literacy; to sink wells, plant trees, erect housing; to combat women's oppression; to carry out land reform; to join others worldwide to free themselves from the imperialist yoke. $20. Also in French.

Revolutionary Continuity
Marxist Leadership in the U.S.
The Early Years, 1848–1917
Birth of the Communist Movement, 1918–1922
FARRELL DOBBS

"Successive generations of proletarian revolutionists have participated in the movements of the working class and its allies.... Marxists today owe them not only homage for their deeds. We also have a duty to learn what they did wrong as well as right so their errors are not repeated."
—*Farrell Dobbs*. Two volumes, $17 each.

Rosa Luxemburg Speaks
EDITED BY MARY-ALICE WATERS

Rosa Luxemburg's place of honor among the great revolutionary Marxist leaders of the twentieth century has often been denied her. Here she speaks for herself, with clarity and wit, taking on political battles that continue to divide revolutionaries from reformists in the workers movement even a century after her murder in Berlin in 1919 by counterrevolutionary militias. $25

PATHFINDERPRESS.COM

CAPITALIST CRISIS AND THE FIGHT FOR WORKERS POWER

Is Socialist Revolution in the US Possible?
A Necessary Debate Among Working People
MARY-ALICE WATERS

Fighting for a society only working people can create, it is our own capacities we will discover. And we will answer the question posed here with a resounding "Yes." Revolution is possible but not inevitable. That depends on us. $7. Also in Spanish, French, Farsi.

Malcolm X, Black Liberation, and the Road to Workers Power
JACK BARNES

"The conquest of state power by a class-conscious vanguard of the working class is the mightiest weapon possible in the fight against Black oppression, the subjugation of women, Jew-hatred, and every form of human degradation inherited from class society." $20. Also in Spanish, French, Farsi, Arabic, Greek.

The Clintons' Anti-Working-Class Record
Why Washington Fears Working People
JACK BARNES

What working people need to know about the profit-driven course of Democrats and Republicans alike over the last three decades. And the political awakening of workers seeking to understand and resist the capitalist rulers' assaults. $10. Also in Spanish, French, Farsi, Greek.

The Teamster Series
FARRELL DOBBS

Four books on the 1930s strikes, organizing drives, and political campaigns that transformed the Teamsters into a militant industrial union movement. Written by the organizer of these battles and leader of the Socialist Workers Party. A tool for workers seeking to use union power and advance the fight for a party of labor. $16 each, series $50. Also in Spanish. *Teamster Rebellion* is also available in French, Farsi, Greek.

Are They Rich Because They're Smart?
Class, Privilege, and Learning Under Capitalism
JACK BARNES

Exposes growing class inequalities in the US and the self-serving rationalizations of well-paid professionals who think their "brilliance" equips them to "regulate" working people, who don't know what's in our own best interest. $10. Also in Spanish, French, Farsi, Arabic, Greek.

Capitalism's World Disorder
Working-Class Politics at the Millennium
JACK BARNES

The social devastation and financial panic, coarsening of politics, cop brutality, and imperialist aggression—all are products not of something gone wrong with capitalism but of its lawful workings. Yet the future can be changed by the united struggle of workers and farmers increasingly conscious of their capacity to wage revolutionary struggles for state power and to transform the world. $20. Also in Spanish and French.

PATHFINDERPRESS.COM

New International
A MAGAZINE OF MARXIST POLITICS AND THEORY

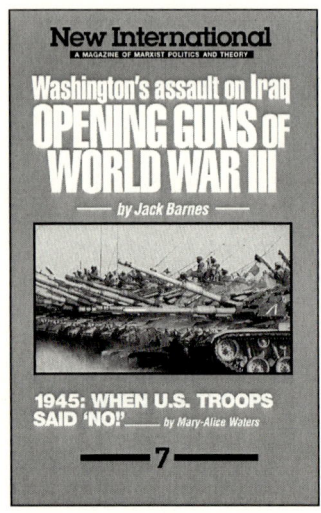

NEW INTERNATIONAL NO. 7
Opening Guns of World War III: Washington's Assault on Iraq
JACK BARNES

The murderous assault on Iraq in 1990–91 heralded increasingly sharp conflicts among imperialist powers, growing instability of capitalism, and more wars. Also includes:

1945: When US Troops Said 'No!' by Mary-Alice Waters
Lessons from the Iran-Iraq War by Samad Sharif

$14. Also in Spanish, French, Farsi.

NEW INTERNATIONAL NO. 11
U.S. Imperialism Has Lost the Cold War
JACK BARNES

The collapse of regimes across Eastern Europe and the USSR claiming to be communist did not mean workers and farmers there had been crushed. In today's sharpening class conflicts and wars, these toilers are joining working people the world over in the class struggle against capitalist exploitation. $14. Also in Spanish, French, Farsi, Greek.

NEW INTERNATIONAL NO. 12
Capitalism's Long Hot Winter Has Begun
JACK BARNES

Today's global capitalist crisis is but the opening stage of decades of economic, financial, and social convulsions and class battles. Class-conscious workers confront this historic turning point for imperialism with confidence, Jack Barnes writes, drawing satisfaction from being "in their face" as we chart a revolutionary course to take power. $14. Also in Spanish, French, Farsi, Arabic, Greek.

THE WORKING CLASS AND THE FIGHT AGAINST JEW-HATRED

The Fight Against Jew-Hatred and Pogroms in the Imperialist Epoch
Stakes for the International Working Class

V.I. LENIN, LEON TROTSKY
FARRELL DOBBS, JAMES P. CANNON
JACK BARNES, DAVE PRINCE

Jew-hatred and pogroms—such as Hamas carried out on October 7, 2023—are part of the social convulsions and wars of the imperialist epoch. The authors explain why fighting Jew-hatred is decisive to the working class and oppressed nations of the world—and *what is to be done to end it*. $10. Also in Spanish, French, Greek.

Imperialism's March Toward Fascism and War
JACK BARNES

"There will be new Hitlers, new Mussolinis. That is inevitable. What is not inevitable is that they will triumph. The working-class vanguard will organize our class to fight back against the devastating toll we are made to pay for the capitalist crisis. The future of humanity will be decided in the contest between these contending class forces." In *New International* no. 10. $14. Also in Spanish, French, Farsi, Greek.

The Jewish Question
A Marxist Interpretation

ABRAM LEON

The battle against reactionary forces aiming to exterminate the Jews remains central to world politics, as shown by the genocidal October 2023 pogrom in Israel. Why is Jew-hatred still raising its ugly head? What are its class roots? Why, as Abram Leon explains, is there no solution "independent of the world proletarian revolution"? Revised translation, new introduction, 40 pages of illustrations and maps. $17. Also in Spanish, French, Greek.

PATHFINDERPRESS.COM

EXPAND YOUR REVOLUTIONARY LIBRARY

New Expanded Edition!
Cosmetics, Fashion, and the Exploitation of Women
MARY-ALICE WATERS
JOSEPH HANSEN, EVELYN REED

"Norms of beauty and fashion are inseparable from the class struggle." That's the title of the opening chapter of this timely new edition of a lively 1950s debate in the *Militant*, a socialist newsweekly. How cosmetics and fashion monopolies rake in profits from social insecurities of women and adolescents. Why women's integration into the workforce and unions is a major advance in the fight for emancipation. A Marxist classic on the origins of women's oppression and the working-class road forward. $15. Also in Spanish, French, Farsi, Greek.

Women in Cuba: The Making of a Revolution Within the Revolution
VILMA ESPÍN, ASELA DE LOS SANTOS
YOLANDA FERRER

The integration of women in the ranks and leadership of the Cuban Revolution was intertwined with the proletarian course led by Fidel Castro from the start. This is the story of that revolution and how it transformed the women and men who made it. $17. Also in Spanish, Farsi, Greek.

Feminism and the Marxist Movement
MARY-ALICE WATERS

From the earliest days of the modern revolutionary workers movement, Marxists have championed the struggle for women's rights and explained the economic roots in class society of women's oppression. $5. Also in Farsi.

Labor, Nature, and the Evolution of Humanity
The Long View of History
FREDERICK ENGELS, KARL MARX
GEORGE NOVACK
MARY-ALICE WATERS

Without understanding that social labor, transforming nature, has driven humanity's evolution for millions of years, working people are unable to see beyond the capitalist epoch of class exploitation that warps all human relations, ideas, and values. Only the revolutionary conquest of state power by the working class can open the door to a world free of capitalist exploitation, degradation of nature, subjugation of women, racism, and war. A world built on human solidarity. A socialist world. $12. Also in Spanish and French.

The Communist Manifesto
KARL MARX AND FREDERICK ENGELS

Communism, say the founding leaders of the revolutionary workers movement, is not a set of ideas or preconceived "principles" but workers' line of march to power. It springs from a "movement going on under our very eyes." $5. Also in Spanish, French, Farsi, Arabic.

The History of the Russian Revolution
LEON TROTSKY

How, under Lenin's leadership, the Bolshevik Party led millions of workers and farmers to overthrow the state power of the landlords and capitalists in 1917 and bring to power a government that advanced their class interests at home and worldwide. Unabridged, 3 vols. in one. Written by one of the central leaders of that socialist revolution. $30. Also in French and Russian.

PATHFINDERPRESS.COM

Lenin's Final Fight
Speeches and Writings, 1922–23
V.I. LENIN

In 1922 and 1923, V.I. Lenin, central leader of the world's first socialist revolution, waged what was to be his last political battle—one that was lost after his death. At stake was whether that revolutionary government and the world communist movement it led would remain on the revolutionary proletarian course that brought workers and peasants to power in Russia in 1917. $17. Also in Spanish, Farsi, Greek.

America's Revolutionary Heritage
Marxist Essays
GEORGE NOVACK

A materialist explanation of the American Revolution, Civil War and Radical Reconstruction, genocide against the Indians, rise of American imperialism, first wave of the fight for women's rights, and more. $23

Pathfinder Press **accessible e-books** for the blind, those with low vision, or other challenges reading print books

For a list of current accessible titles, go to:
pathfinderpress.com/
collections/books-for-the-blind.

Visit bookshare.org for information on how to sign up.

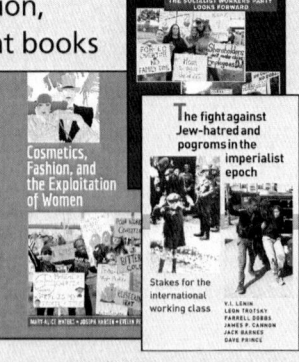

DEFENDING CONSTITUTIONAL FREEDOMS

Under the constitution "the power of censorship rests with the people over the government, not the government over the people."
—James Madison, *1794*

50 Years of Covert Operations in the US
Washington's Political Police and the American Working Class
LARRY SEIGLE, FARRELL DOBBS STEVE CLARK

How class-conscious workers have defended constitutional freedoms and fought the capitalists' drive to build the "national security" state essential to maintaining their rule. $10. Also in Spanish and Farsi.

Socialism on Trial
Testimony at Minneapolis Sedition Trial
JAMES P. CANNON

The revolutionary program of the working class presented in federal court in 1941 on the eve of US entry into World War II. The frame-up charges of "seditious conspiracy" targeted leaders of the Socialist Workers Party. $15. Also in Spanish, French, Farsi.

FBI on Trial
The Victory in the Socialist Workers Party Suit Against Government Spying
MARGARET JAYKO

The record of a historic victory in the fight for political rights, including the 1986 federal court ruling against government spying and excerpts from trial testimony by SWP leaders Farrell Dobbs and Jack Barnes. $17

PATHFINDERPRESS.COM

PATHFINDER AROUND THE WORLD

UNITED STATES
(and Caribbean, Latin America, and East Asia)
>Pathfinder Books, 306 W. 37th St., 13th Floor
>New York, NY 10018

CANADA
>Pathfinder Books, 7107 St. Denis, Suite 204
>Montreal, QC H2S 2S5

UNITED KINGDOM
(and Europe, Africa, Middle East, and South Asia)
>Pathfinder Books, 5 Norman Rd.
>Seven Sisters, London N15 4ND

AUSTRALIA
(and New Zealand, Southeast Asia, and the Pacific)
>Pathfinder Books, Suite 2, First floor, 275 George St.
>Liverpool, Sydney, NSW 2170
>Postal address: P.O. Box 73, Campsie, NSW 2194

BUILD YOUR LIBRARY!
JOIN THE PATHFINDER READERS CLUB

$10 / YEAR
25% DISCOUNT ON ALL PATHFINDER TITLES
30% OFF BOOKS OF THE MONTH
Valid at pathfinderpress.com and local Pathfinder book centers

Go to: pathfinderpress.com/
products/pathfinder-readers-club

Pathfinder
pathfinderpress.com